A Visitation of God

A Visitation of God

Northern Civilians Interpret the Civil War

SEAN A. SCOTT

UNIVERSITY PRESS

2011

OXFORD
UNIVERSITY PRESS

Oxford University Press, Inc., publishes works that further
Oxford University's objective of excellence
in research, scholarship, and education.

Oxford   New York
Auckland   Cape Town   Dar es Salaam   Hong Kong   Karachi
Kuala Lumpur   Madrid   Melbourne   Mexico City   Nairobi
New Delhi   Shanghai   Taipei   Toronto

With offices in
Argentina   Austria   Brazil   Chile   Czech Republic   France   Greece
Guatemala   Hungary   Italy   Japan   Poland   Portugal   Singapore
South Korea   Switzerland   Thailand   Turkey   Ukraine   Vietnam

Copyright © 2011 by Oxford University Press, Inc.

Published by Oxford University Press, Inc.
198 Madison Avenue, New York, New York 10016

www.oup.com

Oxford is a registered trademark of Oxford University Press.

All rights reserved. No part of this publication may be reproduced,
stored in a retrieval system, or transmitted, in any form or by any means,
electronic, mechanical, photocopying, recording, or otherwise,
without the prior permission of Oxford University Press.

Library of Congress Cataloging-in-Publication Data
Scott, Sean A.
A visitation of God: northern civilians interpret the Civil War / Sean A. Scott.
   p. cm.
Includes bibliographical references and index.
ISBN 978-0-19-539599-0
1. United States—History—Civil War, 1861–1865—Religious aspects.
2. United States—History—Civil War, 1861–1865—Social aspects.
3. United States—Church history—19th century.
4. Laity—United States—History—19th century.
5. War—Religious aspects—Christianity—History—19th century.
6. Slavery and the church—United States.   I. Title.
E635.S36 2010
973.7'1—dc22   2010010476

9 8 7 6 5 4 3 2 1

Printed in the United States of America
on acid-free paper

For Heather

Acknowledgments

Writing this book has been daunting at times but also immensely enjoyable. The research alone required traveling thousands of miles and spending countless days sifting through letter collections and straining my eyes at newspapers on microfilm. Needless to say, during three semesters with most of my time occupied in writing lectures or grading papers, I sometimes found myself suffering from archival withdrawal. Now, as I sit each day in the National Archives searching for Lincoln documents, I still recall with fondness the days when I devoted my energies to understanding and writing about religious Northerners and the Civil War. This book truly has been a labor of love, yet I could not have completed it alone. Numerous archivists and reference librarians, too many to name, rendered assistance in locating promising sources. I am grateful to friends and family who provided lodging and fellowship along the way, the Munyons in Wisconsin, the Ices in Minnesota, and especially my father- and mother-in-law Gordon and Linda Wall in Michigan. A Purdue University Research Foundation Grant generously provided funds for a year's writing, and a Faculty Research Grant from Ouachita Baptist University covered costs for securing photograph rights. The Moore family deserves special thanks for giving me a home away from home while at Purdue.

My educational and intellectual debts are many. Without the foundation laid by the grammar exercises, sentence diagramming, and compositions assigned by Mrs. Brown, unquestionably the world's finest and most respected high school English teacher, I probably would never have been up to the task of writing a book. Edward Panosian inspired me to become a historian, and his "ten principles to live by," inscribed by me in the front of the History of Civ. book on the last day of class, still give reason to meditate. Carl Abrams, Linda Hayner, John Matzko, and Caren Silvester all deepened my desire to pursue an academic life, and their masterful lectures gave me much to ponder as a student and emulate as a teacher. John M. Glen's rigorous demands sometimes pushed a young graduate student to the breaking point, yet his meticulous care in reviewing each paper strengthened my prose. His admonition to write a monograph rather than a dissertation could not have been more apposite. Frank Lambert, Michael Morrison, and Ryan Schneider all offered insightful comments on drafts of this work, and Professor Morrison's tip to examine secular newspapers for religious commentary vastly enriched the narrative. Bob May repeatedly proved to be a wonderful mentor, and his example as both a first-rate scholar and an award-winning teacher has set a high standard of professional achievement. I especially appreciate his continued support in helping to advance my career. His careful reading of the text undoubtedly strengthened the work and saved me from numerous errors. The anonymous reviewers for Oxford University Press also offered constructive suggestions, and I trust that the final product reflects their sound judgment. My editor Nancy Toff demonstrated enthusiasm for the project from the outset, and her patience in working with this rookie author should garner her the editor of the year award. I also am grateful to Nancy's assistant Sonia Tycko for patiently answering numerous questions and production editor Liz Smith for guiding the work to completion. The assistance of these superb teammates notwithstanding, any remaining mistakes or errors of interpretation are my own.

The main ideas and themes in chapter 7 have been published in the *Journal of Social History* (Summer 2008), and I thank editor Peter Stearns and his skilled assistant Carol Sturz for permission to revisit them here.

Finally, my parents Steve and Sue Scott have supported me in my chosen pursuits my entire life, and this project has been no different. They tell me that they read to me every night when I was little, but I don't remember it. However, 8 mm film verifies this claim, so I suppose they deserve credit for instilling in me a love of learning. I will be forever grateful. Their financial assistance and moral support along the way cannot be measured. More recently, their willingness to let my wife and me live in their basement for a semester so that I could devote all my energies to writing helped me complete the dissertation and finally secure gainful employment. Opening their home again so that I could revise the manuscript for publication and escape the oppressive heat of an Arkansas summer may have been an even greater blessing. Our cat Ewok, who would have preferred that I never leave home, reluctantly adapted to my coming and going and even learned to share me with this project. I know Mom and Dad will be pleased to receive a copy of this book, but they are much more thrilled to finally have a grandchild. Priscilla already has brought much joy to my life, but she paid no attention when I read to her a few copy-edited pages of this text. Maybe someday after her interests have progressed beyond *Mr. Brown Can Moo! Can You?* she will want to read Daddy's book. My wife Heather has lived with this work since our marriage, and her patience and understanding in allowing me time to write facilitated its completion. Probably more significant, her willingness to live on the meager salary of a graduate student and adjunct instructor represented a greater sacrifice than a new bride should have been asked to make. Her friendship and love made the writing process more satisfying, and she continues to enrich my life in innumerable ways.

Contents

Introduction, 3

Chapter 1. "If God Saves Not Our Country It Must Be Lost"
Providence, Secession, and the Outbreak of War, 11

Chapter 2. "Until the Great Sin...Has Been Removed"
God's Chastening, the Sacred Union, and Emancipation, 35

Chapter 3. "Try to Live the Life of a Christian"
The Personal Faith of Women on the Home Front, 71

Chapter 4. "Christian Patriotism" in Flush
Political Preaching, Antiwar Dissent, and Summer Thanksgiving, 97

Chapter 5. "Exhorting You to Be Faithful...to God and to Men"
Fatherly Counsel and the Path to Christian Manhood, 139

Chapter 6. "Discord Sown among Brethren"
The Appropriation of Scripture, Politicized Religion, and Church Division, 161

Chapter 7. "Earth Has No Sorrow That Heaven Cannot Cure"
Civilian Perspectives on Death and Eternity, 191

Chapter 8. "God Be Thanked the Nation and Humanity Were Saved"
Retribution against Traitors, the Reelection of Lincoln, and the Termination of War, 215

Chapter 9. "How Mysterious Are the Ways of Providence"
Civilian Attitudes toward the Assassination of Lincoln, 245

Epilogue, 265

Abbreviations, 273

Notes, 275

Bibliography, 315

Index, 339

A Visitation of God

Introduction

On April 26, 1860, the *Presbyter*, an Old School Presbyterian weekly published in Cincinnati, ran an editorial entitled "Our Country's Dangers." Editor J. G. Monfort feared that selfish politicians had rejected all avenues of sectional compromise and were preparing to jettison the Constitution and sever the Union if doing so suited their special interests. Intense political feelings had produced hostilities and fostered an atmosphere of violence in some areas of the country, and the writer worried that the rule of law was falling by the wayside. However, he regarded these developments as only superficial symptoms of a more serious malady. Too many citizens had ignored "the authority and will of God as the God of nations," and sin was rampant throughout all levels of society. Monfort implored Christians to pray that God would withhold his "just judgments" from the country, for he believed that the righteousness of the godly might stave off national punishment. In particular, devout citizens could promote Christianity in the political sphere, and he made this clear in no uncertain terms. "Christians must carry their religion into politics," he wrote, "if they would save their country from the wrath of heaven."[1]

This advice was nothing novel, for Protestant church members and attenders had taken an active interest in politics during the antebellum period. Indeed, evangelical Americans helped shape the debates over such politically charged social issues as temperance and slavery and ultimately contributed to the splintering of the second party system, the growth of sectionalism, and the coming of the Civil War. By 1860, churches were influential institutions that shaped the lives and experiences of millions of Americans. For many years, historians focused entirely on the sermons and activities of ministers in order to understand the intersection of religion and the Civil War. But over the past decade, several significant works have illuminated important facets of Civil War religion such as the faith of soldiers, the centrality of theology to the contest, and the inability of religious leaders to develop a moral justification that could have averted war.[2]

This study contributes to the recovery of Civil War religion by examining the conflict from the perspective of civilians on the northern home front. Numerous religious Northerners understood the Civil War as a struggle permeated with theological meaning. The letters and diaries of civilians, both prominent citizens active in public affairs and obscure individuals seemingly forgotten to history, are replete with examples of how faith in a sovereign God who controlled the destinies of nations influenced their views on national events and the war. This book combines the personal opinions of laity and ministers revealed in private correspondence with religious sentiments expressed in public documents such as sermons, church records, and editorials from both the secular and religious press to create a narrative that conclusively demonstrates the importance of religion on the northern home front during the Civil War.

Three overlapping themes run throughout the story line. The first centers on how religious Northerners comprehended God and his working in the world. Many civilians believed that God providentially controlled history, so they attempted to discover how current events revealed his will. Since the Puritans, religious individuals had asserted that God had a special relationship with America. They based this assumption on millennial ideas, which envisioned America spreading freedom and liberty around the world and helping usher in the kingdom of Christ on earth. When war broke out, devout Northerners applied this religious facet of American exceptionalism to the Union and claimed that God favored the North in the military contest. They insisted that God was chastening his chosen nation for its sins, especially for tolerating slavery, and maintained that he would destroy the wicked institution through war.

This mindset fostered the notion that the Union was sacred and had to be preserved at all costs since God would achieve his divine purposes through it. When ministers and laity fervently supported the war, they often acted as if God had sanctioned the Union. Individual churches and denominational assemblies likewise threw their collective weight behind the war effort and made unbridled patriotism a religious duty. In many cases, both preachers and laity appropriated Scripture to prove the righteousness of their cause, and their insistence that all churchgoers evince Christian patriotism contributed to the fusion of religion and politics during the conflict.

The ubiquity of patriotic utterances delivered from church pulpits gave rise to complaints about political preaching from churchgoers who disagreed with the dominant religious interpretation of the war. Some raised legitimate concerns that clergymen had forsaken their primary duty to preach the gospel and therefore deserved to be removed from ministry. More commonly, Democratic members who found that the sermons of their pastors contained political positions contrary to their liking complained that Unionism had infested the churches. Some Democratic laity left assemblies that they alleged had been contaminated by politics, and Unionist members generally rejoiced at their withdrawal. In some cases, Democratic dissidents formed their own religious bodies in which they could worship as they pleased, but political partisanship similarly plagued these new congregations. While some believers regretted the church divisions and lamented that interest in the war had contributed to the decline of spiritual vitality among churchgoers, many ministers and laypeople looked to the nation rather than the church as the instrument through which God was accomplishing his will in the world.

Any account of northern religion during the Civil War would be incomplete without including the beliefs of Abraham Lincoln. His election in 1860 gave rise to secession and opened the floodgates of speculation concerning God's purposes for the country's future, and his assassination produced an outpouring of public religious sentiment possibly unmatched in the nation's history. Since his death, Lincoln's own religious views have intrigued historians and the general public, but this treatment, like those works that preceded it, will not attempt to uncover the deep secrets of his heart. Nevertheless, his speeches, letters, and public proclamations for religious observances reveal a growth in personal faith as well as a sincere conviction that God was central to understanding the meaning of the conflict. Furthermore, his skepticism that man could discern God's ways with absolute clarity provided a sharp contrast to the dominant religious view held by most Northerners and has justifiably earned him the designation as the war's greatest theologian.[3]

This work is confined geographically to the Union states of the Civil War west—Ohio, Indiana, Illinois, Michigan, Wisconsin, Minnesota, and Iowa. The Old Northwest, as it was known in the late eighteenth and early nineteenth centuries, was the new nation's first frontier where the experiment in liberty and democracy could be tested. Although the Northwest Ordinances prohibited slavery in states formed from its territory, settlers sympathetic to the peculiar institution nevertheless flocked to parts of southern Ohio, Indiana, and Illinois. In the 1830s and 1840s, migrations of New Englanders, residents of the Mid-Atlantic states, and European immigrants contributed to a heterogeneous society that resembled "an ethnic and cultural checkerboard" more than the "proverbial melting pot." When combined with individuals who were born and came of age in this area, the Old Northwest might even be called "a region of strangers." Yet if anything helped unify these disparate groups of people, it was the church. Religion offered the bonds of community and fellowship, especially on the early frontier when camp meetings regularly brought together families isolated by great distances. As population grew and cities multiplied, churches, with their domestic missionary endeavors and denominational newspapers, continued to shape society and have a profound impact on the lives of many families. Religion, however, was unable to erase all social and class differences, and disagreements over slavery, in particular, caused a rift between some people in the Old Northwest. Far from being a homogenous region, distinct pockets developed, such as the bastion of antislavery activity in Ohio's Western Reserve and the haven of secessionist sympathy in southern Illinois called Egypt. This diversity of opinion, combined with the dearth of studies on the Old Northwest as a region and the abundance of scholarly analyses steeped in sources from New England and states along the eastern seaboard, makes an examination of these states indispensible for rendering the complexity of the northern home front during the Civil War.[4]

Indeed, when searching for what might have been the typical northern experience during the Civil War, one would not expect to find it in the erudite elocutions of preacher Henry Ward Beecher, the extraordinary combat experiences of soldier Joshua Lawrence Chamberlain, or the insightful and prolific pen of civilian George Templeton Strong. Although their stories illuminate facets of life during the war which we are richer for knowing, they nevertheless are far from representative. Walt Whitman once claimed that "the real war will never get into the books." Yet rather than there being only one valid account of "the real war," there are in fact many story lines that communicate some aspect of that unwritten whole. This study attempts to convey one of those narratives by giving insights into the lives of little-known Northerners—the minister who faithfully pastored a small town church and had only one or two of his sermons printed throughout his entire ministry; the undecorated soldier who dutifully served his country and returned home heralded only by family and neighbors from the local community; and the lonesome housewife who bore increased burdens of childrearing and domestic responsibilities while developing a political awareness and passionately expounding her views in a flow of steady letters to her soldier-husband. On the nation's eighty-fifth birthday, Abraham Lincoln, himself a product of the hills of southern Indiana and plains of Illinois in the Old Northwest, spoke of the war as "essentially a People's contest" dedicated to preserving a Union that offered each citizen the possibility of achieving a better life. Lincoln believed that "the plain people," by and large, agreed with his assessment of the conflict.[5] This book presents some of those "plain people."

The Old Northwest may have best embodied the mix of peoples who constituted the population of the North during the Civil War, but choosing a moniker by which to refer to them as a collective whole was somewhat problematic. Since this story is framed within the context of the Civil War and its North versus South dichotomy, it made most sense to use the designation "Northerner" to describe residents who lived in the Union states of Ohio, Indiana, Illinois, Michigan, Wisconsin, Minnesota, and Iowa. The label "Midwesterner" was rejected because the term was not commonly used during the 1860s. Although often employed by contemporaries when contrasting themselves with New Englanders, the term "Westerner" failed the test because of its modern association with states near the Rocky Mountains or Pacific Ocean. In addition, both California and Oregon had been admitted to the Union prior to 1860. Finally, "residents of the Old Northwest" or "Northwesterners" were simply too cumbersome and more befuddling than enlightening for a twenty-first-century audience.

This study primarily focuses on members of evangelical Protestant denominations because their opinions abound in the available documentary record. Baptists and Methodists dominate the narrative because these churches enjoyed a larger membership than other denominations during the mid-nineteenth century due to their emphasis on the revivalistic methods of the Second Great Awakening. Presbyterians also flourished in the region, and they generally appealed to more educated laity who thoughtfully discussed the intersection of their faith with national affairs. The views of Congregationalists, Episcopalians, Disciples of Christ, and members of the Church of God appear, though much less frequently. Whenever possible, perspectives of groups outside the Protestant mainstream have been included. Because of their numerical strength in parts of Ohio and Indiana, Quakers receive greater treatment than might be expected, and their fellow pacifists, the Mennonites, also earn more than passing mention. The opinions of Catholics, Unitarians, and Swedenborgians have been incorporated when available, but the dearth of primary sources from members of these groups has limited them to the periphery. However, the question remains as to whether or not geography significantly affected the beliefs of the laity. Although the inroads of religious liberalism might have been more prominent in the writings of New England elites, a breadth of theological views existed throughout the entire North. Indeed, the writings of ministers, editors of religious newspapers, or civilians from New England, the mid-Atlantic, or the Old Northwest seem to mirror each other because churches throughout the Union generally gave their full-fledged support to the war. Citizens who opposed the war on religious grounds likewise can be found throughout the North, yet their greater numbers and more vociferous opposition only led to new church movements in the states of the Old Northwest. Rumors of the formation of a northwest confederacy, rather than the machinations of New Englanders as had been the case with the Hartford Convention during the War of 1812, demonstrate that the Old Northwest represented the most volatile region of the North both politically and religiously.

Without the letters and diaries of numerous "average" citizens, this study would have been impossible. In bringing to light the religious ideas and convictions of many people who never intended to have their beliefs scrutinized for the purpose of history, I often have been reminded of my status as an uninvited observer or possibly even an unwelcome intruder, a fact explicitly underscored by one Hoosier female who wrote, "Dear brother this letter is intended for no other eyes than yours."[6] But if I have violated the sanctity of someone's privacy by reading his or her confidential musings, I have done so with the best intentions. I have taken people's words at face value and assumed that they honestly meant what they wrote unless sarcasm or irony could be detected. Since religious beliefs cannot be quantified or measured to gauge the depth of a person's sincerity, I have attempted, whenever possible, to present my subjects through their own words. Furthermore, in trying to acquaint myself as fully as possible with people who lived and died over a century ago, I have attempted to locate many of them in the 1860 census in order to determine their age, occupation, and social status. Because of high literacy rates in nineteenth-century America, class had little bearing on a person's ability to communicate his or her beliefs effectively. However, spelling was by no means uniform, and I have refrained from noting misspellings by cluttering quotations with *sic*. Other than replacing dashes with periods and inserting lower case letters when persons habitually capitalized all nouns, punctuation remains unchanged. Any use of italics denotes emphasis found in the original documents.

Finally, the reader should be aware that I am writing from a perspective sympathetic to the tenets of historic Christianity. I understand the church to be an apolitical institution, established for the purpose of preparing believers for the world to come. To be sure, Christians, as individuals, have responsibilities to government and oftentimes act prudently in giving attention to matters of state. The Apostle Paul, for instance, appealed to Caesar as a Roman citizen, not as a Christian. Yet as a collective whole, the church has no claim to secular power and trivializes its spiritual authority when it meddles in politics. There are no records of first-century Christians devoting ecclesiastical energies to influencing the political debates of the Roman Empire. By focusing exclusively on its spiritual mission, the Christian church spread throughout the world, had a positive impact on Roman culture and society, and outlived the Empire. Even though I personally am glad that the North won the war and greatly admire Lincoln for his insistence on preserving the Union and eradicating slavery, I believe that Christ's church would have prevailed spiritually regardless of the outcome of the military contest and any subsequent alterations of American history. Yet many northern preachers and laypersons, rather than trust that the church, as Christ's redeemed, would endure and ultimately triumph regardless of the rise and fall of any particular nation, instead placed a spiritual significance on the maintenance of the Union because they viewed it as the entity that would help the church in its mission to Christianize the world. Far from sensing a tension between an earthly government and the heavenly city, most antebellum religious Northerners conflated the two and interpreted the Civil War as their opportunity to inaugurate a Christian nation.

I

"If God Saves Not Our Country It Must Be Lost"

Providence, Secession, and the Outbreak of War

Upon the election of Abraham Lincoln to the presidency on November 6, 1860, Elisha Mills Huntington, retired judge from Terre Haute, Indiana, contemplated the nation's uncertain future. Preparing for the worst, Huntington frankly admitted, "I look for trouble." Nearly two weeks later, the editor of the *Chicago Daily Times and Herald*, voicing the concerns of a majority of Americans, wondered "What is to be done?" concerning the extreme positions taken by northern abolitionists and southern fire-eaters. In his Thanksgiving Day address, George Duffield, pastor of Detroit's First Presbyterian Church, asserted that the present crisis held in the balance nothing less than "the dissolution of the Union."

In the closing weeks of 1860, the elevation to the presidency of a sectional candidate who garnered only forty percent of the popular vote produced rumblings of secession in the South and made the plight of the Union the primary focus of national attention. More notably, the similar manner in which a civilian, a newspaper editor, and a minister all framed their understanding of the predicament at hand foreshadowed the blending of religion and politics that would become a defining element of the coming conflict. After expressing his initial fear that difficulties loomed, Huntington promptly added, "But a kind Providence will I trust save us from the horrors of Disunion." In his attempt to convince the public to ignore the rants of abolitionists, the editor of the pro–Stephen Douglas *Chicago Daily Times and Herald* acknowledged that slavery could never be eradicated through human effort. Freedom for the slave lay "in the hands of ONE higher than you or we[,]... hands that will deal with it in the great march of humanity as seemeth best to HIM."

Duffield exhorted his congregation to be mindful of God's "approaching judgments" and repent, hoping that as a result churches would be revived spiritually, patriotism would trump party divisions, and men of integrity would overcome corrupt politicians. But most apparent to Duffield, the prevailing political turmoil clearly evidenced "the ordering of a propitious providence" who "is waiting for this great nation to turn from its evil, and thus give Him occasion for prolonging His care."[1]

A belief in providence, the idea that God controls and guides events in human history, not only characterized the outlooks of these three individuals but also had been an integral story line of American settlement and expansion. From its Latin root, providence literally means "to see before." According to this definition, God knew what would happen before it ever transpired and, as sovereign of the universe, directed events to achieve his intended result. The belief in providence as the impetus for American history originated with the Puritans, who brought the concept from England and applied it to their situation in New England. They envisioned themselves as God's chosen people, a New Israel entrusted with a divine mission to accomplish in the wilderness where God had placed them. As settlement expanded in the eighteenth century, providence shed its provincialism and developed an intercolonial basis for the purpose of achieving religious liberty throughout the colonies. By the Revolutionary era, providence had been transformed completely into a national ideology that emphasized both political and religious freedom as the divine purpose of America. To many Americans of this generation, the cause of liberty equaled the cause of God. After gaining independence, the young republic faced both domestic difficulties and foreign threats, and providence became an effective tool for strengthening American nationalism. Providence was the glue that unified settlers of various ethnic and cultural backgrounds, giving them an identity and role in helping fulfill America's destiny. During the nineteenth century, providence and patriotism became so entwined, according to one scholar, that "the idea of a protecting Providence was *characteristic* of American patriotism." Fourth of July orations abounded with references to providential assistance and reinforced the widespread belief that God showered America with his special favor. God had providentially blessed the Union because liberty would spread through it, not just in America but throughout the world. By the outbreak of the Civil War, the marriage of providence and patriotism had imbued the Union in sacred meaning. Indeed, such a transmutation prompted one historian to claim that "the Union was Providence incarnate."[2]

This providential outlook, which saw God actively participating in American history and promising future blessings for the expanding nation, specifically characterized the optimistic rhetoric of many public figures throughout the antebellum period. For instance, the major speeches of

Daniel Webster are replete with references to God's assistance in America's growth and the sanctity of the Union in God's master plan. Although some historians might categorize the providential language employed by political and cultural elites as civil religion, a genuine belief that God providentially controlled all things prevailed in "the writings of the common man," according to historian Lewis O. Saum. However, unlike leading politicians, common folk seldom thought of providence in terms of historic national events or of a bright future evidently manifest. To them, providence acted on a personal basis and affected immediate circumstances or taught spiritual lessons through trials precipitated by past actions, and its purposes were never apparent but unknown. In Saum's opinion, this pessimistic view of providence produced resignation to the tedious nature of everyday life. It is no wonder, then, that he concludes that the chaotic nature of the Civil War caused "unelevated people" to discard a providential outlook almost altogether. When the providential mind-set persisted, Saum alleges, it was articulated most often by the elderly or by Southerners. He claims that the war contributed to the decline of providence due to a growing lack of faith in an "intelligible order," and luck or chance subsequently dethroned providence as the primary explanation for events.[3]

On the contrary, substantial documentary evidence demonstrates that belief in providence remained vibrant throughout the Civil War. Many religious civilians of all social classes affirmed their conviction that God played a role in the war. Some people focused on the personal aspect of providence in dealing with individuals. Others, including people of the lower class, related the doctrine of providence to national affairs and emphasized the coterminous nature of God and the Union. Some individuals comfortably made applications in both categories. In fact, providence proved to be a remarkably flexible concept and operated on many levels for different people.[4] Some individuals cited in this study testified to undergoing a conversion experience, so their expectation of having a personal relationship with God undoubtedly shaped their providential outlook. Individuals not professing Christianity or affiliated with any particular denomination may nonetheless have ascribed to providence a role in events of the Civil War because of the widely accepted tradition linking providence and the Union. It matters little whether or not these people considered themselves born-again believers, nominal Christians, or altogether irreligious. Whatever the case, the idea of providence played an integral role in how numerous civilians understood the causes, progress, and ultimate meaning of the war.

The months between Lincoln's election and inauguration proved critical to the unraveling of the Union. As a lame-duck president, James Buchanan wielded little power and demonstrated even less leadership. Although he recognized the immanency of secession, his idea to call a constitutional convention in order to assure Southerners that slavery would be protected in the states where it existed and remain open to federal territories was not only impractical but also represented a repudiation of the Chicago platform upon which the Republicans had won office. Many Northerners regarded the president's plan not as a compromise but as a complete acquiescence to southern fire-eaters' demands. Because he believed that the federal government lacked constitutional authority to prevent states from seceding from the Union, Buchanan allowed southern secession to transpire. When South Carolina unanimously passed its ordinance of secession on December 20, the dissolution of the Union had only begun.[5]

Having done little to try to avert the breakup of the Union, Buchanan invoked divine assistance and designated January 4, 1861, as a day for people to fast, pray, and implore God to resolve the crisis that he could not. Some Northerners completely ignored the directive, ostensibly because they lacked all respect for the man who issued it. At two churches in Indianapolis, one Methodist and one Episcopal, the speakers declined to deliver their prepared remarks because too few people were present to warrant the effort. The editor of the *Indianapolis Daily Journal* claimed that lack of interest in the fast reflected the low opinion citizens had of the outgoing administration and not spiritual apathy. George Tuthill officiated at his Congregational church in Pontiac, Michigan, but few churches in the area followed suit. In private, he blamed Buchanan for permitting secession to occur and completely understood why people would disregard the request of a man whom many supposed to be as traitorous as South Carolinians. Other ministers publicly denounced the president for his inability to resolve the sectional crisis. James Smart, Methodist Episcopal pastor in Flint, Michigan, interpreted Buchanan's call for a national day of prayer and fasting as merely an act of desperation befitting one who had "brought the country to the brink of ruin." In Coldwater, Michigan, Presbyterian Horace Hovey portrayed the president as "an imbecile old man wringing his hands" in the White House when the country needed a Jacksonian "*hero*, wielding his sword on the plains of South Carolina."[6]

During the winter of 1860–61, northern clergymen willingly expressed their opinions regarding the political crisis. Several ministers initially hoped that a policy of conciliation would hold the Union together and prevent war. Some of these conservatives, clearly the minority, considered the pulpit an inappropriate place to discuss politics. In his Thanksgiving sermon, Charles Pettit McIlvaine, Episcopal bishop of the diocese of Ohio, dismissed secession as an unsuitable topic for church and focused instead on the necessity of religion as the basis of national prosperity. Although fellow bishop Samuel McCoskry of Detroit's St. Paul's Church agreed that political and sectional topics "are subjects which ought never [to] have place in the house of God," he nonetheless felt it admissible to excoriate abolitionists for causing divisions in the churches and promoting "infidelity" while claiming to be the agents of God. At Milwaukee's First Presbyterian, James Corning concurred that abolitionism had "infested" the churches to the extent that some congregations admitted only antislavery advocates as members. He alleged that the dogmatism of abolitionist ministers contradicted "the charity of Christ" and concluded that "a pulpit that rides anti-slavery will never gain many converts. Men will despise it, and they ought to."[7]

Most ministers disagreed with these conservative positions and unabashedly addressed political matters from the pulpit. Many clerics regarded the country's problems as "dark dispensations of divine Providence" and seized the opportunity to denounce a multitude of national sins deserving divine punishment. For instance, George Duffield decried the Constitution's failure to acknowledge God and considered disunion the obvious result of the doctrine of popular sovereignty with its emphasis on self-government "independent of Jehovah." Duffield surprisingly asserted that the nation's chief crime and root of all its problems was the unjust and unconstitutional removal of the Cherokees from Georgia in the 1830s. This deplorable incident had produced a "spirit of lawlessness" and set a precedent for the violation of contracts and covenants that reached its culmination in secession. James Smart and Horace Hovey likewise catalogued numerous American sins, including political partisanship, the lust for territorial expansion through the Mexican War and filibustering expeditions, and the Fugitive Slave Act, yet each agreed that slavery was the primary cause of sectionalism. Although both men emphasized repentance as the prescription for appeasing the wrath of God and avoiding conflict, Hovey demonstrated an uncharacteristically haughty spirit by claiming that slavery was strictly a sectional sin that the South alone needed to confess. Taking a different tack, Cincinnati Presbyterian S. R. Wilson insisted on the benignity of slavery when compared to the deplorable living conditions of many free blacks and concluded that northern "aggressors" deserved greater blame than southern secessionists for dividing the country. More typical was Illinois Presbyterian L. M. Glover's assertion that God's wrath, when poured out on nations, fell on the righteous and evildoers alike, and this truth demonstrated that all Americans needed to confess both individual and collective sins. Regardless of their views on the place of politics in the pulpit, in January 1861 practically all ministers agreed upon the undesirability of war. Clergymen opposed to slavery could resoundingly approve James Smart's prayer "that God in his providence may devise some means by which slavery may be abolished without the effusion of blood." Without question, northern preachers recognized the gravity of the situation at hand, and most overwhelmingly voiced their political opinions, desiring to influence public debate and secure the preservation of the Union.[8]

Although historians typically have viewed ministers as shapers of public opinion, it seems just as likely that they reflected the popular will as much as molded it. As David Chesebrough has observed, when ministers addressed contemporary matters from the pulpit, they bolstered public opinion by seemingly imparting "divine sanction" to prevailing popular attitudes. Indeed, civilian opinions on the secession crisis abound with the belief that only God's intervention could prevent hostilities from breaking out between the sections. Elisha Huntington exhibited a more pessimistic outlook than most individuals when even before South Carolina seceded he alleged that "the country is already irrevocably divided." He expected "*servile* war" to shatter the Union by early 1861 unless "God save[s] us from these dire calamities." Indianapolis banker Calvin Fletcher similarly thought secession was imminent but accepted that "God has it in his care & I will try & rest with confidence in his directions." Once South Carolina seceded, Fletcher prayed for God to "avert the War" because "it is beyond the power of man." Detroit resident Jane Merick's New Year's petition appealed for "our heavenly Father [to] keep us from contrasting the blessings of peace with the horrors of war." Yet after five states of the Deep South and Texas joined the ranks of secession by early February, war seemed near. According to Martha White Talbert, a Quaker from Westfield, Indiana, the country had become "convulsed with contending factions," creating a division that pitted "the right against might." Although Talbert was uncertain which side would "conquer," she expected "the God of justice and mercy" to "rule in the contest."[9]

But if God providentially planned to afflict the nation with war, religious Northerners wanted to understand his reasons for doing so. Some citizens suggested that God was chastening the nation for unconfessed sins. Andrew Ingram of Lafayette, Indiana, maintained "hope that an overruling Providence will not punish our nation according to its iniquities, but that his chasnings [chastenings] will be tempered with mercy." In Marshall, Michigan, attorney George Woodruff regarded "the impending crisis" as "another signal…of the Divine justice upon national sins."[10] Although the chastening process caused temporary pain, neither of these men sought to avoid it because they understood that it would produce lasting benefits through purification. With its imperfections removed, a purged nation would shine brighter and renew its moral strength to stand more firmly for the right. Because God had chosen the Union to be the beacon of liberty throughout the world, his occasional disciplining gave continued evidence that the divine mission awaited future fulfillment. References to chastening became more common after the war developed into a protracted struggle, but it is noteworthy that a few civilians linked political difficulties with national sins even during the secession crisis.

Belief in God's providence did not prevent northern civilians from holding man responsible for actions that precipitated the political confrontation. To be sure, the doctrine of providence was not identical to fatalism, which held that events happened by chance apart from human free will. Providence, in contrast, struck a balance by placing human responsibility and decision making within the sovereignty of God, thereby demonstrating God's omnipotence by allowing man to make personal choices within his sovereign decrees. For instance, Elisha Huntington blamed both sections of the country for causing the conflict. In his estimation, South Carolina was a "nest of traitors" determined to find the slightest ground for separation, yet "the mad, fanatical and persistent assaults of the North upon the Institution of slavery" had inflamed the South. "The abolitionists of the North & the Disunionists of the South are alike guilty of destroying the best government the world ever saw," he complained. Despite doubting their ability to achieve success, Andrew Ingram nonetheless desired that conservative politicians from both sections continue negotiations in order to reach a compromise. Calvin Fletcher surmised that the government might head off further trouble by offering monetary compensation to emancipate slaves in the border states. Civilian recommendations had little chance of influencing public policy, but Abraham Lincoln certainly possessed the ability to affect the outcome of events. When the president-elect passed through Indianapolis on his way to Washington, Fletcher attended the public rally. He expressed sympathy for Lincoln regarding the difficult position the president-elect had inherited and the grave responsibilities he bore. Feeling moved to pray for Lincoln, Fletcher clearly expressed how man's actions worked within God's providence. "I pray God to direct & that he may thro Mr. L. heal the differences" between North and South. Indianapolis lawyer John L. Ketcham echoed this sentiment when he wished that Lincoln would "be the Instrument in the hands of the Almighty to bring good out of Evil."[11] It seemed logical to these men that God would work through the nation's foremost leader to achieve his intended purposes.

Although Abraham Lincoln had been a public figure in Illinois practically his entire adult life, his personal religion was difficult to classify. Raised in a Calvinistic Baptist church as a youth, Lincoln never joined a church as an adult and was branded an infidel during his successful 1846 congressional campaign against the famous Methodist itinerant Peter Cartwright. He flatly denied the allegation, and during the 1850s he often attended church, replaced his youthful fatalism with something closer to a belief in providence, treasured the Bible for its moral wisdom, and frequently peppered his political speeches with biblical quotes, a habit that drew criticism from Stephen Douglas in 1858. Only two weeks before the 1860 election, Lincoln cited Luke 16:31, "'If they hear not Moses and the prophets, neither will they be per-

Calvin Fletcher (1798–1866) settled in Indianapolis in 1821 and became one of the city's most prominent citizens, active in politics, law, banking, and education. He supported numerous city churches with generous financial contributions and was a strong advocate for Sunday schools. His daily diary, which he kept for more than thirty years, provides a window into the heart of a man truly consumed with the idea of God's providential governing of everyday human affairs. *Indiana Historical Society*

suaded though one rose from the dead,'" to underscore that his prior public declarations were more than sufficient to satisfy Southerners that, if elected, he would abide by the Constitution and leave slavery alone. A month after Lincoln's victory at the polls, an Illinois minister wanted to be certain that the president-elect understood the importance of Scripture and God's providence. William Sloane informed Lincoln that he had detected "the hand of God...in your election," encouraged him to read the Psalms to gain wisdom, and admonished him to remember the psalmist's instruction, "*It is better to trust in the Lord than to put confidence in man*" when choosing his cabinet. Before departing Springfield on February 11 "to assume a task more difficult than that which devolved upon General Washington," Lincoln expressed his dependence on "the same omniscient mind, and Almighty arm that directed and protected" the father of the country. Furthermore, he asked his friends and supporters to petition God's assistance on behalf of the country and "invoke His wisdom and guidance for me." After a week and a half of extemporaneous comments at whistle-stops and formal speeches in major cities along the route to Washington, a wearied Lincoln learned in Philadelphia that his belief in the concept of a protecting providence might be tested. Intelligence had confirmed the existence of a plot to assassinate him in Baltimore, so he altered his itinerary and passed through the city at night. Guarded by his close friend Ward Hill Lamon and detective Allan Pinkerton, the president-elect arrived in the capital without incident on the morning of February 23.[12]

When Inauguration Day dawned ten days later, some religious Northerners balanced their feelings of uncertainty with the conviction that God would preserve the nation. A female resident of Schoolcraft, Michigan, hoped that Lincoln would neither enrage Southerners by outlawing slavery nor conciliate them by allowing "the black pollution" to spread over "*the free* earth" and be thrust upon "unwilling people" in the territories. She placed confidence in the president and believed that a merciful God would "take pity on our miserable condition as a nation and uphold our Ruler by His strong arm." However, if "the plots of the wicked" somehow succeeded in assassinating Lincoln, then she would "expect fire and brimstone to rain down from the Lord...and blot us out of existence." To everyone's relief, an early morning drizzle was the only thing that fell from the skies above the domeless Capitol on March 4. In his address, Lincoln did his utmost to reassure the South that there was no reason for hasty action because he would not confiscate their property or violate their constitutional rights in any way. In a lawyerly manner, he attempted to persuade all citizens who truly loved their country that "the Union of these States is perpetual." Furthermore, he asserted that secession would lead only to anarchy and despotism. Barely mentioning slavery, he avoided making moral judgments that might alienate and divide, and his brief allusions to God were little more than stock phrases. An excellent speech perfectly suited for the political conditions of the hour, the First Inaugural showcased Lincoln the rationalist thinker whose masterfully crafted language could reassure his countrymen that sectional harmony "surely" would be restored when "the better angels of our nature" resounded "the mystic chords of memory" that would "swell the chorus of the Union."[13] After four long years as president, this confidence in man's capacity to solve his problems by drawing on his own strength and understanding would be replaced by a humble acknowledgment of human inability to effect an outcome that God did not intend, for war would transform Lincoln into a spiritual seeker who affirmed that "the Almighty has His own purposes."

While Lincoln deftly sidestepped slavery in his address, some religious civilians pointed to it as the primary cause of the difficulties between North and South. Antislavery advocates understandably thought that disunion ultimately would result in the removal of slavery from American shores. On several occasions during the winter of 1860–61, Calvin Fletcher mused that the peculiar institution was "doomed" and that secession would sound its "death [k]nell." Although Fletcher often wondered what would become of the Union, he was certain that "slavery has brot it to the verge of distruction." W. G. Johnson, a Baptist minister in Geneseo, Illinois, maintained that God "has seen the affliction of his oppressed people in the South...and will send deliverance." He speculated that Southerners, like the Egyptians who enslaved the Israelites, might suffer destruction by "the hand of God." While Fletcher and Johnson welcomed the opportunity to wipe out slavery, other civilians valued peace at the expense of leaving slavery intact. Elisha Huntington preferred to let the South separate from the Union rather than prolong a dispute that he considered to be "all moonshine." When he accused so-called "Black Republicans" of commencing "this war upon slavery," Huntington mirrored those conservative ministers who blasted abolitionists as a principal culprit for the nation's problems. Andrew Ingram likewise was disturbed "that this question about the negro should dissolve our government & plunge us into civil war.... It is ridiculous in the extreme that a sensible people should quarrel over it." Ingram thought it appalling that slavery would sever the Union when the country suffered from greater "evils," in his estimation, "than African slavery."[14] Regardless of their specific opinions on the institution itself, Northerners who ascribed to providence a role in directing political events often agreed that slavery was the chief point of contention dividing the nation.

Religious civilians who applied the doctrine of providence to national events during the secession crisis were continuing a practice dating back to at least the mid-eighteenth century when American Protestants "actively embraced republican ideals" because they believed that "American republicanism appeared not just scriptural but God-given." During the American Revolution, New England clergy had given religious meaning to political matters, even "defining republican liberty as a cardinal principle of Christian belief." According to this thinking, religion reinforced civic humanism because religious precepts helped cultivate virtue in citizens. A virtuous citizenry, in turn, would sustain representative government based on the ideals of liberty and freedom. According to Mark Noll, the concept of Christian republicanism, which had wedded evangelicalism and republicanism during the mid-eighteenth century, motivated many individuals throughout the antebellum period to let their personal faith shape the public discourse over issues ranging from temperance to abolition. One Baptist periodical claimed in 1856 that political involvement by Christians was imperative because "underlying all purely political questions [is] a moral one of paramount significance." Because Christian republicanism cast freedom and the Union in a sacred light, Protestants who espoused this view had a moral responsibility to support and preserve the Union at any cost.[15]

Coincident with this moral justification for political activism lay the potential for risking Christian unity since some individuals rejected the philosophy of Christian republicanism on various grounds. One objection centered on the idea that religious beliefs should remain in a separate sphere from political and social matters, thereby compartmentalizing the sacred and the secular. Although laypersons seldom referred to it by name, theologians invoked the doctrine of the spirituality of the church when opposing the mixing of religion and politics. According to this view, the church should be apolitical and limit itself to addressing only spiritual matters such as disseminating the word of God. Individual believers possessed freedom of conscience when dealing with all other issues of life. Another complaint against Christian republicanism arose from pacifist groups such as Quakers and Mennonites, whose opposition to war left them in a predicament concerning how to demonstrate support for the Union without condoning a war to maintain it. As Thomas Curran explains, these "perfectionist pacifists" opposed the dominant "sentiment of Christian republicanism" by remaining true to their biblical convictions that Christ taught nonresistance. Probably most common, though, was the fundamental division between adherents of the Democratic party and ministers whose public pronouncements championing the Union caused resentment and produced accusations of warmongering and sectarianism for discussing political matters in church. For example, in his annual message before the legislature of Indiana in January 1861, outgoing Democratic governor Abram A. Hammond denounced "profoundly ignorant" clergymen who allegedly disturbed the public peace by meddling in politics. When Indianapolis Baptist James Simmons, who had begun a sermon series on Christ's sufferings before the politician's address, came to the story of Christ before Pilate, he responded to Hammond's criticism by noting that Jewish leaders had accused Christ of stirring up excitement among the people for simply preaching the truth. Simmons took satisfaction in being charged with the same offense as the Savior, and he advised Hammond to study closely the teachings of Christ in the New Testament and to learn from history "the character and fate" of the Roman governor.[16]

The secession crisis quickly made apparent the antagonism between northern ministers who commented on political subjects from the pulpit and laymen who viewed these utterances as inappropriate for the house of God.

When John Funk attended Chicago's Third Presbyterian Church in late December 1860, he heard Reverend Swazy deliver "a regular old revolutionary sermon" challenging the North to stand firm against the South. Raised in a Mennonite background, Funk was uncomfortable with the tone of the message and regarded most Northerners as "blood-thirsty and anxious enough to fight without such injunctions being sent forth from the sacred desk." From the opposite perspective, clerics who adhered to Christian republicanism often learned firsthand the perils of political preaching. One Democrat walked out during George Tuthill's fast day sermon, and the patriotic Congregationalist refused to allow the local paper to print his address because of the editor's reputation for "vilify[ing] any minister who speaks for the slave." Despite "misgivings" about his chosen topic, Perry Hall, minister at Central Christian Church in Indianapolis, decided that his pastoral "duty" compelled him to deliver a sermon on the "present crisis in our national affairs" for the evening service on January 13, 1861. Two days after preaching to "a crowded house," Hall received threats of tar and feathering from some enraged listeners, and a few days later one of his deacons resigned over the sermon's content. Nevertheless, Hall publicly defended his decision to preach a political message and dismissed his detractors as being in error and "afraid of the light." Indeed, he even refused to make amends when offended individuals threatened to leave his church unless he apologized for his political sermon.[17]

A number of themes emerged during the secession crisis that foreshadowed future developments. Many northern civilians looked at the country's political troubles through a theological grid that placed God at the center of the action, guiding events for the nation's benefit. Ministers frequently expressed their political views from the pulpit, sometimes alienating members who disagreed with the content of their sermons or considered political preaching altogether improper. Both civilians and clergy generally expressed unequivocal support for the Union, and while they made clear their desire to reach a diplomatic compromise to avoid armed conflict if possible, they insisted that the Union was worth fighting for if necessary. Several of these religious-minded individuals even designated slavery as the central issue causing the country's division. Most significantly, the line between religious beliefs and patriotism was becoming blurred so that many Northerners considered the Union to be sacred. These developments produced a "tragic quandary" for northern religion because war seemed to be the only viable option for accomplishing the twofold objective of preserving the Union and fulfilling America's divine mission to spread freedom. Instead of offering a voice of impartiality, many northern clergy rushed into the charged political atmosphere and had their judgment obscured by the prevailing patriotic fervor.[18] Coincidently, a majority of northern laity seemed unconcerned that patriotism had become sacrosanct and religion had been politicized.

Immediately after his inauguration, Lincoln faced a dilemma regarding Major Robert Anderson's request for reinforcements and supplies at Fort Sumter in Charleston harbor. Unwilling to surrender federal property to the newly formed Confederate government, the president decided that by sending provisions only he would force the Confederacy to reveal its hand. If Rebel batteries fired on a ship executing a strictly humane assignment, then the South would be entirely guilty of starting the conflict. However, if Sumter were successfully reprovisioned, then the North would gain a moral victory and Lincoln would deftly diffuse a volatile situation. Confederate president Jefferson Davis ultimately decided that the time for action had arrived and authorized Brigadier General P. G. T. Beauregard to demand the surrender of Sumter and to attack the fort if Major Anderson refused to comply. Anderson held firm, and on April 12, 1861, Confederate batteries opened fire on Sumter and for the next thirty-three hours poured shell into the fort. Undermanned, nearly out of food, and lacking sufficient ammunition, Anderson surrendered the fort. In response, Lincoln called for 75,000 militia to assist the government for ninety days in order to quash the rebellion. Intoxicated by the war spirit, a majority of the northern populace rallied to preserve the Union.[19]

After months of waiting and anxiously following political developments, the northern masses erupted in displays of unionism during the weeks after the attack on Sumter. Calvin Fletcher described Indianapolis as being in a whirl "of great excitement. Men doing nothing but walking up & down the street greatly angery at any one who intimated a favor to the South." His son Elijah, a Methodist minister in New Albany, Indiana, directly on the border with Kentucky, considered himself in no danger because the residents of southern Indiana were "staunch patriots." The younger Fletcher thought that Louisville's inhabitants were clouded by a "strange blindness" if they expected Indiana to favor the South. At Indiana Asbury University in Greencastle, John Poucher had difficulty concentrating on his studies with patriotism at such a high tide and "nearly all our time...absorbed in reading political papers." Within a few days of Sumter's surrender, about one hundred students had left campus, either enlisting or returning home. A Grand Rapids, Michigan, resident swelled with patriotic devotion after hearing Baptist preacher Abel Bingham pray for the country and "the subjection of those *ambitious, proud,* and *imperious spirits*" who commenced the war. Wisconsin senator James Doolittle notified Lincoln and Secretary of War Simon Cameron that "nothing can exceed the enthusiasm and united determination of every man, & of every party, and of all churches & ministers, to sustain the administration. They feel it is obeying God, and if an angel from Heaven had spoken there could have been no more hearty response than we now see to the Presidents proclamation" calling for troops. So strong was the patriotic fervor in Chicago that it began to annoy John Funk, who had to endure the singing of "My Country Tis of Thee" five times at various meetings and social gatherings he attended. To his amazement, the Sunday school superintendent even "preached a war sermon to the children."[20]

Fostering patriotism among children was only the tip of the iceberg for most northern churches, which wholeheartedly threw their support behind the Union. The *Chicago Tribune* discerned no "distinction of sect, creed or denomination" among religious supporters of the war. In the weeks after the surrender of Sumter, numerous ministers assured their congregations and enthusiastic soldiers preparing to head off to camp that America was God's chosen nation. S. W. Lynd, Methodist Episcopal pastor in Mt. Auburn, Ohio, reminded his city's home guards that "our beloved Union is the offspring of special providence. God guided our fathers to this land of promise." Consequently, God would sustain the Union army in its righteous war against the rebels. William Goodrich, pastor of Cleveland's First Presbyterian Church, crowed, "I *know*, that with this host goes forth the unseen presence and the might of a just God." Although Goodrich did not claim that victory would be immediate, he assured his congregation that God "has no providence which sides with traitors," and "in his own way and time, he will turn back the tide of rebellion, and give the victory to our arms." Horace Hovey told members of the Coldwater, Michigan, Light Artillery and Zouave Cadets that God would dispense his "thunderbolts of Justice" to "destroy the traitors, and give his beloved a peaceful home again." Preaching to Company A of the 1st Michigan Volunteers in Detroit's Christ Church, Benjamin Paddock noted how God's chosen nation Israel had often experienced war, and he concluded that Israel's "*cause was always just and the necessity* [of war] *inevitable.*" Drawing a parallel to the present conflict, Paddock reminded the troops to trust God to assist their "holy cause" as he had guided Israel in the past. Some ministers flagrantly appropriated Scripture in order to bestow divine sanction on northern patriotism. Horace Hovey took his text from Psalm 60:4, "Thou hast given a banner to them that fear thee," and extrapolated that the Star Spangled Banner was a *"sacred"* flag which "*God* gave...to this Republic for a holy purpose." According to Hovey, that "holy purpose" was the cause of freedom, a cause that might even require the shedding of blood. The patriotic salvos discharged from northern pulpits in the aftermath of Sumter portrayed the Union war effort as a religious crusade. The connection between God and country had become so airtight that patriotism was considered a Christian obligation. Goodrich concluded, "In this cause, the consecration of ourselves to our country's service, may be the noblest duty we can render to our Redeemer and our God."[21]

The enthusiastic ecclesiastical support for the mobilization of Union arms caused one sympathetic Presbyterian to conclude that northern churchgoers had interpreted the sectional conflict as "a religious war." The practice of collecting funds for soldiers on Sundays, the abundance of prayer meetings where members of all denominations supplicated God to uphold the government and protect soldiers, the steady enlistment of church members and prevalence of commissioning services after which new recruits left for the field with Bible in hand, and the sustained commitment to visit soldiers in camp in order to minister to their spiritual needs all demonstrated the "profound religious significance" that northern Christians perceived in what at first glance appeared to be a struggle strictly over political and constitutional questions. The writer maintained that such an enormous expenditure of effort would be entirely misguided and even sacrilegious if undertaken merely to sustain human government. In his opinion, preserving a government "*upon foundations and under conditions consistent with Christ's Kingdom*" was the fundamental issue at stake for most religious Northerners, for in the end churches would benefit from a revitalized government based on moral principles such as justice and love.[22]

The Presbyterian's utopian, millennial vision was far from at variance with mainstream opinion on the war's meaning, for by the spring of 1861 even secular newspapers of opposing political persuasions distinctly manifested the extent to which the mixing of religion and politics had permeated northern culture. The *Rockford (Illinois) Register*, a Lincoln organ, defended the principle of the equality of man, insisting that it was a God-given right that applied to all humans, including blacks. In advocating equality, Republicans countered the "political atheism" of Democrats. Furthermore, Republicans claimed that their "political action is made conformable to, and sanctified by a truly religious life," in effect admitting that religious principles motivated their political activities. "We are, in short but pursuing the straight-forward course of duty toward God and our fellow man that shall open our hearts and understandings for the reception of a larger measure of the Divine life." In contrast, the editor of the *Niles (Michigan) Republican*, a Douglas mouthpiece, alleged that Republicans had built their party on a "rotten foundation" when they maintained that the Declaration of Independence intended equality for blacks. Moreover, the editor questioned Republicans' religious motivations when they affirmed that God providentially had determined to end slavery. From the Democratic standpoint, if slavery were indeed a sin as Republicans contended, then why had God given victory to the colonies in the American Revolution and knowingly allowed the creation of a government "dedicated to slavery?" The editor jabbed, "Truly, these fanatics are wiser in their own eyes than God himself." In reality, the editor asserted, slavery had proven beneficial to Africans, and God had used it to Christianize them and spread the gospel to Africa.[23]

Several secular newspaper editors who weighed in on the incident at Sumter employed providential terminology when seeking a satisfactory explanation for what had transpired there and what it all meant for the nation's future. In Columbus, Ohio, the editor of the *Daily Capital City Fact* gave Major Anderson little chance of holding out against the Rebels unless "the work of a special Providence" upheld him. After the surrender, the editor of the *St. Clairsville (Ohio) Gazette and Citizen* asserted that "the God of their fathers... protected them," for "the interposition of Divine Providence" provided the only plausible explanation to account for the preservation of every life amid such a bombardment. Despite opposing the war, the Democratic editor thought it might provide a potential providential benefit if it became "the means by which he [God] intends to rid the earth of this cursed faction [Republicans]." Of course, the Republican-leaning *Evansville (Indiana) Daily Journal* came to a different conclusion concerning God's purposes. The editor confidently professed that "the fearful commotion that is now shaking the country to its foundation, is incomprehensible to human understanding, except as interpreted in the light of Divine Providence." Although God's plan could not be known with certainty, "it may even be possible that Providence designs by means of these troubles to put a summary end to slavery." In Madison, the *Wisconsin Daily Patriot* offered a different take and focused on political corruption as the nation's foulest blight. The editor grounded his argument in the biblical concept that the penalty for sins required a blood atonement, so the "blood-letting" of war might be the means "that an Allwise Providence has ordained... to cure the fatal malady." Alluding to the most recognizable verse in Scripture, John 3:16, the editor declared that "the blood of God's only Son was offered up as an atonement for the sins of the whole world, and nothing but blood can now purify the corrupted political atmosphere."[24] By drawing a parallel between the death of Christ and the nascent war, this editor clearly illuminated the pervasiveness of religion in the political discourse.

Not to be outdone by clergy and secular newspaper editors, many northern civilians espoused a religious view of the outbreak of war by defining it in providential terms. Calvin Fletcher deemed the fall of Sumter "no great loss" because he had "faith [to] believe all is right." He simply trusted God's ability to direct the nation that "He has never forsaken." John Poucher lamented "the horrors of civil war" but reassured himself that "the country is subject to the will of God." As northern states quickly filled their enlistment quotas, Henry Demaree of Johnson County, Indiana, foresaw a "ruined cuntry" unless "God saves" it. Although Lizzie Little of Aurora, Illinois, blamed "those rebelious Traitors" for causing the war, she knew that ultimately "God ordains[,] that he ruleth and reigneth[,] and that we are in his hands." No human could ascertain God's reasons for allowing hostilities to commence, so believers in the doctrine of providence simply had to trust that God knew what was best. Andrew Ingram noted the futility of trying to debate the *how*'s, *why*'s, or *what if*'s of the conflict, for "the ways of Providence are inscrutable." The past could not be altered, so it behooved man to "have faith to believe that He, in his own way and in his own time will settle it aright, and that good will in the end come of it."[25]

Despite the scriptural teaching that God concealed his purposes from the minds of men, many religious civilians nonetheless formed their own conclusions as to why he had permitted the onset of war. Belief in providence did not discourage a person from seeking to understand earthly events; indeed, it more likely encouraged speculation and stimulated the desire to draw applications in order to find transcendent meaning in life's happenings. Furthermore, with each individual left to his or her own imagination, a plethora of explanations resulted. This diversity of meanings ascribed by northern civilians to the inception of war attests to the pliable nature of the doctrine of providence and its usefulness for comprehending such alarming national events. The most obvious question on people's minds concerned which side deserved blame, and Northerners seldom needed help in finding the answer. John Poucher concluded that the North was indeed justified in pursuing war because the South had initiated it. By provisioning Sumter, the federal government had merely attempted to maintain its rightful property from being illegally "seized by the 'fire eaters.'" Calvin Fletcher implicitly agreed with this conclusion that the government had acted within its proper bounds and therefore prayed for God to "give *the right power.*" Other perplexities involved the prospects for the government's preservation and God's intention in allowing war in the first place. Fletcher assumed that the corrective hand of God fell on both North and South and postulated that his "just retribution...may be to bring us to a sense of our dependence" on him. William Patrick, mayor of Urbana, Ohio, possessed "an abiding confidence and faith" that God would sustain the government and not "permit this unholy war brought upon us by the mad schemes of that Calhounian origin, to result in...its overthrow." Although the war might have been "unholy" in its secessionist roots, Patrick conceded that God could have used wicked means to bring about a divine end. "Perhaps in the wise dispensations of his providence he may see a necessity of chastening all of us for past sins & for our future good." Cyrus McCormick, Chicago industrialist and inventor of the reaper, discerned an opportunity for repentance in the face of "this great affliction and scourge.... We must be humbled, feeling that it is the hand of the Lord, though brought about by wicked instrumentalities, and deserved on account of the sinfulness of the people."[26]

Although Patrick and McCormick anticipated that some unknown good would derive from the divinely inspired reproof and admitted the existence of sin in general, other civilians immediately drew specific connections and made concrete applications. In John Poucher's opinion, any deaths resulting from the war would be in vain unless accompanied by "the abolition of slavery and all its doctrines." Thomas Barland of Eau Claire, Wisconsin, pontificated to his sister Betsy, who had resided in Kentucky during the 1850s and had many slaveholding friends, that "when the Lord...take[s] up the cause of the poor [slaves] into his own hands, he will sooner or later carry it through in a manner glorifying to himself & destructive to every obstacle...of his kingdom." Where Barland barely hinted at the idea that the war and the eradication of slavery were only secondary matters compared to the primacy of Christ's millennial kingdom, other northern civilians explicitly employed apocalyptic language. Therese Elstine unmistakably interpreted the inauguration of hostilities as a sign of the imminent Apocalypse, disclosing to a friend "that we are fast approaching a period that is refered to by Christ when wars and rumors of wars shall have spread all over the Earth." Regardless of what martial cataclysms the future held in store, she urged "Cristians to pray that good may be brought out of these great commotions in the affairs of men." Ann Conkling, a family friend of the Lincolns from Springfield, similarly found millennial overtones in the severing of the Union. Although God alone knew the country's "future destiny," she perceived "that he is fulfilling the purpose of his own kingdom" and would continue to "overturn" human affairs until "*he shall* reign on earth."[27]

Regardless of God's intentions in the war, whether punishment for unnamed sins, the predestined destruction of slavery, the harbinger of the Apocalypse, or even something entirely unanticipated, the specific application mattered little when one possessed confidence that God supported the Union and would give victory to her arms. Thomas Barland did not fret over the outcome but took comfort "that sooner or later God would interpose by his mighty power & in his infinite wisdom to...show on what side he had always been." Elisha Huntington called for swift military action, presumptuously claiming, "Nor can the Gates of Hell prevail against us." This excessive bravado, found more often among the clergy, seems to have been the exception among northern civilians. Although believers in providence expected God to inevitably bring good out of troubling circumstances, their faith in an eventual happy ending did not prevent periods of doubt or hide feelings of uncertainty. Elijah Fletcher carried "a heavy heart" because he "felt that as the 'United States' we had ceased to be." During the "love feast" at the church John Maine attended in Mansfield, Ohio, "there were but few dry eyes in the house" because "allmost every one that spoke said something about our now distracted but once happy Country." The disruption of the Union caused Nettie Fowler McCormick's "pride" for her once "great & glorious" country to be replaced by "mortification,...terror,...[and] alarm."

Martha White Talbert even wondered if the revolutionary generation had fought and died for naught since the country they struggled to found had been torn apart. Worse than doubting the Founding Fathers, Andrew Ingram questioned America's divine calling. "Those high expectations of our Countrys future glory, prosperity and renown and her mission as an exemplar among the nations of the earth are—I greatly fear—likely to prove a mere phantasm." Ingram despaired that the Union's breakup had forfeited America's elevated position among the world's nations, because civil war would reveal "our utter incapacity for self government."[28]

Adherents to the doctrine of providence accepted that God possessed ultimate control of events, but they also recognized the place for man's free will within that sovereign plan. Therefore, it naturally followed that northern Unionists would blame Southerners for their choices and actions that led to war. Thomas Barland condemned "wicked" southern preachers for teaching the "corrupt doctrine" of slavery and "leading the[ir] blind" followers to the brink "of immense worldly disaster" in the form of civil war. While these clergy claimed to be "worshippers of God," in reality they were "workers of iniquity" awaiting "the manifestation of God's judgemant." By attacking the clergy, Barland implied that southern Christianity itself was a false religion because it had been defiled by and remained under the dominion of the sin of slavery. With southern religion thoroughly contaminated, it was not much of a stretch for Lizzie Little to attribute "all this misery" to "those rebelious Traitors...which his Satanic magisty uses to do his feindish work."[29] As strange as it seems, Little's accusing secessionists of being emissaries of the devil harmonized with the doctrine of providence. God could permit Satan to work his evil temporarily while inevitably overruling his devilish designs for the accomplishment of the divine will, hence the oft-heard prayer for God to bring good out of evil.

In some cases, Northerners' abhorrence of the Rebel cause corrupted their view of Southerners themselves, sometimes even degenerating into outright hatred. One week after Federal troops occupied Alexandria, Virginia, Chicago resident Thomas Bryan warned his parents to keep up their guard because he suspected all "disunionists" of being "full of both wiles & wickedness." If the Confederates ever retook Alexandria, he presumed that they would not hesitate to engage in "acts of violence upon unoffending citizens known to indulge Union sentiments.... I feel painfully assured that the hotheaded secessionists of V[irginia] would delight in persecuting Union families whenever they may fall in their power." Depicting the enemy as barbarians from the safety of Chicago was one thing, but only the Ohio River separated Elijah Fletcher from many southern-sympathizing Kentuckians. Fletcher recognized his potential danger as "a Methodist minister of the church North." He conjectured that if "the rabble of the other side make in roads" into New Albany, he "would be precious game to them." Nevertheless, Fletcher did not hide his true feelings regarding Southerners, but fumed, "The very sight of a *Southron* makes me mad. Their long hair, supercilious bearing,...tobacco-spit[ting,] brandy-red faces make me sick at my stomach." While some Northerners were content to denigrate Southerners in general, Lizzie Little reserved her contempt for their leader. Little principally blamed Jefferson Davis for the war and estimated that his removal might cause the rebellion to collapse. Consequently, she concocted a scheme to assassinate Davis and revealed it to her future husband, George Smith Avery. Although she admitted the plot might be farfetched, Little figured that, at worst, she would be killed, but success "would immortalize my name" and possibly end the war. After Avery scuttled her plan, Little concluded that the next best thing she could wish for was "a hell of *real fire & brimstone*" for all Southerners.[30] When discussing Southerners during the war's initial stages, religious Northerners tended to let their carnal passions supplant a forgiving spirit and preferred vengeance to mercy.

The fervency of Union sentiment in the months immediately following the surrender of Sumter eventually waned, and dissenting voices cautiously emerged. For Democrats and people of southern heritage, living in the North, especially the states of Ohio, Indiana, and Illinois, became a difficult and sometimes perilous experience. Because they controlled the reins of national government, many Republicans refused to tolerate dissent in any form. According to Melinda Lawson, Republicans viewed Democrats' slavish "devotion to party at the expense of nation" as endangering "the very existence of the Union." Consequently, Republicans often branded all Democrats as disloyal and even treasonous for remaining faithful to their party. A. H. Davidson, a native Virginian living in Indianapolis, directly felt the stress of the charged political atmosphere immediately after Sumter. Although Davidson prudently avoided political rallies, he nevertheless considered his position "anything but...pleasant" because "very few...sympathise with me, and I am obliged to be very guarded in my speech." Henry K. Wilson, a Democratic state senator from Sullivan County, Indiana, waited until the end of May before feeling secure enough "to whisper his opinion about the causes of this war, without a threat of being bayoneted." His senate colleague Smith Jones of Bartholomew County complained that rabid Republicans labeled "the friends of peace" as traitors and tried to intimidate them with threats of hanging. Therese Elstine described the "frightful" tumult created by "wild" Republicans in Mt. Carmel, Ohio, who had "secretly threaten[ed] a couple of citizens here with mobing and tar and feathering...for expressing themselves against the Administration." How often intimidation ended in violence is anyone's guess, but Republicans certainly made Democrats aware of their minority status as political outsiders for failure to support the war.[31]

Excluded from the political mainstream by Republicans, Democrats and war dissenters refused to let Unionists appropriate the doctrine of providence. Opponents of war trusted that God's providence would prevent armed conflict and altogether rejected the idea that he had sanctified the Union cause. Having lost "confidence in men in high places," meaning Republicans, a despondent Smith Jones hoped that "Divine Providence...[would] interpose in such a visible manner" and preserve the government. Indeed, Unionist Northerners who audaciously declared to know God's purposes for the conflict struck many war dissenters as sheer arrogance. A. H. Davidson presumed that northern war proponents, specifically "the *ultra* wing of the Republicans," sought "to subjugate" the South. Their boasting of the North's easy triumph and slavery's certain overthrow within six months was "heart sickening" to Davidson, who disbelieved that "a Just God [would] permit such men to succeed in their hellish designs." Republican leaders could be expected to make bellicose speeches, but Davidson especially took offense when members of the clergy uttered similar sentiments. He identified a coterie, "mostly made up of professing christians and christian ministers, who are hounding on the war spirit in hope of crushing out what they call 'the Slave Power,' who say 'There can be no peace without the shedding of blood.'" Smith Jones complained of "fanatical Ministers of the Gospel rejoicing and exulting" over war, and Henry K. Wilson concurred that the clergy were stoking the war fever by "proclaiming that this is a war in which providence is engaged, that his hand will carry it through on the side of the North."[32]

Possibly no minister was more vocal in promoting war or infuriating its opponents than Cincinnati Methodist Granville Moody. Invited to speak at Brookville College in Indiana on June 15–16, the man who would earn the moniker the "Fighting Parson" because of his command of the 74th Ohio Infantry directly addressed antiwar critics and Democratic editors who accused preachers of instigating war with their abolitionist sermons. Moody presumptuously crowed, "I believe it is true, that we did bring it about and I glory in it." The Democratic press pilloried the cleric for this imprudent boast and for his dubious interpretation of John 18:36, "Jesus answered, My kingdom is not of this world: if my kingdom were of this world, then would my servants fight." This text was a favorite of peace-loving religious Northerners, but Moody asserted that the verse taught that Christians, as citizens of an earthly government, had civic responsibilities that included fighting to preserve freedom and overthrow slavery. A local editor countered by citing Christ's rebuke to Peter that all who took up the sword would perish by it, and he suggested that the decapitating begin with Moody and his fellow "abolition priests." Even more offensive to his Democratic detractors, Moody claimed that blacks deserved to be treated as brothers, for they were included in the command to love one's neighbors. With no biblical support to contradict this latter assertion, the editor simply fussed and fumed about the "miserable abolition harangue" that had sullied the reputation of the college and community. Democrats could not tolerate ministers like Moody or religious periodicals that linked the war with the destruction of slavery, and they often complained that the mingling of religion and politics had sapped the spiritual vitality from the church. Moody's discourse prompted one listener to complain that "the churches languish" because many ministers failed to follow Christ's example or "preach the truths of revelation."[33]

The Bible, however, contained much information about war, as a correspondent to the *Presbyter* noted. Biblical warfare generally indicated that God was punishing a nation's sins, and the writer urged Northerners to repent while they had the opportunity. For all practical purposes, many citizens would have discounted this admonition, for most Northerners, including religious ones, presumed that the war would be brief and anxiously awaited news of the one battle that would end the conflict. The government's call for ninety-day enlistments certainly confirmed this popular opinion. Some religious civilians simply doubted southern manliness and underestimated their will to fight. John Funk forecast minimal fighting because "the Southerners are too great cowards to stand much rough useage." Benjamin Webb, a Quaker in Richmond, Indiana, concluded that "after the South gets whipped pretty badly in one or two battles they will want to compromise." In spite of widespread predictions of the war's speedy termination, a few prescient Northerners envisioned a prolonged conflict. A woman in Whitewater, Wisconsin, presumed that the North would prevail against an "underrated" Confederate army after a struggle "more protracted than many think," but she conceded that the exact duration of the contest was "known only to Him who doeth all things well." William Patrick feared that "much blood" would be shed "before this struggle can be settled," yet he expressed faith "that God who is ever merciful" would sustain the government.[34] Despite their disagreement on the length of hostilities or intensity of the fighting, religious Northerners remained confident of success in battle because of the justice of their cause and the mighty arm of their God.

However, when the armies finally met at Manassas Junction on July 21, 1861, the North received a rude awakening. After pushing back Confederate forces most of the day, the Union attack stalled because of failure to coordinate its movements or dispatch reinforcements. When the Rebels counterattacked late in the afternoon, the Union line broke, and what began as an orderly Federal retreat deteriorated into a rout as panicked soldiers fled in disarray. Northern responses to this unexpected setback included disappointment, concern, outrage, and plenty of censure. From the extremely jaded standpoint of John Funk, the defeat was "a hasty step forced on by politicians & unsophisticated and medd[l]ing men—while at the same time our Government and [elected] offices were thronged with traitors all working together for our defeat." Elisha Huntington regretted that the "blunders at Manassas has given the South courage." When Calvin Fletcher heard the "very sad intelligence" that the Union army "had taken a fright & run," he immediately was "overwhelmed" by the blow. Scarcely knowing what to do, he summoned Methodist bishop Edward Ames, and the two "felt it the[ir] duty to fall before the Lord" and confess "great national sins." After time had elapsed for him to ponder the meaning of the setback, he concluded that the "repulse...was a necessary providential dispensation.... We had not seen the horors of slavry, the real cause of the war[,] till our prisoners fell into the slave holders hands."[35]

Although the outcome of Manassas surprised many religious Northerners, it ultimately increased their resolve to support the Union and pursue war until the rebellion was crushed. Milton Marsh, a missionary with the American Sunday School Union, claimed that residents of Oshkosh, Wisconsin, earnestly believed "that the *Government must be sustained* at all hazard." With unwavering confidence, he affirmed that "God will order all things for the ultimate good of our nation." The defeat at Manassas might have been "necessary to humble us for our sins & wickedness," Marsh acknowledged, but God would never "utterly forsake us." In his estimation, "great good to the world, is yet to be accomplished by this nation." Because individuals such as Marsh still clung to the belief in America's divine purpose and providential destiny, they concluded that it was only a matter of time before God would providentially provide the victory. The war, Marsh informed a soldier friend, "is Gods work & must succeed in the end."[36]

2

"Until the Great Sin...Has Been Removed"

God's Chastening, the Sacred Union, and Emancipation

In February 1861, Reuben Hitchcock attended the Washington Peace Conference as a member of the Ohio delegation. Dubbed the "Old Gentlemen's Convention" due to the presence of several men long since removed from the political limelight, most notably former president John Tyler, the conference accomplished nothing apart from demonstrating that Republicans would not bow to the wishes of conservative politicians by accepting any compromise that would give slavery permanent constitutional protection. Hitchcock's correspondence during the convention reveals him as a man of principle who strived to place the good of the country above party loyalty or personal ambition. When he sensed that some Republican delegates wished to divide the party by escalating the tension between the factions around William Seward and Salmon Chase, he refused to allow such political maneuvering to influence him or draw his attention away from the potential calamity that awaited the nation. "What is the life of one man or of a thousand, compared with the multitudes that must be destroyed, & the untold misery that must arise, if this disunion is not stayed," he pondered soberly. When two fellow Ohioans interrupted his writing with dire predictions of "destructive war" between the sections, he reiterated his intention to do his utmost to procure an honorable peace. "God forbid that I should in any way become responsible for such [bloodshed]," he asserted.[1]

After human effort failed to prevent the outbreak of war, Hitchcock, like many religious Northerners, promptly accepted that God had permitted the disruption of the Union and concluded that such a seemingly disastrous event from man's perspective must have been the divine will for the nation. Having witnessed firsthand the rancor that existed between politicians of each section, he was convinced that peace would prevail only after the South had been "thoroughly whipped." Although he presumed northern victory, he conceded that God alone knew the long-term consequences of the war. "A God of justice & infinite power rules amid all the hosts of heaven and in all the armies of the Earth," he affirmed in August 1861. "He sees the end from the beginning, and will do right, and in his own way will accomplish his purposes, all of which aim at the highest & best good of the Universe."[2] Hitchcock trusted that God would sovereignly direct events to achieve his intended objective, and this conviction reinforced his patriotism. Only six months earlier he had labored to negotiate a settlement to avert hostilities, but August found him consenting to his twenty-one-year-old son's enlistment to fight for the preservation of the government.

Reuben Hitchcock's interpreting the Civil War through a religious grid was anything but atypical. Moreover, his unconditional support for war naturally resulted from his premise that God had allowed the conflict in the first place. Indeed, his religious outlook worked hand in hand with his patriotic inclinations to make sacred a war that on the surface seemed to comprise political disagreements over constitutional provisions. From the aftermath of Manassas in July 1861 to Abraham Lincoln's issuing the Preliminary Emancipation Proclamation in September 1862, numerous northern civilians affirmed their belief that God controlled the unfolding of the war. By ascribing to God the governance of human affairs, religious Northerners could comprehend events beyond their control. A theological understanding of the war justified the conflict, offered hope during dismal periods of defeat, and infused their instinctive patriotism with godly zeal. By maintaining that the war was a divinely sanctioned contest, they could claim the moral high ground and denounce national sins, particularly slavery, without compunction or apology. Yet in sanctifying the war as a holy crusade blessed by God to purge the nation of iniquities and to overthrow slavery, they risked compromising the spiritual effectiveness of the church and alienated many Democratic members. Nevertheless, few individuals showed concern over upsetting Christian unity, for their confidence in God's support for the Union and America's unique place among the nations of the world rendered all opposing viewpoints irrelevant, unpatriotic, and even sacrilegious. Since God never acted purposelessly, religious Northerners sought to discover his intentions, and many presumed that he ordained the war to destroy slavery. When the president himself, after suffering through months of frustration caused by the indecision of his generals, enduring repeated military reversals, and mourning the loss of thousands of soldiers as well as his twelve-year-old son, admitted that he had reached the same conclusion, the God-centered perspective of the war had gained credence from a source that no seer would have ever predicted.

The months after the Federal repulse at Manassas witnessed the strengthening of the bond between religion and patriotism. Already, some religious Northerners stressed the justness of the Union cause and explicitly referred to it as a holy undertaking. When a college classmate volunteered in September 1861, William Cline of Hartford City, Indiana, eased the sorrow of their parting with the thought that his friend had "enlisted in a Holy cause" that deserved "the sympathy of every true American." Elisha Huntington claimed that not only loyal Americans but Christians around the world would acknowledge the righteousness of the Union war effort. "The judgment if not the sympathy of all Christendom will pronounce our cause just and holy." Granville Moody informed President Lincoln that the "people of the West" considered the war to be "*a righteous cause*" to preserve the government, and they pledged to "follow the President along the terrific path over which Providence is leading us to a more glorious future." At his church in Daviess County, Indiana, Franklin Alford regarded the spiritually mature members to be those "good soldiers of the cross who will stand in defense of the caus[e] of truth and righteousness and importune...the God of our fathers to guide and guard our armies."[3]

Convinced of God's support and willing to submit to his sovereign direction, religious Northerners needed only to trust his infinite wisdom and accept his perfect timing, which might require suffering additional defeats and bearing the loss of loved ones before gaining ultimate victory. When a regiment of volunteers departed New Albany in mid-August amid the cheers and tears of family and friends, Elijah Fletcher contemplated the "day of reckoning" that awaited "those men who have brought this curse [of war] on our land." Although he resisted the temptation to make specific predictions, Fletcher nevertheless expected a final outcome that would prove beneficial to the country despite the hardships it must first endure. "I stand to day more firm than ever in the faith that God will bring us into a large place," he maintained, borrowing a biblical phrase used by David that attested to God's special favor in delivering him from King Saul. "My comfort is that He knows better than we do; & is far more merciful to us than we are to ourselves." Elijah's father Calvin likewise comforted himself by meditating on God's sovereign care both for his family, especially during the days of uncertainty after the capture of his son William, and for the country. "God knows what is needed....He has the present & future of my dear country in his keeping," he affirmed at the end of August. "The good of the nation, he will promote. The stripes it now recieves may yet (I believe it) be its future glory." With such optimistic expectations of God's projected blessings on America and a firm conviction in the rectitude of the war, some Northerners took the next logical step and insisted that Union victory was guaranteed. Mary Chittenden of Hartsville, Indiana, professed her belief "that the over ruling providence of the most high will guide our armies and lead them on to certain victory."[4]

While faith in the assistance of a sovereign God caused some religious Northerners to consider Union defeat impossible, others wondered what God intended to accomplish and questioned why he allowed setbacks to occur. "Darker and darker gets this night of war and confusion," Serena Wright lamented from Minnesota in late August. "People are asking 'How long, Oh Lord! how long'—and what will the end be when it does come?" The absence of any clear revelation of God's purposes allowed individuals to divine the signs of the times, and some identified issues that prevented the nation from immediately receiving God's blessings. A female resident of Albion, Illinois, deemed that the nation had grown haughty and had failed to acknowledge God for its prosperity, and he had permitted the war to humble the country and remind it to rely on him. "I cannot but hope this war will end in great good to our nation, teaching us our dependence on God for the blessings of freedom," she asserted. "We have been too proud and boastful, too much inclined to think our own right arm hath done all this, and now we are being justly humiliated." When Calvin Fletcher visited with two bishops of the Methodist Episcopal church in mid-August, the men radically differed over the anticipated duration of the war, with Fletcher speculating that it would conclude in fewer than seven years and the bishops conjecturing that it would last as many as fifteen or even thirty years. Regardless of its length, all three "agreed that God in mercy would do all things right & that it might justly appear that we of the north had become so wicked...[and] corrupt that we were to bleed, bleed, bleed."[5] In the months after Manassas, many Northerners who affirmed the divine origins of the war constantly returned to the concept of justice. In the first place, they considered the war a just and holy crusade against the traitorous South to preserve their constitutionally established Union. Coincidentally, they conceded that God was entirely just in punishing the nation through afflictions brought about by war. However, antislavery Northerners regarded the preoccupation with justice as hypocritical while slavery remained protected.

The national debate over slavery erupted anew after General John C. Frémont issued his unauthorized proclamation of emancipation on August 30, 1861. Believing that the civil government of Missouri lacked the ability to curb violence caused by Rebel marauders, Frémont declared martial law in the state and ordered that any person found in arms against the government would have his property confiscated, including his slaves, who would be liberated. This edict went beyond the Confiscation Act passed by Congress earlier that month, which stipulated that only slaves actively assisting the Confederate army could be confiscated. Fearing that such an inflammatory proclamation might alienate border state slaveholders and compel Kentucky to join the Confederacy, Lincoln diplomatically asked Frémont to revise his decree to conform to the Confiscation Act. When the headstrong general refused, the president amended the order himself and shortly thereafter removed Frémont from command in Missouri.[6]

Lincoln's decisive response and political perceptiveness helped keep Kentucky neutral, but in the process he alienated many northern Republicans, particularly religious individuals who favored abolition. Calvin Fletcher immediately hailed Frémont's proclamation as "an important step" in the process of securing freedom for slaves and hoped that similar measures would be enacted in all states of the Upper South. Denominational bodies such as the Illinois Conference of the Methodist Episcopal church even joined in the formal commendations and "unanimously" passed a resolution applauding Frémont for his emancipation edict. However, frustration quickly replaced this exuberance as news of Frémont's downfall, often premature but eventually confirmed, circulated throughout the North. Although Alice Grierson considered the general's dismissal to be "very unwise," she gave Lincoln the benefit of the doubt and affirmed her faith that eventually all would work out for the best. Others, in contrast, lacked her forgiving spirit. J. S. Scoland of Miamitown, Ohio, recounted the story of a local judge who used the occasion of Frémont's ouster to take a backhanded slap at the president. According to Scoland, the judge cited Isaiah 3:4, "Children shall be their Princes and *babes* shall rule over them," in such a way that none present misconstrued the intent of his barb. While antislavery advocates had every reason to applaud Frémont's proclamation, conservative Northerners considered it a misdirected effort to make abolition into a war aim. Elisha Huntington regarded Frémont as little more than a pawn in the hands of "Black Republicans" who nonetheless was "vain enough to think he will be Dictator." Regardless of the various opinions of the man himself, the excitement caused by Frémont's proclamation demonstrated that the topic of emancipation would remain in the public discourse for months to come.[7]

One week after Frémont's edict stirred the hearts of numerous antislavery Northerners, General George B. McClellan, commander of the Army of the Potomac since the debacle at Manassas, issued an order that received widespread approbation from religious citizens. McClellan decreed that officers and enlisted men alike should make every effort to observe the Sabbath by suspending all nonessential military maneuvers, attending religious services, and creating an atmosphere conducive to rest. He stipulated that adherence to this directive should be motivated by a sense of "sacred duty" to God rather than be grudgingly complied with as a mere formality that reinforced dominant social conventions. "We are fighting in a holy cause," the general asserted, "and should endeavor to deserve the benign favor of the Creator." Most churchgoers wholeheartedly agreed with this assessment and in several cases had pointed to the Union army's fighting on Sunday as the reason for defeat at Manassas. J. G. Monfort, editor of the *Presbyter*, noted that the results of several momentous battles over the last one hundred years—the British at Quebec, the Americans at Monmouth, the British on Lake Champlain and again at New Orleans, the French at Waterloo, and the Mexicans at Buena Vista—all proved that armies which attacked on Sundays met resounding defeat. He considered it "utterly vain and presumptuous" for Union forces to expect to receive God's blessings if they continued to initiate combat on Sundays. Religious bodies such as the Illinois Conference of the Methodist Episcopal church and the United Presbyterian Synod expressed their approval of McClellan's action by sending resolutions to the president, who dutifully presented the latter document to the cabinet.[8]

During the autumn of 1861, the government also afforded Northerners the opportunity to examine publicly the country's relationship to God. Nearly three weeks after Manassas, the Federals had suffered another humiliating defeat at the battle of Wilson's Creek in Missouri, and Lincoln responded to this second repulse by consenting to a congressional recommendation calling for a day of national fasting to be observed on September 26. With providential language, the president summoned Northerners "to recognize the hand of God in this terrible visitation" and humble themselves in order to gain military victories and "be spared further punishment, though most justly deserved." On one level, the presidential proclamation in no way violated the separation of church and state, for it merely invited Americans of all faiths to seek God's blessings on the Union. To be sure, Lincoln clearly stayed within his constitutional limits because no particular denomination received preferential governmental assistance. Indeed, his language lacked emotion, and his writing was devoid of personal conviction, resulting in an overall tone that was mechanical and read like an agglomeration of "religious catchphrases...pasted...together in the excessively clausal style of a legal brief." Nevertheless, by employing the providential motif that many Northerners sincerely affirmed, he presented an ideal opportunity for ministers and the religious press to interpret his action as proof "that the United States was a Christian nation as much as if it had been written in the Constitution."[9]

Numerous published sermons delivered on the day of the fast attest to the northern clergy's widespread acceptance of the war as a just and moral cause worthy of the support of all loyal citizens. Oftentimes these jeremiads presented little noteworthy content, typically addressing such standard themes as America's providential destiny, cataloging the ever present sins of national pride, greed, governmental corruption, and Sabbath-breaking, and emphasizing the need to repent in order to regain God's favor. However, the sermons of four pastors—J. B. Bittinger of Cleveland's Euclid Street

Presbyterian Church, Cincinnati Presbyterian M. L. P. Thompson, William W. Patton of Chicago's First Congregational Church, and Indianapolis minister James Simmons of First Baptist Church—merit attention because of their insistence that slavery was the chief cause of contention that ultimately had provoked war.

Bittinger based his sermon on the principle found in Numbers 32:23 that sin would always reveal itself and result in eventual punishment. He asserted that because slavery had been allowed to fester unattended for decades, it had led to numerous political sins such as the annexation of Texas and the Mexican War, had destroyed completely the Whig party and crippled the Democrats, and had generated wicked legislation that defined humans as property and prevented slaves from being taught the Bible. In Bittinger's opinion, the war would eradicate slavery, and God had given the North the opportunity to "immortalize" itself by assisting in this providentially inspired task. Thompson and Patton both blamed the Founders for abandoning the principle of equality after winning independence and allowing slavery to gain a secure foothold in the republic. According to Thompson, the failure of the United States to expunge slavery at the constitutional convention mirrored Israel's disobedience of God's command to wipe out all idolatrous inhabitants of Canaan upon entering the Promised Land. Both nations suffered dire consequences by allowing the source of future judgment to remain in the land when it could have been exterminated. Patton even alleged that God had punished the Union with military reverses "because our government has evinced no determination to make this war bear on the final destruction of slavery." Simmons preached from Isaiah 58:6, "Is not this the fast that I have chosen? to loose the bands of wickedness, to undo the heavy burdens, and to let the oppressed go free," and focused solely on the North's complicity in supporting the sin of slavery. In his most condemnatory point, he alleged that rampant antiblack sentiment in the North had helped contribute to "the continued degradation" of slaves. As evidence, he cited Indiana's revised constitution that prohibited blacks from taking residence in the state. In addition to discriminatory laws, most Hoosiers, including church members, held blacks in "haughty disdain" by refusing to follow the scriptural injunction "'to condescend to men of low estate'" and in many cases incriminated themselves by regularly using "the reproachful epithet 'nigger.'" Simmons concluded that Americans needed to genuinely repent by embracing "the work of emancipation or suffer the destruction of the Republic." Far from being abolitionist rants, these four sermons demonstrated the growing sentiment, even in racially conservative northern states, that the war's purpose transcended the constitutional issues over which it had begun and would somehow, in a way only God could foresee, undermine the institution of slavery.[10]

If the primary purpose of the fast was "to promote patriotism," as Harry Stout maintains, then it effectively accomplished its mission. After listening to his sermon, Patton's congregation adopted several resolutions, one of which expressed gratitude that so many Christian men had taken up arms to defend the country. In Greencastle, Indiana, the address of "an old gray headed Patriot" swelled the patriotism of a student at Indiana Asbury University. "I find that I am feeling more and more of an intrest in this my native country than I ever have felt," he acknowledged after contemplating the many "priveleges" he enjoyed that derived from "the strugle of 76." In some cases, patriotic displays of support for the Union war effort lacked evidence of genuine repentance or humbling before God and proved to be little more than efforts to repair national pride. However, some religious civilians observed the fast in all sincerity. Alice Grierson outwardly complied with the spirit of the proclamation by eating only a peach until supper. Others underwent serious soul-searching both for themselves and the country. As he observed the fast with other believers, Franklin Alford noted that "the solemnity that was manifest...and the fervency of the prairs of the brethren on that occasion is never surpassed and seldom if ever equaled." Calvin Fletcher marked the day by abstaining from food and confessing his personal "weaknesses short coming[s] & sins before the Lord" as well as "those of my nation."[11]

From the clergy's standpoint, the government's consecrating a day for the country to implore God for his blessings solidified in their minds their responsibility to discuss political matters that dealt with moral issues. Many ministers, such as J. B. Bittinger, resented being "stigmatized as 'political priests,' and fanatics" for preaching to their congregations about the "moral duties" of citizens. Bittinger considered it both natural and necessary for a person's faith to influence all aspects of life, for it was absurd to think that "men ceased to be citizens when they became Christians." James Simmons defended himself against the charge of political preaching by stressing his pastoral obligation "to *infuse the eternal principles of righteousness from the pulpit into politics.*" He contended that the faithful minister would instruct his congregation that the "all-pervading presence and power" of Christianity should motivate their actions as much "at the *caucus* and the *polls*, as at the *prayer meeting* and the *communion table.*"[12]

Clergymen seldom needed to worry about being reprimanded for overstepping their bounds when addressing political matters from the pulpit, for annual denominational sessions often officially sanctioned this practice. Ministerial delegates assembled for the North-Western Indiana Conference of the Methodist Episcopal church, meeting in South Bend only two weeks after the fast, resolved "to exert our influence in sustaining our Government in this trying hour, by all proper means in the sphere of our calling."

The Indiana Synod of the Old School Presbyterian church, also meeting in October, urged its ministers to promote loyalty to the government and deemed that the didactic mission of the church legitimately included messages dealing with slavery. At the October meeting of the Presbyterian Synod of Northern Indiana, John Lowrie, pastor from Fort Wayne, delivered a keynote address on the duties of Christian citizens. Citing Paul's injunction in Titus 3:1 that ministers needed to remind their congregations to obey civil authorities, Lowrie claimed that pastors who neglected to confront political issues of moral significance were contributing to "the ruin of the nation." Since rebellion and treason were sins, ministers were obligated to denounce them and to "vindicate a war...forced upon us." For the bulk of his discourse, Lowrie expressed little of substance to differentiate himself from a score of other patriotic orators, but he deviated from the norm with his closing reminder that a minister's primary duty was to preach the gospel, not to inundate his audience with a continual flow of patriotic utterances. Lowrie maintained that pastors could be "outspoken in supporting the government" without providing a weekly review of political matters from the pulpit. Sunday messages should concentrate on spiritual topics and worship, and Lowrie implied that some clergymen had induced their flocks to give greater heed to war news than their spiritual welfare.[13]

In some cases, this warning came too late as complaints of religious apathy sparked calls for revival among members of several denominations. A letter circulated in 1861 by John Dunham of the Monticello Regular Baptist Association in northwestern Indiana bemoaned the "great stupidity and coldness...common among professors of godliness." The author blamed the excitement of "the present political crisis" for distracting people from their spiritual devotions and yearned for a renewed piety leading to "a general revival of religion." The clerk for the Old School Presbyterian Synod of Ohio wholeheartedly agreed with this assessment and, while not condemning patriotism, grieved over the tendency of church members to "become so absorbed in these public interests as to allow the cause of Christ to languish." A Methodist minister in New Albany, Indiana, concluded that "this wicked war...excites wild commotion in our hearts, but all the time tends to freeze our religious feelings. I fear that we, as a church, have less interest in God's cause and less sympathy for suffering humanity than ever before." Only six weeks after commending the fervent devotion displayed during the fast day service, Franklin Alford lamented the low attendance at prayer meeting. He regretted that people were "so eas[il]y drawn off from the place where they should meet." Peter Demaree of Johnson County, Indiana, concurred that the war should have been motivating Christians to pray more fervently, but instead he discerned a "coldness" and spiritual impotency in the church, even implying that God might have withdrawn his favor and guidance.

"It semes that we ar left to our selves to go a stray," he opined dishearteningly.[14] In the autumn of 1861, most ministers had convinced themselves that the fast confirmed America's special relationship with God, and they regarded it their duty to reinforce the nation's flagging confidence in the Union. While this effort bolstered spirits for a short time, some Northerners craved a rekindling of genuine spiritual devotion, for they recognized that public displays of religiosity did not foster sincere reliance on God, let alone guarantee battlefield victories.

Even for civilians who possessed a steadfast belief that God would work out all things for the good of the nation, the events of late 1861, other than the capture of Port Royal Sound off the coast of South Carolina in early November, did not offer much reason for optimism. The Federal defeat at Ball's Bluff in October, fears that the *Trent* Affair might provoke war with England, and an overall lack of faith in the nation's civil leaders caused public morale to languish. Cincinnati resident Amanda Wilson admitted to having "very gloomy feelings in regard to the war" at the end of October. "Lincoln does not seem the man," she grumbled. "God have mercy upon us!" As the year came to a close, Mary Logan, wife of Democratic congressman and future general John A. Logan, remained "disgusted with Seward" and the rest of the national leadership in Washington. "There seems to be no hope for the Government to retain any respect if they keep on," she murmured, probably referring to the administration's recent release of Confederate commissioners James Mason and John Slidell after an imprisonment of one-and-a-half months. Convinced that the seizure of Mason and Slidell fell within the bounds of international law, Calvin Fletcher hoped the government would not submit to "dishonorable" terms. The prolonged negotiations and possibility of British intervention on behalf of the Confederacy made national prospects "look gloomy" to Fletcher, and he could only implore "God [to] save us from a conflict with other nations" by "turn[ing] the hearts of men as the rivers of waters." When the two Rebel agents gained their freedom the day after Christmas, Fletcher was relieved that "the agony is over," yet he remained unimpressed with William Seward's handling of the situation, alleging that the "Secretary of State has lacked a manly...bearing towards England." With such negative opinions of the leadership abilities and effectiveness of the country's foremost public servants, these individuals could appreciate Hoosier Frances Ely's counsel to pray fervently that "God [would] grant all, and even more, than the wisdom of Solomon to our rulers in this mighty emergency."[15]

Civilian confidence in the army and its commanders did not rate much higher during the closing months of 1861. Because the flurry of enlistments in the spring and summer months facilitated a successful mobilization of the entire North, many individuals expected immediate results, especially considering the prevalent expectation of a quick war. However, little of consequence occurred on the battlefield, and the president was not the only Northerner growing impatient. Calvin Fletcher noted disapprovingly that Federal and Confederate troops seemed to be doing little more than "looking at each other" from their entrenched positions. The blame, many people felt, rested squarely on the shoulders of General McClellan. An excellent administrator, McClellan had organized the disarrayed forces that he inherited, removed inept officers, and whipped the army into fighting shape. Nevertheless, he consistently exhibited a reluctance to use this war machine, instead believing reports that greatly inflated Confederate numbers. In late September, Fletcher supposed "that the immense force of McClellan ought to...enable him to be aggressive if he desires," but he gave the general the benefit of the doubt, conceding that "his knowledge is better than ours." When the aged war hero Winfield Scott somewhat reluctantly submitted his resignation as general-in-chief at the end of October, opening the way for McClellan to assume the position he had coveted for some time, Fletcher immediately expressed delight that the "old inbecel man" had stepped aside. However, he already had lost a degree of confidence in the young commander's ability to lead the army because of his repeated hesitation to fight. Admitting that he lacked certainty that McClellan was "the man," Fletcher hoped that "God [would] indue him with the true spirit." Similarly disgusted with the army's sluggishness, J. S. Scoland sought evidence of the biblical principle that genuine faith would be validated by appropriate works. "I am only provoked at the assurances of McC[l]ellan and Sewar[d] that a few months will close the war—an assurance which seems to rest wholy on faith—*not works.*"[16]

Some civilians lacked faith in their political and military leaders because they believed that both the government and the army had been corrupted thoroughly. In the first place, ministers often publicly excoriated politicians and reminded their flocks of the degrading influences of the political sphere. In his fast day sermon at the Baptist church in Franklin, Indiana, Silas Bailey suggested that many elected officials had drawn "the nation away into practical political atheism." Indeed, he alleged that most people associated the terms "'politician,' 'office-seeker,' [and] 'office-holders'" with individuals whose qualities "no moral man would wish himself...to possess." To be sure, many contracts signed by the War Department exuded graft and corruption, and charges of profiteering plagued Secretary of War Simon Cameron and eventually forced his resignation in early January 1862. When Edwin Stanton, a former member of James Buchanan's cabinet, replaced Cameron, John McCullough of Bureau County, Illinois, took this as evidence of the South's continued influence over the federal government. "I certainly think that we are sold to Jeff Davis," he imagined naively. "I wish that Washington was sacked and old Abe too." Like McCullough, many Northerners seldom cared to ascertain the validity of accusations of corruption or disloyalty and simply presumed that the privileged class was abusing the powers of office, sometimes at the expense of soldiers. Margaret Ross of Lebanon, Ohio, who deeply regretted that she had allowed her son to enlist, vented her frustration on Washington social elites. "While the raskely Politicians are living at there ease and Mrs Lincon [is] prepairing her diamonds and sattins for evening parties, our boys is suffering in Western Va. for the want of food and clothing, and what is to become of them this winter God only knows." Calvin Fletcher was concerned that God's "just judgments" directed at "our corrupt men" would fall upon the army and hinder it from gaining victories because "rogues who have lived for years by bribing Congress & state legislatures have...[become] army contractors." On another occasion in late December, he attempted to cheer a discouraged friend, reminding him that "God would not abandon us" simply because of the corruption of "our officers in high places." Relying instead on God's mercy and willingness to "hear & answer" the petitions of "thousands [of] good praying people in the background," Fletcher implied that the virtue and piety of the average American citizen would counterbalance the vices that contaminated many public positions.[17]

This underlying faith that God was using the war to accomplish certain purposes buoyed the spirits of many northern civilians during dismal periods of the war's first year. To be sure, having sins publicly exposed was humiliating for the country, but the expectation that repentance and eventual blessing would follow fostered optimism for the future. As 1861 came to a close, religious Northerners based their hope on two principles. The first rested on God's sovereignty, which encompassed the infallibility of his nature and his inherent capacity to direct all things to achieve an intended good. William Patrick admitted on Christmas Day that he had "passed through such a long scene of mental suffering, gloom and despondency...all growing out of the state of the times." But when he confessed this sin of faithlessness in God's sovereign control, his melancholy vanished. "We must not suffer ourselves to murmur at God or distrust his Providence," he affirmed, for "He will do all things right." Reuben Hitchcock conceded in late November that although "the present is dark" and "mystery surrounds the future," he could take comfort that "a God of infinite love,...wisdom, &...power is at the helm" of the nation. Since God could "cause the wrath of man to praise him," he trusted completely that God would "overrule this rebellion for good."[18]

As an extension of the foundational truth of divine sovereignty, the second assumption emphasized God's special favor to America. This unique relationship afforded the assurance of supernatural assistance in the conflict. Indeed, its very existence confirmed the righteousness of the Union cause, for God would never sustain or sanctify an unjust enterprise. Taken to its extreme, this idea underscored the nation's sacred mission to advance Christ's millennial kingdom. In his Thanksgiving Day sermon, Presbyterian minister John Agenbroad stressed that the future would reveal the great extent to which "God especially worked for this nation & people." Furthermore, he maintained that "God has set the special seal of his favor upon our armies," and as evidence he pointed to numerous clergymen whose service as chaplains had helped spark an "extensive revival of religion" among the soldiers, ostensibly resulting in scores of conversions in each regiment. Reuben Hitchcock commemorated Thanksgiving while on business in Pittsburgh, where he listened to a sermon in which the minister documented the errors of the South and contrasted their plight with the hope possessed by the North. According to Hitchcock, the preacher demonstrated that "of course the God of Heaven was on our side, in him was our refuge, and we must be successful." Meditating on the certitude of victory through God's support, Hitchcock revealed a distinct postmillennial bent. "I have long believed that it was his [God's] purpose that the people of this nation should perform an important part, perhaps be the leading instrument, in the great work of this worlds redemption." God intended war to instruct his people and prepare them for the "glorious results" that would "grow out of this rebellion." In a war sermon preached in early December at Cincinnati's Ninth Street Baptist Church, twenty-eight-year-old minister E. T. Robinson asserted that "the very severity of the testing" demonstrated that the nation had "a sublime mission unfulfilled." By combating rebellion, the country was performing its providential role in hastening Christ's kingdom. Indeed, recent events appeared to fulfill the descriptions of John's Revelation. "All the triumphs foreshown in the Apocalypse seem to be sounding at once on the air," Robinson alleged. From a human perspective, the war was merely a tragedy, but the discerning individual could distinguish beneath the surface the hand of Christ preparing the way for his earthly kingdom. Although Robinson never predicted Union victory, his expectation that biblical prophecy encompassed American history turned Federal soldiers into emissaries of God.[19] At the conclusion of 1861, most religious Northerners never paused to consider the significance or long-term consequences of fusing patriotism and religion, and for many, any impulse to do so had long since passed.

As 1862 commenced, religious Northerners reiterated their conviction that God governed the affairs of nations. In fact, they often identified God as the central actor in the war, leading the Union army, giving it victory, and mapping the course of America's future. When Joseph Beebe of Jackson, Michigan, looked for evidence that war might terminate shortly, he found only unprincipled politicians periling the country for their own personal advancement. Since men were unreliable, he had faith "that God the disposer of all things will so overrule the wrath of man and give wisdom to our rulers that soon the end may come." In Fredericktown, Ohio, Phebe Mount possessed less hope for a favorable outcome and even doubted that the country was worth saving. "I do sometimes think that if this whole united states was turned over into the ocean and seas I would be sadisfied," she confessed to her husband Charles, a soldier in the 20th Ohio. "Let the Lord destroy the whole face of this country and begin here a new a gain." Calvin Fletcher had concluded months before that God controlled the war, yet he wondered what a new year would bring. "Thus far God has restrained any great onset except [the] battle of Bull's Run when neither army was prepaired," he reflected. "The result of the [armies'] great movements towards each other God holds for the unknown page yet to be written." Hannah Bingham recollected back a half century to the War of 1812 and England's unsuccessful invasion from Canada and defeat at the battle of Plattsburg. "God was on our side & we gained the victory," she asserted matter-of-factly. Presuming that God had not changed his allegiance in the interim, she expected a similar outcome. "If god is for us now who can be against us." Her husband Abel, a former missionary to the Ojibwa and current Baptist minister in Grand Rapids, Michigan, could have been mistaken for a priest of ancient Israel as he consecrated his son-in-law Claude Buchanan and the 8th Michigan to God's care. "May the LORD of Hosts be your Leader, ever inspiring both officers and men with true patriotism, and [supplying] a confident reliance on the Divine arm in evry emergency, and mak[ing] you brilliantly triumphant in evry combat."[20]

While Abel Bingham merely borrowed the language of the Old Testament, Cleveland Presbyterian F. T. Brown drew an explicit parallel between Old Testament Israel and America. In a sermon on Psalm 20, Brown claimed that "the Hebrew Church" sang this "war psalm" when the soldiers of "the Hebrew State" went forth to subdue their enemies. Brown reasoned that since God had chosen Israel to be his special people, then both their political and religious institutions belonged to him. Consequently, "it was the privilege and duty of the *Church* of Israel" to support the armies who defended the government. Convinced that America was "a Christian nation" similar to Israel, the patriotic preacher asserted that the republic's churches were obligated to sustain its military in any way possible. In his zeal to justify the vocal Unionism of the majority of northern congregations, Brown took liberties with Jewish history and inserted the church, an institution not introduced until the New Testament, into Old Testament Hebrew worship. His extrapolation paled in comparison to an outright falsehood foisted on one inattentive editor. According to the account reprinted by a Republican

A veteran of the War of 1812, Abel Bingham (1786–1865) served as a missionary to the Ojibwa in Sault Ste. Marie from 1828 to 1855. Sent by the American Baptist Missionary Society, he relocated his family to the wilds of Michigan's Upper Peninsula and built a home, a church, and eventually a school. As a septuagenarian, he spent the last decade of his life preaching in Grand Rapids, a firsthand witness not only to the nation's territorial expansion but also to the westward movement of the church. *Clarke Historical Library, Central Michigan University*

newspaper, a Baptist preacher pointed out the contemporary fulfillment of a biblical prophecy from Haggai 4. "'Behold there shall be rebellion in the South,... and her *rice fields shall be wasted and her slaves set free*. And behold, *great ships from the North* shall devour her pride,... and her dominion shall be broken.'" If a scriptural reference to rice fields did not seem dubious enough, a quick thumb through the Old Testament would have shown that the book of Haggai contains only two chapters. Some Democratic editors relished the opportunity to discredit their political rivals, whom they impugned for using the pretense of religion to justify war.[21]

Extensive ecclesiastical promotion of a biblical mandate for war may have inspired citizens on the home front, but it did not produce results on the battlefield. Winter limited military maneuvers, but the commander in chief impatiently waited for his idle army to exert itself. On January 27, Lincoln issued General War Order No. 1, dictating that aggressive military offensives begin by February 22. This directive shortly bore fruit in the western theater as a joint army—navy operation led by Brigadier-General Ulysses S. Grant and Flag-Officer Andrew H. Foote captured Fort Henry on the Tennessee River and Fort Donelson on the Cumberland River. Besides taking approximately twelve thousand Confederate prisoners, Grant's victory at Fort Donelson opened Kentucky and most of Tennessee to Federal occupation and finally gave the North cause to celebrate. Hoosier Emma Ely did just that, despite having neighbors who considered it "unchristian-like to rejoice" because the Union had suffered nearly three thousand casualties, including five hundred killed. In her estimation, the dead had gained glory, and the triumph had confirmed her belief that "God is always on the side of the right." In New Albany, Elijah Fletcher's "heart burn[ed] like fire at the glorious news" of the fall of Fort Donelson, prompting him to erupt in praise to God. "'Bless the Lord oh my soul; & all that is within me bless his holy Name,'" he extolled. Ammi Williams, schoolmaster in Fremont, Ohio, regarded the Union success at Fort Donelson as "a splendid afair." "The government seems to be making progress against the enemy now days," he reckoned. "God grant it may be a death blow to rebellion." L. B. Gurley, Methodist pastor in Galion, Ohio, declared as much to his congregation, imprudently claiming that the fort's capitulation was "the sure harbinger of approaching peace." About a week after the surrender, over three thousand prisoners of war, described as "miserably clad...poor [and] dirty" by Calvin Fletcher, arrived in Indianapolis to be detained at Camp Morton. Fletcher thought it entirely providential that these Southerners from Tennessee, Alabama, and Arkansas could view firsthand the advantages of northern society. "I can perceive how God in his mercy & for the purpose of perpetrating [preserving] our good republic has & will send the lower class of the South here to see the effects of freedom from Slavery."[22]

The problem of slavery had been weighing heavily on the minds of many Northerners in recent months, and its import seemed to increase almost daily. In November 1861, Lincoln privately developed two proposals whereby the legislature of Delaware would request federal remuneration to phase out slavery by either 1867 or 1893. But in his annual message to Congress in early December, the president publicly reiterated his opinion that preserving the Union was his "primary object." However, he urged Congress to designate as "free" those contrabands seized in accordance with the Confiscation Act and to provide for their colonization on a voluntary basis. Two days later, Senator Lyman Trumbull of Illinois introduced a measure that would become, after seven months of heated debate, the Second Confiscation Act, which authorized the expropriation of the property and slaves of all traitors. Even some state governments, hoping to incite the federal government to action, agitated against slavery by sending resolutions to Congress. The Michigan legislature, for instance, unequivocally called for slavery to "be swept from the land." Not to be outdone by politicians, several northern denominations took every opportunity to denounce slavery. During its April meeting at Fort Wayne, the North Indiana Conference of the Methodist Episcopal church resolved that slavery was the "root and origin of this war," and delegates expected the conflict to continue "in the providence of God" until the nation's bane was *extirpated.*" In late May, the Washtenaw Baptist Association of Michigan accused the Confederacy of fighting "in defence of...the extension of human bondage." God would prevent this wicked purpose from succeeding, these Baptists declared, for his strong arm "is stretched for the triumph of freedom." If necessary, he would supernaturally intervene as he had often done for Israel in order "to secure the victory of the right."[23]

Many religious civilians likewise gave close attention to the matter of slavery and frankly expressed their feelings on the subject. Alonzo Hudson, a Protestant Episcopal minister in Portage, Wisconsin, petitioned President Lincoln to resist any impulse to take action against slavery, concluding that the war itself would destroy slavery in due time. Hudson opposed "even attempting any legislation for *general* emancipation by Congress" because he believed that slavery fell within the jurisdiction of the states, and federal interference would "needlessly provoke" some loyal citizens "into acts of rebellion." In his estimation, "the utter destruction of slavery" would prove to be an "incidental, yet natural and inevitable" outcome of the war. The government needed only to "provide asylum" and educational opportunities to slaves freed "by the stroke of war." C. M. Hatch of Sault Ste. Marie, Michigan, disagreed with Hudson and asserted that Congress possessed the authority to deal with slavery. "The institution of Slavery is a Sin...against the law of God, and the law of our better nature, but it is *not* a sin against the Law of our Land." Hatch viewed the war as a conflict over the rule of law, and despite the inherent wickedness of slavery, it could only be removed through appropriate legal proceedings. Calvin Fletcher had been prognosticating the demise of slavery since the secession crisis, and regardless of the government's attempt to sidestep the issue, he remained confident that "God...intends...that his African childrin are to go out from bondage." For too long, Fletcher maintained, the North "endeavored to live in peace with the South & let the institution of slavry alone." Despite controlling the reins of government for thirty years, the South "at last determined to rule or [face] ruin" and instigated the war. Although the North "has abhored slavry as a people," it nonetheless deserved God's chastisements. However, for "a pure free Republic...to exist in north America" again, "in some way poor Africans...[had] to be liberated." Fletcher calculated that the government, as a last resort, would "be forced" to arm blacks.[24] Although they differed over the government's policies and course of action regarding slavery, these religious civilians assumed that the war, in some way or another, would render slavery obsolete.

Not all devout Northerners concurred with their brethren who asserted that slavery needed to be eradicated as a result of the war. Antiblack sentiment had remained especially strong during the 1850s as the Indiana and Illinois legislatures passed exclusion laws attempting to bar blacks from settling there. Indeed, the intense emotions generated by the topic of slavery threatened to sever even the closest relationships. In the war's early months, Lizzie Little often praised her beau George Avery for his courage, patriotism, and manliness while deprecating those "loafers" and "effeminate Dandies" who would benefit from George's sacrificial service. Always concerned for his safety, she nevertheless considered the risking of his life justifiable because "humanity calls loudly for aid...to avenge their wrongs." This oblique reference to slavery sufficed until the war dragged on into 1862 when she explicitly disclosed her contempt for the government for failing to free the slaves. "If our Administration does not declare the Slaves emancipated ere four weeks pass by I fear we are lost," she complained to George in mid-January. "Never was American freedom at so low an ebb, & yet if the root of this evil be removed we can...do much to leave our country free." Less than a week later, Lizzie revisited this subject, alleging that "the South herself will print emancipation upon her banner" before Congress would get the nerve to act. Nevertheless, she preferred to have him daily facing danger, suffering hardships, and "marching to the music of freedom [rather] than living a life of ease & luxury." As the only members of God's creation possessing eternal souls, humans "should have higher aims" than serving as "'aproned waitors,'" she insisted, and nothing could be "nobler than purchasing Freedom for all mankind."[25]

At this point, George had tolerated as much of her antislavery blather as he could take and straightforwardly revealed his reason for fighting and his abhorrence of blacks.

> You must not make an Abolitionist out of me. I fear you do not comprehend my real motives for engaging in my country's service. I will assure you of one thing that it is not for the emancipation of the African race I fight. I want nothing to do with the Negro. I want them as far from me as is possible to conceive. Already we

have more colored population in the northern states than is agreeable or profitable, then why fight for more. Slavery is acknowledged to be a local institution hence it is governed by local law. This being the case we the people of the free states have no right even if we were so disposed to interfere with that "peculiar institution."... I would not sleep one night in the "Tented Field" to free every slave in America if they were to remain on our soil. You can have a more favorable opinion of the African than I have[, for] it is your right. No Lizzie, I am simply fighting for the Union as it was given to us. I want nothing more—I will have nothing less. When President Lincoln declares the slaves emancipated I will declare myself no longer an American citizen.

Lizzie was undeterred by George's transparent Negrophobia and refused to retract her claims that the war must destroy slavery. Shortly thereafter, she alleged that "every [Rebel] victory rivits the chain of the Slave tighter," escalating the bloodshed and prolonging the suffering of slaves. Without genuine repentance leading to the overthrow of slavery, the nation's prospects for success, she estimated, were "uncertain" at best. Unwilling to allow their disagreement over slavery to diminish their love for each other, George recommended that they "let no differences of opinion, however great they may be, lessen our affection." However, he remained uncompromisingly opposed to abolition and warned Lizzie "not [to] presume for a moment that I can ever endorse your doctrine—it is tinctured to[o] much with John Brownism." Furthermore, like a majority of Northerners, he underscored his absolute abhorrence of the idea of black equality. "I cannot believe that you have so much sympathy for the *African* as is indicated in your language...[or] that you wish to associate in any way with that race," he marveled bewilderedly. "If your doctrine were carried out how long would it be before you would have to extend to them the hand of fellowship." Reminding her that he did not want to argue over this subject again, George sought to have the final word on the matter by personalizing his most damning accusation against abolitionism. "Let me say just here, that this war has been brought on mainly by persons advocating the same doctrine which *you* (My Lizzie) endorse."[26] Overlooking this rebuke, Lizzie remained personally devoted to George and manifested the depth of her convictions by mentioning emancipation on later occasions. George even conceded that the preservation of the Union was worth ending slavery if blacks were colonized in Africa. Most importantly for themselves, they recognized that dissimilar interpretations of the war's meaning and contested ideas regarding the status of blacks in society need not keep them apart, and they married during George's furlough in the summer of 1863.

As more and more Northerners convinced themselves that the nation's offense in countenancing slavery had necessitated a brutal war to destroy it, some individuals wavered, albeit momentarily in most cases, in their conviction of America's uniqueness and questioned the country's ability to serve as an exemplar among the nations. In February 1862 Milton Buswell, farmer and engineer from Warren, Minnesota, pointed out the rank hypocrisy "in proclaiming 'Liberty'... while holding in the most servile bondage millions of our fellows...[made in] Gods immuge." Although this blatant sin did not nullify America's status as "a Christian nation," he nonetheless regarded it as indefensible, an utter "shame on civilization[,]... Christianity [, and]... Justice." In his opinion, the nation deserved "the piercing wounds of her revengeful sword" for "standing up before the face of our Maker and upbraiding him by striving to feter and bind... [those] he has made free." Ohioan James Meharry even began to doubt the country's divine mission to help usher in Christ's earthly kingdom. He regarded "the bloody buchering battlefield in this cristian ninteenth centaury" as a nadir in world history, lower even than the so-called Dark Ages, when Islam and Roman Catholicism "rained and no bright intalects graced the *world*." Instead of nations "beeting there swords into plowshears" as characteristic of the millennial kingdom, man kept "inventing most deadly weapons of death." Despite this apparent setback in the progress of the kingdom from a macrocosmic standpoint, local events gave Meharry reason for hope. A revival at one Methodist church yielded forty conversions with the addition of the same number to the membership rolls, and another congregation increased by almost thirty souls.[27]

Indeed, from most outward appearances, interest in spiritual matters remained high, and certain evidence confirms this impression of ecclesiastical vibrancy. For instance, numerous civilians attested to their regular church attendance and sometimes revealed the topics of the sermons they heard, thereby substantiating that many ministers performed their duties throughout the course of the war by addressing appropriate theological topics. In March 1862, Lizzie Caleff wished that her soon-to-be husband Madison Bowler of the 3rd Minnesota could have listened to an explication of Job 19:25, "'I know that my Redeemer liveth.'" Edwin Rice recorded that the Chicago Congregationalist Jonathan Blanchard exposited on the Abrahamic covenant and stressed the continued necessity for Christians to practice infant baptism. Clergymen who preferred a less heavy subject matter could never go wrong with a simple gospel message. John Funk appreciated William W. Patton's reminder of the urgency to heed the call to salvation. The upheaval caused by war, financial downturns, or any such trial, Funk recounted Patton as declaring, "should especially bring to us the fact that this is the accepted... day for salvation."[28]

Proclaiming the gospel and making disciples constituted the church's primary task, and many congregations continued to evangelize throughout the war. In some instances, ardent preaching and the intense atmosphere of revival meetings provided a unique opportunity to reap a harvest of souls in a short period of time. As a result of a Methodist protracted meeting in Greenfield, Indiana, that lasted more than four weeks, more than ninety individuals joined the church, resulting in a noticeable change in the community. Letty Longnaker noted that many people now attended church each night rather than going to frivolous social gatherings. At other times, soldiers home on furlough involuntarily fell prey to the religious emotionalism that often characterized revival meetings. Ann Cavins of Bloomfield, Indiana, described how one soldier, who had formerly teased his companions for succumbing to the revival enthusiasm, became "powerfully convicted and had the real old fashioned 'jerks.'" Although she had read of such a phenomenon, she had never observed it personally. On this occasion, the man "was happily converted" only a few days after being afflicted with this mysterious malady, "and the jerks left him in an instant."[29]

Unlike the previous examples, not all efforts to win the lost or to fan the flames of revival bore immediate fruit. After listening to a message aimed "for the salvation of souls," a female resident of Wisconsin surmised that the pastor had "cast...[his] bread upon the waters, with no immediate prospect of a return." Highly skeptical of organized religion, Jacob Thorna of Belleville, Illinois, grew tired of local revivalistic activity. When a Methodist church commenced a protracted meeting on the heels of a Baptist campaign, Thorna seemed annoyed that another crusade had begun, especially after entering its second week with no visible results. "No one has joined the church yet nor gone up to the mourners bench," he jadedly noted. "How long it will continue the gods only know." At a meeting in April 1862, representatives from the Muncie, Indiana, Presbytery lamented the absence of any sign of revival in the district's churches. On the contrary, the war seemed to have "distracted the minds of our people, and hindered the cultivation of a devotional spirit." Furthermore, delegates alleged that the presence of nearby military camps contributed to "the increase of intemperance and Sabbath desecration."[30]

Combating hedonistic impulses and diminishing the influence of worldliness on its members had presented a challenge for the church since its inception. While some churches might have blamed the war for exacerbating these problems, in most cases it would be difficult to prove a direct connection between the war and the escalation of behavioral sins. In addition to continuing to evangelize the lost throughout the war, some congregations diligently disciplined members who succumbed to worldly temptation and thereby damaged the reputation of the local assembly as well as marred the testimony of Christianity in general. Most cases of church discipline concerned the commission of conspicuous sins involving conduct considered taboo for professing Christians. By publicly confronting the erring brother or sister, the assembly hoped to bring them to repentance and restore broken fellowship. However, when the accused person refused to confess wrongdoing, that individual could be removed from the church by vote of the other members. For instance, a report surfaced in February 1862 that George Larimer of Deer Creek Regular Baptist Church in Miami County, Indiana, had been intoxicated and uttered profanities. According to witnesses who questioned Larimer about his alleged misbehavior, he demonstrated "a very bad spirit" and gave them "no satisfaction whatever." Although he admitted to sharing a quart of whiskey with some friends, he denied the charges of drunkenness and swearing. Nevertheless, the congregation believed the testimony of his accusers, and a motion was offered and unanimously approved to expel Larimer from the church. Furthermore, in order to make clear the church's position on alcoholic consumption, the members adopted a resolution that branded the "drinking [of] intoxicating liquors" as "an act worthy of discipline." Later in the war, members excommunicated Calvin Ogburn for deserting from the army. By neglecting his duty and breaking a solemn oath, he had made himself "unworthy of Christian fellowship." Although many churches were abandoning disciplinary action in order to avoid unpleasant confrontations, those congregations that continued to practice it possessed significant authority over their members.[31]

While some churches remained focused on spiritual matters such as evangelism, discipleship, and church discipline, others wholeheartedly embraced the war spirit. Whether passing resolutions supporting the Union or preaching on political matters on Sundays, these churches departed from traditional Christian practice by closely identifying themselves with secular affairs. For those church members who approved the war and regarded the preservation of the government as a sacred cause, the mixing of religion and politics seemed natural and entirely acceptable. Alice Grierson thought it completely appropriate when her pastor applied verses from the famous passage on faith in Hebrews 11 to the current conflict. The minister drew a parallel between Old Testament Israel, which "'put to flight the armies of the aliens'" by exercising faith in God, and the Federal army, which could expect to gain victories if it would only rely on God instead of its own might. Some individuals became so accustomed to political commentary from the pulpit that they expected to hear it on a regular basis. After moving from Ohio to Sparta, Wisconsin, William Kennon quickly discovered that local residents seemed to accept that political matters belonged in the church, but they disagreed over how frequently such topics should be discussed. "The only question which I have heard debated with much bitterness," he informed a relative in Ohio, is whether or not "a *preacher* should pray *every* Sunday for the abolition of slavery or only *occasionally*." N. C. Burt, Presbyterian pastor in Cincinnati, perceived better than most laypersons the inherent tension between spiritual and political matters and the war's noticeable effect on the church. From a spiritual standpoint, he regretted that "the distractions of the times seem almost fatal to conversions." Yet as a loyal citizen of the Union, he considered "this rebellion as a grand iniquity...[upon] which it might be eminently proper for the church to speak." In fact, he had become so convinced of "the justice, the expediency, indeed the necessity of the war" that his mind "never was clearer about anything not specifically revealed" in Scripture. Such a view was anathema to Burt's correspondent, conservative Presbyterian Henry Van Dyke, and his less than subtle claim that the righteousness of the war obliged churches to actively support the government, possibly to the temporary detriment of spiritual progress, in order to achieve "the regeneration of the country" must have rankled the Brooklyn Democrat to no end.[32]

Northern Democrats especially contended that churches had compromised their spiritual mission and sold their souls to the Union war effort. Ira Borton of Yellow Creek, Indiana, complained that "the religion of this country has got so enshrouded in the spirit of the war that it is about all smothered to death and gone by the board." Borton expected Christians to demonstrate brotherly love toward one another, so he found it particularly ironic that a local Methodist minister had organized a company of soldiers, many from his own congregation, to go South to "meet their brother Methodes[ts] there &...forgive them their tresspasses" by shooting at them. Republican church members often recognized that Democrats felt ill at ease attending services where the preacher unabashedly identified himself with the pro-war party, but they made little effort to check such vocal Unionism, preferring instead to let offended members find a new place of worship. When a Mr. Edwards left the Presbyterian church she attended in Springfield over political differences, Ann Conkling blamed him for failing to put his spiritual welfare above temporal matters. "Politics I fear will prove a terrible snare to his soul," she claimed. Some ministers clearly regarded their reputation as outspoken supporters of the war as a badge of honor and seemed indifferent to concerns of Democrats who withdrew from the church because of their political pronouncements. "Mr. Battelle of Wesley Chapel asked me whom I had *driven* out of church yesterday," Perry Hall related without the least hint of compunction. He did not care if some citizens detected "a preconcerted move among the preachers" to infuse the pulpit with political discourse. Unfortunately for religious Democrats, the stance taken by ministers like Hall only foreshadowed greater harassment that they would face as the war progressed.[33]

With political differences dividing northern Christians who should have manifested unity in Christ, it is no wonder that conservative, moderate, and radical politicians remained at loggerheads over the future of slavery as the summer of 1862 approached. But as the Union army continued to be swarmed by contrabands seeking freedom, a combination of legislative design and military necessity would help decide the issue. President Lincoln, whose views on the constitutional parameters for dealing with slavery were far from settled in early 1862, did his utmost to find a satisfactory solution to the problem. However, the Delaware legislature rejected his plan for compensated emancipation, and the other border states ignored his congressionally approved offer of federal monetary assistance for gradual manumission. Although the states could determine their own course of action regarding slavery, the District of Columbia fell under the legislative jurisdiction of Congress, and in April Radicals steered through a bill that freed nearly three thousand slaves in the nation's capital. Despite his preference that the matter be submitted for a public referendum, Lincoln applauded the measure for providing three hundred dollars compensation per slave and for tendering free passage for settlement in Haiti or Liberia. Colonization had been a favorite program of Lincoln's for years, and numerous northern Christians of a conservative stripe supported it as well. Because it was grounded in the ideas of racial superiority and segregation, colonization remained a popular scheme among some clergymen for eliminating the blight of slavery while preserving the North for whites.[34]

Some whites may have believed that colonization had merit, but most blacks emphatically opposed the idea. After passing a resolution thanking God for the action of Congress and the president in abolishing slavery in the District of Columbia, members of Terre Haute's African Methodist Episcopal church explained why colonization lacked any appeal. As people "born on American soil," they considered America their "natural...home" and had no inclination to leave, despite the many injustices they had suffered. Ignoring the protests of most black Americans against any colonization venture, Lincoln kept his options open and spent considerable effort promoting a project in the Chiriquí coal region of Panama, only to be rebuffed by both black clergymen from the nation's capital as well as the governments of Honduras and Nicaragua. In June 1862, Willis Revels, pastor of the A.M.E. church in Indianapolis, outlined eight objections against colonization to Haiti that epitomized the prevailing African-American opposition to leaving their country. Cognizant of "the vile spirit of Negro hate" that motivated whites to seek the removal of blacks, Revels underscored the impracticality of sending native-born Americans to a foreign land with a different language, culture, and religion. In his opinion, his people continued to show "evidence of vitality, of self-appreciation, [and] of progress" in America, and he firmly believed "that God's providence designs...to provide for them an ample home in conjunction...with the numerous other races of men to be found here."[35]

In early June, Ohio Democratic congressman Samuel S. Cox employed biblical allusions to describe the pitfalls of emancipating blacks in a sometimes humorous speech that captured the essence of northern Negrophobia. He claimed that the nation's brave soldiers had given their lives in "a holy cause" for the preservation of the government, and it would insult their memory to make the war into an abolition crusade. In his opinion, "slavery agitation,... the worst crime since the scene on Calvary," had caused the conflict. Trying to assign the greater portion of blame between northern abolitionists or southern secessionists would be like attempting "to apportion the guilt of the crucifixion between Judas and the Roman soldiers." Cox insisted that the extremism of abolitionists had infected political moderates, and just as the demons whom Christ cast out of the Gadarene man entered into a herd of pigs which ran headlong into the Sea of Galilee and drowned, so too northern "fanatics... sated with negroes, taxes and blood" were leading the country down the path of self-destruction. After briefly discussing the status of Ohio's blacks, who were generally "vicious, indolent, and improvident," Cox turned to the issue of emancipation in the District of Columbia. His fellow Ohioan John Sherman had asserted before the Senate that the capital was "*a very Paradise for free negroes*" because they received better treatment there than in Ohio or Indiana. However, Cox maintained that "if the rush of free negroes to this paradise continues, it would be a blessing if Providence should send Satan here in the form of a serpent, and an angel to drive the descendants of Adam and Eve into the outer world." Then, there would be no one left "but Congressmen and negroes, and that will be punishment enough." After the laughter in the House chamber died down, he added, "You will have to enact a fugitive law, to bring the whites to their capital." By using scriptural analogies to convey his racial fears, Cox demonstrated that conservative Northerners had not surrendered the Bible to antislavery militants.[36]

Although prohibiting slavery in the District of Columbia represented an important breakthrough that Radical Republicans had labored tirelessly to achieve, many abolitionist civilians, wearied by the slowness of the political process and alarmed at the ever-increasing number of Union casualties, unrealistically expected Congress to take further, immediate action against slavery that would produce sweeping results and hasten the end of the war. After a neighbor's son fell in battle, Lizzie Little wondered why the nation's leaders still allowed "the corner stone of all this immense suffering" to remain intact. Since she considered them to be reluctant to act against slavery, she welcomed "every reverse of our arms," reasoning that the government "must be compelled through *self interest* to do *justice*" to the slave. An easy victory, she reckoned, would never bring about the destruction of slavery.[37]

If Lizzie Little truly regarded Union defeats as beneficial, then Confederate General Thomas J. "Stonewall" Jackson had been giving her plenty to celebrate as he repeatedly confounded Federal forces in the Shenandoah Valley throughout May and early June. Jackson's wily maneuvering kept 60,000 Union men occupied and prevented Irvin McDowell's corps from joining McClellan's massive army of over 115,000 bluecoats laying siege to Richmond. Beginning June 25, these forces would encounter General Robert E. Lee's army of less than 90,000 in a series of engagements called the Seven Days' battles. After combined losses of more than 36,000 casualties that portended the coming of many such costly encounters, Lee's Army of Northern Virginia succeeded in driving McClellan and the Army of the Potomac away from the Confederate capital. Before she received news of this terrible slaughter, Rhoda Southworth of Belle Plaine, Minnesota, had been contemplating the horrifying probability that "thousands...[of] lives must be thrown away" with the armies in such close proximity in Virginia. The thought of this carnage became even more intolerable to her because "the great sin which...has brought upon us all these fearful judgments of God" still existed. After accounts of the tactical defeat during the Seven Days' reached the North, a female resident of Peoria, Illinois, wondered if the Union would even survive because "the *plague spot* has festered *so* long." "I fear an an[ni]hilation of our Government can *alone* end this war," she glumly confessed before rallying her spirits with the remembrance that God sovereignly ruled and could still "up rear a government so *perfect* in its regulations that *it must abide.*" According to abolitionist Christians, only a Union purged of slavery deserved divine preservation, and military setbacks should have been expected as long as slavery existed. Calvin Fletcher noted that "God seems not to prosper our arms" because "we have not done justic[e] to his colored childrin." Nevertheless, he speculated that the demoralizing loss during the Seven Days' would prompt the government to modify its strategy for conducting the war to include granting liberty to blacks. In all likelihood, this "military necessity" would even result in the arming of African-Americans to assist in procuring their own freedom.[38]

Fletcher's prediction proved true, and as a consequence of McClellan's unsuccessful Peninsula Campaign the government radically changed its war policy. In the summer of 1862, the army discarded its initial practice of trying to conciliate southern civilians by treating them as loyal citizens and upholding their property rights in hope of reducing support for the Confederacy and implemented a pragmatic policy of doing whatever was necessary to gain battlefield victories regardless of the impact on civilians. Congress signaled this transition to a harsher prosecution of the war with passage of the Second Confiscation Act on July 17. After months of debate and compromise, the bill finally passed authorizing the confiscation of slaves of traitors. However, the provision stipulated that individuals accused of treason had to be brought to trial in a federal court, a logistical impossibility that rendered the act impracticable. Furthermore, Southerners who professed loyalty to the Union before the measure became law could still keep their slaves. Far from sweeping away slavery with one broad stroke, the Second Confiscation Act, according to one historian, was "an imperfect instrument" and "confused piece of legislation." Most congressmen admitted as much, with Ohio senator John Sherman even conceding that it represented "a declaration of policy" more than "an act to be enforced." Nevertheless, the Second Confiscation Act gratified many religious Northerners who had long yearned for an emancipationist policy. The editor of the *Western Christian Advocate* lauded Congress for having the backbone to attack the root cause of rebellion and urged Lincoln to seize the opportunity to become "a minister of the Gospel to millions of our race" by securing liberty for the enslaved. Willis Revels thought the new legislation marked "the beginning of the end of American Slavery," yet he tempered his optimism by stressing that "the entire people will have to humble themselves before god and ask forgivness for the sins of the nation" before "the preservation of the government" would be assured. Other citizens explained the new policy as evidence of God's working through human agency to achieve his divine purposes. According to Franklin Thorpe of Springfield, Illinois, many of the nation's leaders had sought in vain to preserve the Union while protecting slavery, but God, wanting to demonstrate "that Liberty is not a name but a truth," overruled their schemes and refused to allow a purportedly free country to maintain humans in bondage any longer. Calvin Fletcher likewise interpreted the enactment of the Second Confiscation Act as evidence of God's imprint on national affairs and marveled at his inherent ability to do all things perfectly. He claimed that God had "brot to straits" Lincoln, some of his cabinet, and generals like McClellan who favored conciliation toward the South by sovereignly dictating that federal policies should "comply with the prayers & intreaties of the thousands who have wept for Africa & begged they [slaves] might...be free."[39]

In accusing Lincoln of attempting to spare slavery, Fletcher had misjudged the president entirely. On the contrary, Lincoln had become convinced that emancipation was necessary to win the war and save the Union, and he actively and consciously exercised his executive powers in order to destroy slavery. By skillfully managing his cabinet and outmaneuvering Congress, he maintained personal control over any question relating to the status of African-Americans. Careful to abide within his constitutional parameters and ever sensitive to public opinion, Lincoln acted against slavery at a time when the nation was ready to accept an expanded purpose for the war. While this apparent sense of perfect timing confirmed his greatness to many observers, it also bore the marks of Lincoln's growing providential awareness. To be sure, much has been made of his theological unorthodoxy and failure to unite formally with any denomination during his lifetime. Nevertheless, his thinking on providence and God's role in history evolved during the war, and he acknowledged that God purposefully intervened in human affairs to achieve his intended result, an outcome that might possibly be different from what man anticipated. An exchange shortly after the defeat at First Manassas revealed the first indication that the president was no longer interpreting providence as a distant cosmic force but as a personal, albeit mysterious, being whose ways defied man's comprehension. When his Illinois friend Orville Browning, who had been appointed to fill the Senate seat of the late Stephen Douglas, prodded him to attack slavery in order to gain divine assistance on behalf of the Union, Lincoln retorted, "Browning, suppose God is against us in our view on the subject of slavery in this country, and our method of dealing with it?"[40]

This uncertainty regarding his ability to discern God's purposes distinguished Lincoln from the vast majority of northern Protestants, who confidently claimed to know the mind of God concerning the war's meaning and often declared as much to the president. When a group of Quakers urged him in June 1862 to abolish slavery "under divine guidance," Lincoln admitted that he had contemplated how he "might be an instrument in God's hands" for achieving the goal that they desired, but he supposed it equally likely that "God's way of accomplishing the end [of slavery]...may be different" from what the Quakers envisioned. Sometime after the Union army's devastating repulse at Second Manassas, Lincoln elaborated on this idea of God's sovereign prerogative to fulfill his decrees in a manner incomprehensible to man. Having reached the point where all human wisdom, effort, and resources had seemingly proven incapable of helping him lead the nation to victory, Lincoln plumbed the depths of his soul and composed a penetrating essay containing what Mark Noll calls "the most remarkable theological utterance of the Civil War."

> The will of God prevails. In great contests each party claims to act in accordance with the will of God. Both *may* be, and one *must* be wrong. God can not be *for*, and *against* the same thing at the same time. In the present civil war it is quite possible that God's purpose is something different from the purpose of either party—and yet the human instrumentalities, working just as they do, are of the best adaptation to effect His purpose. I am almost ready to say this is probably true—that God wills this contest, and wills that it shall not end yet. By his mere quiet power, on the minds of the now contestants, He could have either *saved* or *destroyed* the Union

without a human contest. Yet the contest began. And having begun He could give the final victory to either side any day. Yet the contest proceeds.

In this "Meditation on the Divine Will," Lincoln rose above the shallow, pretentious assertions of most northern clergymen by humbly conceding that God's ways were inscrutable. Without presuming or even needing to understand the divine purposes for why the war commenced or what it ultimately meant, Lincoln simply accepted that it continued according to God's will for reasons far beyond his finite comprehension. Where most northern ministers and religious civilians automatically assumed that God favored the Union, thereby making the war effort a sacred cause, Lincoln demonstrated greater theological acumen, for he understood that God, having concealed his plans from men, might not be supporting either side as both claimed.[41]

Indeed, later in September when a delegation from Chicago, including Congregational pastor William W. Patton, presented Lincoln with a petition signed by Chicagoans from many different denominations calling for a presidential proclamation for immediate emancipation, Lincoln challenged their assumption to know not only God's will for the country but also the precise course of action he should take. "If it is probable that God would reveal his will to others, on a point so connected with my duty," the president tactfully pointed out, "it might be supposed he would reveal it directly to me." To be sure, Lincoln reminded them, he coveted nothing more than "to know the will of Providence" concerning how to deal with slavery. "*And if I can learn what it is I will do it!*" he added emphatically. However, he did not anticipate receiving "a direct revelation" because "the days of miracles" had long since passed. Therefore, he had no alternative but to "study the plain physical facts of the case, ascertain what is possible and learn what appears to be wise and right." Although Lincoln raised objections concerning why a presidential proclamation freeing the slaves would prove unsatisfactory and ineffective, he underscored to his visitors that he did not oppose the idea entirely. In fact, he had already taken steps in the direction of emancipation two months previously and was merely waiting for the proper moment when God would employ his "human instrumentalities...to effect His purpose."[42]

The development of Lincoln's theological interpretation of the war coincided with the evolution of his thinking regarding slavery and emancipation. According to Richard Carwardine, Lincoln's "understanding of providential intervention" helped him make the pivotal decision to expand the war's objective to include emancipation and strengthened him to see it come to fruition. During a private carriage ride with William Seward and Secretary of the Navy Gideon Welles on July 13, Lincoln dropped a bombshell, disclosing for the first time his willingness to free the slaves by a presidential proclamation as a "military necessity" for winning the war. Although Welles did not comprehend at that exact moment the full weight of Lincoln's revelation, he recognized that it signaled "a new departure" in the president's thinking regarding his policy toward slavery. However, in public Lincoln seemingly remained committed to a moderate course of action. In a meeting the previous day with representatives from the border states, he had urged them to accept compensated emancipation with colonization before that opportunity passed them by completely, but as before his plea fell upon deaf ears. The Second Confiscation Act proved equally disappointing, and he only withheld his presidential veto after Congress revised the bill to ensure that the confiscation of property could not extend beyond the lifetime of the offender and was limited to those individuals who were found guilty of treason after the law's enactment. While these efforts for dealing with the peculiar institution proved unsatisfactory to Lincoln, it mattered little, for he already had determined to exercise his presidential war powers under the Constitution to strike a lethal blow to slavery. During a cabinet meeting on July 22, he read a draft of his Preliminary Emancipation Proclamation, which declared free all slaves in states in rebellion against the government effective January 1, 1863. Lincoln did not care that some members of his cabinet received the announcement unenthusiastically while others opposed it altogether, for he was not seeking their "advice." He "had resolved upon this step" to move against slavery, and only Seward's recommendation to suspend a public declaration until after a military victory in order to avoid the appearance of desperation gave him reason to delay.[43]

The Union army's lack of success on the battlefield during the summer of 1862 not only forced Lincoln to wait for the public unveiling of his emancipation scheme but also generated much discouragement on the northern home front. At times, several religious individuals seemed to lose confidence in the ability of the army to achieve success, and they often reaffirmed their conviction, probably as much for their own waning morale as for the benefit of their correspondents, that God still controlled the outcome and would cause their arms to triumph eventually. Lizzie Little thought the war had hurled the country into "a wild, mad vortex" unsurpassed by any other calamity the world had ever witnessed. "'Tis a terrible lesson we are learning," she admitted, "but I believe God teaches." In her estimation, military leaders had not risen to the "the magnitude of the work" that God had set before them, and she hoped that in the future they would prove to be "true & efficient men, not Traitors or Dolts." Tired of reading about the army's lack of progress and yearning for the return home of her husband Claude, Sophia Buchanan prayed for "God [to] grant a speedy termination to this unholy war." Nevertheless, she reassured herself that the North would prevail "in the end" because "we have 'God & right' on our side." From all outward appearances, that end was by no means near, for the next major engagement at Second Manassas in late August resulted in a decisive Federal defeat. Under Major General John Pope, who after coming from the western theater in late June immediately humiliated his new troops by crowing that the western armies had "always seen the backs of our enemies," the newly organized Army of Virginia met defeat at the hands of wily Robert E. Lee, whose superior generalship more than exposed his counterpart's braggadocio. By boldly dividing his outnumbered forces, Lee surprised Pope's army and drove it from the field, in the process bringing the Rebel army to within twenty miles of Washington.[44]

An aura of gloom unmatched thus far in the war pervaded the North in the aftermath of the loss at Second Manassas as Lee's Army of Northern Virginia crossed the Potomac and made its way into Maryland during the first week of September. By invading the North and gaining victories there, Lee hoped that Maryland might join the Confederacy and proponents of peace in the North might triumph in the fall elections and prod the Lincoln administration to seek a diplomatic settlement to end the fighting on southern terms. Under such ominous circumstances, even northern civilians who trusted in God's superintendence of events found it difficult to maintain a positive outlook. "I feel to-day as if the Devil might as well take our Country," Serena Wright seemed to despair after learning of the recent reversal. "For my life, I cant see what it is worth." Promptly regaining her perspective, she encouraged her husband George to refrain from "desponding for *any* reason" because "we are so blessed above other people." Having grown so accustomed to frequent Federal repulses that she received such news with "a kind of dispairing indifference," Rhoda Southworth emphasized the necessity for the nation to place itself in right relationship with God in order to reverse this undesirable trend, for it was futile to fight against the Almighty. "With God on our side we should be strong tho all the world were against us," she maintained, but if "all the world were in league aginst him...[it] should surely come to nought." In order to gain the assistance of the invincible Ruler of the universe, the nation still needed to humble itself, repent of its sins, and turn to God so that victories would be won. "I could see...the reason why god does not seem to be with us in our Battles," Hannah Bingham theorized, for "we as a people have forsaken Him & have not had respect to His laws." Instead of relying on God's strong arm for deliverance, the nation had swelled up with pride in its own martial strength and forgotten that it was God who had enabled the United States to triumph in previous wars. Hannah's husband Abel agreed that the nation had stubbornly refused to call upon God or depend on him as its sole support. "We are not sufficiently humble yet, and do not in a national capacity mourn over our sins as we ought, nor as a nation implore the Divine aid & protection as we should." In his opinion, patriotic fervor manufactured at "War meetings of *Hurrah*" did little to further "our cause" and proved useless for "drawing down the blessings, and aid from on High." Despite the nation's unwillingness to repent and acknowledge its dependence on God, Abel Bingham presumed that God ultimately would prosper the North and continue to be long-suffering until the country saw the error of its ways. "We act as if we did not...have Israels God for our God," he marveled, "but I believe that He is the same God still.... Let us place our trust & confidence in Him, as His people did in ancient times, and He will as assuredly grant His aid."[45]

As the war's second summer concluded, most religious civilians readily admitted that the North had done nothing to deserve God's favor. Nevertheless, the majority of them unflinchingly clung to their belief that God supported the Union in the war. "Did I not believe that our cause is just, and has the approbation of the God of Justice and of battles, I should despair," Reuben Hitchcock informed his wife. "But relying on Him, I am yet confident of success," no matter that "it may come through seas of blood." Despite the temporary hardships and destruction engendered by the conflict, Hitchcock considered them as little more than bumps on the road to future progress. "Although so fraught with present evil[,] righteous wars...are made of God...[to be] the instruments of great good in the advancement of the world." However, before national and world conditions could reach their apex, sin had to be eradicated, which required divine chastening. For many Christians, the concept of chastening underpinned their idea of God's special relationship with America. According to Scripture, God's children could expect fatherly reproof in their personal lives to convict them of unconfessed sin and help them grow in their Christian walk and pursuit of holy living. This process of loving discipline, though painful for a time, benefited the Christian in the long run and confirmed that a person truly was a child of God. In the same manner, if God had indeed chosen America to be an exemplar among the countries of the world, then national chastening should be expected periodically to purge away sins. By interpreting the war as a form of chastening, many Christians found resounding evidence that God had not cast off America. Before God would make the North victorious, "he may discipline us thoroughly first," Reuben Hitchcock recognized, emphatically adding "and we need it." Somewhat less confident than Hitchcock, Sophia Buchanan thought she discerned God's hand of correction in the war, which helped invigorate her wavering faith in the army's ability to prevail through God's assistance. "I...do not put that confidence & trust in our God, which I ought," she confessed, "that though he willingly afflicts us now, it is for some wise purpose, which he only understands." After "we are sufficiently punished, will he not help us conquer?" she asked rhetorically, "for are we not in the right, & does not God battle for the right?"⁴⁶

While Lee's foray into Maryland served to legitimize the northern war effort for Sophia Buchanan and only reinforced her faith in the indestructibility of the government because of its unique position in God's sight, it had the opposite effect on Calvin Fletcher and even prompted him to revise his outlook on the North's prospect of survival. Throughout the early stages of the war, Fletcher had often affirmed his conviction that God at some point would deliver the Union, but an invading Rebel army seriously shook his confidence in the righteousness of the northern crusade against southern rebellion to the point that he momentarily questioned America's divine destiny. "I had been sure we had the justice of the cause, that we...were in the eyes of God...bound to maintain the integrity of the union," he recalled, showing signs of doubt. "I may have been blind & not seen the weakness of our cause or its injustice." Waiting for news of the result of the engagement at Antietam clearly unsettled Fletcher, and he attempted to prepare himself for the worst, expecting to hear that the Army of the Potomac had been put to flight once again. "I have slept badly. Have been a little sick & sad.... I have concluded...that the Southern confederacy is a fixed fact. I pray I have grace to meet the status & character of one of a conquered nation." As Fletcher's angst over the country's future mounted during the uncertain weeks of September 1862, his hope for emancipation plunged precipitously. If the North sued for peace, he realized, the chains of slavery would become "more firmly fixed than ever." This sobering thought dealt a serious blow, albeit temporarily, to his presumptuous tendency to think he could decipher God's intentions from events of the war.⁴⁷

Like Fletcher, many other Northerners had been contemplating the future of slavery over the past two months. Almost immediately after Lincoln announced to the cabinet his decision to emancipate slaves, reports of a significant development, some intentionally made public by the president himself in order to gauge the popular reception of his intended policy, spread throughout the country. Nevertheless, few Northerners who caught a glimpse of what had transpired during the July cabinet meeting pressed Lincoln to pursue immediate emancipation. After guessing what was afoot, Horace Greeley delivered the most notable critique with his *New York Tribune* editorial that challenged Lincoln to do nothing other than enforce the Second Confiscation Act. In his famous rejoinder to "The Prayer of Twenty Millions," Lincoln cut to the heart of the matter. "My paramount objective in this struggle *is* to save the Union, and is *not* either to save or destroy slavery. If I could save the Union without freeing *any* slave I would do it, and if I could save it by freeing *all* the slaves I would do it; and if I could save it by freeing some and leaving others alone I would also do that." After shrewdly disarming his critics by classifying them as opponents of the Union if they questioned his method of managing the war, Lincoln explained that his *"official* duty" required only that he preserve the Union. His *"personal* wish," however, encompassed universal freedom for all.[48]

Although this concluding statement was a thinly veiled hint to the course Lincoln shortly would take, few individuals were astute enough to recognize it. In typical Lincolnian fashion, the letter was enigmatic enough to reassure conservatives, moderates, and radicals that their views on slavery coincided completely with the president's. Back home in Quincy, Illinois, Senator Orville Browning reported that the people of his state, with the exception of a few ultra-radicals, "are all with and for you." Even a prominent local Democrat related that the reply to Greeley had produced "general joy" among the opposition party and satisfied them that Lincoln would not jeopardize their support by declaring emancipation. Antislavery denominational bodies seemed just as hopeful that Lincoln supported their position, and during a ten-day period in September they bombarded his office with resolutions beseeching him to enforce the Second Confiscation Act or abolish slavery immediately. Not to be outdone by ecclesiastical organizations, a group of Christians from Lamoille, Illinois, tried to impress upon the president the magnitude of his responsibilities in possessing the God-given authority to abrogate slavery. "Almighty God...has a controversy with us," they contended, and unless Lincoln appeased his wrath by freeing the slaves, the nation could not count on divine assistance.[49]

Of course, not all civilians who might have read the exchange between Greeley and Lincoln took comfort from it as Orville Browning alleged. In Minnesota, an uprising of the Sioux was wreaking havoc on frontier settlers during the latter half of August, and some residents believed rumors that Southerners had incited the Sioux to revolt as an ancillary diversion to the main fighting. Although Serena Wright personally supported emancipation and later actively participated in the Freedman's Aid Society, she thought it inappropriate for the cabinet to be "diddleing over the negro question" at a time when "our enemy opens the very gates of Hell" on northern civilians. As polar opposites on the antislavery position, many socially conservative whites, animated by their Negrophobia and determined to exclude blacks from the North, vehemently condemned any talk of an emancipation policy. Elisha Huntington regarded Lincoln's "foolish twaddle about Emancipation" as a sign of desperation and confirmation of the growing national influence of "Niggerism from Greeley to Fred[erick] Douglass." After mentioning how infrequently several denominations held religious services and deploring that the meetings on those occasions typically resulted in the preaching of "a War Sermon or a recruiting lecture for volunteers," a female resident of Ohio reflexively transitioned to her antipathy for black refugees who had settled locally. "I think if Old Abe would visit this colony here and see how they live he wouldn't want no more niggers free and here among us." In contrast to individuals of both extremes who paid close attention to political developments and kept abreast of newsworthy items, some antislavery Northerners seemed unaware of the reports of impending emancipation and continued to criticize the Lincoln administration for what they considered to be a dereliction of duty in ignoring slavery. "Till some measures are taken to abolish slavery," Ella Johnston of Ashtabula, Ohio, complained to a soldier with the 105th Ohio, "every man upon our side who dies in battle, is wantonly sacrificed." Rhoda Southworth lamented that the government continued to spurn "the great principle[s] of justice and humanity and liberty" while "clinging to the great sin which has brought upon the nation His righteous judgements and makes him our enemy." In her opinion, Lincoln had been trying to wage war while relying on his own intellect and abilities, and unless he made God his source of strength and wisdom, he would continue to lead the country down the path of destruction. Southworth yearned "to whisper in Lincoln's ear" scriptural injunctions such as Psalm 118:8, "'It is better to trust in God than to put confidence in man.'" Indeed, she had practically given up hope that Lincoln would ever turn from his own understanding and seek God's face, even comparing him to the wicked fool described in Psalm 52:7. "I fear it must be written of our president 'Lo! this is the man that made not God his trust.[']"[50]

Rhoda Southworth could not have been more mistaken. After several months of pondering the role of providence in the war and seeking to discern the divine will, Lincoln decided to put God to the test. On September 17, Lee's undermanned Army of Northern Virginia fought McClellan's Army of the Potomac to a tactical draw during one of the bloodiest battles of the war, inflicting 24,000 combined casualties. With Lee forced to retire to Virginia, the North claimed victory, giving Lincoln the opening for which he had been waiting. Addressing his cabinet on September 22, the president astounded everyone by disclosing that he had covenanted with God to announce publicly his emancipation policy if the army gained the upper hand at Antietam Creek. Like Gideon laying out a fleece to seek confirmation of God's will, Lincoln had received his "indication of [the] Divine will," having "satisfied" himself that "God had decided this question in favor of the slaves." As of January 1, 1863, the proclamation read, all slaves in areas held by the Confederacy would be declared "forever free." Although the words themselves were useless apart from the delivering power of Federal forces, the principle they represented gave many individuals, black and white alike, reason for hope. When a group of well-wishers saluted Lincoln two days later, he declared to them, with a mixture of unpretentiousness and ambivalence, "I can only trust in God I have made no mistake." Despite this note of uncertainty, Lincoln's decision to move forward with emancipation should not be construed as an irrational, reckless bargain with God. For months he had carefully weighed the matter in his mind and reasoned through the potential ramifications of such a critical measure. By coming to regard providence as a personal God who purposefully acted in human affairs, Lincoln gained a new perspective that enabled him to act on moral precepts, principles that he could believe with some certainty coincided with the divine will. Thus, by adding to his constitutional duty to preserve the Union the moral imperative to abolish slavery, Lincoln infused the war with a sacred mission, an action that many religious Northerners had long awaited and which only reinforced their propensity to interpret the war from a theological mind-set.[51]

3

"Try to Live the Life of a Christian"

The Personal Faith of Women on the Home Front

Born in Youngstown, Ohio, in 1828 and raised in the home of a loving but authoritarian father active in the Disciples of Christ denomination, Alice Kirk formed strong family ties and valued the importance of personal piety from an early age. After becoming engaged to Benjamin Grierson, she realized she could not marry him because of his "indifference" toward religion and his indulgence in the vices of drinking and smoking. When the Grierson family moved to Jacksonville, Illinois, in 1849, Alice and Ben decided to break off all communication, and their separation seemed final. But as "Providence" would have it, in 1853 Alice accepted a teaching position at a girl's academy in Springfield, Illinois. While making his rounds as a band conductor, Ben discovered Alice's name on a school advertisement and immediately tracked her down. After courting for a year and gaining the permission of her father, who realized that his twenty-six-year-old daughter would either marry Grierson or die a spinster, the couple wed.

Marital bliss faded quickly as myriad trials overwhelmed the newlyweds. Alice struggled to establish a Christian home, failing to reform Ben's character flaws or break through his religious apathy. Further complicating this endeavor, Ben's inability to support his wife on the meager salary of a music teacher necessitated that the couple board with his parents. Before long, Alice's growing discontent at living with her in-laws and unexpected pregnancy convinced Ben that he needed a regular income. He borrowed money to buy a share in a dry goods store in Meredosia, Illinois, and for the first time managed to provide a home for his family. Unfortunately, the Panic of 1857 crippled the local economy, and he was stuck with a store overstocked with goods purchased on credit. His indebtedness continued to increase, and by 1861 creditors had taken not only the store but also his home. Forced to move his family back to his parents' residence, Ben Grierson's future looked bleak.

The war, however, provided an unexpected opportunity to start a new life, and Ben took a position as aide-de-camp to Brigadier General Benjamin Prentiss. Alice instantly opposed this decision to join the army and contended that Ben had a responsibility to stay with his family. "The separation of families," she lamented in July 1861, is "one of the great evils of war." Even more distressing, she feared that the dissolute atmosphere of camp would corrupt Ben's morals even further. Despite these objections, Alice's growing sense of patriotic duty convinced her that her husband's service was both commendable and needful. Although Ben's absence from home produced additional cares, Alice's personal faith in a sovereign God enabled her to give him up and bear increased burdens, knowing that she endured these hardships for the country's good. "God alone knows how great must be our individual sacrifices, in this just, & necessary, war," she reminded Ben in August 1861, "but whatever they may be, may he give us strength and patience, to...bear them cheerfully, having faith that what he willeth is best."[1]

Alice Grierson's response to the effects of the Civil War on her family closely resembled the experiences of many northern women. Sincere religious devotion characterized the lives of numerous women, and this pietistic outlook was an integral component of daily life. In letters to soldiers, devout women emphasized the value of prayer, the importance of spiritual growth, and the necessity of relying completely on God when suffering through trials. However, recent scholarship has tended to overlook this more personal and individualistic aspect of faith and focused instead on the increased public roles of women during the war. Furthermore, several historians have emphasized how the Victorian ideals of domesticity and the cult of true womanhood motivated women to become guardians of morality and the home. This is surely the case with some women, but others inquired about the spiritual health of soldiers because their personal faith motivated a desire to know that loved ones were prepared to meet God. Attempts to convert unsaved family members and efforts to confirm that professing Christians had made peace with God clearly demonstrate a concern that derived from genuine personal piety rather than accepted social norms. Admonitions to refrain from various vices, albeit grounded in conventional morality, superseded the standard trope when framed in relation to the seriousness of preserving one's testimony primarily for the sake of Christ and only secondarily as a product of feminine persuasion. Because many women developed their religious beliefs independent of clergymen or the dominant social and cultural constructs of the day, they cultivated an individualized "spiritual orientation to God" that allowed them to apply their faith in a multitude of ways.[2] By concentrating on the theme of domesticity, some historians have ignored the genuine pietism that stimulated many women's religious instruction to soldiers. Establishing the authenticity of northern women's personal faith and understanding their religious dialogue with soldiers as a primarily spiritual undertaking that coincidentally conformed to Victorian ideals of domesticity creates a more balanced representation of northern women and illustrates the centrality of religious convictions in helping them cope with changes engendered by the Civil War.

The absence of husbands and sons from home was probably the most fundamental challenge many women faced. As the only method of maintaining personal connection with their menfolk, women's correspondence often renders an unvarnished glimpse of their inner spiritual struggles. In candid missives and private diaries, many women disclosed their core religious beliefs, in the process revealing the significance they attached to spiritual matters both for themselves and their loved ones. Mary Ann Hobbs of Orangeville, Indiana, regretted that her husband William, an assistant surgeon with the 85th Indiana Volunteers, could no longer "enjoy the same privileges and blessings" of shared church attendance. Nevertheless, she took comfort in the doctrine of God's omnipresence, believing that God was "evry where present" and would uphold William whether he was "in the tented field or on the weary march." She also emphasized the importance of relying on God's grace in every circumstance and reminded him that grace "will be suficient for your day and trial." From her own admission, she followed this advice and depended completely on grace. "I am satisfied that it takes more grace to sustain me at the present time than it ever did before." With two sons in the Union army, Cornelia Chase of Elsie, Michigan, often felt lonely. "If it was not for the presence of god my Savior," she affirmed, "I should indeed be alone." After failing to receive word from her son George after an engagement at Murfreesboro, Tennessee, she sincerely implored God to supply grace and strength to bear "the agony of suspense" and yearned to place George's safety in God's hands. Upon learning that George had been wounded, she confessed that her constant cares for "my dear boy in the hospital" drew her attention away "from heavenly things." Yet in the midst of this trial, she steadfastly professed, "Still my hope is in God and in him will I trust." Hoosier Margaret Smith complained to her husband George of the 12th Indiana that a prolonged illness weakened her so that she could "hardly sit up to write" him, and her sorrow at being "left alone" during her sickness was "more than I know how to stand." Nevertheless, she determined to persevere, believing that "God...is helping me every day." Emilie Gleichmann, a recent emigrant from Germany, had made few close friends in Evansville, Indiana, and sometimes regretted having allowed her husband

John to enlist with the 136th Indiana in 1864. "I can hardly write from crying," she divulged on a particularly lonely occasion, "and if the dear Savior wouldn't be my friend, I would despair."[3]

When difficulties arose or trials increased, a reliance on God's sovereignty allowed women to trust in his perfect care and absolute control instead of their own insufficient strength or limited understanding. Eliza Porter of Lattaville, Ohio, did not attempt to hide her true feelings when she wished that her brother John's regiment would not be sent far from home or be put in the path of danger. "My heart shrinks from the prospect of living in this sinful dark friendless world without you." But at the same time, she recognized her need to accept "that our Heavenly Father should do as he thinks best with us" and determined that it profited nothing to worry about her brother's safety or "anticipate sorrows." "God has promised strength only for today," she concluded, "and in infinite mercy, He shuts the future from our view." God's foreknowledge of future events gave assurance that nothing could transpire without his permission, including the protection of soldiers if he so willed. "I know the Lord can save you on the battle field as well as in the quiet home," Rhoda Eggleston reminded her son Hubert, who was fighting the Sioux with the 6th Minnesota. "It is a great comfort," she added, "that you...trust futer events to him who overrules all things for the best good of all his children." Louisa Semple reminded her brother Ben Grierson that God's understanding was both infinite and intimate. "Even the hairs of your head are all numbered," she pointed out, alluding to a teaching of Jesus' recorded by Matthew and Luke. Consequently, no bullet could find him "by accident" but only if permitted "by the Divine Will." After her husband Claude, a lieutenant with the 8th Michigan, had survived several battles during the first two years of war, Sophia Buchanan could honestly affirm that "God has indeed been good to us." When she contemplated all that had transpired since Claude enlisted, she could not help but discern God's hand of guidance and protection on their lives. "He has led us along by a way that we knew not," Sophia perceived. "Often when I have feared that you would be killed in battle, I have said to myself, if God has been our friend thus far through life in pleasant places, can he not still be our comfort & protector, when trials come."[4]

Women concerned about a soldier's safety or seeking grace for their own trials found solace most often in prayer. Prior to the Civil War, there had been a renewed emphasis on public prayer during the Businessman's Revival of 1857–58, a predominantly urban, middle-class religious awakening. In his study of the revival in Boston, historian John Corrigan describes the prayer at these public meetings as being an emotional "performance" or "spectacle" in which "persons gave the heart to God in prayer and expected God, in turn, to grant a request." According to Corrigan, both men and women viewed prayer as a business transaction with God. By offering their hearts to him in emotional displays of public prayer and boldly petitioning him for both spiritual and temporal blessings, they expected God to grant their requests and fulfill his part of the contractual exchange. In contrast to this earlier community-wide movement, the prayers of women for soldiers were completely private in nature. Although their petitions certainly involved emotions, these women never considered themselves as entering into negotiations with God and presuming that he would answer in the manner they desired simply because they asked. Instead, women's prayers convey a sense of coming before God in humility and revering him for his awesome power and majesty. Entering into an attitude of prayer could quiet the heart and bring relief from cares and distractions of the world by drawing a person's mind to spiritual matters. "I found much peace and happiness last night in prayer," a rejuvenated Alice Chapin extolled. "I seemed so to feel the *nearness* of *Christ*." Without presuming upon the goodness of God, women could trust him to answer the requests of his children offered in accordance with his perfect will. Sophia Buchanan avouched, "I have learned to trust in him, & to feel that he is...ready, willing & able to answer prayer."[5]

The safety and protection of soldiers in battle seems to have been the most frequently mentioned request and most desired result of the prayers of northern women. Ohioan Eliza Mears informed her husband in November 1862 that she considered it a "privilege" to bring him and other loved ones before the "Mercy Seat, and there present Them to a kind Covinent keeping God for protection & Preservation while surrounded with disease and Death." After John Griffin of the 17th Illinois had a "narrow escape" in battle in the summer of 1863, Emma Stevens of Keithsburg, Illinois, concluded that her prayers were indeed efficacious. "Truly we have every reason to believe that our prayers have so far been heard and answered." A female friend informed James Hill of the 33rd Indiana that the prayers of citizens of Putnamville were like "a blessed shield of defense" screening him from harm. Prayers, however, did not guarantee safety, and when God withheld his hand of protection, the loss of a loved one understandably left questions that lacked easy solutions. Upon learning that a friend's cousin had died at the battle of Resaca, Georgia, in May 1864, Therese Elstine reflected, "I often think it so strange that the earnest and constant prayers for such are not more effectual." Her musings led her to contemplate the dilemma of how finite human beings could ever comprehend the intentions of a transcendent God. "We cannot know what God purposes by any of His acts," she abruptly concluded. Other women, in contrast, had their faith in the value of prayer strengthened even under adverse circumstances. After her son Jacob was wounded at the battle of Murfreesboro, Margaret Bender rededicated herself to prayer. "I have committed him anew into the hands of God and pray that He may be with him and preserve him from all danger." Even "if it's our dear Saviour's Will that he should die," she added, "my prayer is...that I may become reconciled to His Holy Will."[6]

Few women left more explicit evidence of personal reliance on God during trials than Alice Chapin, who buried her seven-month-old son less than seven weeks after her husband Lucius enlisted with the 4th Indiana Cavalry in August 1862. Finding "much comfort" in prayer during her "hour of sore trial," she sought, like David in Psalm 61, to take refuge on "'the Rock that is Higher than I.'" Instead of questioning God or losing faith, she turned her attention to her inner life and resolved, with "*God* being my helper[,] to put down all the selfishness in my heart, and try to bear patiently the trials he calls upon me to bear." Her increased devotion was undoubtedly bolstered by Lucius's positive attitude after he responded to the news of his son's death by reaffirming that "God is good *to me*...and is still my support my comfort my peace my *all*." Alice also took consolation from Scripture and gained perspective for her own situation from the unparalleled sufferings of Job, a righteous man who refused to curse God despite losing his possessions, physical health, and ten children. She deemed that "the blessed realities of Truth expressed in the Bible" and "the *comfort* of its Holy pages" strengthened her "Faith to trust Gods promises." Yet for all her noble intentions to live as a victorious Christian, she often complained of the weakness of her flesh. "I am sometimes *astonished* at myself...to think I even *dare* ask God to pardon my sins." Although disappointed by her frequent spiritual shortcomings, Alice did not despair over these failures, for she knew that God extended mercy and granted forgiveness "even when we have been *so wicked* and...go astray from him." Alice's determination to persevere in her Christian walk was reinforced by the encouragement she received from Lucius, who emphasized God's sovereignty over all aspects of life and reminded her that God disciplined Christians through trials that resulted in personal betterment. He directed her to Philippians 1:6, which confirmed that God "would school" Christians through afflictions for the purpose of making them "perfect...in Jesus Christ," an unattainable end "in this life" that would only be realized in eternity. By pointing out the constructive nature of trials and the impossibility of achieving earthly perfection, Lucius hoped to convince Alice that her circumstances, though truly difficult, were bearable through the grace of God.[7]

After suffering through the death of her infant son, Alice Chapin's hardships continued to mount throughout the war. Lucius's brother Coy Chapin fell at Nashville in April 1863. Monetary limitations necessitated that Alice and her two-year-old daughter Ally move in with her parents in Terre Haute. Hoping to ease the family's financial burden, she even considered teaching school for a term to earn an additional forty dollars. However, the care of sick family members demanded most of her attention over the winter of 1863–64. She nursed her sister Hannah to health, agonized over the condition of Ally, who seemed "in the very jaws...of death" as she suffered through a debilitating illness that kept her bedridden until early spring, and witnessed her father's deteriorating health bring him to "the brink of the grave." Throughout that "*trying* winter," Alice felt as if "the grim Monster [death] hovered so closely round our loved ones...that certainly he would take *some* of our number." The aforementioned all managed to elude death, but in June 1864, George Chapin, another of Lucius's brothers, was killed in uniform. This second blow fell hard on the Chapin family, especially Alice's mother-in-law Sarah, who had given two sons to the slaughterhouse of war in exchange for "tribulation and nothing else[,] tribulation too that cannot be relieved in this life." During this period, which Alice described as "one of the saddest and most anxious seasons of my life," she despaired that it would "seem almost a miracle" if Lucius survived the war. Her consuming desire was for his safe return so that they could "try to live for God & his glory" and die peaceably at home. But until that day arrived, she did not want to lose sight of her present responsibilities and forfeit the chance to hear God say, "'Well done good and *faithful* servants, enter into the joy of thy Lord.'" Over the course of the war, Alice learned to accept her trials, do her duty as a Christian, and, as Lucius advised, "leave the consequences with God."[8]

Alice Chapin's emphasis on her abject sinfulness and the unmerited nature of God's saving grace manifested her solid grounding in the doctrines of the Calvinistic strain of orthodox Christianity. A housewife in her mid-twenties who embraced such a view was becoming increasingly uncommon, for over the first half of the nineteenth century theologians had subtly modified or altogether rejected aspects of Reformed theology. Doctrines such as total depravity were more apt to be espoused by older believers like seventy-year-old Hannah Bingham, who avowed in July 1864, "I am convinced more & more of the utter helplessness as a sinner to do anything for my own salvation or that will in the least bring me into favor with god." "My only hope," she professed, "is in the atonement of the son of god."[9] Women of Alice Chapin's and Hannah Bingham's ilk represent a religious category that historian Richard Rabinowitz has labeled as doctrinalist or orthodox because they stressed the importance of a proper understanding of theology as essential to their personal experience of religion. Doctrinalists considered the soul's salvation to be their primary spiritual concern, for only through a conversion experience could a person be brought into a right relationship with God and secure eternal blessings.

But as nineteenth-century society moved further away from its Puritan heritage and adjusted to the individualistic ethos of the expanding nation and religious democratization caused by the Second Great Awakening, many

As the wife of a frontier missionary in Sault Ste. Marie, Hannah Bingham endured numerous hardships. Her diary entries attest to a strong faith in God to supply her physical and spiritual needs. During the war, she often affirmed her belief that God was directing the conflict to free the slaves. *Clarke Historical Library, Central Michigan University*

people yearned for a more activist, anthropocentric religious experience. Proponents of moralism underscored their own ability to alter their behavior and achieve personal reformation rather than believing that only God could change their hearts. In contrast to doctrinalists' focus on metaphysical concepts such as living for God and his glory, moralists sought to live virtuously because of practical benefits that would accrue in the present life as a result of appropriate conduct. By establishing patterns of virtue and gradually developing godly habits, moralists would become Christians through a process of behavioral change rather than by undergoing a climactic conversion experience. Antoinette Cobb of Mantua, Ohio, illustrated this viewpoint when giving childrearing advice to a friend in August 1862. She asserted that vigilant maternal care would help cultivate suitable behavior in a child but conceded that some children would misbehave regardless of parental instruction. In her opinion, childhood disobedience did not confirm "the doctrine of Total Depravity," for she believed that everyone possessed "*some good*..., although it may be very difficult to find." Nevertheless, this innate virtue "*is* hid away in the secret chambers of the heart." Periodically throughout life, "the doors of the heart will be opened, and the *good* will be made manifest."[10] As a parent, Cobb sought to draw out the child's natural predisposition toward moral living and through proper nurture direct the youngster down the path that would lead to a virtuous life.

In addition to doctrinalism and moralism, devotionalism emerged in the 1840s as a third discernible category of religious thought. Devotionalism placed emotions at the center of religious practice and attempted to make the process of developing a devotional spirit an end in itself. By primarily emphasizing feelings, devotionalists minimized both doctrinalists' objective to apply theological truth and moralists' resolve to practice virtue. Instead, devotionalists sought to be religious simply for its own sake and for the positive feelings it produced. Because of the subjective and sentimental nature of devotionalism, the desire for repeated episodes of communion with God made obsolete the necessity of a single conversion crisis. After reading her Bible on a Sunday morning in April 1863, fifteen-year-old Hattie Godfrey prayed to God and expectantly waited for an infusion of emotional encouragement. "I fail in doing and being as I would like," she admitted, "but I hope before long to feel forgiven of my many sins." Three months later, she thought she sensed spiritual progress but could not know with certainty. "I begin to feel as though I could almost give myself up to Christ. Oh how I wish I was one of his flock."[11] Familiar with doctrinalist terminology, Godfrey nonetheless trusted her own subjective experiences to measure her devotion. To be sure, these three categories are ideal constructs, not impermeable divisions. Doctrinalists, for example, expected Christians to model moral behavior and sometimes exhibited traces of devotionalism in their personal walk with God because these outward signs were evidences of conversion and demonstrated growth in grace. Since they were not regarded as ends in themselves, virtuous conduct and pietistic acts in no way detracted from doctrinalists' overarching goal of living out theological truth.

The most easily identifiable area of divergence found in the views of doctrinalists, moralists, and devotionalists pertained to conceptions of soteriology. Orthodox Christianity, as illustrated by the testimonies of Alice Chapin and Hannah Bingham, maintained that salvation was by grace alone through faith in Christ, who was completely God and completely man at the same time, lived a sinless life, died on the cross, and rose from the dead. No amount of good works could merit favor with God, for only Christ's atonement provided the way for man's salvation. The moralist, in contrast, emphasized the individual's effort in seeking to change one's character in order to become a Christian. For instance, Amanda Chittenden attended church sporadically once the war began as she moved from one Indiana community to another while staying with various relatives during her husband George's stint as a surgeon with the 16th Indiana. However, the shock of finding her brother lying in his own vomit in a drunken stupor roused her from spiritual slumber in the autumn of 1861. Amanda lamented that her upbringing, in her opinion, had lacked examples of genuine religious affections, for she had only heard her father offer mealtime prayers that "never reache[d] Heaven," only seen her parents attend Sunday service but never prayer meeting, and not once witnessed them "go to the communion table and consecrate their lives, and services to the Saviour." Convinced that George's childhood had been more devout, she blamed her religiously deficient home environment for her having heretofore "lived a purposeless life." Because of her brother's disgrace, she vowed to "try and live a christian," and if George outlasted the war, she hoped he would join her in this endeavor at moral improvement. But after embarking on this quest, Amanda quickly found it to be more difficult than she expected. "My progress is backwards instead of forwards," she admitted, and consequently appealed to George for "some kindly words of encouragement to help me onward and upward." Where a doctrinalist like Alice Chapin had examined her life and found herself to be an unworthy sinner by nature who could never merit salvation, Amanda uncovered only "little errors that lead the soul away from the paths of virtue." Staying on that proper course, she believed, simply necessitated that they "be christians," which they ostensibly could attain without divine assistance.[12]

In contrast to Amanda Chittenden's assumption that she could become a Christian by her own moral effort, Serena Wright expected to find God revealing himself through a devotional experience as she kept her heart open to him. However, she exhibited elements of both doctrinalism and moralism as well. When referring to the "cares and toils" of everyday life, Serena expressed a perspective well within the bounds of traditional Christianity. With her husband George away from their home in Fergus Falls, Minnesota, in December 1862, she demonstrated a reliance on God to provide her daily needs, encouraging herself with the promises of Matthew 6:32–33 that "'Your Heavenly Father'" knew them in advance and would provide accordingly if she would "'seek...first the Kingdom of God and his righteousness.'" But after hearing a message in November 1863 about the death of a just man, she was convicted by her own moral "poverty" and sought "for a better and higher way of living." Although she expressed sorrow over her sins and bemoaned the daily occurrence of "good resolves broken and destroyed," she focused solely on her motives and works as the solution to her failures, thinking that by "earnestly" yearning "to live better" she would find spiritual success. Serena attempted to reform herself despite reading in the Gospels that Jesus not only claimed to be "*able to save* to the uttermost all who come unto him" but even forgave a lame man's sins. Notwithstanding Jesus' assertion of his deity and ability to save, she was undecided "whether he be God or not." Befitting one who was the adopted daughter of a Unitarian minister, she concluded that he possessed "marvelous power" only. Her "doubts and questionings" regarding the person of Christ did not concern her nearly as "much as the fear that we shall not live up to the light we have, and do faithfully the things *we know* we ought to do." In her estimation, a devotional experience would settle the matter of knowing how to live uprightly. "My prayer is...that God will lead us, is rather that we will submit to be lead by Him, and that all necessary truth will be taught us." For this to take place, she had to keep her heart sensitive and gain a greater awareness of God's working. As a result of her "praying daily for his guidance," she concluded, "he will keep our hearts ready to receive and welcome his truth, as he shall see fit to reveal it." In Serena's estimation, a devotional experience was the secret to the Christian life. Once it had occurred, proper actions would follow. Precise doctrine mattered little, she assumed, for "we cannot seriously err in beliefs" as long as we "give ourselves unreservedly to Our Heavenly Father."[13] Whether classified as a doctrinalist, moralist, or devotionalist concerning the way of salvation, many women relied on personal faith that understandably influenced other aspects of their lives throughout the Civil War.

Women often demonstrated their faith by becoming involved in various forms of benevolent work that supported the war effort. Although some women's participation derived from sheer patriotism, others indicated that a spirit of Christian charity and compassion motivated their efforts. Ann Conkling took blankets, clothes, and religious tracts to soldiers hospitalized at Camp Butler in Springfield. She considered ministering to soldiers as an opportunity for Christian service and hoped that other "Christians will awake, and labor with diligence in the new field...that has been opened to this Nation" because of war. In Jacksonville, Illinois, Elizabeth Duncan provided sick and wounded soldiers with "maps of scripture," assuring herself that men "who never read God's word at home...are delighted with the truths" contained therein. She viewed the war as "a precious time to work" and underscored the spiritual nature of her benevolence, concluding that she would "never regret working in God's vineyard." Because of the close-knit nature of local communities during the mid-nineteenth century, women took a keen interest in the welfare of hometown soldiers and especially sought to furnish their basic necessities. For instance, the women of Grace Church sent the 3rd Ohio Volunteers a package of homemade goods containing three dozen pairs of socks, twenty-two "woolen drawers," and ten pairs of mittens to be distributed to the neediest soldiers. Besides assisting soldiers, aid societies sought to care for their destitute families as well. Illinoisan Mary Cheney participated in a strawberry festival that raised three hundred dollars for families of poor soldiers. When a little girl came begging at her door, Mary followed her home and found her mother ill in bed, "too proud" to beg for food for her three children. Mary helped them as best she could, sent for a doctor, and notified the soldier's aid society, to which she had been contributing a dollar for eighteen consecutive months. Although her service might have seemed insignificant to some, Mary clearly recognized the importance of her contributions to the war effort. She personified the advice that she once gave to a disheartened friend, encouraging her to remember that her only obligation was to "do all you can in the place God has put you."[14]

In addition to devoting their time to benevolence, many religious women considered the enlistment of their men as the highest sacrifice females could make for their country. Since women could not fight (although a few successfully disguised themselves as men), allowing their men to serve was the most heroic act of patriotism they could perform. Sophia Buchanan frankly asserted that "we wives did a good deal for the war in letting our husbands go." When she failed to receive letters from her husband Claude as frequently as she wished, she acknowledged that she could "put up with such things" for the sake of the country. Ellen Woodworth echoed this sentiment when attempting to reconcile her struggles with loneliness and her patriotic pride at being a soldier's wife. "I too am doing something for our Country," she confided in her diary. "I have given all... for the cause of Liberty & freedom." Although Rhoda Southworth often counseled her eighteen-year-old son Eli to seek a discharge and return home, especially after he had become ill and was confined to a hospital in Missouri, she nonetheless remained "willing to make sacrifices for our beloved country." When her son Rufus joined the 21st Indiana, Sarah Dooley gave him "to the Lord and laid him on the alter of his country," trusting that God would "do what is rite" and enable her "to submit to his will." She endeavored to bear her son's absence "with cristian fortitude," knowing that he was serving "in a glorious cause."[15]

In contrast to these examples of feminine patriotism, not all religious women felt inclined to make sacrifices on behalf of the country. Some women disagreed with the choice of their sons and husbands to enlist but were powerless to prevent it. Elvira Aplin, who was estranged from her husband, chided her eldest son George for joining the army instead of remaining in Burton, Michigan, to fulfill his responsibilities as head of household and provide for his younger brothers. Although Elvira promptly came to accept George's decision and supported him wholeheartedly thereafter, other women faltered in their devotion to the cause. As the war dragged on into the autumn of 1864, Lizzie Bowler of Nininger, Minnesota, grew weary of the long separation from her husband Madison, and her letters began to show it. "You seem to be wholly absorbed in the one idea of getting me out of the army and getting me home," Madison reproved her. Thinking that she had been influenced by "those who are ever finding fault with the Government," he admonished her to write encouraging letters and "be a true union heroine." But Lizzie had tired of making personal sacrifices, and with Madison being ill, she desired for him to think of his health foremost. "I do not want to be any more patriotic than I now am," she retorted bluntly. In her opinion, his primary duty was to return home to his family, and she did not "feel willing to sacrifice" his life for the country.[16]

Lizzie Bowler's patriotism only waned for a short period of time toward the end of the war, but Ohioan Ann Cotton struggled from the moment her husband left home. Hoping to gain some practical medical experience, Dexter Cotton enlisted as a surgeon in the fall of 1862. Shortly thereafter, Ann manifested her displeasure at this decision and continued to harp on the subject for months. "I daily regret having given my consent to your going away," she complained. "I do not know what possessed me." Ann seemed unconcerned about the impact of her bitterness on Dexter's spirits and frankly insisted that his service would render little "benefit to you or any one else." Adding insult to injury, she insensitively pointed out his less than homelike living conditions. "It is dreadful to live as you are doing," she jabbed, "& all for nothing too." When Ann was in a less spiteful mood, her transparent honesty revealed that her affection for Dexter trumped her love for country. "I am more a wife than a patriot, & although I do care for my country, I care for you much more." Despite admitting her selfishness in wanting to keep Dexter at home, Ann considered this an instinctive and therefore completely appropriate feeling. In her mind, "civic obligation" paled in comparison to family duties and her "domestic happiness." The division of her loyalties between her husband and her country proved to be a gap that only the passage of time could bridge, and then only incompletely. Although her resentment had softened by late February 1863 to the point where she felt "more satisfied" to be without Dexter than she had initially, Ann nonetheless continued to suffer through periods of despondency. After Dexter became ill in the summer of 1863, she confessed that at times she wanted him home so severely that she almost ceased to "care...what became of the country." Ann's seeming indifference to the nation's future was more pretense than reality, for she developed a keen political awareness and closely followed war developments beginning in the summer of 1863. Nevertheless, Ann Cotton can only be labeled a "reluctant patriot" at best, for she indisputably regarded her more than two-year separation from Dexter as a "great sacrifice," too burdensome for her to bear on the country's behalf.[17]

While Ann Cotton barely tolerated having her husband in the army, Phebe Mount never came to terms with the absence of her husband Charles and took every opportunity to demonstrate her extreme displeasure. A mother of five, Phebe understandably complained of increased domestic duties and a lack of adult conversation. "How dreary long and tedious is *my* life," she grumbled shortly after Charles joined the 20th Ohio. Phebe wondered if his decision had been prompted by her failure to make their home comfortable and underscored that she had done her best as a housewife. Similar to Ann Cotton, she could not ascertain that Charles was "doing any good" in the army. "I hope you may never find any thing to do," she asserted spitefully, but "sit there and fold your arms untill you are ready to come home to stay." Charles tried to make amends by asking forgiveness for enlisting without her permission and neglecting to consider that she would be "called upon to make a greater sacrifice" due to his absence. Despite this plea, Phebe remained upset and contended that she could "never... be reconsiled" to his absence. Moreover, she felt "that you done me wrong" by leaving home, in the process inflicting "a wound that cannot heal over." Phebe's outlook continued to darken over the course of Charles's service, and she confessed that "every week leaves me further from anything like enjoyment or happiness." At one point she became so depressed that she even bemoaned the day of her birth and despaired that "the world and eternity would be better off without me." Her only consolation during this period seems to have been her "great comfort and happiness" that Charles had a "hope of life everlasting beyond the grave through Jesus." This assurance of Charles's salvation, however, did not go far in revitalizing her melancholy spirit or alleviating her domestic hardships. By juxtaposing these seemingly unrelated themes at the end of a letter, Phebe Mount illustrated how personal faith did not guarantee a capacity to bear trials more easily or preclude periods of extreme discouragement. She signed off one letter, "May God save your soul in heaven for Christs sake is the prayer of your wronged and grieved and burdened wife."[18]

Whether enthusiastically supporting a husband's enlistment or regretting the day he left home, wives often complained of the difficulties of raising children alone. A frustrated Ann Cotton informed Dexter that he could "assume the whole responsibility of training the children" once he returned, for she had "had enough of it." She urged him to come home and make their fifteen-year-old daughter Ella start obeying, as she had gone out four times in one week and was doing "just as she pleases about everything." Although Ella's independent streak and alleged misbehavior might have been legitimate grounds for requesting assistance, such childrearing problems also gave Ann an excuse for pressuring Dexter to return home. "The children will almost forget that they have a Father if you stay away much longer," she warned in April 1864. Alice Chapin asked Lucius to pray that she would have wisdom in disciplining their daughter Ally because she often demonstrated a will of her own. Sophia Buchanan offered a similar plea in dealing with her son Claudie, who "seems to be more turbulent & noisy than ever." Although she desired to exercise "more faith in my saviour" and sought "wisdom & strength" from above in knowing how "to guide him aright," she also yearned for her husband's "strong arm to help" her. When her husband William Starr, a colonel with the 9th West Virginia, intimated that she was neglecting her parental duties, Quaker Anna Starr of Richmond, Indiana, rebutted that their boys came to the dinner table with clean hands, combed hair, and brushed teeth. Furthermore, they always hung up their hats and placed their schoolbooks in the proper place. "I have not an idea *why* thee thinks I am relaxing in my care," Anna wondered perplexedly. "I only *know* that I am *increasing* my care and feel *more deeply* every day the *necessity* of increased watchfulness." In her estimation, she had the "*double* responsibility of *acting* [as both] Father and Mother," a task made more burdensome by her "delicate state of health." Instead of faltering under the weight of this additional strain, Anna was infused "with increased energy and *determination* to bear *my* part of the great sacrifice we are *both* making for our country."[19]

Regardless of their feelings concerning a husband's or son's absence and the degree to which they were able to cope with subsequent domestic hardships, religious women made a sincere attempt to ascertain the spiritual state of their loved ones. Efforts to present a clear gospel witness that salvation came by faith in Christ demonstrate the importance of evangelism as the primary concern for women who recognized that death might prevent them from ever seeing their family members face to face on earth again. After reminding Ben that he had "*no assurance*" of surviving the war, Alice Grierson compassionately asked him if he could "in all seriousness answer, 'I am ready'" to enter into "that other world." Without belaboring the point or pressuring him to make an immediate decision, she gently expressed her desire for God to "grant..., through faith in his Son," that Ben would "be ready when that hour" appointed for his death came. Often concerned about her son Eli's safety, Rhoda Southworth comforted herself by praying for his conversion. She trusted that God was convicting Eli of his need for "true repentance" and sovereignly "pursuing that course, which by his grace will be instrumental in bringing you to himself." Although Rhoda realized that her "prayers cannot save you," she hoped that Eli would be "persuaded to seek him [God] now while you may." If she could only have assurance that Eli, through the combination of divine election and human responsibility, had made God his "*Savior*," she would be able to "bear all things" and endure her trials in peace. From evidence in a letter she had received, Mary Stork surmised that her friend James Hill, a lieutenant with the 33rd Indiana, had made "peace...with God" and given his heart "to the Savior." If, however, she had inferred incorrectly, she urged him not to wait until "some future time" to trust Christ, for that opportunity "may never come" again or his heart might be "less inclined" to accept Christ if a second chance presented itself. After having been recently converted herself at a revival meeting in the spring of 1864, Ellen Woodworth set to work on her husband Samuel, who was serving in Alabama with the 1st Michigan Engineers and Mechanics. When instructed by his wife to "look to Jesus," Samuel replied that he recently had been on his knees, shedding "repentant tears" and longing "to live a christian life." Interpreting this news as evidence of spiritual conviction, Ellen commended him for being "on the right path" of *true genuine* repentance." Although she encouraged Samuel to "seek" God's "love & forgiveness," she made it clear to him that he could not "change" his own heart "from a sinful to a spiritual state" by his own effort. Shortly thereafter Samuel put his faith in Christ, and Ellen rejoiced that they now possessed "a firmer foundation to build upon" and shared "a faith that...centers our hopes & joys on a risen Redeemer."[20]

Unlike the previous examples, not all women concerned about a soldier's personal salvation specified that redemption could be obtained only through Christ. Almira Dart of East Pontiac, Michigan, instructed her brother George Howell of the 22nd Michigan to "seek God with all your heart & He will be found of thee." If George would only offer himself "unreservedly to God," then "he will forgive your sins." Dayton, Indiana, resident Anna Seawright first inquired of her brother James Rizer whether he had any physical needs she could meet, but she was more interested in discovering his "condition spiritually." Although Anna had no uncertainty regarding the depth of James's patriotism, she hoped he would leave similar proof of his religious devotion. "You have left evidence to us that you love your country, and her laws—but I ask [you] to leave an evidence that above all you consecrate your soul, and body to God." Four months after her marriage to Madison Bowler during a furlough in late 1862, Lizzie Bowler beseeched her new husband "to take into serious consideration" her "one request" that he would "become a christian." However, Lizzie neglected to provide specific instructions as to how Madison should seek to effect this transformation. She seemed to indicate that for Madison to satisfy her wish, he needed only to "care less for things of this wicked world and pay more attention to Heaven." After her son Arthur died from battle wounds in the summer of 1864, Elvira Aplin expressed hope that his death would "result in the conversion of all the rest of the family." While in the hospital, Arthur had spoken with his chaplain and "had made up his mind to be a christian," and Elvira hoped that her other son George would "take care" of his soul before he was wounded. She reminded George that his faithfulness in performing his duties, his honesty, and his temperance amounted to nothing apart from a conscious decision to "repent of his sins and give his heart to God."[21] The preceding examples demonstrate the lack of theological precision that resulted from the religious and denominational fragmentation of the first half of the nineteenth century. Although some women remained familiar with the language of theological orthodoxy, such as when stressing the necessity of repenting from sin, they failed to present the gospel clearly and completely, instead offering only snippets of gospel truth blended with moralist instructions or sentimentalist emotions.

Mary Collett's attempt to witness to her brother T. E. Smith, a lieutenant with the 79th Ohio, illustrates how jumbled a person's presentation of salvation could become. In November 1861, their seventy-five-year-old uncle died "without leaving his friends one word of evidence...of any change of heart" or preparation to meet God. Nevertheless, Mary hoped that God might still have mercy on him, for only the possibility of universalism could offer her any "consolation" that he might eventually be saved. In bringing up this matter to her brother, she hoped that he would examine himself and make his spiritual peace while time remained. "Twill be much easier to change your thoughts & give your heart to your God now than when you grow old," she asserted. Reminiscing about their mother, Mary remembered how she had prayed for them on her deathbed and concluded that nothing could possibly go wrong for them spiritually because of the sincere prayer of a dying mother. "I cannot but believe that we will all be guided & led in the propper paths," she insisted. However, this statement struck her as too deterministic, so she promptly added, "You know how firmly we believe in free agency—we must do something ourselves." This being the case, she hoped that he would take the initiative in securing his salvation, for she prayed nightly that he would "acknowledge" his sins and "ask with *faith* and penitence." If he would only do this, she was confident that he would "be blessed & pardoned from sin" and "feel Gods love in your heart."[22] Mary Collett's letter contained a patchwork of theology that demonstrates how women often possessed the intent to evangelize without having a clear understanding of the content of the gospel itself. Her muddled effort combined orthodox elements such as the need to confess sins, added a heavy dose of the language of sentimentalism with its emphasis on the feelings of the heart, stressed the importance of man's free will in the process of salvation, and even left open the chance of universal redemption.

While concerned women such as Mary Collett hoped to direct their loved ones to salvation by means of persuasive missives, Christians in the army had been thrust into a vast harvest field of souls. Hannah Bingham hoped that her son Judson, a chaplain with the 10th Massachusetts, had been permitted to visit the sick and wounded after the battle of Fredericksburg in order to direct "some dying soldier to the Lamb of God that taketh away the sin of the world." The duty to evangelize did not fall to chaplains only but included men in the ranks as well, for the possibility of impending death gave greater urgency to sharing the gospel to soldiers who were unprepared for eternity. Coldwater, Michigan, resident Mercy Bates urged her son George White of the 19th Michigan to be a light to the lost whereby he "might be the meanes of saving soles from eternal distruct[ion]." Alice Chapin likewise reminded Lucius to maintain an excellent personal witness so that all his companions would *"know* & see and feel that you are a Christian & be able to *easily* discern by your daily walk that you have been with Christ & have learned of him." Since Lucius had taken a public stand for Christ, Alice advised him to guard his testimony even more carefully, for "they of the world do *watch* the Christian *very* closely," seeking to expose hypocrisy in order "to justify their own *evil* deeds." For this reason, she prayed for him to "be firmly...established in all *good* works" so that his flawless example would "constrain" others "to acknowledge that you are governed by a higher power than they know of." In addition to living out a godly example, she expected him to make a concerted effort to share his faith verbally as well. "I hope you will not fail to exhort your mess mates and all whom you may be associated with." Alice's zeal for Lucius to win converts remained high even after he became ill in July 1863 and was confined to a field hospital in Nashville for two months. She regarded his incapacitation as entirely beneficial because it presented the opportunity to evangelize other convalescents and potentially "lead *one* soul to *Christ*."[23] By emphasizing the personal nature of actively spreading the gospel on an individual basis, Alice Chapin instructed Lucius to follow the exact method of evangelization that Christ had prescribed to his disciples.

Although they lacked Alice Chapin's precision in their instructions for soul winning, other women desired similar results. Rhoda Southworth sought confirmation that Christians in the army were "striving to do good" and "exerting a saving influence upon their fellow soldiers" by both example and witness. When Elvira Aplin heard in May 1863 that religious meetings in the 35th Illinois had increased in attendance and soldiers were "enquiring what they shall do to be saved," she considered this spiritual awakening "much better than any war news." For evangelistic-minded women, even seemingly negative circumstances could prove beneficial when they resulted in the salvation of souls. Hoosier Elizabeth Mendenhall believed that her uncle's imprisonment in the South had been instrumental in his "coming over to the knoledg of truth." After returning home in late 1863 following several months as a prisoner of war, he received baptism and joined a Baptist church. In Elizabeth's estimation, it had "bin a blessing to him to be shut up in prison." Although "it seamed heard to the naturel man" to suffer physically for a time, the adversity led to the spiritual awakening of his inner man. When Dorothy Blinn visited her wounded son John at a field hospital, she found him in good spirits, encouraging his comrades to continue to fight for the country and pleading with them "above all to *seek* the savior." In this instance, the family's suffering at his loss was mitigated by his deathbed witness and his testimony in dying as "a happy Christian rejoicing in the Savior."[24] This ability of some women to view the horrors of war as a prime opportunity for evangelism clearly demonstrates the depth of their spiritual outlook on life.

Many women stressed the importance of Christian soldiers being salt and light because they viewed the military camp as a morass of wickedness. Camp life threatened to corrupt Christian morals by presenting numerous temptations to sin. Stories of men losing their faith or developing degrading habits reinforced the typical female assumption that negative influences and the alluring, irresistible appeals of iniquity pervaded camp. For instance, Rhoda Southworth heard that there had been three "praying men" in Eli's company when it left Minnesota, but by the summer of 1862 all three had "abandoned praying." One of the men was subsequently numbered among "the most profane" members of his regiment. Once soldiers acquired immoral habits in camp, so the thinking went, they proved almost impossible to break. Devout soldiers often reassured their wives that they had not abandoned the faith or violated their moral principles while away from home. John Gleichmann informed Emilie that he had been mocked for praying publicly at a religious service. "From then on they called me the Saint and made fun of me. I let them ridicule me but I did not give up praying," he testified. "I... am not ashamed to acknowledge my Savior." When George Avery returned to the field after marrying his sweetheart Lizzie Little during a furlough in June 1863, he could not help but note the prevalence of moral degeneracy in his camp at Little Rock, Arkansas. George observed firsthand "the progress of human depravity" as soldiers endeavored "to gratify their sensual desires," caring "little whether or not there is a comingling of the races." In his estimation, many soldiers lived for pleasure while expecting their wives at home to remain chaste; he, on the other hand, reaffirmed his love for and devotion to Lizzie.[25]

In some instances, contextual evidence confirms the findings of historians who have emphasized how some women were motivated by ideas of domesticity and redemptive womanhood, for moralist admonitions for men to guard their character and abstain from vice that lacked any reference to a higher religious purpose must be considered as nothing more than feminine efforts to exercise domestic influence. For example, Anna Starr regarded camp as a place where a man could either "*rise above* a great deal of evil" or "*lower himself*" by joining in its corrupting practices, and she exhorted her husband William to return home with his virtue intact for his family's sake. "Thee has *need* of *all* the refining and endearing influences of wife and little ones at home to counteract the many temptations and coarser influences of a soldiers life." In her correspondence with her future husband Henry Van Sellar, Sallie Pattison of Paris, Illinois, never hinted at having any personal faith and only brought up religious subjects when referring to her desire to skip church. "My seat will be found vacant at *Church* tonight," she admitted in July 1863, because "I find more pleasure in writing to a friend than going there and yawning half the time." A few months later she "made no sacraf[ice]" to remain home from meeting to write him again and confessed that she only liked to attend because of the opportunity to socialize and meet other young men. "I often look over the congregation and cannot see a gentleman who I would like to entertain while walking home.... If I am with a Gent that I am proud of," she disclosed, "I like to go [to church;] if not I beg to be excused." In late December, Sallie's father "became alarmed" over her prolonged absence from church and feared that his daughter might be losing her *"religion."* After Sallie and Henry were married in February 1864, her attitude toward spiritual matters remained one of indifference. She referred to the new pastor at their church as "a perfect old grunt" and an "old fogy" not "worth a cent. He is one of the storming staving old Methodist[s] who wants to preach religion into you whether you want it or not." Despite this personal lack of interest in spiritual matters, Sallie nonetheless wanted Henry to follow a strict moral code in the army. She cautioned him not to use profanity or become drunk and believed that he would comply simply out of deference to her wishes. Sallie's example effectively demonstrates that personal piety was not a prerequisite for demanding moral behavior from soldiers.[26]

Although historians have been quick to highlight numerous examples similar to the previous illustrations, they have neglected to note instances when contextual evidence overwhelmingly demonstrates that women addressed moral issues primarily out of religious motivations with the clear intention of helping soldiers maintain their Christian testimonies. Unambiguous references to living as a Christian and avoiding wicked behavior in order to please God confirm that some women denounced the sins of camp because they desired to cultivate Christian devotion. In these instances, a careful analysis of the overall context of letters conveys a genuine concern for soldiers' spiritual lives as opposed to merely depicting attempts to exert domestic authority in accordance with Victorian social standards.

Because some women assumed that their men already knew how to act properly when away from home, they refrained from mentioning specific behavioral prohibitions and simply admonished them to lead an upright Christian life. "Do not let the dutyes you owe to your God bee neglected,"

Elizabeth Stevens of Oskaloosa, Iowa, admonished her husband Simeon. "Remember they are more binding than military dutyes." Ann Cotton warned her husband Dexter that he had better return from the army "with a clear conscience" regarding his personal behavior and the activities in which he engaged himself. "You know that the *greatest* objection I had to you entering the army," she reminded him shortly after he had left home in October 1862, "was the fear that you would not lead a truly Christian life while there, & I know you will find it hard to do so.... I would a thousand times rather hear of your death, than have you live dishonored & disgraced." Rhoda Eggleston straightforwardly entreated her son Hubert to make certain that none of his actions ever brought "reproach upon the cause of Christ." Putting a positive spin on the same advice, Hoosier Mollie McPheeters counseled her husband John to make certain that his "walk and conversation" caused others to take notice that he was "a follower of Jesus." Ellen Woodworth exhorted her husband Samuel "to be *firm* in your principles" and to "be morally & religously strict in keeping an unblemished character." By fulfilling his "duty as a true Soldier in the sight of man, & the fear of God," he would receive God's blessings and "return home a '*christian soldier.*'"[27]

On other occasions, women stressed the importance of relying on God for strength to refrain from succumbing to sin's enticements. "Be strong in resisting the snares and temtations that are around you," Sarah McLean of Jersey County, Illinois, urged her son Edgar. "Trust steadfastly in him who alone hath power to protect and save." Elvira Aplin offered comparable guidance to her son George. "Look to God for help in all times of trouble," she advised, "and thank Him for delliverence from the same." When her nephew suggested "that the influences of the army must be adverse to growth in grace and christian experience," a Hoosier female countered that "the [biblical] promise, 'My grace shall be sufficient for thee' will apply to every emergency of every loving, faithful, conscientious, crossbearing christian." Either a bit naive in discounting the depths of human weakness or overflowing with faith, Lucy Bradford expected her husband William of the 57th Indiana to handle temptations with relative ease. "I am glad you resist all the temptations to which you are exposed," she complimented in January 1862, "but I have never had the least fear of your fall for I know your firmness and of your trust in One who is a present help in every time of need." Other women emphasized the power of prayer in helping soldiers stand firm in the faith as a result of God bestowing his grace in times of need. Mollie McPheeters apprised John that she petitioned God to "give grace to enable you to overcome every temptation to which you are exposed in camp." Sarah Dooley similarly supplicated that God would prevent her son Rufus "from sinning against him and his holy laws."[28] These sincere admonitions clearly demonstrate the seriousness that Christian women attached to their soldiers preserving a godly testimony principally for their own spiritual benefit.

Although the two previous categories seem quite orderly, they fail to relate the complexity of the situation. More often than not, women's instructions to soldiers regarding their conduct in camp were stimulated by both religious convictions and conventional morality because the two inevitably overlapped. On one occasion, women might emphasize the importance of resisting temptations in order to honor God or to preserve a Christian testimony. At other times, they urged proper behavior for the benefit of fulfilling their personal wishes or doing right for its own sake. This lack of a habitual, specific application of religious motivations should not be interpreted as spiritual inconsistency or a decline in devotion. Neither should it be understood as a simple appeal to domestic authority, unless such a view harmonizes with the entire context of a woman's correspondence. Instead, it is reasonable to assert that religious women did not always consider it necessary to explicitly frame their comments within an overtly religious context in every letter. In the end, abstaining from alcohol or avoiding evil companions out of consideration for wife or mother accomplished the same purpose as if it had been done for spiritual reasons. For instance, Ann Cotton informed Dexter that an Ohio colonel in their acquaintance was humiliating his wife by his inappropriate conduct. She reminded him that he would make her "perfectly happy" if he always comported himself "as a true patriot & christian should." Sarah Dooley challenged her son Rufus to "come home a sober and virtuous...man [so] that your parents may be proud of you and feel like thare prayers are answerd." Mary Stork seconded this appeal and implored Rufus to remember his upbringing so that he would make proper decisions when tempted to sin. "Your parents and friends have taught you all your life the right from the wrong way so that you can not fail to know what is right." If he would live honorably, he could return home a soldier whom "none of us [will] be ashamed of."[29]

Few women rivaled the forthrightness of Elvira Aplin when it came to denouncing the temptations of camp life. "I think that those men who do not take especial pains to keep their morrals alive will soon be worse than heathens," she forecast in January 1863. In her estimation, soldiers required frequent reminders of the numerous threats to their personal character. "Unless I give you a lesson on morrality once in a while," Elvira insisted to her son George, "you will forget there is such a thing." Women like Elvira criticized camp life because they worried that their soldiers would fall under the influence of profane comrades who would lead them into various sins. When Alice Grierson first learned that Ben had enlisted, she expressed immediate concern that the degeneracy of camp would exacerbate his ongoing struggles and make permanent his moral deficiencies. "I have known & felt for years that the men with whom you have been most intimately associated, had a bad influence over you," she bluntly asserted in May 1861. "They were not only intemperate in the use of liquors, tobacco &c, but with two or three exceptions, they were men, not governed by religious principle." Now that he was removed from "the restraints of home," she feared that he "might be under even worse influences." In order to alleviate her misgivings, Ben took a temperance pledge, and Alice supplicated him to consider this vow "sacred" as one made "between you & your Maker." While reading the *Parke County Republican* in June 1864, Sarah Dooley discovered the name of her son Rufus on the list of local soldiers who had embraced temperance. Heartened that her son possessed not only bravery on the battlefield but also "the courag to abstain from the intoxicating glass," Sarah suggested that fulfilling this promise would bring him respect and an honorable reputation. In her opinion, Rufus had avoided "the first step to ruin" by refraining from drinking alcohol. George Aplin likewise supported temperance, a decision that his mother approved even if it cost him a promotion. Elvira seemed to regard the officer's corps as little more than a drunk tank, for on several occasions she cast aspersion on "our drunken and dissolute officers." She preferred to have George remain in the ranks with his integrity intact rather than purchase a "Genls commission with liquor."[30]

Although alcoholic consumption might have been deemed the most enslaving of sins, it was by no means the only one censured. Alice Grierson repeatedly berated Ben to stop smoking cigars before he formed another vile habit. Smoking was not only a loathsome practice, Alice maintained, but it also demonstrated Ben's prodigality in light of the family's economic troubles. While Alice had been scrimping at home, Ben had spent a whole dollar on cigars for his own indulgence, and she challenged him to name an instance when she had purchased anything "for my own exclusive gratification." Mary Stork regarded card playing as the greatest peril to a soldier's moral downfall and charged Rufus Dooley to "let the cards alone for they lead to every other vice." Indeed, gambling became a serious problem for some soldiers. Ben Grierson discovered in January 1862 that some men in his regiment had squandered most of their pay playing cards. In order to halt this practice, he authorized the arrest of any soldier who gambled in camp. Amanda Chittenden went beyond card playing and condemned all types of recreational amusement. "How heartily I disapprove of *games*," she disclosed to her husband George. Although formerly she had played checkers, she had quit because, from her "inmost soul," she now considered such diversions to be "a great evil." Amanda's prohibition of games might have been extreme, but the dangers of illicit sex most assuredly merited the warnings of concerned women as camp followers and city prostitutes abounded and threatened to entice soldiers to sin. Offering spiritual encouragement to her son-in-law Claude Buchanan, Hannah Bingham passed along her prayers for God to protect him from the "traps of immorality." Alice Grierson denounced the officer's parties Ben frequented, fearing in part that women in attendance might be morally loose. Whether condemning drinking, smoking, gambling, swearing, or whoring, women at home forcefully contended that soldiers need not "follow vice as a means of pleasure." As Mary Stork reminded Rufus Dooley, "Better [to] do without pleasure than to do that which your Father & Mother would be grieved about."[31]

In addition to admonitions to abstain from the rampant wickedness of camp life, women of faith also offered spiritual encouragement to help soldiers combat these temptations and foster growth in godliness. Gentle directives to read the Bible and heed its counsels seemed the most effective way to keep spiritual matters fresh in a soldier's mind. "Read your testament & heed its counsels," Almira Dart instructed her brother George Howell. "You will find every thing there to encourage you & it will cheer you & keep up your spirits." Having few personal belongings while in the field, a Christian soldier would value his Bible highly. Elvira Aplin expected George to keep his Bible from being "spoiled with rain," for "it will be the best companion you can possibly have. Peruse its pages often and try to become familiar with its teachings." Soldiers who were well-grounded in the truths of Scripture, she believed, would be better equipped to resist temptations and increase their spiritual discernment. "A soldier is surrounded by everything that has a tendency to make him forget God," Elvira asserted, "and those who do not make His word their study and guide will loose much of their morality." Lucius Chapin expressed appreciation for the Bible that Alice sent him, and she rejoiced that he took such delight in reading it. "I am glad your Bible is a comfort to you," she penned. "You will become far more advanced in knowledge of its divine truths than your wife," she speculated on account of her many domestic responsibilities. Nevertheless, Alice asked Lucius to tell her what book of the Bible he was reading so that she could study the same passage simultaneously. In cases where soldiers were unlikely to open the pages of Holy Writ, devout women had to content themselves with referencing Scripture in their letters. Alice Grierson maintained that Ben's battlefield successes stemmed in part from his obeying Ecclesiastes 9:10, which she paraphrased as "'do with your might, what your hands find to do.'" Taking advantage of a didactic opening that could have been interpreted as a not-so-subtle slam, Alice observed, "That is one command of scripture which you obey, whether you know it or not."[32]

By their own acknowledgement, many northern women possessed a sincere faith in God and demonstrated their genuine devotion to him by caring for the spiritual welfare of soldiers. Whatever their theological differences might have been, they confirmed that personal faith motivated their admonitions to soldiers. To be sure, some women acted strictly out of a desire to exercise domestic authority and promote morality for its own sake, and historians have given considerable attention to this angle. However, the perspectives of women whose faith informed their entire outlook on life merits notice as well. Whether seeking grace to endure trials, witnessing to loved ones, or encouraging soldiers to resist temptation, these women considered spiritual matters to have paramount significance. Nevertheless, personal faith did not always guarantee that women would be enabled to cope with the absences of loved ones, overcome domestic hardships, or receive answered prayer. In early March 1863, Alice Grierson professed her belief that Ben would survive the war and "be a better man in the end" because of "all the rough teachings, hard experiences, and many temptations" that he would encounter. Although he escaped the war with his physical body untouched, he never underwent the spiritual transformation for which Alice had yearned so earnestly, yet she persisted in imploring him to be converted even in July 1865. As far as her own spiritual condition, Alice could probably still agree with the assessment she had made during the summer of 1863. Her tribulations, no doubt, had been numerous and burdensome, but she trusted the promise of Hebrews 12:11 that ultimately they would produce "'the peaceable fruits of righteousness'" in her life. At such a point, she could consider it "good" indeed "that I have been afflicted."[33]

4

"Christian Patriotism" in Flush

Political Preaching, Antiwar Dissent, and Summer Thanksgiving

Shortly after Lincoln issued the Preliminary Emancipation Proclamation in September 1862, the *Western Christian Advocate* confidently proclaimed the coming of "the Year of Jubilee." With slavery eradicated, "the American Republic will go forward fulfilling her high destiny," finally able to honor the founding principle "that 'all men are created equal.'" Furthermore, the Union could "expect the Divine assistance" since the nation finally had forsaken its chief sin. Without the support of slave labor, the Confederacy would not long endure. The combination of moral rectitude and military necessity had roused the president, "the agent in the hands of God," to obliterate "the very soul and life of the rebellion." Still, the Methodist editor knew that political malcontents would attempt to discredit the edict and convince credulous citizens that it would open the floodgates of African-American refugees to the North. In his desire to reassure conservative whites that they should fear no such sable horde, the editor revealed the limited scope of equality as defined by numerous religious, antislavery Northerners. In the first place, the proclamation encouraged voluntary colonization, which would discourage the preponderance of "wandering vagabonds." In addition, blacks preferred warmer climates, so most would choose to enjoy their liberty in the South. Finally, this extension of freedom's boundaries would prompt northern blacks to flock to the sunny South. Having assuaged any concerns over race amalgamation, the writer matter-of-factly confirmed that the provision made no pretense to securing political equality for blacks. Wholly satisfied that this deathblow to slavery constituted the nation's lone duty to African-Americans and placed the country in proper relation to God, the editor anticipated that God would bring the war to a swift end and "help us in restoring the Government to more than its former glory."[1]

Many religious civilians agreed that the Preliminary Emancipation Proclamation signaled a new direction in the war, for now slavery had to be destroyed for the North to claim victory. Churchgoers who had asserted all along that God was withholding his blessings from the Union army until the slaves went free rejoiced. Some individuals found the news almost too incredible to be true. Twenty-two-year-old Sophia Southworth thought that Lincoln must have undergone some mysterious transformation that caused him to reverse his policy capriciously and issue "the most manly" decree of his presidency. She initially feared that the document might be misconstrued to limit its effectiveness but accepted at face value that the nation's "last curse" finally had been removed since the government had determined to obey God's command to "let my people go." Closely following the war's development from Minnesota's remote northwestern corner, Milton Buswell claimed that Lincoln would lose all credibility if he rescinded this pledge. With the "bleeding cancer" of slavery removed from its shores, America could "proclaim *liberty* without hypocrisy" for the first time in its history, a landmark that angels would hail with songs of "Glory-Hallelujah" while freedmen joined in the chorus. These two commentators seemed unconcerned about or unaware of the limited reach of the proclamation, but even an editor of a religious weekly who recognized the document's practical impotence without first making Southerners a "conquered" people did not regard this as a shortcoming. In his opinion, the theoretical value of having a presidential declaration to destroy slavery and the moral significance of a condemnation of "human bondage as a principle of the American Government" more than compensated for any actual weaknesses of the proclamation.[2]

Many denominational bodies likewise echoed their approval of the president's measure and in the process reaffirmed their commitment to prosecute to the bitter end what they perceived to be a God-ordained conflict. At their annual meeting, Indiana Methodists interpreted the Preliminary Emancipation Proclamation as evidence of God's sovereignty and confirmation of "the justness of our cause." In fact, the language of some resolutions sounded as if God himself and not Lincoln was carrying out the order. In early October, Reformed Presbyterians in Illinois affirmed that "the most high God, Ruler of Heaven and Earth,... has arisen to set the oppressed in safety." The assembly charged its members, "as Christians and patriots," to assist in the work of quelling the rebellion for the purpose of eradicating slavery. The Old School Presbytery of Logansport, Indiana, viewed the document as proof that God was using the war to judge the nation for countenancing the sin of slavery before he brought about its final destruction. U.S. Senator James Doolittle, a member of the Wisconsin State Baptist Association, informed his spiritual brethren that Lincoln's manifesto had paved the way for God to begin blessing the Union army with victories.[3]

Most Democrats, war opponents, and racial conservatives challenged any notion that God had endorsed, let alone inspired, the Preliminary Emancipation Proclamation. Some individuals branded it as unconstitutional, while others seized on the document as a new opportunity to denounce abolitionism for causing the conflict. Although he personally disliked slavery, Jerome Brown of Hartford, Michigan, condemned the war as an attack on southern rights and feared that the "old constitution" had been annulled. In the process of destroying that worthy document, abolitionists had fashioned a god in their own image, one who delighted in violence and struck down his enemies, proving to Brown's satisfaction that "an abolition God... is no God at all." Critics of emancipation contended that the triumph of abolitionism had not only produced a false deity but also wrecked the government. Henry Cobb, a farmer in Mantua, Ohio, complained that "a military despotism rules us" and had wiped away all "freedom & liberty." He indirectly blamed slavery for producing an unnecessary war that "artful & scheming" politicians were manipulating for personal gain. "What a blessing to the world," he imagined wildly, "if Africa had sunk 500 years ago—or more recently, [if] Northern traitors, had grinned through a hempen cravat." An editor in Circleville, Ohio, agreed that supporters of emancipation should be hung and considered it "a pity that there is not a more tormenting hell than that kept by Beelzebub for such abolition fiends."[4]

In the autumn of 1862, uncertainty about the nation's future hovered like a dark storm cloud over the home front, and outbursts of political discord periodically dotted the landscape. In particular, the draft drew the ire of many Democrats. The responses to the draft by members of the Cobb family typified the political and racial outlook of conservative Northerners. Antoinette Cobb thought that military service would break the health of her forty-one-year-old husband Henry. She regarded the draft as the administration's reckless attempt to "kill off this generation" and abhorred any abolitionist policy that necessitated "the sacrifise of so many of our white Brothers." Her sister-in-law Ann almost despaired when contemplating the thought of losing her husband to conscription. "What shall I do if Nute is drafted[?] The Lord only [k]nows." Impervious to religious scruples when his life potentially hung in the balance, thirty-eight-year-old Newton Cobb vented his frustration against "the Damn Abolishin thieves" who had deceived Lincoln. He claimed that these radicals deserved to fight until completely annihilated, "both men & women." The Cobb brothers escaped the draft in Portage County, Ohio, but forty-nine men from their township "were dragged from their houses & families" in order to become cannon fodder, Henry later reported with disgust. Opposition to the draft likewise ran high in parts of Indiana. A mob allegedly in cahoots with a sympathetic local sheriff disrupted the proceedings in Blackford County and chased off the enrolling officer and provost marshal. Although Democrats generally condemned the draft, at least one newspaperman found a silver lining therein. After one local minister had his number picked, the editor of the *Cincinnati Enquirer* claimed that the lottery had proven an effective method for revealing God's will concerning whether or not clergymen should be exempted from conscription. He hoped that men of the cloth who formerly had clamored for war from the safety of their pulpits would be sent forward to the heat of the battle like Uriah, where either they would learn to regulate their loose tongues or have them permanently silenced by the enemy.[5]

In mid-October, citizens infuriated by the draft had the opportunity to voice their displeasure at the polls in Indiana and Ohio. Democrats took back the legislature in Indiana and won all state races by a large majority. Staunch Unionists, of course, feared that an ascendant Democracy would undermine the war effort. Calvin Fletcher branded the entire Democratic ticket in Marion County as "secession candidates" and claimed that all nominees lacked "religious & moral" character. Members of both parties, however, portrayed their opponents as religious infidels. After federal authorities arrested sixty-year-old Dr. Edson Olds without legal justification in August, the former state legislator and congressman from Ohio immediately gained fame in Democratic circles as a martyr to Republican tyranny. A devout Methodist, Olds ran for office while imprisoned and won election to the Ohio legislature. Finally released after five months of incarceration, he recounted to his supporters in Lancaster, Ohio, that his coldhearted captors had even denied his request for a Bible. Peppering his speech with biblical allusions, Olds noted that Christ had commended peacemakers in the Sermon on the Mount, yet the current administration ignored this principle and pursued war. Leveling his most condemnatory accusation in a manner that vindicated his own actions, he claimed, "Had Old Abe and Dave Tod lived in the days of our Saviour, the chief priests and Pharisees would not have been compelled... to find false witnesses against the Lord of Glory; they would have nailed him to the cross for discouraging enlistments." By characterizing his political opponents as willfully disobedient to Scripture, Olds attempted to secure the moral high ground for the Democratic party. Despite his best efforts to silence his detractors by depicting them as religious infidels, Olds remained an easy target of ridicule. Dripping sarcasm, the editor of the *Cincinnati Daily Commercial* thought it a moral outrage that the government had prohibited "a hardened sinner" like Olds from reading the Scriptures or some other religious tract, such as "[A] Call to the Unconverted" by seventeenth-century English Puritan Richard Baxter, while he languished in "the bowels of an Abolition Bastile." In an attempt to disarm his critics, Olds countered with a letter to the Democratic *Cincinnati Enquirer* that attested to his good standing over the previous two years in a Methodist assembly whose leaders differed with him over politics yet received him as a brother in the faith. Finding more fuel for the fire, the *Commercial* marveled at the aged doctor's fortitude in enduring the teachings of "a Black Republican pulpit" and "taking his religion, mixed with Abolition politics" for two whole years.[6] Although both parties claimed to embody the spirit of true religion, neither considered that using religion to further partisan political ends cheapened and trivialized genuine faith.

Of all northern Protestant denominations, the Episcopal church had earned the reputation for being immune to political controversies. When its General Convention assembled in New York in October 1862, even the secular press closely watched its proceedings for signs of political entrapment. As expected, the high church element within the denomination attempted to set the tone, but several resolutions, including one by a layman from Minnesota who sought to prohibit "the introduction and discussion of all political subjects...as inimical to Christian unity," did not carry. The Committee on the State of the Country and the Church recognized that deliberately ignoring the nation's present crisis demonstrated a ludicrous denial of reality. By meeting's end, the adoption of Charles McIlvaine's pastoral letter cut the ties of traditionalism and gave the denomination a fresh outlook on church-state relations.[7]

Handpicked by President Lincoln to serve as an unofficial diplomat to England in the fall of 1861, McIlvaine returned to Ohio after nearly eight months of successful lobbying for British neutrality. This experience strengthened his unionism and broadened his understanding of how to balance properly his duties as a citizen of both an earthly state and a heavenly kingdom. McIlvaine's Pastoral Letter indeed signified a radical shift from the customary reticence of the Episcopal church regarding civil affairs, but the views expressed therein steer clear of the excessive patriotism and sanctifying of the Union that characterized most denominational pronouncements during the Civil War. The bishop's epistle stands as a monument to careful biblical exposition, and his emotional restraint and evenhanded treatment of the Christian's sacred and secular obligations set him apart from most other religious leaders.[8]

After introductory remarks, McIlvaine examined the war within the context of the age-old mystery of how divine sovereignty and human responsibility could function simultaneously. In his opinion, God used the war to punish the nation for its sins, yet he brought this about through human agency. Scripture clearly demonstrated the validity of this reasoning. When

Charles McIlvaine (1799–1873) graduated from the College of New Jersey and studied at Princeton Seminary before taking his first pulpit at Christ Church, Georgetown, in 1820. His congregant John C. Calhoun, then secretary of war, arranged for him to become chaplain and professor at West Point, where he taught Jefferson Davis, Robert E. Lee, and other notable Civil War officers. He was appointed Episcopal bishop of Ohio in 1832 and remained in that post until his death. In addition to serving as a special deputy to England in the autumn of 1861, McIlvaine volunteered with the U.S. Christian Commission and preached to troops on the front lines during the war. *Library of Congress, LC-DIG-cwpbh-02476*

Peter preached at Pentecost, as recorded in the Acts of the Apostles, he explained that Christ had been " 'delivered' unto death 'by the determinate counsel and foreknowledge of God,'" yet the crucifixion was carried out " '*by wicked hands*' " of men. Having established that God could superintend a war begun by men, McIlvaine turned to a brief delineation of the nation's sins.

Most northern Protestant ministers would have instinctively harped on slavery, but the bishop suppressed his antislavery sympathies and focused on "that one great sin," the refusal to accept Christ as the Savior and only "sacrifice of propitiation for our sins." By envisioning the wrath of God coming upon man solely for his personal rejection of the Son rather than the manifold fruits of such unbelief, he followed the apostolic example of preaching the unadulterated gospel and letting its transformative power effect social change. America, in McIlvaine's estimation, had forgotten God's prior blessings and begun to believe that the nation had prospered through its own skill. Only humility, repentance leading to salvation, and complete reliance on God could restore the land to its former greatness.

McIlvaine knew that he opened himself up to the charge of meddling in politics with his remarks on human culpability for the war. Therefore, he grounded his argument in the Bible in order to disarm his critics in the high church party. Most loyal Northerners, he assumed, would concede that the South had violated the Constitution, and in repudiating the highest law of the land they had broken Paul's injunction in Romans 13 to obey earthly authorities as "ordained of God." According to the text, those transgressing this precept would "receive to themselves damnation." With scriptural backing, McIlvaine could assert that southern rebellion was sinful. Having arrived at this point, most Protestant clergyman typically jumped to the following conclusion: if rebellion equaled sin and the North opposed rebellion, then the Union cause must be righteous. Not only did he resist this logic, McIlvaine also stipulated that church members should not transfer their hatred for the sin of rebellion to individual Southerners, for Christ had commanded his followers to love their enemies and do good to them. McIlvaine's message rang loud and clear. Instead of sticking their heads in the sand and acting as if no danger existed, devout Episcopalians could support the nation in its hour of need without scrapping the doctrine of the spirituality of the church. However, vigilant believers would resist the temptation to become overly enamored with the city of man and constantly keep sight of the kingdom of God. By relying on God's grace for help in present difficulties, faithful pilgrims would yearn even more for their heavenly reward and the termination of earthly struggles.[9]

In the following weeks, high church leaders censured McIlvaine for his "political manifesto," an allegation that of course caught the attention of the Democratic press. The *Cincinnati Enquirer* claimed that the devil, disguised as "an angel of light," deceived the bishop into thinking that throwing ecclesiastical support behind the government's war would benefit the Episcopal church. Instead, McIlvaine had betrayed the church's spiritual calling, confused the roles of church and state, and forfeited his position of respect within the community to become "a Republican clerical politician" no different from most other northern preachers. Not surprisingly, the *Cincinnati Daily Commercial* defended the loyal bishop. McIlvaine simply had acted as any Christian patriot would have done if placed in his position. Moreover, only the *Enquirer* would find something "fearfully Satanic" in the church seeking to sustain the Union. Both newspapers doubtless drew attention to this incident to promote their partisan agendas and overlooked the God-centered focus of McIlvaine's letter, which underscored that no matter how critical the times, nothing should detract from a Christian's duty to love God supremely and "be followers of Him who, when *we* were [his] enemies, died for us."[10]

While the draft, religious controversies, and editorial polemics polarized the home front, the Army of the Potomac, still licking its wounds from Antietam, gazed listlessly into Virginia from the safety of its camp in Maryland. In early October, after personally inspecting "General McClellan's body-guard," Lincoln urged his inordinately cautious commander to take the offensive with his 135,000-man juggernaut. Like the president, many northern civilians had grown tired of the army's inertia and McClellan's excuses and impatiently waited for the campaign that might end the war before year's end. Having decided the past spring that McClellan lacked the necessary "genius" and "skill" to be an effective leader, by late October Lizzie Little had lost all confidence in the general and outright accused him of "imbecility" for wasting the opportunity to destroy Lee's forces after Antietam. Sophia Buchanan thought it "strange" that the army had remained immobile for so long and maintained that soldiers faced a higher risk of dying from exposure to winter weather than from Rebel guns. When Little Mac finally set his troops in motion on October 26, they edged forward so sluggishly that Lee maneuvered James Longstreet's corps between Richmond and the Federals while still keeping Jackson's forces in the Shenandoah Valley on McClellan's flank. His patience finally exhausted, Lincoln cashiered McClellan on November 7 and elevated Ambrose Burnside. Some civilians heartily approved of the firing. Robert Rice, a medical student at the University of Michigan, credited McClellan with superbly training the army but hoped that Burnside, in contrast to his "ineffective" predecessor, would know how to employ such a potent force in battle. Manifesting lofty expectations that shortly would prove misplaced, Rice optimistically claimed that Burnside possessed "the opportunity of becoming a second Father of his Country."[11]

Some civilians affirmed their confidence in the abilities of the new commander, but several stipulated that God alone controlled the war's outcome and the nation's destiny. After endorsing Burnside's appointment, Sophia Buchanan promptly added that her "only trust" for military success rested in God, who "is ever on the side of right & justice." While he hoped for a second incarnation of Washington, Robert Rice admitted that only the One "who builds up and pulls down thrones at His pleasure" could determine the final outcome of the war. Other civilians expressed their conviction that God was directing human history to its culmination, the millennial reign of Christ on earth. Sarah Hall of Mendon, Michigan, prayed that "the Lord [would] hasten the time" when instruments of war would be recast into agricultural implements and "Christs kingdom" would be established among men. Indianapolis resident Charlotte Conner yearned for citizens and soldiers alike to rely on God, for she believed that the Union army would never triumph unless the entire nation began "appealing to God" and "acknowledging him as King." In her opinion, the war represented the age-old conflict between good and evil that had begun when "the first secessionist" Satan rebelled against the righteous rule of God. In subsequent manifestations, tyranny had raised its monster head against the principle of personal freedom, as exemplified in the English Civil War. Conner considered this incident to be highly illustrative for the present struggle and asserted that Federal soldiers needed to imitate "stout old Cromwell smiting his enemies in the name of the Lord of Hosts" in order to gain the divine favor that secured victory. Until this transformation occurred and the nation's leaders invoked God, she would ruminate on the biblical truth that "God chose the weak things of this world to confound the mighty and the foolish things of this world to confound" the wise.[12]

Whether or not Conner had the president specifically in mind cannot be known, but it is undeniable that Lincoln knew his Bible and could quote it just as readily. Nevertheless, he sometimes refrained from appealing directly to Scripture even when an opening presented itself. Shortly after a group of ministers complained about the irreligious atmosphere in many army camps, Lincoln issued an order in mid-November urging members of the military to make every attempt to observe the Sabbath properly. Instead of invoking the fourth commandment of the Decalogue to justify this measure, he cited a precedent established by Washington during the American Revolution as sufficient explanation for the proclamation. However, it does not follow that the president was being disingenuous and merely gave the directive for the sole reason of catering to the interests of a host of religious citizens. In fact, the document contained a serious warning, for Lincoln suggested that God might withhold his blessings if the army and navy desecrated his day of rest. In all likelihood, the decree to honor the Sabbath espoused a view that Lincoln personally endorsed, yet it also furthered his goal of preserving the Union by strengthening support for the military among religious civilians who abhorred the worldly environment that their loved ones sometimes endured. Yet as war progressed, Lincoln's announcements relating to spiritual matters, which initially were grounded in the rationale of civil religion, would manifest astonishing theological depth.[13]

The enactment of one religious edict, though appreciated, probably satisfied few churchgoers, for in their minds the Sabbath proclamation fell far short of making amends for the nation's numerous sins and prolonged disregard of God's laws. In a sermon entitled *Humiliation and Hope* presented to members of the New School Presbyterian Synod of Michigan, George Duffield emphasized the need for national repentance for such long-standing sins as Sunday mails, intemperance, and slavery. According to the text Psalm 79:8–9, God's gracious act in forgiving his genuinely penitent children brought glory to his name by manifesting to the heathen his abundant mercy on his chosen people. The context of the passage clearly refers to Israel, yet Duffield applied it to America and claimed that "God's honor and glory seem to be deeply and intimately involved in the preservation of this land, and of the union of its several States." Confident of America's future role in promoting religious liberty and world missions, Duffield explained how the eradication of slavery might be providentially intended to promote the exaltation of God's name throughout the world. Although some men might question the wisdom and feasibility of the Emancipation Proclamation and fret over its long-term consequences, they needed to accept it as coming from "the hand of Providence" via the instrumentality of man. Instead of wildly speculating about doomsday scenarios such as the decline of southern agriculture or the seeming abomination of black suffrage, Northerners should trust the sovereignty of God in destroying slavery and accept that he intended it to be "a real and lasting blessing." By challenging his denominational constituents to ponder such difficult issues as social and political equality and to view them in relation to God's inscrutable acts, Duffield looked beyond the war to a radically altered postwar world that God was effecting for his own glory. The Presbyterian cleric grounded his optimism in God's desire to shed his grace abroad and receive praise for his wonderful works and underscored that the North needed to "lay hold upon the arm of God, and link the interests of our country with His throne" in order to secure a prosperous future.[14] Of the scores of published sermons on the war, Duffield's discourse on this occasion merits attention for his painstaking care in exegeting the text. Few conservative biblical commentators would find fault with a hope founded on God's delight in showing mercy to his repentant children in order to glorify his name. Furthermore, Duffield showed remarkable restraint by forgoing any impulse to make a direct application to Southerners in his explication of this lamentation psalm in which the writer implored the Lord to punish Israel's oppressors and enemies.[15]

The hope that Duffield sought to inspire in his listeners in mid-November appeared as a theme of some Thanksgiving Day addresses two weeks later. In particular, Duffield's Presbyterian colleague Faunt Le Roy Senour of Rockford, Illinois, asserted that hope abounded because several "indications of reason and Providence" demonstrated that the rebellion would fail. Senour selected as his text the prophecy from Isaiah 21:11–12, which he characterized as "abrupt, concise, obscure...[yet] sublime." The passage describes an Edomite, a descendent of Esau, calling out to a Hebrew watchman, "What of the night?" and receiving the answer, "The morning cometh." Senour interpreted this exchange as signifying how Israel's own flesh and blood, now its "bitter enemy," gloated over the desolation of the land. Drawing the parallel to the present, Senour preached that the North's own countrymen had caused the night of "death, ruin and devastation" to settle over the once thriving land. But just as the watchman asserted that the morning would bring an end to suffering and inaugurate the rebuilding of Jerusalem and its temple, so too would the Union shortly be restored to its former greatness. While Duffield envisioned a chastened and spiritually revived America promoting the glory of God, Senour pictured God working to exalt the illustrious name of the Union. "In the history of this rebellion," he concluded the message with a flourish, "we see the hand of God, repairing, strengthening, adorning, and covering with glory, our grand old Temple of Liberty." Although he may have tickled his listener's ears with soothing words taken from Scripture, Senour played fast and loose with the text in an attempt to instill hope. Most problematic, he ignored four crucial words that completely altered the meaning of the verse. After replying that "the morning cometh," the watchman added "and also the night." Israel's deliverance, according to the prophet, would be transitory, a brief period of renewal followed by the return of affliction.[16]

Senour's sermon demonstrates the extreme lengths to which some northern ministers went to make little-known Old Testament passages relate to the Civil War. In addition to butchering the gist of the text, Senour misled his congregation by suggesting that God valued national prosperity over spiritual vitality. In fact, ensuing events shortly would prove that Senour might have looked much more prescient had he included the phrase about approaching night. On December 13, Ambrose Burnside met Robert E. Lee at Fredericksburg and sent wave after wave of his brave troops to their deaths. Attempting to dislodge the entrenched Rebels with an overpowering frontal assault, the Army of the Potomac instead suffered a lopsided defeat, taking 12,600 casualties in the process. News of the devastating loss deflated the optimism of some individuals. Permelia Gordon reported to her husband Samuel that many residents of Hamilton, Illinois, were glum "because the rebels beat us in nearley every battle." After the account of the setback reached her in Minnesota, Serena Wright complained, "Our war news dont amount to shucks, only in the slaughter of precious lives....Oh Burnside." A widowed minister's wife in Yellow Springs, Ohio, accused the ill-fated commander of recklessly sending his troops "into a Butcher shop." Despite severe disappointment, some civilians focused on God's sovereign rule over the affairs of men in order to maintain perspective. Calvin Fletcher admitted that the unfathomable carnage made him too sorrowful to contemplate the details of the battle, so he turned his attention to prayer and immediately felt burdened over the nation's political corruption and aversion to emancipation. Trusting that "a just & wise God" could not err, Fletcher reaffirmed his belief that deliverance would come only from God rather than the army.[17]

January 1, 1863, inaugurated a new era for those who insisted that God was using the war to bring about the destruction of slavery. The much-anticipated final draft of the Emancipation Proclamation even contained a new closing addendum that appealed to "the gracious favor of Almighty God" in validating the declaration that slaves living in the rebelling states were now free. John L. Ketcham applauded the order, for it indicated that "this blessed land will yet be the light of the world." On a more practical level, the new policy would demoralize the South by taking away laborers who formed the backbone of the southern economy and employing many freedmen as auxiliaries to Federal forces. Calvin Fletcher erroneously assumed that this last provision would furnish blacks an immediate opportunity to become soldiers and fight side by side with whites. He expected God to "raise up a Moses" from among the sable ranks whom even whites would admire. Completely rejuvenated in spirit, Serena Wright dared Jefferson Davis to devise some counter proposal and challenged England and France to come to the South's rescue. "Abraham Lincoln with God on his side is mightier than they all," she crowed. George Tuthill rated New Year's Day 1863 as one of the most pivotal days in world history but doubted that all Northerners grasped the significance of the moment or the "greatness of the deed." To be sure, some individuals feigned indifference, yet an honest evaluation of the situation betrayed their genuine concern. "If it were not for the serious consequences that may result from it, one might suppose it one of the jokes of the buffoon at the White House," a resident of Corydon, Indiana, quipped sardonically. "None here seem to notice it in any way," he added unconvincingly. In contrast to those who denied the magnitude of the proclamation and acted as if they could wish it into oblivion, other racial conservatives such as Ethan Brown ardently deplored the altered war policy embodied in the document. Brown grudgingly admitted that support for the edict had been growing in southwestern Michigan, yet most of his acquaintances in Berrien County agreed that "we have fought long enough and killed white men enough for the d—d niggers."[18]

The battle lines drawn by the Emancipation Proclamation were unmistakably clear. Christian abolitionists often professed that either the Union would survive the war and dismantle slavery, or treason and tyranny would triumph over "the last best, hope of earth." As Lincoln poignantly had declared a month earlier in his annual message to Congress, by "*giving* freedom to the *slave*, we *assure* freedom to the *free*." Defined in these stark terms, the war embodied a conflict between good and evil, light and darkness. According to Sophia Buchanan, the inability of individuals to discern this moral truth could be attributed only to the diabolical work of the Archfiend. She imagined "Satan himself...loose in our very midst," deceiving the credulous multitude into accepting the pernicious doctrine that slavery should be tolerated. Accusing the South of "fighting to maintain slavery forever" and likely intending to spread it across the continent and reopen the "abominable" slave trade, she affirmed with certainty that the Union possessed the moral high ground and waged a just war against "this accursed sin slavery." Her father Abel Bingham concurred with this assessment and added that "the holy scriptures" confirmed the righteousness of the cause. The present difficulty, then, centered on why victory proved so elusive. His thorough explanation epitomized the theological understanding of the war that had become ascendant among religious Northerners.[19]

In a long discourse to his son Judson, chaplain with the 20th Massachusetts, Bingham began by stressing that he had entreated God to impart divine understanding and remove all "selfish & false views" from his mind. Making no pretense to prophetic capabilities, the aged Baptist minister nonetheless wrote as one having spiritual authority. Bingham constructed his argument on the presuppositional truth that "Jehovah [existed] as the Sovereign Ruler of the Universe." As potentate of heaven and earth, God superintended "the rise & fall of nations." Therefore, a country flourished when God bestowed his bounty upon it. Similarly, a country suffered tribulation when God punished its sin in order to prepare it for a glorious future mission. This concept rested on the principle found in Proverbs 15:33 that humility preceded honor. Since the North had not provoked war but merely opposed the spread of slavery into free territories and defended federal property, the evidence clearly demonstrated to Bingham's satisfaction that the Union "cannot be on the wrong side." The only explanation for the lengthiness of the conflict pointed to manifold "national & individual sins" that needed to be confessed and forsaken. Once sufficiently humbled "in His school of discipline," the government could expect to accomplish that noble work for which God was preparing it, specifically to be "His honored agent to give the last & finishing stroke to the gigantic institution of slavery." Bingham's confidence that he had comprehended the meaning of the war exemplifies how many northern Christians sanctified the American government and made it God's emissary among the nations. By assuming that man could decipher God's macrocosmic intentions with relative ease, Bingham furthered the simplistic view of providence that demystified God.[20]

The views espoused privately by Bingham oftentimes made their way into pulpits across the North and inflamed the longstanding controversy over what constituted acceptable subject matter for a sermon. Supporters of the Union generally approved the minister who promoted the war effort or condemned slavery from the pulpit. Indeed, some congregants grew so accustomed to patriotic messages over the course of the war that they offered no objection even when core biblical doctrines acquired a political application. Christian Kohlsaat, a law student at the University of Chicago, did not bat an eye when his pastor politicized the simple gospel text of John 3:7, "'Marvel not that I said ye must be born again.'" In emphasizing that only those individuals who had experienced the new birth could enter heaven, the minister noted how absurd it would be if unconverted sinners could reside in a perfect environment. To illustrate his point, the preacher selected the southern aristocracy, the archetype of sinners for many northern pulpiteers. Claiming that "slaveholders would be kidnapping the negroes" if all men gained admittance into heaven, the preacher painted a mental picture that overshadowed the soteriological significance of his text. If, perchance, any hearers missed this political dimension of the sermon, he adjourned the service by supplicating God to "save us from the blackhearted democrats and rebel sympathisers." Twenty-year-old Nancy Mitchell of Harrison County, Ohio, summed up the outlook of many Unionist churchgoers regarding discourses that might be construed as political lectures. After hearing an exposition of Malachi 3:9, "'Ye are cursed with a curse; for ye have robbed me[,] even this whole nation,'" she observed matter-of-factly, "Let 'Rebel Sympathizers' say what they may[;] he found it in the Bible."[21]

Opponents of the war instinctively condemned such preaching as inappropriate for Sunday services. Some may have genuinely believed that the spirituality of the church was being compromised, but most merely resented having to listen to political views that they considered offensive. Peace Democrats urged their followers to withdraw from such fraudulent and polluted places of worship. Some Democrats in Brown County, Indiana, officially resolved to silence "clerical incendiaries" who promoted war by leaving their churches and terminating their financial contributions, reasoning that a lack of food and money made demagoguery less appealing. In one speech, Ohio Democrat Clement Vallandigham ranted that "the Churches had departed from the doctrines of Christ and him crucified, and taken up the nigger and him glorified!" Moreover, he claimed that abolitionists even had overrun many Sunday schools and exploited them "to upset Democracy." The embattled politician consequently admonished attentive parents to "keep your children at home" rather than expose them to an impure gospel. Some churches effectively dealt with disgruntled members in a manner agreeable to both parties and thereby prevented the entire congregation from combusting into flames of partisan fury. In February 1863, First Baptist Church of Canton, Ohio, amicably parted ways with Peter Bitzel after his "differences of opinion" with several other church members regarding the war convinced both sides that a peaceable separation would serve the interests of all. The assembly therefore suspended its normal rules governing the removal of members and granted Bitzel a letter of dismissal attesting to his status as a member in good standing. Emphasizing that the church had no desire "to take action on political questions" and that all efforts to reach a compromise and achieve reconciliation had proven futile, the congregation severed its ties with Bitzel by sending him off with its prayers for him to "have an abiding attachment to the cause of the Redeemer" and wishing for him to "find a people that he can co-operate with." From all appearances, the Canton church skillfully handled this potentially disruptive affair without drawing negative attention to the ministry. However, their example of demonstrating Christian charity to brethren who differed over matters not essential to doctrine had few parallels throughout the North.[22]

Oftentimes, both Unionist church members and their Copperhead counterparts seemed to revel in denouncing one another and furthering division. A resident of Vincennes, Indiana, reported that the town's Presbyterian church had split after a minister from Kentucky wreaked havoc in it, and the "secesh party" retained control of the sanctuary because of greater numbers. The ousted faction procured a new building and resumed assaults on their former brethren with a fervor better suited for combating the devil. According to the correspondent, the modest size of the Episcopal church there precluded any possibility of a formal separation, so members "pray together in church and abuse each other out of church." Some Republican laypersons took every opportunity to deride churches that they regarded as little more than traitorous, if not sacrilegious, assemblies. "I suppose the northern rebles have got a church," Samuel Borton of Stark County, Ohio, quipped. "They call it the South Carolina Church." In extreme cases, clergymen who failed to express support for the war to the degree that their congregation demanded sometimes became a shepherd without sheep (or, more accurately, a shepherd looking for sheep of a different political stripe). In Fremont, Ohio, the disgraced Reverend Heller had only a handful of people present to hear "his '*farewell sermon.*'" Lizzie Rice informed her husband that Heller "quit the preaching and is now acting out '*secesh*' pretty strong.... Guess he always was more of a '*slink*' than a preacher," she added with contempt. Even ministers who held positions of authority within their denominations recognized their inability to check the congregational demand for politically themed discourses. While visiting parishes under his care, George Upfold, Episcopal bishop of the Diocese of Indiana, learned that parishioners in Mishawaka were dissatisfied with their rector because of his unwillingness to attend Union meetings and blabber over politics like local ministers of other denominations. The church members, Upfold related, "think and talk of nothing else than politics," particularly extreme abolitionism. He explained to them, probably to no avail, that their rector would incur his displeasure by mixing politics into his sermons. Although Mishawaka garnered specific condemnation, all the parishes under his oversight suffered from a deleterious preoccupation with political matters. "It is my painful experience," the bishop grumbled, that "this accursed war is doing religion and the Church serious injury."[23]

Some observers agreed with Upfold's pessimistic outlook regarding the state of religion. However, Methodist minister William Graham of Crawfordsville, Indiana, differed with the bishop over the primary cause of ecclesiastical decline. He contended that "attributing the lukewarmness and inefficiency of the Church" to the war overlooked deep-rooted spiritual issues such as the tendency of many Americans, including churchgoers, to place their temporal well-being and security over the condition of their soul and preparation for eternity. In Graham's opinion, personal spiritual apathy coupled with the demise of "the holy influences of religion" in public life would engender extreme factionalism, reproduce chaotic conditions of the French Revolution, and ultimately cause "the star of American freedom [to] go down to rise no more." While most members of the laity discerned no such dire consequences, they nonetheless perceived the need for spiritual awakening. On the eve of commencing a protracted meeting in Galena, Illinois, Sarah Kohlsaat hoped for a revival of devotion, for "a death like lethargy seems to pervade the churches." After returning from Sunday services in February 1863, Cornelia Chase reached the same conclusion and implored God to "have mercy on us" and remove "the stupor that rests over the Church." Others resolved to combat with all their power the secular forces of division that endangered the unity of the church and threatened to diminish the fervor of the saints. A female resident of Carroll County, Ohio, informed relatives in Indiana that "the war and the nigger questen has nearly destroyed our churches tho I em detarmend to not let et destroy my soul."[24]

Yet while political partisanship and concerns over the war sapped the religious zeal from some assemblies, others seemed to effervesce with spiritual vitality during the early months of 1863. Some churchgoers reported a noticeable increase in religious interest, and revival campaigns oftentimes produced conversions, baptisms, and accessions to the membership rolls. At a protracted meeting in Orangeville, Indiana, several people made professions of faith while other backsliders were "reclaimed" from the world. "It was the best meeting that I have been at for years," one regular attender apprised her husband. Baptist clergyman W. G. Johnson detected a renewed desire for spiritual matters in his congregation in Illinois and anticipated "a revival of God's work among us." The secular press even took note when a religious awakening seemed to sweep over a local community and turned people's attention to their sacred responsibilities. The *Franklin Democrat*, published in Brookville, Indiana, reported the initial stirring and continued fervency of revivals in the Methodist and Presbyterian churches there. Several residents had been converted already, and "many more are seriously enquiring the way to be saved." Although some people might have been caught up in the emotion of the moment and made an insincere decision, others demonstrated the depth of their new convictions by altering their lifestyle to conform to ecclesiastical mores. Eliza Harrell of Leesville, Indiana, testified that she had gone to meeting as "a poor Sinner" and "Seeker of Salvation" but left a changed person. As evidence of this, she vowed to abandon worldliness, which meant never attending another party again. Furthermore, she promptly attempted to proselytize her sister by admonishing her to conform to the same social restrictions. Several churches could praise God for showering them with blessings during a dry season of war, death, and political dissension, but few enjoyed a harvest of souls comparable to that of Bethel African Methodist Episcopal in Indianapolis. With contrabands streaming into the capital, Pastor Willis Revels found himself laboring in a larger field. After protracted meetings in which thirty persons claimed salvation, the church returned to its normal service schedule. However, "a revival broke out" suddenly one Sunday, and daily weeknight meetings resumed. An additional forty-two individuals declared faith, and several more "anxious souls" continued to seek "the way of life."[25]

Northern churches often raised money to assist freedmen, but much of it ultimately went to support evangelistic efforts in the South rather than help blacks settle in the North. In most instances, individual church members had to take personal initiative to aid contrabands in their vicinity. Calvin Fletcher provided lodging on his property or helped black refugees find shelter with other families, hired some as workers on his farm, and donated money for their support. This conscientious steward viewed his wealth as a gift from God and consistently engaged in acts of charity in order to demonstrate his desire to be "a servent & follower of Christ." For example, he made available a cabin for an escaped slave from Arkansas and referred to the aged freedman as a "friend" most likely "sent of God." Because of his personal friendship with Willis Revels, he even attended a baptismal service on the heels of the A.M.E. revival. After his son Keys, a soldier with the 133rd Indiana, compared the frolicking he observed at a contraband camp near Nashville to "looking at a big cage full of Monkeys" and complained about the "*cussed niggers*" who rode horses while suffering soldiers walked, the offended father determined to address the matter of racial tolerance in a future letter. Despite this goodwill toward blacks, Fletcher did not refrain from reprimanding those who deserved it. He criticized blacks who "behaved very badly" at the baptism and dismissed a hired hand and a female domestic who engaged in illicit sex.[26]

Fletcher's benevolence to contrabands living nearby set him apart from most churchgoers in racially conservative Indiana. Many white laypersons had no desire to see blacks enter their churches or communities. Ann Cotton, who attended the churches of several denominations while her husband served as a surgeon in the army, heard that slaveholders had been sending their slaves farther south in order to prevent them from being liberated by advancing Union forces. This suited her fine, for she wanted them "kept away from our free states" so that she did not have to look upon "their black ugly faces." In fact, she thought the war had dragged on long enough that the time had arrived "to take the Negroes & let them die & be killed off instead of our best men." Rubbing shoulders with blacks caused some individuals to alter their formerly sympathetic feelings. Having previously contemplated going south to educate contrabands, Ella Johnston of Ashtabula, Ohio, declined to teach in the local Union schools because they "savor too strongly of Africa." As a student at Oberlin College, she had grown tired of the preferential treatment that had "spoiled" blacks there, and she now found them all "particularly disagreeable." When a black student from Oberlin transferred to Antioch College, an institution in Yellow Springs, Ohio, begun by religious free-thinkers, some white students "kicked up a fuss" and about a dozen withdrew from school in protest. However, the faculty supported the black student, and one professor threatened to leave if Antioch failed to integrate. "I think it is too bad the 'niggers' can't stay where they belong," Mary Ladley groused. Learning that blacks had been admitted to some northern colleges would have baffled many whites who continued to accept the fiction of African-American intellectual incapacity. After her son's experiences with contrabands in the South confirmed her own prejudices, Ohioan Eliza Rice conceded that blacks, despite being "another people and perhaps by natture inferior," nonetheless were members of the human race and therefore possessed a right to liberty. This concession notwithstanding, conservative laypersons agreed, whether asserted explicitly or tacitly implied, that black freedom should not extend north of the Ohio River.[27]

While some religious Northerners directed their enmity toward blacks, others reserved their indignation for Copperheads. Describing life in Iowa for her Quaker relatives in Indiana, Sarah Shively reported that several neighbors feared the freedmen would "flock...like wild geese" to their agrarian paradise. For her part, she believed that God willed their freedom, and if they did migrate to Iowa, their presence "would be as agreable as some of the democrats." In some families, political loyalties trumped biological ties, and heated debates over the war erupted. Sarah Dooley informed her son Rufus that his Copperhead uncle had written her a letter blaming abolitionists for the war. The feisty Unionist responded with a message intended to "stir up his [w]rath," for she would not suffer such "abuse" without returning "a sharp rebuke." Copperheads always fell under suspicion whenever calamities befell Unionists, regardless of whether the damage might have resulted from an unforeseen accident as easily as a criminal act. "A Methodist church burnt last week and old Solomon Lusk had 4 hay stacks burnt," Sarah Dooley relayed the local news on another occasion, "and it is generly believed that the Butternuts done it." Many Republicans erroneously characterized all Democrats as Copperheads, and War Democrats especially bristled when family members questioned their loyalty. A self-professed "Union Democrat" in Holmes County, Ohio, unequivocally expressed his zeal for prosecuting the war to the bitter end, for he despised the "villainous, traitorous, so-called Democrats who have sold themselves to the demon of Secession as well as to Beelzebub." Despite his solid Unionism, his father had accused him of Copperhead sympathies, and he hoped that his brother would read their correspondence in order to clear his name from the taint of disloyalty. Public denunciations of Copperheads grew more frequent as the fighting dragged on, and one minister in Michigan even used the occasion of a soldier's funeral to castigate citizens opposed to the war. Henrietta Wheeler informed her son William, a soldier with the 26th Michigan, that Reverend Hamp, feeling compelled to "preach the truth," "laid it down pretty strong on the Southern sympathizers," which provoked some to leave the service. After an impassioned political rally in Cincinnati attended by over four thousand Unionists, Presbyterian pastor M. L. P. Thompson exulted that "not a copperhead hissed." He thought it prudent for them to lay low if they valued their safety because "the wrath of loyal people is pretty nearly up to the exploding point," and "a general smashing of them" might commence straightway. In his opinion, the "scary rascals" would no longer "hatch treason" in broad daylight as had been their custom.[28]

In fact, rumors of seditious Copperhead activity already had struck terror into the hearts of some civilians. The Knights of the Golden Circle, a secret society of alleged insurgents, had become the bugaboo of the Republican imagination. In early 1863, Indiana Governor Oliver P. Morton helped spread the rumor of a KGC plot to topple his administration and ultimately create a northwest confederacy. The governor hoped to use the threat of Democratic insurrection to rally his party after its poor showing in the fall election, a goal he accomplished, but in the process numerous Hoosiers feared the worst. A woman in northern Indiana expected that her soldier-husband would have to come home to fight the menacing traitors, who according to hearsay boasted 90,000 "armed" members in the state. Although this number was greatly exaggerated, the KGC indeed existed. An abundance of documentary evidence confirms that political dissidents organized themselves into small bands for the purpose of disrupting the home front and undermining the rule of law. When a federal marshal apprehended ten men in southern Illinois in 1862, one person confessed outright to having joined the KGC. A preacher among the group arrested, taken in a fit of rage uncharacteristic of a man of the cloth, reportedly declared that he would select "the Demons of Hell" for his companions before stooping to consort with "the abolition and Lincoln party." From the perspective of a correspondent to Greencastle, Indiana's *Putnam Republican Banner*, the minister and his ilk soon would fraternize with the devil's minions. Referencing the story of Joseph's sale into Egypt by his jealous brothers, the writer applied the truth of God's sovereign control over history to the war, slavery, and the activities of disloyal citizens. Just as God brought good out of the evil actions of Joseph's brothers, ultimately using that nefarious scheme to preserve Israel during famine, so the treasonous plotting of leading antiwar Democrats such as Clement Vallandigham would be brought to naught. Despite their best efforts to employ the KGC to bring Ohio, Indiana, and Illinois into the Confederacy, their "Northern conspiracy" would produce "the total destruction" of Copperheads, slavery, and rebellion. "The Lord has rolled a great National evil back upon itself," the man asserted, "and it is all tending hell-ward together." Rather than merely speculate about the aims of Democratic dissidents, James Weiler actually infiltrated a secret meeting in Allen County, Indiana, in the spring of 1863. He discovered about forty Copperheads congregating at a schoolhouse that he had helped build and decided to investigate. At first, he feared that the blackguards might kill him, but their leader, a minister, intervened and allowed him to stay. After hearing speeches supporting Jefferson Davis, treason, and draft resistance, Weiler concluded that all secret assemblies opposing the government's prosecution of the war originated "in H—l" and had as their leader "Beelzebub the chief of Devils."[29]

In contrast to this rare account of a clandestine rendezvous, most official Democratic meetings occurred in broad daylight, were publicized in party newspapers, and generally remained free of illegal or traitorous activity, though Republican organs sometimes claimed otherwise. A typical gathering, like one held in Johnson County, Indiana, in March 1863, professed loyalty to the Union and condemned secession. At the same time, the opposition party decried the federal government's increased authority and unwanted interference into the daily lives of its citizens. Condemning the usurpation of state sovereignty, emancipation, arbitrary arrests, suspension of the writ of habeas corpus, and national conscription recently passed by Congress, these anxious Hoosiers charged the president with wielding "dictatorial power." Instead of calling for violent reprisals against the perpetrators of these perceived wrongs, party leaders merely expected their supporters to voice their disapproval at the ballot box. On rare occasions, some rallies turned ugly. At a meeting in Greensburg, Indiana, in early May 1863, Senator Thomas A. Hendricks and other Democratic leaders addressed about one thousand followers at the courthouse. As the meeting disbanded, shots rang out when "Republican rowdies" provoked a Democrat. A witness of this assault, described as a "peaceable, quiet" Presbyterian church member, drew his pistol in an attempt to restore order but instead received a nonfatal bullet to the abdomen. Unionist home guards, drilling nearby, had to be brought in to arrest the upheaval.[30]

Although the political views espoused at Democratic rallies could not have differed more markedly from those heard at Union functions, speakers for both groups often appropriated religious terminology to justify their partisan convictions. At a Democratic meeting in Jackson County, Indiana, in March 1863, Cyrus Dunham, former congressman and colonel of the 50th Indiana, invoked religion to support his racist views. The colonel assumed that God had created blacks inferior to whites and claimed that no amount of abolitionists "between heaven and hell" could alter this divine blueprint and elevate blacks to full equality with whites. General Henry B. Carrington, bane of Copperheads and military commander of the District of Indiana, adopted the same tactic in a letter written for public reading at a Union meeting in Indiana. In it, the general asserted that "this most righteous war" waged for the principle of "universal freedom" would triumph, that "the Providence of God" intended the liberation of all slaves, and that humanity should therefore "bless the Providence" and not obstruct moral progress. Whatever their viewpoint, by sprinkling their speeches with references to God, many orators appealed to the religious sensibilities of their audience in an attempt to gain political capital.[31]

Some ministers came to sound more like stump speakers than expositors of Scripture as they cursorily mentioned a verse or biblical incident before embarking on a long political discourse. Commemorating the second anniversary of the attack on Fort Sumter during a Sunday evening service at Plymouth Church in St. Paul, Minnesota, Silas Hawley extracted a phrase from Psalm 83:4 that enabled him to berate the Confederacy. In the text, the psalmist describes how Israel's enemies conspired to "cut them off from being a nation." Some of these antagonists had descended from Abraham and therefore were rebelling against their own homeland. The wording chosen by the translators of the Authorized Version must have jumped off the page when Hawley's eyes came upon the key phrase of the next verse, "They are confederate against thee." According to the Congregationalist minister, ancient Israel exemplified progress while the surrounding nations exuded barbarity. Similarly, the southern regime rationalized its tyrannical reign over blacks and poor whites according to antiquated principles that also fueled their ambition to subjugate the North. Alleging that the overarching design behind secession and the firing on Fort Sumter was southern determination to establish a North American monarchy, Hawley claimed that the war pitted proponents of republican government against champions of aristocracy, the American ideal of self-government versus European-style despotism. Functioning more as a civic guardian than a spiritual shepherd, Hawley closed by urging his congregation to lay aside party differences and join forces to form patriotic leagues in an effort to preserve the nation. In this discourse, Hawley cited Holy Writ as mere formality, for he drew no spiritual application. He likely selected the passage for the sole reason that it referred to a belligerent confederacy, and his choice of Scripture ultimately undermined the entire argument. Denouncing monarchy, he put himself in the tenuous position of endorsing ancient Israel and having to recast it as a "Jewish Commonwealth" fighting rebellious states. In reality, after Israel spurned its theocratic origins and adopted the monarchical model of its neighbors, it eventually fell into idolatry during the reigns of wicked kings. Although the specific alliance mentioned in the passage may not have annihilated Israel, foreign invaders ultimately conquered both portions of the divided kingdom and exiled its inhabitants. Far from confirming Hawley's assertion that "the nation is to be saved," the passage should have served as a warning that even people chosen by God, as many Northerners presumed they were, sometimes received severe punishment.[32]

Civilians hungering for more spiritual nourishment than the crumbs offered by Hawley and his ilk could find heartier fare from an unusual source. In response to a Senate resolution, the president issued a fast day proclamation on March 30, 1863, that contained more theological profundity than most patriotic sermons. Alluding to Psalm 33:12, Lincoln affirmed his belief in the scriptural precept that only nations that acknowledged God as Lord received his blessings. In light of this "sublime truth" confirmed by history, the country needed to repent of its sins, specifically pride that led to complete disregard of the God who had elevated the United States to prominence. Selecting words pregnant with soteriological meaning that likely derived from his Calvinist upbringing, the president admonished his countrymen, "We have become too self-sufficient to feel the necessity of redeeming and preserving grace." To most Protestants, this terminology would have connoted the salvific work of the Savior, a surprising allusion for a man who rarely spoke of Christ. Lincoln, of course, had no intention of expounding on theology or endorsing a particular brand of Christianity. Nevertheless, his straightforward call for personal spiritual examination contained more to ponder and apply than most addresses delivered from northern pulpits.[33]

Some Northerners took to heart the exhortation to seek divine forgiveness that only individual and national repentance would bring. Elvira Aplin anticipated that "the prayers of the righteous" would have greater efficacy in opening the floodgates of God's mercy and drawing the war to a successful conclusion than the futile strategies of the "drunken and dissolute officers in the Army." Ann Conkling, in contrast, did not share Aplin's faith in the penitence of the people. She concluded that too many citizens lacked the humility necessary to mark the occasion "in a proper spirit." Furthermore, she speculated that northern clergy would abuse the fast by discussing war topics such as slavery, proclaiming "the righteousness of our cause," or enumerating the transgressions of Southerners. Conkling desired for sincere confession of sins that would placate God's wrath, thereby making it possible for him to transform the suffering of war into blessing. She agreed with Lincoln's assessment that Americans had "vainly imagined" that their "superior wisdom and virtue" had produced national greatness and reflected on Daniel's warning to the haughty Babylonian king Nebuchadnezzar. "'Thy kingdom shall be made sure unto thee *after that thou hast learned that the heavens do rule.*'" Somewhat surprisingly, the Democratic sheet *Indianapolis Daily State Sentinel* likewise drew attention to the president's assertion that the nation had "forgotten God." With such being the case, no minister should presume "to teach God" by designating specific sins such as slavery as the source of national woe. Genuine humility would manifest itself in acknowledging the limits of human understanding and relying on the infinite reservoir of God's wisdom for direction in terminating the war. While some opposition papers might have questioned the president's sincerity or blasted him for engaging in rhetorical casuistry, this editor accepted the proclamation at face value, limited himself to a mild reproof of political preachers, and expressed an unfeigned desire for heartfelt repentance that, through God's enabling, would lead to national restoration.[34]

Instead of fulfilling the *Sentinel*'s wishes, few ministers, surviving reports indicate, steered clear of subjects that could be construed as political. At least one preacher who conscientiously attempted to avoid controversy left a listener slightly peeved. Richard Brown of Monticello, Indiana, informed a chaplain friend that his pastor had denounced "national sins" and underscored the need for repentance with a "manly" address. Despite its suitableness overall, the message, according to Brown, suffered from "one very serious fault," namely, the speaker's repeated insistence that no one should interpret his discourse as "an antislavery sermon." Many other clerics, in contrast, flaunted their abolitionist credentials with gusto. In Cincinnati, Swedenborgian Chauncey Giles asserted that the nation's primary sin was its failure to view all men as "created in the likeness and image of God." Since America's "special work" entailed spreading freedom around the globe, slavery had to be extirpated because it prevented blacks from exercising their God-given right to live freely by keeping them in a state of perpetual childhood. Old School Presbyterian Edward Barr of Frankfort, Indiana, charged the North with "complicity" in the southern sin of slavery, specifically widespread aversion toward blacks. Demanding equality of treatment and recognition of the humanity of African-Americans, Barr distanced himself from many within his denomination with his progressive racial views. Indiana Methodist H. B. Collins argued that America was a Christian nation established by God and governed by scriptural principles. Nevertheless, sin had secured a foothold from the outset when the Founders reluctantly incorporated slavery into the Constitution. The spirit of "practical atheism" had grown under the influence of the southern "Goliath" John C. Calhoun, and the violation of the Missouri Compromise demonstrated its ascendancy. Collins cited Isaiah 58:1, "Lift up thy voice like a trumpet, and show my people their transgression" to justify his decision to condemn slavery. Indeed, anyone who accused him of political preaching had fallen under the influence of the slave power. According to his reasoning, loving slavery meant hating God, which amounted to outright atheism. Repentance was imperative, for God never would preserve a nation that sanctioned slavery or practiced atheism.[35]

Measuring the public reception of the fast is difficult to gauge. Charles McIlvaine detected more "earnestness & prayerfulness" exhibited on the last Thursday of April than on any previous day since the war had commenced. To be sure, some individuals truly sought to consecrate the day and "implore divine mercy" on the nation's behalf. Calvin Fletcher gave his hired hands a free afternoon so that they could attend services. However, the sermon from Job 23 preached at Roberts Chapel earned only a "fair" rating from the discriminating Methodist. Other citizens might have conformed outwardly to satisfy the expectations of family or peers. Sixteen-year-old Alice Ladley, daughter of a Disciples of Christ minister, seemed less than enthusiastic about the fast but nonetheless expected that she would be compelled to comply with its observance. While some larger churches in urban areas may have packed their pews, others opened their doors with little response. Samuel Hibbard, a circuit-riding Methodist in southeastern Michigan, noted that "very few" heard the "spirited" discourse on national affairs delivered in his hearing. The lack of listeners for that particular topic might not have been too regrettable, for he believed that a message emphasizing the importance of individual examination and making personal application had more value than a political homily. Indeed, the political themes of numerous sermons in Chicago prompted a scornful review from the *Chicago Times*. The writer found it odd that so many preachers shared similar political views while disagreeing markedly on theology. Surely God did not "instruct them alike in secular affairs" but leave the more significant matters of faith and eternity to their varied preferences. If they truly deserved the title "Divine ambassadors," how could some clergymen advocate election and others free will, some affirm the triune nature of the Godhead and others endorse Unitarianism, or some maintain the existence of hell and others teach universal salvation? Wondering if any one denomination held the "orthodox" position in both politics and religion, the author narrowed the field to Congregationalists and Methodists since these groups had been represented by William W. Patton and John Dempster when Chicago Christians presented their emancipation memorial to Lincoln the previous September. The Democratic wag concluded that Patton, based on his "stump speech" on fast day in which he maligned the memory of Stephen Douglas, must have been chosen by Lincoln as the minister who "possessed the Divine afflatus." The fulminations of this sarcastic newsman after the presidential fast captured the frustrations of all Northerners who believed that the churches had abandoned their spiritual function in order to become the handmaiden of politics.[36]

While some civilians petitioned God for his mercy or vented their frustration over the mingling of politics and religion, the Army of the Potomac finally was preparing to engage the enemy. Having replaced Burnside in late January, Major General Joseph Hooker moved his troops across the Rappahannock and Rapidan rivers, flanking Lee's army, and converged at the crossroads known as Chancellorsville. On the night of April 30, Hooker congratulated himself on performing a successful offensive maneuver that had placed the now vulnerable Confederates firmly within his grasp. "God Almighty could not prevent me from winning a victory tomorrow," he reportedly boasted in a manner that undercut the spirit of humility that the fast had attempted to create. Presuming to have removed God from the equation, Hooker ignored the biblical proverb that pride goes before destruction. Over the next few days, Robert E. Lee gave him ample reason to consider the adage. The Confederate commander deduced Hooker's strategy from intelligence reports and devised a daring counteroffensive that defied military logic. Leaving a skeletal force of 12,000 men to defend his lines against potential assault by nearly 120,000 bluecoats, Lee again divided his army. Led by Stonewall Jackson, 44,000 Rebels audaciously marched across Hooker's entrenched front to an attacking position on the enemy's unprotected right flank. Union scouts detected Jackson's movement but mistakenly interpreted it as a retreat, an error that cost them the chance to destroy Lee's entire army with one quick strike. Instead, Jackson's battle-hardened veterans broke from the woods and overwhelmed Oliver O. Howard's bewildered Eleventh Corps, composed mainly of untested German immigrants. Only the darkness of night saved the Federals from suffering a greater reversal on May 2. His right flank decimated, Hooker never recovered his nerve and was even knocked unconscious for thirty minutes when a shell struck the Chancellor home. By early morning on May 6, the Army of the Potomac had retreated across the Rappahannock. Despite his brilliant victory, Lee suffered the loss of his best commander when Jackson was mortally wounded by friendly fire. With more than 23,000 combined casualties, neither side had much cause for rejoicing.[37]

The mood in the North was glum indeed. When Lincoln received news of the resounding setback and flight of the army, he exclaimed, "My God! My God! What will the country say!" Mary Cheney conveyed the sentiments of many citizens when she confessed that the "reverses on the Rappahannock sicken me." She momentarily questioned the idea of America's status as a divinely chosen nation and wondered, "Has God forsaken us, or is He only trimming the lamp that it may burn more brightly?" Attempting to save face and put a positive spin on the retreat, General Hooker applauded his men for their accomplishments on the field and sheepishly claimed that any inability to measure up to loftier expectations resulted from unanticipated developments that could not have been "prevented by human sagacity or resources." The general's lame attempt to whitewash a defeat failed to satisfy the editor of the *Cincinnati Enquirer*, who assumed that the vanquished commander wished the country "to hold Divine Providence responsible" for the army's reverse. Far from giving consolation to northern citizens, the proclamation proved to the editor that Hooker's "piety [was] equal to his skill in strategic warfare."[38]

While the Army of the Potomac continued to disappoint, soldiers in the western theater were beginning to make headway. Since late 1862, General Ulysses S. Grant had probed in vain for a weak spot in the defenses of Vicksburg, the Confederate citadel overlooking the Mississippi River. Deciding upon a bold offensive that severed his own supply lines, Grant bypassed Vicksburg and marched his army deep into Confederate territory with the goal of isolating the city and preventing additional reinforcements. His army of forty thousand moved toward the state capital of Jackson and overwhelmed General Joseph E. Johnston's outnumbered troops, who abandoned the city with only token resistance. Two days later, a successful Union stand at Champion's Hill prevented General John Pemberton's forces guarding Vicksburg from linking up with Johnston's. Forcing Pemberton to withdraw to the safety of the Rebel stronghold, Grant positioned himself to lay siege to the city on May 18. A pair of costly and ineffectual assaults over the next four days convinced the determined but patient commander to cease all frontal attacks against entrenched positions there, and he set his army to work digging trenches in preparation for the long siege that would starve the city into surrendering.[39]

As a symbol of impregnability, Vicksburg was integrally linked to the morale of both sides. Numerous northern civilians believed that the defeat of this Confederate bastion would signal the closing stages of the rebellion. Therefore, the public watched its torturously slow developments with "intense interest" and oftentimes great "suspense." In late May, a female resident of Indiana anticipated the day when "God [would] give us a victory there... that will strike a death blow to rebeldom" in the west. While reading at home on May 24, Calvin Fletcher counted one hundred salvos from a cannon near the state house and immediately assumed that it announced tidings of some notable triumph. However, he had learned to temper his initial excitement because of frequent false alarms. "We are most sure to be made victims on Sunday," he noted skeptically. "Even ministers have announced victories when we have afterwards found they were defeats." Stepping outside, he encountered a soldier who reported that Governor Morton had received a wire that Vicksburg had fallen. Entirely unconvinced, Fletcher nevertheless remained hopeful that "*God had given* us the victory," for he knew better than to place his trust in feeble men. The siege's demoralizing effect on southern civilians caused Mollie McPheeters to reflect on the brutality of war. Having heard about the awful conditions being endured by women and children, she correctly concluded that their mere presence would not incline Grant to prevent the full brunt of his iron-fisted policy from falling on all inhabitants. She considered it "a pity that innocent children should suffer," but the women, "the very worst of rebels," deserved to feel the oppressive burdens of war. The anxious housewife from southern Indiana concluded that "rebels are rebels" regardless of gender, and the faster Vicksburg fell, the sooner her husband could return home.[40]

Although two years of fratricidal war had taken a heavy toll on the northern populace, many patriotic civilians expressed their determination to persevere to the end no matter what the cost. An Iowa woman estimated that half of the citizens of Oskaloosa had worn black at some point for friends or relatives killed in "this unholy rebellion." Similar to the Apostle Paul, who loved his countrymen so much that he offered to damn himself eternally for their spiritual preservation, she expressed willingness to sacrifice her own life if it would terminate the war in an honorable manner. Knowing that such a hypothetical exchange could never occur, she pledged to do all within her power to help the soldiers and "leave the rest with God." A schoolteacher in Cambridge, Illinois, informed John Griffin, a private fighting at Vicksburg with the 17th Illinois, that she sometimes wished herself a man in order to "fill one place left vacant by some brave soldier." Upon hearing news of "the fearful loss of life" after each engagement, an all too frequent occurrence in civilian life, she often had difficulty fulfilling her domestic responsibilities. Nevertheless, each time she resolved to struggle onward and viewed the completion of each task as her personal contribution that in some small way helped maintain a semblance of normalcy on the home front. Despite long separations from loved ones and the constant anxiety that death might sever all earthly communion, religious Northerners trusted that God was directing national events for a higher purpose and would sustain his children through their trials. Alice Chapin recognized that although "*war*... may cost *us* our *dearest* objects of affection," that sacrifice was worth the price of remaining "a *law* abiding country."[41]

The home front seemed like the front line of battle to some Unionist civilians, and the longer the war dragged on, the bolder Copperheads became. After returning from Sabbath school the first Sunday in May 1863, J. H. Stoneburner of Clay County, Indiana, informed soldier James Hartley that Union-loving men at home were combating a demonically assisted foe. "It appears that the Devill is let loose in this part of the world, [for] we are sore persecuted with the copper heads." Such pesky adversaries tested his faith, but he determined, with "the assistance of God," to contend against the enemy as a courageous soldier. Indeed, Stoneburner assumed that battling these political opponents would merit him a spiritual reward, for those who overcame the evil one would "receive the crown." Asa Sutherland borrowed a phrase from Paul's second epistle to Timothy to describe conditions in Lawrence County, Illinois. "Perilous times" were experienced there when two Copperheads brazenly attacked a staunch Republican and Presbyterian church member riding to a friend's residence after dark. Fortunately, the fiends only meant to frighten the man, cutting up his saddle but letting him go unscathed. Nevertheless, Copperheads were armed to the teeth while Unionists lacked the means for self-defense since local authorities had forbidden the purchasing of weapons. One "tory" neighbor reportedly sat in his home with cocked gun ready to shoot any Republican who dared approach. The wretched state of affairs caused Sutherland to identify with Paul when he anticipated his martyrdom and attested to having discharged all his earthly duties as a devoted soldier of Christ. Despite his overarching desire to have God remove him from his difficult circumstances, Sutherland recognized that he must face his trials. Paul had likened the Christian to a soldier and an athlete, consequently he needed to fight using the full panoply of the spiritual armor and run the race of the Christian life with discipline and endurance despite living "in a land of tories." Saturating his letter with biblical allusions, Sutherland superbly demonstrated how personal faith applied to experiences on the home front. Moreover, he perceived that the war was testing the verity of certain scriptural principles. "The bible is certainly a vain book," he proffered, unless southern rebels and northern traitors received a fitting recompense for their heinous crimes. The cardinal doctrine that "sin must reap its reward" convinced many Northerners that the day of judgment for the wicked would come eventually and the cause of righteousness would triumph.[42]

A few civilians, however, found the idea of a righteous conflict utterly offensive and adamantly affirmed that nothing morally honorable ever resulted from war. Members of pacifist denominations such as Quakers and Mennonites historically opposed war on religious grounds. To be sure, some Quaker men set aside their religious scruples against fighting and served in the Union army. Others, after intense soul-searching, determined to uphold the principles of their faith no matter what the personal consequences. When a female cousin asserted that paying the $300 commutation fee allowed by the Enrollment Act was an honorable method for avoiding fighting, Cyrus Lewis summarily rejected her logic. Even this alternative would violate his pacifist principles, for he made no distinction between contributing money to support an unjust war and actively participating in it. Attempting to correct his cousin's assumption, the philosophical young Quaker from West Liberty, Ohio, concluded that adherence to conscience outweighed all pragmatic justifications when considering the propriety of a specific action. "Thee says thee sees no reason that we should not use our earthly blessings to prolong our lives that we may do more good in the world and serve God better. Now I will ask thee if a life preserved by means which thou believed to be in direct opposition to the commands of God would be likely to add to the Glory of God or the advancement of Christianity?" Briefly taking her side for the sake of argument, Lewis conceded that a man might gain forgiveness for "great and grevious sins," even that of acting contrary to the dictates of conscience. However, in committing the questionable deed, a man might sear his conscience so deeply that he no longer felt inclined to seek pardon for his iniquity. Furthermore, caving in to peer pressure during a time when all of humanity was watching events in America would betray the historic tradition of Quaker pacifism. "The society of Friends have for centuries held up to the world the doctrine and principles of universal peace and born a strong testimony against the taking of life in any manner whatever," Lewis reminded her. To compromise these tenets during the present hour would merit such severe judgment that the "Society of Friends would be blotted from the earth." Although persecution might come to those who stood for their beliefs, it probably would be minimal. He knew of two Quakers recently drafted who refused to report for duty and spent a few days in the guardhouse at Camp Dennison in Cincinnati before receiving honorable discharges as conscientious objectors.[43]

Unlike Cyrus Lewis, some pacifists had no qualms about supporting the war financially if it helped secure their exemption from fighting. Writing on behalf of deacon Jacob Nold and other Mennonites in Columbiana County, Ohio, Bishop John M. Brenneman of Allen County had drafted a petition to President Lincoln in the summer of 1862 explaining the well-established Mennonite stance against war. Professing complete loyalty to the government, he did not ask that the group be excused from all civic duty but offered to help pay the costs of war in lieu of military service. Brenneman had heard that conscripted Mennonites in Virginia had been taxed two percent of their property value instead of being forced to fight and hoped that Lincoln would be gracious enough to approve a similar settlement for Ohioans if not show them more mercy by reducing the percentage. In addition, their compassion for the needy compelled them to voluntarily assist the families of soldiers who lacked necessities of life. Lest the president think that Mennonites considered themselves superior to other religious sects, Brenneman stressed that they did not "censure, judge, or condemn other denominations, or Christian professors" but merely sought liberty in matters of conscience. Despite taking time to craft this thoughtful appeal, the bishop apparently expected it to accomplish little and in fact never sent it to Lincoln. He cautioned Nold to resist the temptation to rely too heavily upon the help of man in seeking a solution to the threat of conscription and reminded his friend that "God is certainly more to be depended on than the President." With language that shortly would prove all too prophetic, he observed that Lincoln was nothing but "a poor dying mortal like ourselves, and if we lean intirely upon him for help, I fear we would lean on a broken reed."[44]

In 1863, Brenneman published a tract entitled *Christianity and War* in which he sought to encourage his brethren to hold fast to their pacifist principles. He based his entire argument on Scripture and asserted that genuine followers of Christ would keep his commandments. The Sermon on the Mount contained the key teachings on interpersonal relations and culminated with Christ's directive to love one's enemies by doing good to them and praying for them instead of returning evil for evil. Furthermore, the Savior had come to establish a spiritual kingdom and had prepared his followers for spiritual warfare only. Since no New Testament precedent existed for Christians wielding carnal weapons, Brenneman asserted that even if the South overran the North, destroyed homes, and killed civilians, no resistance should be made. Possessions and even life itself mattered little when compared to eternal rewards that awaited the faithful. The Bible declared that those who lived by the sword would die by it, if not in the present life, then by "'the sword of Christ's mouth'" when he judged the lost and condemned them to hell. Of course, Brenneman reached the predictable conclusion that true believers could not war against their enemies or kill a man without willfully violating the essence of New Testament Christianity. It logically followed, then, that those who hated their enemies exposed themselves as "children of their father the devil." Betraying his innermost convictions that had to be concealed in his petition to Lincoln, Brenneman suggested in less than subtle terms that members of other denominations fighting in the present conflict were undeniably not Christians regardless of their personal professions of faith. This assertion demonstrated that an unbridgeable gulf separated extreme pacifists and the majority of northern churchgoers regarding a Christian's proper duty to government. Despite this glaring disparity, Brenneman emulated mainstream Protestants by claiming that the war represented divine judgment for national sins. Furthermore, by raising the possibility that slavery might have been the leading cause of the conflict and its destruction the war's ultimate purpose, he indirectly gave credence to those Christians who viewed war as a last resort and necessary evil through which positive results such as the preservation of the rule of law and eradication of the sin of slavery could be accomplished.[45]

Brenneman had been encouraged to write his treatise by his young protégé John Funk, who earlier in 1863 had composed a tract that equated war with worldliness and alleged that the devil had deceived most men into thinking that their religion pleased God when in reality it led them down the path of destruction. Funk had strayed near that path after moving to Chicago in 1857 to make his fortune in the lumber business. Converted the following year, he attended the churches of several denominations, including William Patton's First Congregational, because the city had no Mennonite assembly. A keen observer of politics and frequent commentator on the war during its early stages, Funk practically ceased to mention the war in his diary after the spring of 1862. The following autumn he traveled to Elkhart, Indiana, to receive communion at a Mennonite church and heard Brenneman preach. Inspired by the bishop's message, Funk began contemplating more seriously the basic tenets of pacifism, and his intellectual search culminated with his return to his family's religious roots. Despite regular attendance at Protestant churches for more than three years, including time spent teaching in the mission school of Chicago's Third Presbyterian Church, he condemned his former associates in his tract *Warfare*. Funk cited many of the same verses that Brenneman would employ and charged "false teachers" with deluding courageous men into enlisting and ultimately throwing away their lives. In his opinion, Christianity and war had as little in common as heaven and hell. Indeed, the ministry and life of Christ plainly exposed the prevailing clerical belief in a sacred war to be an entirely unbiblical and oxymoronic position that Mennonites would reject if they valued their eternal salvation.[46]

The extreme pacifist principles of universal peace and nonresistance had minimal chance of gaining popularity throughout the North to begin with, but bald-faced denunciations of mainstream Protestants guaranteed that few individuals would pause to consider the views expressed by Brenneman and Funk. Nevertheless, the pacifist message contained elements that could have benefited some northern churchgoers. Although the preservation of the Union might have demanded fighting a war against

John Funk and Chicago Sunday school pupils, 1862. After a brief association with Protestant churches, Funk embraced his family's faith, denounced politicized religion, and eventually became one of the leading Mennonites of his day, publishing the *Herald of Truth* beginning in 1864 and becoming a bishop in 1892. *Mennonite Church USA Archives*

Rebels, no cause existed for physical aggression to spill over into churches themselves. However, scattered episodes of violence proved that some northern assemblies and communities suffered from a dearth of brotherly love. A mob of Copperheads "armed with knives and revolvers" made good on a threat against a certain circuit rider who ventured back into rural Crawford County, Ohio, to conduct services in late May 1863. Breaking down the door of the church during the opening prayer, the ruffians scattered the congregants, shattered windows, destroyed some of the makeshift pews, and finally dismantled a few logs of the building's framework. Not content with this damage, the gang of Copperhead miscreants reportedly turned to arson, razing a German Methodist meetinghouse north of Bucyrus because of the minister's penchant for delivering political messages, an allegation he unequivocally denied. Several incidents at churches in Hancock County, Ohio, demonstrated the severe partisanship that plagued small communities there. Individuals in several congregations received beatings, and after one such assault in Jackson Township, Copperhead thugs reportedly stood on the pews and hollered, "'Hurrah for Hell and Vallandigham.'" Wary churchgoers began to take precautions against potential disruptions, which resulted in the disarming of fourteen would-be assailants in Arlington and the whipping of another band of Butternuts who had harassed a singing school in Liberty for three consecutive weeks. In some instances, the physical conflict resulted from encounters between individuals within the church rather than with outsiders. According to the local Democratic press, a female congregant at Mount Zion Church, quite eye-catching in her ten dollar dress, attended service one Sunday in mid-July "for the express purpose of 'picking butternuts,' and kicking up a row." Lingering by the church door at the conclusion of the meeting, she and a friend began to tussle with two girls sporting butternut pins. Without masking its approbation, the paper declared the Butternuts victors in the fracas and took great delight that the expensive dress "got considerably mussed."[47]

Although excited eyewitnesses or partisan editors likely embellished specific details in order to portray their opponents as contemptible scoundrels, the frequency of politically motivated confrontations at church makes it evident that relations between Unionists and Copperheads had deteriorated significantly by the middle of 1863. In all likelihood, the increasingly hostile rhetoric employed by some religious Unionists against Copperheads contributed to violent incidents. Mary Sutton, a Sunday school teacher in Montgomery County, Indiana, considered it unpleasant enough having to work with the Copperhead secretary, but she absolutely refused to allow the children of Copperheads in her class, preferring to segregate them with their own kind. "If any of them goes to come in my class I will tell them I wont teach copperheads," she threatened adamantly. According to the opposition press, Congregational pastor Edward P. Goodwin of Columbus, Ohio, indoctrinated his Sunday school pupils with the dictum that they had a "duty to help fight the Copperheads." Even the Catholic bishop of Iowa publicly denounced Copperheads in a Sunday sermon and threatened to excommunicate parishioners who had joined the KGC if they did not break off all association with the clandestine group within two weeks. In Cincinnati's *Catholic Telegraph*, which had received criticism from Catholic newspapers in New York, Philadelphia, and Boston after officially adopting an emancipationist stance in the spring of 1863, editor Edward Purcell advised a concerned member not to worry about causing "dissensions amongst Catholics and disturb[ing] the peace of the Church" by promoting an antislavery position.

He confidently affirmed that the Catholic church would survive any internal spats over slavery, so the parishioner should stand boldly for "human liberty" regardless of any protestations by an offended brother. A Catholic resident of Gibson's Station, Ohio, confirmed that political factions had developed in the local parish, for "zealous defenders" of the peculiar institution had branded both Purcell and their "patriotic pastor as 'Black Abolitionists'" for their outspoken opposition to slavery.[48]

Indeed, many Democratic editors seemed predisposed toward depicting clergymen as bloodthirsty demagogues who had lost all interest in spiritual matters. Serving a small community in central Ohio, the *Newark Advocate* published an article about a conference of New York Methodists in order to accentuate the editor's contention that most ministers sought to drub Democrats. After complaining about "the infamous Copperheads" in his neighborhood being "as thick as blackberries," one cleric admitted that "he often hoped within himself that thrashing a man well might become one of the Christian virtues." This clever remark brought laughter and applause from his fellow preachers, and the hand clapping and feet stomping that punctuated the proceedings whenever orators denounced Copperheads caused the presiding bishop to become "most disconcerted" on account of the improper deportment of delegates. When two courageous ministers voiced their opposition to a resolution condemning slavery, the enraged clerics hissed their disapproval.[49] The editor chose to relate this account because it underscored two important ideas. First, rank-and-file Democrats needed to proclaim their political beliefs unashamedly, even if it meant being ostracized by their acquaintances. In addition, the anecdote conveyed the impression that most ministers had abandoned their religious calling and left many churches spiritually bankrupt. The tendency of Democratic editors to unearth and broadcast a bevy of inflammatory statements against Copperheads made by laypersons and clergy alike strained the limits of mutual toleration within some northern churches, and before year's end several new church movements would emerge.

For most Northerners, church disputes paled in significance to the news that Robert E. Lee and his Army of Northern Virginia had embarked on their second invasion of the North beginning June 3. Hoping to provide relief to war-weary Virginians, ease the burden on the Confederate treasury by feeding his men from the bounty of Yankee farms, and possibly gain a resounding victory that would convince the Union government to sue for peace, Lee launched the campaign with high expectations. However, the aura of invincibility that had seemed to hover over him vanished like a mist as his 75,000-man army set foot on free soil. As expected, many northern civilians anxiously awaited news of the precise whereabouts of both armies. Although he confessed that the "serious & frightful" Rebel incursion worried him,

Calvin Fletcher regarded it as a potential blessing in disguise, for it would help unify the northern populace and decisively reconfirm in their minds the necessity of crushing the rebellion and preserving the Union at all costs. After learning on June 29 that Confederate forces had entered Pennsylvania, Fletcher recalled the previous Sunday's sermon from Psalm 55:22, "'Cast thy burthen upon the Lord & he shall sustain thee.'" He applied this verse to the present emergency and reaffirmed his conviction that the nation needed to trust in God alone, for "He will direct all for the best." To be sure, the opinionated banker found little reason to place confidence in man's abilities. In his estimation, the government and the army possessed nothing but "very weak instruments" for God to work through.[50]

In fact, one of those weak instruments had been set aside recently. Because of disagreements over strategy with Lincoln and General-in-Chief Henry Halleck and growing personality conflicts with the latter, General Hooker abruptly submitted his resignation in an ill-devised attempt to gain leverage to pursue his own strategy. Instead of caving in to his mercurial general, Lincoln selected the unassuming George Meade to command the Army of the Potomac. Momentarily stunned by his promotion and immediately saddled with the unenviable duty of matching wits with Lee, Meade could only conclude that his unforeseen appointment "appears to be God's will for some good purpose." A Presbyterian minister in Indiana hoped as much and supplicated God to make Meade "our *Joshua*" in order to avoid a "ruinous" setback on northern soil.[51]

Meade's premonition that a beneficent end lay in store for the North proved true, and he triumphed over Lee at Gettysburg. The retreat of this battered Confederate army, coupled with the surrender of Vicksburg on July 4, made for an Independence Day unparalleled since 1776. Great rejoicing ensued as news of the victories spread. A cable from the War Department signed by Lincoln urged that "He whose will...should ever be done, be everywhere remembered and reverenced with profoundest gratitude." According to one observer, Methodist minister William Godman of Marion, Ohio, "seemed to be inspired" with patriotism as he read this dispatch and passed along the latest details from Pennsylvania during Sunday services on July 5. In a stirring prayer, he "gave the disloyal their due portion" and made some convicted listeners squirm with unease. The heroic Union stand at Gettysburg revitalized Sophia Buchanan's conviction that God had chosen America to accomplish "a great work" among the nations. Her sister Angie Bingham expressed thankfulness that God had shown his favor by granting success to Union arms, but the sobering reality that the earth had been "deluged in precious blood" diminished her elation. The 51,000 combined casualties suffered at Gettysburg prompted Serena Wright and scores of others to offer prayers for "the poor tortured, breaking hearts" across the nation.[52]

After more than two years of war, many civilians had become all too familiar with the carnage and bloodletting that would have been unimaginable in peacetime. Some individuals recognized that war had altered their thinking and dulled their sensitivity to the suffering of others. With Vicksburg fallen, Indianapolis resident Martha White Talbert anticipated the speedy capture of the Rebel citadel guarding Charleston, South Carolina. "My heart would once have recoiled at the thought of such a result," the meditative Quaker admitted, "but there seems to be no alternative... but bloodshed and the destruction of property" in order for "this unholy rebellion" to be crushed. Of all places, the brutal devastation visited New York City in mid-July when disaffection over the draft snowballed into four days of mob rule that at first targeted leading Republicans and their party organs. By the second day, racial tensions stoked the rampage in the streets as bands composed primarily of Irish immigrants directed their hatred at unsuspecting African-Americans, killing at least eleven and razing the Colored Orphan Asylum. With the city's police force unable to halt the rioting, several regiments that fought at Gettysburg had to be brought in to restore order. In less than two weeks time, the bright rays of victory that had bathed the country in hope were eclipsed by the dark clouds of anarchy and racial intolerance that took the lives of at least 105 people. On the one hand, most northerners received the news with utter horror. Angie Bingham wondered if "the Evil One" had been given liberty to wreak havoc in America for an undisclosed period prior to the inevitable reckoning when "the judgements of Heaven must fall upon such wickedness." Calvin Fletcher, on the other hand, considered it fitting that the "sink of iniquity N. Y. City" had brought "condign retribution on its self." Convinced that the draft riots would compel the "timid administration" to prosecute northern traitors and anarchists more vigorously and thereby bring the war to a swifter conclusion, Fletcher interpreted the domestic upheaval as further evidence of God's intention to crush all Union adversaries in short order.[53]

While the streets of New York City were convulsed with civil insurrection, residents of southern Indiana and Ohio discovered to their dismay that civil war threatened to engulf their own communities. Confederate marauder John Hunt Morgan disobeyed orders from his superior Braxton Bragg, crossed the Ohio River on July 8, and entered Indiana with about two thousand horsemen. Attempting to pull off some heroics that would bring him personal glory as well as terrorize the northern populace, the Rebel cavalry leader rode forty miles north to Salem, the seat of Washington County, where his veterans saw the backs of local home guards who attempted to resist his advance. One participant confessed that "the Rebs made us skedaddle," but he nonetheless took pride that his fleet-footed steed prevented him from being overtaken. "The bullets whistled all around me but I was not scare[d]," he boasted to an army surgeon two weeks after the danger had passed. From her home in Livonia, ten miles west of Salem, Mollie McPheeters anticipated the capture of the dishonorable "thieves and murderers" who deserved to be "caught and hung" without being given the opportunity to be exchanged or paroled. But instead of continuing north and getting himself trapped in the Hoosier heartland, Morgan veered east and meandered in a northeasterly direction until he crossed into Ohio on July 13. Had he ventured north from Salem and set his sight on Indianapolis, which lay roughly eighty miles ahead, the Kentuckian would have encountered approximately 20,000 home guards whom Governor Oliver Morton had mobilized from around the state and stationed in and below the capital. Tens of thousands of additional men awaited marching orders to rush to the city's defense if necessary. About fifty miles to the west in Parke County, Sarah Dooley reported that men were "taken out of the harvest field right into battle." In reality, the local guards merely mustered for action but never left the county. Nevertheless, the excitement caused by the movements of the "wicked rech" Morgan gave Hoosiers something to remember for years to come.[54]

Reaching Ohio, Morgan's men looked the worse for wear. Since beginning their romp in Kentucky and continuing through southern Indiana, they had been in the saddle almost 400 miles, and some of their mounts showed it. If Morgan had anticipated southern sympathizers rushing to his side and showering his men with provisions, he was mistaken. The Copperhead element may have opposed the war, but they by no means supported the Rebels. As Morgan rode through Harrison, he stole several horses, including one belonging to sixty-five-year-old William Jessup. The government promised to reimburse loyal men for any loss of property, but Jessup preferred to keep the broken-down nag left by Morgan. Nevertheless, he was required to file paperwork with a Lieutenant Nash, who asked the farmer his political leanings. Responding that he was a Democrat who favored the Constitution as it was and supported Vallandigham for governor, Jessup sensed the officer's growing hostility. This encounter made it evident to him that difficult times lay ahead for those citizens branded as disloyal because of their political beliefs. Recounting this confrontation to his son William, a captain with the 5th Ohio Cavalry, the elder Jessup asserted that "it will take the bayonet to prevent the election of Val, and with that resort, God save the just." Although he expected to be persecuted for his views, Jessup encouraged his son to "keep the faith steady,... and we will win and save the country."[55]

Morgan's raid not only put pressure on some Democrats but also tested the resolve of Quakers. With the Rebel outlaws only twenty miles north of Cincinnati, Governor David Tod called on all able-bodied men in the vicinity to assemble at Camp Dennison. One Ohioan was appalled at the derision directed at her brothers and other Friends who "reluctantly" reported for duty. "O how some of them did glory in seeing the Quakers brought in by force. They said one man is no better than another." Cyrus Lewis complied with the order but stressed that he had no intention "to take up arms." The lack of trust initially shown his company insulted him, for a guard even kept watch over their sleeping quarters in order to prevent any attempt to return home secretly. In spite of this indignity, the two-and-a-half day stint with the militia did not cause him to violate any of his pacifist convictions. "Fortunately for us Quaker boys there were not arms enough in camp for all," he related with relief after being excused from drill.[56]

In the meantime, Morgan had ranged 150 miles across southern Ohio with Union cavalry in hot pursuit. Unable to cross the Ohio River at his intended destination because of the presence of a Federal gunboat, he was forced to head north, having suffered the loss of over 800 men when blue-clad horsemen hemmed in his rear guard at the river. Desperately fleeing for their lives, the approximately 700 ragged riders managed to evade capture for six more days. To the very end, Morgan's presence caused rumors to fly as anxious inhabitants of numerous sleepy towns and villages throughout Ohio wondered where the elusive Rebel would appear next. Still grieving over the death of her eleven-week-old son only ten days earlier, Marilla Wells Leggett initially viewed the commotion over Morgan as an invigorating diversion. Men and boys from Montville scrambled to join in the hunt on July 23, and "amusing" stories spread around town. The flurry of activity subsided the following day and caused Leggett to lose all interest in the affair, which now seemed "like childrens play." By the third day, the entire community had grown weary of hearing about Morgan and acknowledged "the folly of getting up such excitements." The chase ended near Salineville on the morning of July 26, when Colonel James Shackelford's cavalry, "by the blessing of Almighty God," bagged the man whom Calvin Fletcher described as "the most daring gurrella of the war." Of course, Fletcher agreed with the colonel's assessment that God should receive credit for Morgan's apprehension, for unseasonable heavy rains had elevated the water level of the Ohio to impassable depths in most places along his route except for a few fords defended by Union forces.[57]

With recent victories at Gettysburg and Vicksburg and the arrest of Morgan, Union prospects indeed looked bright. Even the oft melancholic and sometimes pessimistic Ann Cotton, who three weeks earlier had anticipated a Union defeat in Pennsylvania, conceded in late July that "the war *seems* near its close." In an abrupt about-face, she affirmed, "I now think we will conquer the rebels, & even the *thought* makes me happier!" Other civilians grounded their optimism in the belief that God finally had showered his blessings on the cause he had supported from the outset. In a sermon preached at Milwaukee's Plymouth Church, C. D. Helmer asserted that Christians individually and the church collectively should take the utmost interest in the war because "the welfare of the kingdom of God" hung in the balance. When the undiscerning multitudes raised a ruckus in public celebration for victories that to them appeared to result from chance or good fortune, those who detected "the Hand of God in this conflict" should "cry out amid the noise, 'Give God the glory,' 'The Lord is a man of war, He has given us the victory.'" Iowan Mary Vermilion singled out the administration's recent decision in late May to employ blacks as soldiers as the sole explanation for God finally granting battlefield successes. Confident in the Union's secure possession of the moral high ground, she asked rhetorically, "Is it not a good thing to have God on our side?" In contrast to those who had become "too sanguine" and deluded themselves that the North had struck a decisive blow to the Rebels, Indianapolis philanthropist Ovid Butler recognized that the war might continue indefinitely. The Confederate army, though battered, remained a potent force and could prolong the conflict another year. At such a juncture, the expiration of three-year terms thinning the Union ranks and political divisions at home over the presidential election might prove a lethal combination that could cripple the northern war effort. Even if this worst-case scenario played out, Butler saw no reason to fear because he believed that a sovereign Ruler would "defend the right." "God reigns—Let the Earth rejoice," he extolled. "None but the guilty need tremble."[58]

Resuming his role as national theologian, Lincoln summoned the people to direct their thoughts heavenward by observing a day of thanksgiving on August 6. The president's proclamation depicted an active Godhead who unmistakably functioned as the primary cause of all things. In the first place, God had answered the petitions "of an afflicted people" by giving military successes that indicated the ultimate preservation of the Union. "The presence of the Almighty Father and the power of His Hand" had not only subdued the enemy but also served as the means of comfort to numerous grieving hearts throughout the land. The assertion that God the Father had been working to achieve his purposes for the nation imparted nothing new that the general public had not heard in sermons or even previous presidential fast proclamations. Lincoln, however, entered uncharted theological waters by drawing explicit attention to the work of God the Holy Spirit in carrying out divine objectives. The Spirit could "change the hearts" of Southerners by breaking their resolve to continue the fight, confer understanding to the nation's leaders as they governed, strengthen and reassure soldiers who had endured great physical pain and mental anguish, and guide the country "through the paths of repentance and submission to the Divine Will," which the president believed to be nothing less than "the perfect enjoyment of Union and fraternal peace."⁵⁹

The exceptional nature of Lincoln's thanksgiving proclamation caught the attention of at least one admirer. Charles McIlvaine found it especially gratifying that Lincoln grasped the significance of "the being & influence of 'the Holy Spirit'" in the present conflict. Now that the third Person of the Trinity had received due credit in an executive pronouncement, likely for the first time ever, the only remaining deficiency to be rectified in some future state paper was "a distinct acknowledgement of Christ as the Saviour of sinners." Although his wish for a public declaration along these lines may have been a long shot, the evangelical Episcopal bishop nonetheless expressed his personal desire for Lincoln to possess "the full enjoyment of the precious hope" of salvation in Christ. Members of the laity may not have perceived the theological depth of the announcement of thanksgiving, but they nonetheless appreciated its purpose. "I was so delighted with Lincoln's idea of Thanksgiving," Elizabeth Duncan informed her sister-in-law. "I think we ought to give God the glory for he alone has been our help in this hour of need." Some regular churchgoers sensed that many citizens had ignored the president's call to offer gratitude to God. Alice Chapin was disappointed that the proclamation received "little attention generally" in Putnam County, though she determined to keep the spirit of the day regardless of the prevailing indifference around her. A resident of Henry County, Indiana, reported that no Copperheads were present at the service he attended. In his opinion, "all genuine Christians" offered thanks to God daily for his many blessings, but the "miserable tools of the slave holding oligarchy" found nothing to celebrate in the outcomes of Gettysburg, Vicksburg, or Morgan's raid and would have to wait until "Jeff's day of fasting and humiliation comes round" to express their religious devotion. While this Unionist Hoosier used the occasion of national thanksgiving to make a political statement in the local newspaper by publicly denouncing Butternuts, Mennonite Daniel Brenneman found himself in a quandary different from that of alleged southern sympathizers. Because he maintained a belief in the incompatibility of fighting with several scriptural commands, he certainly could not offer thanksgiving for martial victories without violating his pacifist convictions. Maybe for this reason he erroneously referred to August 6 as a fast day, subconsciously thinking that a nation at war had ample cause for penitence. However, Brenneman detected "little of that contrition and humility of heart" in the townspeople of Bremen, Ohio, that characterized the inhabitants of ancient Ninevah, who fasted and repented in sackcloth and ashes after the prophet Jonah pronounced God's judgment upon them. In truth, obtaining man's approval by showy demonstrations of religiosity may have reaped a temporary reward, but only God could determine the sincerity of a person's motives in complying with the proclamation. A female resident of Terre Haute, Indiana, understood that the genuine essence of "public thanksgiving" lay solely in gaining "the approbation of Him who has all hearts in his hand."⁶⁰

Because they viewed the war as a struggle to maintain the Union handed down by the Founding Fathers, preserve the only democracy on earth, and extend freedom around the world by destroying slavery, it is no wonder that many Northerners believed America to be standing at the crossroads of history. When some ministers emphasized God's role in history as the theme of their thanksgiving addresses, it only confirmed the prevailing notion that God was preparing his chosen people to accomplish a momentous work. Addressing an interdenominational gathering in southwestern Michigan on the subject *God Our Leader*, Presbyterian pastor Sefferenas Ottman traced the hand of God in American history from Columbus through the Pilgrims and the Revolutionary War to the current contest. Even Lincoln had "seemed compelled, as if by a Divine impulse," to abolish slavery in order to preserve the Union. Ottman asserted that the country simply needed to "follow the leadings of Divine Providence" in order for victory to be assured and the cause of universal freedom furthered.⁶¹

In the nation's capital, the proclamation's author likewise heard a sermon that expounded on the overarching purposes of God in history. At New York Avenue Presbyterian Church, Phineas D. Gurley applied Proverbs 16:9, "A man's heart deviseth his way: but the Lord directeth his steps," to several biblical incidents. Selecting the construction of the tower of Babel, the sale of Joseph into Egypt, and the crucifixion of Christ to illustrate God's ability to overrule the designs of man to accomplish his higher objectives, Gurley demonstrated the all-encompassing scope of God's sovereignty throughout biblical history. Known for his scripturally oriented messages, the Princeton Seminary graduate did not disappoint on this special occasion. However, he appended some final thoughts showing how the text applied to the present war. Although Southerners had rebelled to establish their own nation, God was using their wicked actions to preserve the Union whole, in the process refining and equipping it "for a blessed mission and a splendid destiny." Indeed, much cause for hope existed, for the same God who worked out his perfect will in former times "has ever been manifestly and marvellously the Guardian-God of this Republic." Gurley's optimistic reliance in God's sovereign care for the country did not go unnoticed. Lincoln left the service impressed by the fervency of his pastor's conviction that the North would prevail in the conflict.⁶²

By the late summer of 1863, many religious Northerners had affirmed their belief that God was the controlling influence in and over the war. Recent victories had convinced them that a glorious future lay ahead for the revitalized Union, which, purged of slavery, would be prepared to enter, if not initiate, the coming millennial kingdom. In mid-August, Henry McPheeters of Orleans, Indiana, exulted, "It looks like the God of Battles is on our side and I hope *He* will continue to bless our Government untill the last rebel will lay down his arms and Peace and Harmony shall Reign... never to be broken while time lasts." McPheeters clearly anticipated that the cessation of hostilities in America would inaugurate millennial conditions throughout the land. Living in perfect conditions untouched by war or sin, "we shall become a People fearing God, and working righteousness." But before that idyllic world could be gained, the rebellion had to be crushed. During this season of rejoicing and expectation, even the simple faith of a child demonstrated the prevalence of a God-centered view of the war. Schoolteacher Emma Stevens explained to her students that class would be canceled on the day of national thanksgiving so that families could thank God for granting victories. Within moments, she overheard her pupil Charley say to his friend Chauncey, "Aint you glad God is going to stop the war?" The latter, a bit startled by this bold revelation, wondered out loud if God in fact could end the bloodshed. Without a hint of uncertainty, Charley replied, "Yes I expect so, we are all going to ask him to stop the war tomorrow." Although few Christians would presume that their petitions could force the hand of God to halt the slaughter, they nonetheless believed that he alone possessed the power to reestablish peace and would do so "in his own good time."[63]

5

"Exhorting You to Be Faithful...to God and to Men"

Fatherly Counsel and the Path to Christian Manhood

Many Civil War soldiers left their homes as unproven youths who had seen little of the world beyond their local communities. Instead of maturing to adulthood through the typical process of acquiring their own land to farm, learning a trade, or, for those from families with economic means, graduating from college and entering a profession, they proved their manliness on the battlefield. Although this initiation by fire into the ranks of manhood might have signaled a new phase of personal autonomy and parental independence for some soldiers, many others remained in the shadows of their fathers. Christian fathers especially felt compelled to continue their sons' moral upbringing by encouraging them to live virtuous and godly lives while in the army. Indeed, the idea of Christian manhood stressed the father's duty to raise his sons to become upright citizens. For several years, historians of women have portrayed antebellum mothers as primary in child rearing. As rulers of the domestic sphere, mothers bore the responsibility of instilling into boys both republican values and moral precepts. More recently, historians studying masculinity have challenged this interpretation and demonstrated the interdependence of gender spheres. Without doubt, fathers, especially those influenced by revivalistic religion of the antebellum era, played an integral role in the upbringing of their sons.[1]

Letters written by religious fathers to their soldier-sons reveal much about their parental philosophy. To be sure, some fathers played a noticeably less active part than did mothers. Furthermore, fathers generally wielded more influence over the lives of unmarried sons than of those sons who had left home and started families of their own. Despite these differences, the emphasis on maintaining religious devotion and preserving moral virtue as a demonstration of both physical and spiritual maturity remained a constant theme that Christian fathers stressed for soldiers of all ages and ranks. Although a soldier was engaged outwardly in brutal warfare that resulted in killing the enemy, he could remain spiritually upright inwardly by cultivating virtue and resisting temptations of camp life. This unlikely combination blended the competing images of restrained manhood and martial manhood that characterized antebellum America.[2] While these categories sometimes overlapped prior to the Civil War, they converged by necessity during the war in order for Christian soldiers to be able to fight while preserving their religious values. Christian fathers considered it part of their parental duty to remind their sons that genuine manhood consisted of fulfilling both the secular responsibility to serve faithfully as a soldier and the spiritual discipline to live like a saint. In addition to biological fatherhood, ministers oftentimes acted as spiritual fathers to their church members, and their individual responses to how they should best discharge their civic and sacred duties during wartime had a great impact on the lives of their spiritual children in the church.

The authority of fathers over their sons was particularly evident in the aftermath of the attack on Fort Sumter. War fever engulfed the North and infected numerous patriotic youths, many of whom hungered for excitement and a chance to share in the glory of a quick and easy victory. College campuses especially overflowed with martial enthusiasm as hundreds of students exchanged their books for rifles. At Wabash College in Crawfordsville, Indiana, Ransom E. Hawley, two months shy of his seventeenth birthday, longed to join the approximately sixty schoolmates who had enlisted already. He knew full well how remote his prospects were of gaining his parents' approval to enlist and therefore framed the matter in terms of patriotic necessity. His grandfathers had served the country, so he too desired to follow in their footsteps and answer the call to duty. Besides, most of his friends had left school, and the frenzy of the moment made it impossible to study. His parents should not object simply because of his youth, for he had seen boys younger and smaller than he enroll in the ranks. "If I am small I can fight," he contended, "and I have just as much Patriotism in me as any grown man." Despite his best effort to sound mature and independent, Hawley's letter unmistakably conveyed his filial submission when he, like a schoolboy seeking permission to join his friends in their revelry, begged, "*Can't I go? Can't I go?*"[3] Needless to say, Hawley finished the term.

When the summer of 1862 arrived with no sign of war's end, Ransom Hawley again set his sights on the army. In the spring, Hawley had converted during a revival at college, but his newfound faith did not change his outlook about military service. He wanted to enlist with an acquaintance who possessed "good moral principles" and would hold him accountable spiritually, for he sincerely desired to live for Christ. Instead of entreating his parents as he had done the previous year, Hawley approached the subject as if he already had determined to fight but hoped his parents would sanction his decision. Possibly without their total support, he joined the 78th Indiana in late July and served three months, suffering a leg wound in battle.[4]

After recuperating, Hawley returned to Wabash in the spring, seemingly content with continuing his studies. However, Governor Oliver P. Morton's call for six-month volunteers in the summer of 1863 revived his martial spirit. Still two weeks away from turning nineteen, the young veteran again felt compelled to seek his parents' blessing. He figured that they likely had guessed his intentions but nonetheless dashed off an urgent letter in which he anticipated their objections, namely "that wayward Ransom wants to enlist." Torn between his filial duty to respect his parents' wishes and his growing desire to be his own man, he almost perfunctorily asked for their "permission" before asserting forthrightly, "If I enlist (as I shall probably), I will try and make you a visit before I leave." He promised to take final exams before enrolling and attempted to convince them that further military service would not prevent him from earning his degree or alter his intention to become a minister. Moreover, the army would help him mature both physically and spiritually. He would receive training that no college course could offer, gain practical experience that he needed immensely, and learn to "trust in God" for help in living a morally upright life. After making his appeal and affirming his willingness to die for the country if necessary, he closed by repeating his request for their "full consent." Hawley served six months with the 115th Indiana beginning in August 1863 and completed an additional three-month stint with the 133rd Indiana during the summer of 1864.[5] As a son still under the authority of his father but coming of age as a soldier, Ransom Hawley had difficulty finding a proper balance between honoring his parents by following their advice and establishing his manhood by choosing his own course in life.

Although the Hawley family supported Ransom's decision to volunteer, however begrudgingly at first, other families adamantly opposed the enlistment of school-aged sons. In the spring of 1862, Sarah Kohlsaat expressed great concern that her son Christian, a law student at the University of Chicago, would be tempted to join fellow classmates who had enlisted. She confessed that the thought of him joining the army caused her physical distress. "I tremble all over & cannot settle down to any kind of work." Even though Christian's father Reimer thought that his wife was overreacting and should be proud of her son's willingness to serve, he concluded that Christian should remain in school and devote "*every energy*" to his studies. Furthermore,

Christian's uncle Diedrich, who helped pay his tuition, agreed with this decision. Christian quickly assured his parents that he would continue in his present course for another year, for even his professors regarded the completion of his degree to be more pressing at the moment. Nevertheless, he did not eliminate the possibility of future military service should "providence open the way." With calls for additional troops in the summer of 1862 and the establishment of national conscription with the Enrollment Act of 1863, opportunities to fight abounded, but Christian stuck to his books. While traveling as an agent for the Chicago Bible Society in the summer of 1864, Reimer acknowledged that his wife's opposition had likely been the deciding factor in dissuading Christian from enlisting. "It is very well that you were kept back by your mothers stronger antipathy to have you cut or shot to pieces." Even if he had not been as vehement in his opposition as his wife, he nonetheless had shared her sentiment and continued to object to Christian joining the army unless God plainly overruled him. "When he needs you for the horrors of war, he will so hedge up the way to *force* you into it, [but] at present I dont feel as if I could spare any one of my dear ones." The call for 500,000 more troops in the summer of 1864 again threatened to pull Christian into the conflict. When Reimer received the "refreshing" news in late September that Christian had avoided the draft, he saw indisputable evidence of God's mercy in delivering his son from conscription.[6]

Young men who enlisted without parental consent risked not only disappointing their entire family but also upsetting the daily routines of home life. When twenty-seven-year-old Sam Evans of Brown County, Ohio, secretively joined the 70th Ohio in February 1862, he openly rebelled against his father's authority. As the eldest son of Andrew Evans, Sam had remained at home to run the family blacksmith shop and flour mill in addition to assisting with farm chores. This willingness to stay on the family homestead enabled two younger brothers to pursue their own careers and freed up a third for military service with Andrew's blessing. Knowing that his father would not release him from his familial duties or transfer his work load to his eighteen-year-old brother Amos, Sam acted independently and followed his own conscience, in the process removing himself from under his father's control. Andrew reacted as expected to this violation of his patriarchal supremacy and rebuked Sam for his poor judgment, especially after learning that Sam had contracted measles shortly thereafter. Although Andrew did not doubt his son's patriotism or good intentions, he maintained that a person with a weak constitution should have known better than to take on the physically taxing duties of a soldier. In his opinion, Sam had made a "rash" decision as a result of becoming enthralled by the sight of crisp new uniforms and mesmerized by the sound of martial music. Lying incapacitated in a field hospital did nothing to help the government that he sought to serve but instead proved to be an unnecessary "burden." Although Andrew lectured his son for what he regarded to be a lack of discernment, he ultimately came to support Sam after learning of his valor and comportment at Shiloh. The consequences of Sam's action fell hard on Amos, who also desired to fight but refused to violate his father's orders against enlisting. When Amos was drafted later that fall, he felt disgraced for having to be classed with men forced to serve against their will. Nevertheless, he notified Sam that he had done right "by obeying my Parents" and would bear the stigma of conscription "with Christian fortitude as Job bore all his affliction."[7]

Sam again engendered his father's displeasure after he accepted an officer's commission with the 59th Colored Infantry. Although he felt confident that he had chosen wisely, he belatedly asked for his father's input and cited time constraints as an excuse for not seeking this advice earlier. Andrew protested that he would have preferred to remain ignorant of this alleged promotion to "a degraded position" but bluntly gave his opinion since Sam had requested it. "I would rather clean out S__t houses at ten cents pr day, than to take your position with its pay." In his response, Sam capably defended his decision and insisted that he did not want to withhold relevant information from his father. "If I have done wrong it is not your fault but mine," he added, "and [I] will be accountable to God." Andrew retreated somewhat from his stance of total opposition and conceded that he preferred the deaths of black soldiers to those of whites—indeed, that he rather "would have the [black] race extinguished than to loose a single Co. of the white soldiers." Instead of hanging his head after again disappointing his father, Sam continued to do his duty and kept Andrew apprised of his men's natural abilities and military progress. By war's end, Andrew had not only discarded his racist language but also notified Sam that he wholeheartedly supported the Thirteenth Amendment. After the war, while Sam remained south for five months working for the Freedmen's Bureau, Andrew even espoused his willingness to support black suffrage. Sam's determination to choose his own course in life and stand by his decisions enabled him to successfully emerge from his father's shadow, to establish his identity as an autonomous man, and, ultimately, to influence and shape Andrew's political views and social values. Looking back on his family's role in the war, Andrew did not dwell on the sometimes strained relations but focused on the bravery and commendable records of his sons, exclaiming, "God knows I am proud of them!"[8]

The Hawley, Kohlsaat, and Evans examples superbly reveal the various tensions and emotions that families felt when a son confronted the decision to enter the army or stay home. Ministers, too, oftentimes underwent significant soul-searching when weighing the choices between remaining in their pulpits or exchanging their clerical garb for a soldier's uniform. Some concluded that spiritual duties trumped patriotic sentiments and chose to continue to feed their flocks at home. "If I did not feel that God's providence directs me to stay here and labor on in these two feeble churches," Ohio Presbyterian John French asserted, "I should enter the army at once." J. F. Weishample Sr., a field agent who visited Church of God congregations throughout Ohio, Indiana, Illinois, Michigan, and Iowa, similarly viewed his current work as a higher calling than defending the country but conceded his desire "to go forth to preserve the Government as a soldier" if not engaged in the gospel ministry. As war progressed, some clergymen who preferred to serve at home but, like Amos Evans, did not want to bear the stigma attached to being drafted, had to reevaluate their position. Illinois minister William Wright viewed the chaplaincy as a legitimate option if he were conscripted, but his father Nathaniel attempted to persuade him that even religious service in the army was inappropriate for him. In addition to pointing out his son's weak constitution that made him ill-equipped for army life, the Cincinnati lawyer insisted that the individual talents and civic contributions of some men, including most ministers, necessitated that they remain civilians. "The nation must be taken care of *within* as well as *without*," he advised. "To neglect all at home for the sake of fighting for the country, is to make the country not worth fighting for."[9]

Other ministers, in contrast, determined that their duty as citizens compelled them to take up arms to defend the Union. It is difficult to know precisely how many northern clergymen left their churches and joined the Union army as soldiers, but their presence was both noticeable and significant. The 73rd Illinois even became known as the "Preachers' Regiment" because ninety-one ministers, primarily Methodists, served in its ranks. Shortly after war commenced, J. L. Boyd, Methodist itinerant in the North-Western Indiana Conference, enlisted as a private "after much prayer and candid debate with myself." He regarded the defense of country as an imperative possessing as much consequence as his religious "duty to preach and pray with the people." Indeed, after only a few weeks in camp he realized he had entered "a greater missionary field" than he ever would have encountered in his preaching circuit. Although he believed that God providentially directed him to a place of greater service, he nevertheless harbored a lingering doubt about his decision to bear arms and beseeched readers of the *Western Christian Advocate* to advise him whether or not a preacher of the gospel could kill a fellow man during time of war without violating his ministerial office. An answer came two months later from a pastor in Athens, Ohio, who asserted that a minister could enter the army as a chaplain but should never enlist as a soldier. He maintained that because God called men to the gospel ministry, voluntarily leaving the pulpit represented abandoning a sacred vocation to follow an inferior profession. Moreover, army life would subject a minister to Sabbath desecration and cause him to forfeit his position of moral authority. Indeed, the reverend from Ohio employed the most condemning language when he classified all preachers such as Boyd as rebels against God who, "as divinely-called standard bearers in the army of Jesus[,] have seceded and joined the armies of their country."[10]

Few religious Northerners took such an extreme position but generally insisted that clergymen should be free to act according to the dictates of personal conscience. God, rather than man, ultimately would judge their motives to determine if their priorities aligned with his will. After underscoring his personal opposition to having ministers take any military assignment other than the chaplaincy, J. G. Monfort, editor of the *Presbyter*, admonished laypersons to resist the temptation to criticize a preacher who volunteered. Indeed, he concluded that pastors who publicly supported the war would find it difficult "to stand like mile posts, pointing others to the army without moving themselves." Democratic editors, who often blamed ministers for inciting war with their antislavery sermons, commended clergymen who followed their own counsel and purposed to fight. When B. C. Ward, a Congregational pastor in Illinois, determined to raise a company composed only of ministers, he received the hearty endorsement of the *Cincinnati Enquirer*, whose editor hoped that he might fill an entire brigade with his brethren. Lewis Glessner, who edited the *Hancock (Ohio) Courier*, scoffed that Ward would wait an eternity before finding one hundred preachers with enough backbone to put their lives in danger for the cause they so passionately espoused.[11]

Unlike these Democratic detractors, some congregations lamented the absence of their spiritual fathers from their places of service. Larger churches likely found replacements with relative ease, but assemblies in small communities who lost the services of an itinerant might be without a preacher indefinitely. In September 1862, delegates to the annual meeting of the Indiana Presbytery reported that nine churches lacked regular ministers because three men had joined the army. With no local residents able to fill the void, they recommended recruiting qualified preachers from out of state. Sometimes this loss of leadership lasted only for a short period of time. For instance, twenty-one ministers of the North Indiana Conference of the Methodist church served as officers or chaplains at some point during the war, but twelve of them resigned in less than a year. Unaccustomed to the physical demands of army life, numerous clergymen became ill and returned home before their enlistment expired, but others disliked aspects of their new field of service and deemed that their ministerial opportunities had diminished. After his discharge from the chaplaincy, Ohio Methodist L. C. Matlack explained that "the opportunity for extensive usefulness" practically ceased after the men left camp and commenced a campaign. Because "much of the time and most of the Sabbaths were a blank," he began to yearn "for the privileges and labor of a preacher among the people again."[12] Although Matlack managed to resume his ministry to a local congregation, other pastors never returned from the ranks. Religious weeklies often carried obituaries of clergymen and lay exhorters who had vacated their leadership position in a local church to defend their country, only to fall in battle or succumb to disease. It is impossible to measure the long-term effects of these losses on individual congregations, but as a whole the church undoubtedly missed the experience and wisdom of seasoned ministers, the energy and enthusiasm of young men entering the ministry, and the collective abilities and service of believers of all ages.[13]

Despite the possibility of permanent loss, most congregations and Union-loving men on the home front made every effort to convey their wholehearted support to ministers, relatives, or friends who enlisted. Since most fathers of soldiers had reached at least their midforties and therefore had passed the age limit for military service, they immensely appreciated the sacrifices of the younger generation. Many fathers recognized the importance of helping sustain morale by sending upbeat letters to soldiers and emphasizing their patriotic pride in sons who had willingly left the comforts of home to defend the country. When fifty-nine-year-old Joseph Ankeny of Millersburg, Ohio, learned in August 1861 that his son Henry, an Iowa farmer in his midthirties, intended to join the army, he experienced ineffable satisfaction that Henry offered himself "freely and cheerfully" to uphold the government. Caleb Mills, a college professor and former state superintendent of public education in Indiana, heartily commended his students at Wabash College who enrolled in the army and demonstrated his continued admiration by corresponding regularly with several of them. Volunteers earned the respect of their elders because they exhibited the courage and manliness that the older generation would have liked to display had they been in their physical prime. Most aged patriots scorned young fellows who lacked legitimate reasons for taking up arms. Thomas J. Anderson, a judge and son of a Revolutionary War soldier, thought Marion, Ohio, contained few "young men of worth" in the fall of 1862. Only "the trifling ones whom we could well spare" remained "lounging about town" while all the estimable youths had gone to war. In an instance of rare candor, one Indiana man admitted his failure to live up to the ideal of manliness embodied by soldiers. "So you are a bold soldier boy—God bless you for it. I never felt so *small* in my life," Joseph Noyes confessed to soldier John Ballard in early June 1861. "I'm ashamed of myself, *sneaking* around here at home when better men are ready to die. If the Lord will forgive me the *craven* part I have played thus far in this glorious game, I will try and do better in the future."[14]

Although religious fathers viewed physical manliness as an essential quality in their soldier-sons, they stressed that genuine manhood necessitated religious devotion as well. On numerous occasions, fathers juxtaposed admonitions to fulfill the responsibilities of a soldier with reminders to live for God. Franklin Alford straightforwardly exhorted his twenty-two-year-old son Warren to "act the Man and discharge your whole duty to your God and your Country." Before his eighteen-year-old son Rufus even left camp, Indiana farmer Silas Dooley encouraged him to be brave in battle and obedient to his officers. A soldier could be "just as good a christian" while in the army as during civilian life. After completing nearly five months of service with the 115th Indiana in 1863, Ransom E. Hawley was implored by his father to be a "faithful" soldier who cared about the welfare of his comrades and committed himself to living "a godly life." Cognizant of the many difficulties and inconveniences of army life, the elder Hawley emphasized that Ransom should "bear the yoke in youth" in order to build character and prepare himself for future success. Ohio farmer Harrison Kellar counseled his twenty-one-year-old son John, stationed with the Union Light Guard in Washington, D.C., to remember that religion elevated a person's moral worth and signified a mark of true manhood. "Take a *high* religious course and associate with it all that is *noble* and *dignifying*," he asserted, for "a *Christian* is the highest style of man."[15]

Sons raised in Christian homes immediately noticed the degenerate atmosphere of camp. After spending a few days in camp with the 22nd Iowa, twenty-one-year-old George Remley informed his father James, a Baptist minister, that soldiers ate their meals without offering thanks to God. Even worse, he estimated that he had overheard more swearing in a few days in camp than over the previous two or three years combined. His older brother Lycurgus agreed that their company contained some of "the most vulgar, obscene, profane fellows you ever saw." Without elaborating on the sordid details of his surroundings, Wayne Alford, a month shy of his twenty-first birthday, asserted plainly, "The wickedness in camp disgusts me." He asked his father to pray that he would continue to follow God in spite of the dissolute conditions. His brother Warren agreed that the prevalence of sin in camp made the army "a very unpleasant place" for Christians. He trusted that God would give him grace to endure his undesirable circumstances.[16]

Because decadence pervaded camp life, fathers often underscored the necessity of resisting the numerous temptations as a proof of Christian manliness. Far from being killjoys, they prohibited certain conduct because of their firm conviction that bad habits ruined the Christian man by sullying his virtuous character. Silas Dooley warned Rufus to "shun" the evils of camp like a "dedly poisen." Consuming alcoholic beverages, using tobacco, gambling, swearing, and engaging in illicit sex all threatened to corrupt the soldier who yielded to them. Silas rejoiced to learn that Rufus had rebuffed a soldier who wanted to play cards in his tent. Although the social interaction and camaraderie affiliated with drink, tobacco, and cards might have made them seem like innocent "amusements," in reality they were "delusive snares" that drew the moral man "away from the path [of] duty & of virtue." The model soldier would be temperate in all things, Silas stressed, for his self-control enabled him to keep a clear conscience before God and perform his duty well for his fellow man. Harrison Kellar underscored the danger of even becoming familiar with sin. After learning that John, who had noted the wickedness of the nation's capital in a previous letter, had set foot briefly in one of its numerous brothels, he cited Proverbs 7 as a solemn reminder that only foolish youths succumbed to the charms of immoral women. "Better to fall in battle with the enemy" and preserve a virtuous reputation, Harrison forewarned, "than fall by them Prostitutes that infest Washington."[17]

Despite having been trained to abstain from the iniquities that surrounded them in camp, some young men, freed from the restraints of home for the first time, disregarded their prior instruction. Shortly after nineteen-year-old Benjamin Mills became a first lieutenant with the 49th Colored Infantry in the spring of 1864, he described in detail to his father Caleb his new surroundings and daily routine, emphasizing that his captain did not drink or use tobacco and scarcely ever swore. This report likely eased some of the fears of the elder Mills, who encouraged his son nearly two months later that withstanding a temptation once would make it easier to gain victory during subsequent trials. It must have shocked him considerably when Benjamin confessed that he had been chewing tobacco regularly but had decided to stop because "the habit had grown" uncontrollable. Although Caleb refrained from berating his son at that time, he later reiterated upon "the slavery & curse of tobacco" and sent a book that documented the evils of the weed. Alcohol too enticed Benjamin, and he freely admitted to his father that he imbibed because the doctor had recommended blackberry brandy to help cure diarrhea. However, he concealed from Caleb that one of his official responsibilities entailed inspecting the soldiers' whiskey ration. On one occasion in January 1865, Benjamin recorded in his diary that he had examined fifteen gallons of liquor and sampled all of it. Leaving the impression that he did not dislike the assignment, he acknowledged that by the end of the day he "was pretty full and could not drink any more for fear of getting drunk." When Benjamin asked his father to send him some gin whiskey that same month, Caleb, puzzled by the request and somewhat perturbed, responded that he had thought his son to be fully recovered from his illness and no longer in need of medicinal spirits. Far from obliging his son's petition, Caleb lectured him about abstaining from drink. "Nothing would break your mothers heart & bring my grey hairs with sorrow to the grave than a whiskey drinking son. *Let it alone*," he ordered emphatically. "Don't disregard the counsel."[18]

Caleb Mills (1806–79) was a strong proponent of public education in Indiana and the state's second superintendent of public instruction. As professor of Greek at Wabash College, he influenced several young men who enlisted in the war and regularly corresponded with them. A devout Presbyterian, he expected the United States to further God's divine plan for the ages. His view of the war can be summed up in a statement made on the day of Lincoln's second inauguration. "The world moves & God's hand is in all these wonderful events." *Ramsay Archives, Wabash College*

Much like the Apostle Paul, who often likened the Christian life to soldiering, some fathers compared the struggle to resist temptation to warfare. Dependable soldiers had to be alert to the movements of the enemy, so Christians needed to be wary of the Devil's assaults. Caleb Mills drew a parallel between a sentinel standing on picket duty and a vigilant Christian combating the Tempter. A soldier on picket had to watch attentively for an enemy attack, but after a few hours a fresh sentry would relieve him so that he could rest. Spiritual warfare, in contrast, was waged continuously, for Satan, "a subtle, wily & watchful foe" more dangerous than any Confederate soldier, never gave up his surveillance but waited patiently and attacked the moment his prey let down his guard. Only "the shield of faith in the power & promises" of God could block his "darts," Caleb stressed to Benjamin. As a firm believer in the depravity of man, the elder Mills sought to convince his son that he had to combat even his own flesh which predisposed him to sin. Because "'the heart [is] deceitful above all things & desperately wicked,'" Mills explained, citing Jeremiah 17:9, fallen man would rebel habitually against the commands of God and constantly yield to evil desires without regenerating grace. Like Mills, other devout fathers underscored the necessity of trusting in God alone to overcome temptation. Even after Warren had testified to the vibrancy of his spirituality after more than two months in the army, Franklin Alford nonetheless reminded him that God was "a strong tower" in which he could "fly for refuge" in times of spiritual peril. Having enlisted in the early summer of 1861 because of his opposition to secession, Rufus Dooley could appreciate the imagery of dual warfare. Silas knew that his son would never tolerate any "compromise with rebbles," and he urged him to be just as unwavering when confronting the prevalent corruption of camp life.[19]

While the Christian soldier strived to resist vices that led to the formation of wicked habits, he also needed to cultivate godliness by establishing upright patterns of behavior. Fathers therefore reminded their sons that shunning the worldly pleasures of camp would be easier if they spent their leisure time engaged in spiritual activities. Reading the Bible helped fill the mind with invaluable principles that would guide the godly man throughout life. Harrison Kellar advised John to "get the knowledge of your Bible," for it contained the map of "the Highway to the Kingdom." Following its truths would lead to eternal rewards and enable John to become "an heir of God and joint heir with Christ." A son who cherished the Scriptures and attempted to live by its precepts brought peace of mind to fathers concerned about the detrimental influences of camp. Shortly after enlisting, George Remley notified his father James that he had purchased "a good polyglot reference Bible" for a quarter, a clear indication that he intended to engage in serious Bible study while in the army. Sure enough, he earned a reputation for enthusiastically devouring the Word daily. After George's death at Winchester, Virginia, in the fall of 1864, an adjutant related to James Remley that his son had been "very fond of his Bible" and read it each night before bed and throughout the day when "a leisure moment" presented itself. Indeed, he had carried his Bible with him at all times until it wore a hole in his coat pocket. Having lodged with George and observed him closely for several months, the adjutant concluded that he had modeled "a christian soldier in every sense of the word."[20]

In addition to receiving moral instruction in letters from home and in Scripture, religious soldiers could obtain spiritual guidance from the regimental chaplain. During the war's first year, the chaplaincy suffered from a lack of professionalization, and men without religious credentials gained appointments and often disgraced the office by their scandalous behavior. However, over the course of the war, chaplains provided valuable service and contributed to the spiritual welfare of the troops. Devout fathers regarded chaplains as allies who could assist their sons in the spiritual battle against sin. James Remley wondered why Lycurgus had never mentioned his chaplain after over two months in the army. He judged that his sons would benefit from befriending him "if he is a good christian man." Lycurgus responded that he had known the gentleman for some time and attended outdoor services regularly, but the chaplain, who seemed like "a good man," had struggled to procure a tent for preaching once cold weather arrived. This noticeable ineptness caused many in the regiment to regard him as "almost a cipher," so his influence over the men was practically negligible. By the next spring, the chaplain had reinstituted Sunday services in addition to conducting midweek prayer meeting. From all indications, James Remley never inquired about him again, for he likely assumed that boys as well-grounded in the faith as his own had little to learn from such an ineffective preacher. In contrast to Remley, Thomas Barland became so troubled by the absence of a chaplain from his son John's regiment, the 16th Wisconsin, that he complained directly to the president. After John became ill, Thomas visited him at Vicksburg, noticed the absence of a chaplain, and learned from a colonel that the rolls listed a man named Livermore as regimental chaplain. Livermore had preached five or six times but had been away on "other business" for the greater part of two years, apparently padding his pockets "advancing the free labor cotton colony business in the South." Barland attempted to impress on Lincoln the gravity of his letter and implored him to remove this feckless imposter and appoint a competent man who would take his responsibilities seriously. "I feel that if I neglect any more what conscience points out as my duty to these injured men," the concerned father confessed, "I will be guilty of a great sin."[21]

The shortage of effective chaplains in some regiments only underscored the importance of supporting those men who faithfully ministered to soldiers. Caleb Mills held reliable chaplains in high esteem and on several occasions urged Benjamin to "honor and encourage" his chaplain by attending services unless official duties precluded. The devout Presbyterian viewed the chaplain as God's representative in the army; therefore, listening to his messages demonstrated reverence to God and a desire to keep his Sabbath holy. Mills implied that those who deliberately disregarded the Lord's command to observe his day of rest should not "expect blessings," for they had rejected an available "means of grace." Administrative responsibilities occupied most of Benjamin's Sunday mornings, but he enjoyed spending the afternoons reading religious periodicals and considered this activity to be completely "proper" for marking the Sabbath. Stationed near Vicksburg, he frequently attended services in town on Sunday evenings and rated the sermons as satisfactory, though he rarely discussed their content with his father. In May 1864, sounding somewhat perturbed that Caleb harped on supporting the chaplain, Benjamin claimed that attending regimental meetings was "impossible." In the first place, officers had difficulty obtaining seats since none were reserved for them. Furthermore, "the *atmosphere* of the room is such that a white man cannot breathe there," for the church "is always crowded with Negroes." Despite his interest in helping African-Americans transition to freedom, Benjamin nevertheless suffered from racist attitudes, especially in considering blacks as intellectual inferiors. On another occasion near the war's conclusion, he marched the "whole company" to a church nearly forty-five minutes away in order to hear their chaplain. The preacher rewarded his effort by delivering "a very good sermon" on an intellectual level that his troops "could understand," a skill that few ministers, he believed, had mastered.[22]

Denominational differences sometimes disinclined soldiers from developing close bonds with their chaplain. About two weeks after enlisting with the 6th Indiana in the autumn of 1861, Lafayette Alford, nearly nineteen years old, described to his father Franklin his first encounter with the chaplain. After preaching a fine message, the chaplain formed an interdenominational regimental church with membership based on adherence to the Apostle's Creed. Unfamiliar with that ancient confession of faith, Lafayette recalled that it affirmed the "supremacy" of Christ, his virgin birth, crucifixion, burial, and resurrection from the dead for man's sins. Raised in the Disciples of Christ tradition, he detected nothing of questionable doctrine. However, when forty or fifty soldiers from several denominations, including "some from the world" with no church affiliation, stepped forward to join, the chaplain accepted them all. Declaring that each man should set aside temporarily his particular denominational teachings, he exhorted them "to live together as Christians" until the war ended. He promised to inform their pastors at home of their determination to live uprightly while in the army, and those men lacking church affiliation he would baptize according to the mode of their preference. Already disturbed by the inclusion of unbelievers and the injunction to abandon denominational distinctives, Lafayette lost all respect for the chaplain when he removed the phrase concerning the resurrection of Christ in order to accommodate two Universalists who presented themselves for membership. This blatant compromise sealed his decision to remain separate from the ecumenical assembly.[23] Although Lafayette knew with certainty that his father would disapprove of him joining such an inclusive church, he nonetheless reported the incident and anticipated further advice. Away from home for the first time, Lafayette appreciated his father's reassuring counsel.

A chaplain's official duty may have involved preaching and caring for the spiritual health of the troops, but Christian soldiers likewise could help improve the moral conditions of camp by living as godly examples. Some fathers believed that the faithful testimonies of their sons might motivate others to embrace religion. After Lycurgus Remley started a prayer meeting that five or six other soldiers attended, his father James encouraged him to "persevere" in the work, for he might help foster religious affections in his companions. Harrison Kellar commended his son John for praying publicly at a service, an act that demonstrated "moral courage" through his voluntary identification of himself as a Christian. This desire to lead by example, Harrison claimed, manifested John's sensitivity to "the spirit of your Master and the leadings of your noble nature." Since the army could be viewed as a mission field of souls needing to be evangelized, other fathers wanted their sons to be even more assertive by aggressively sharing their faith with unbelievers. Alexander McPheeters exhorted his son John, an assistant surgeon with the 23rd Indiana, to "speak a word for the Saviour on every fitting occassion." He suspected that opportunities to witness were manifold and challenged John "to seek" such openings. In so doing, he would refresh his own soul spiritually, gain friends, and ultimately help others make peace with God.[24]

Christian fathers with unconverted sons carried a heavy burden, for they knew that at any moment a Rebel bullet might send an unprepared son into eternity. Caleb Mills went to great lengths to try to persuade Benjamin to trust Christ. In late August 1864, he brought up the parable of the prodigal son in order to illustrate the path to salvation. The prodigal represented natural man, who existed in a "helpless & hopeless" state, alienated from God. However, a loving Father stood with open arms, ready "to receive every poor sinner." Groveling in the hog pen, the prodigal had nothing by which to save himself. Likewise, man lacked any ability to merit salvation but relied solely on the person and work of Christ for redemption. Caleb entreated Benjamin to put himself in the position of the helpless prodigal and run to God, who would "clothe you with the robe of Christs righteousness, [and] put on your hand the ring[,] token of his everlasting covenant of love & mercy." Although he emphasized man's responsibility to answer the general call to salvation by coming to God, Caleb balanced this with the recognition that God divinely enabled a person to respond. "God give you wisdom & strength to...act promptly," he added, and "leave the result with Him who bids you come."[25]

Three months later, Caleb renewed his evangelistic effort by attempting to demonstrate how "becoming a Christian" was essential to finding fulfillment in life. During both seasons of blessing and periods of adversity, he affirmed, followers of Christ possessed joy that sprang from a living faith, and it not only sustained them throughout life but also gave assurance at death of an eternal home. Before enlisting in the army, Benjamin had weighed the costs of serving the country, knowing full well the hardships but also the potential for rewards. Similarly, he needed to consider the long-term effects of embracing Christianity. Continuing the martial analogy, Caleb paralleled Benjamin's study of military manuals as preparation for success in war with the necessity to heed the instructions in God's handbook in order to gain spiritual victory. In particular, the Bible promised that God would give wisdom and the Holy Spirit to those who asked, that knowing the Scriptures prepared a person for saving faith, and that Christ beckoned the lost to come to him for salvation. Caleb averred that those who trusted Christ would never regret it. Moreover, he would rejoice exceedingly to learn that Benjamin had been converted.[26]

Caleb's evangelistic witness failed to elicit a positive response from Benjamin, but the unexpected news of an aunt's death in early 1865 softened his resistance by bringing home the realization that all people must die. Oddly enough, Benjamin admitted that, despite his experience in the army, death had seemed remote to him before his aunt's demise. Having engaged in several discussions with his captain regarding "the certinty of death and the doom of the wicked," he nevertheless kept postponing "to the dim future" his need to "become a Christian," the deferral of which might not lead to a favorable result. However, he acknowledged his frustration at his moral shortcomings and confessed that he aspired to live virtuously. Still content to try to earn his own salvation by reforming himself from within, Benjamin asked his father to "pray...that I may be a better boy." Patient as ever, Caleb reiterated that man could do nothing to merit salvation. He counseled Benjamin to read Isaiah 55:1–7, which set forth man's "hopeless condition" and God's invitation to come to him for life. "Christ came to seek & save" those who could not satisfy their own longings for fulfillment. Seizing upon the opportunity presented by Benjamin's request for prayer, Caleb advised his son that he needed to offer only one petition, the humble publican's desperate plea recorded in Luke 18:13, "'God be merciful to me a sinner.'" After explaining the gospel again as clearly as he knew how, Caleb appealed to his son's reason, hoping to demonstrate the inconsistency of Benjamin's actions. "You are periling your life for your country to aid in subduing a rebellion against the government," Caleb pointed out, but "at the same time *you yourself* are a confessed rebel against a better government...of the Infinite, Eternal, & ever Blessed Sovereign of the Universe, who has so loved you that he gave his only begotten Son to suffer & die that you might live."²⁷ Based on existing correspondence over the next few months, Benjamin never accepted his father's theology that branded him a rebelling sinner in need of salvation through Christ alone but remained convinced that he could live a moral life on his own strength.

Many fathers concerned about the spiritual welfare of soldiers and the moral corruption of camp underscored to their sons the doctrine of God's sovereignty, both on an individual basis and on a national level. From a personal standpoint, God could protect soldiers from harm, and devoted fathers reminded their sons to entrust their physical safety to his keeping. Numerous letters reveal that religious Northerners often prayed for God to deliver soldiers from death in battle. While eagerly awaiting the details of a skirmish in Virginia in the fall of 1861, Franklin Alford expressed his longing to know that the God "who is able to shield his children from dangor" had preserved Warren. That next spring, he reminded his son to "give God the glory" for bringing him safely through another battle. As the war progressed, Andrew Evans mentioned matters of faith more frequently, and with the knowledge of Confederate threats to kill white officers commanding black troops, he especially feared for Sam's safety if captured. "May God preserve and protect you...from a foe so fiendish and hellish," he petitioned. Even when a soldier received a wound, he should not presume that God had withdrawn his hand of protection or somehow failed him in time of need. Iowan David Lough admitted to his wounded nephew James that it was difficult to accept that his injury occurred in the sovereignty of God, but an infallible God "cannot do wrong" and should not be questioned. Although he had prayed repeatedly for James to emerge from battle unscathed, David believed that an omniscient God had permitted the bullet to hit him, and a loving God would "sustain and uphold" his children during trials if they relied on him for support.²⁸

Several fathers asserted that God, in addition to possessing the power to protect the lives of soldiers, ultimately determined their personal success while in the army. Without espousing a completely deterministic view, these men encouraged their sons to fulfill their duties as best as humanly possible and leave the result with God. Man could strive with all his might to achieve a certain goal, but unless God willed him to attain it, his attempt would result in failure. "Dont seek promotion," Alexander McPheeters emphatically charged John. Instead, he should work "quietly,...punctually and energetickally," always giving his best and "trusting in God" to bring about recognition when it suited his timing. When John Ketcham learned that his twenty-year-old son Willie might be made adjutant of the 13th Indiana or promoted to captain in another unit, he offered no guidance as to which position would be preferable. "I dare not advise," he wrote, but will let "you and Providence manag[e] the matter." Harrison Kellar reminded his son John that exemplary conduct would enable him to gain promotion over men of lesser character, yet in the end only "the Lord whom you serve can open your way" to advancement. "True greatness consists in serving God," he stressed on another occasion, and "God will take care of them that *will* do right." Harrison clearly expected his son to make a name for himself and accomplish great things, but he underscored that God would bless only those who relied on him and would enable them to make significant achievements because of this dependence on divine strength. Yet in his zeal for a son's personal success, even the most spiritually minded father could emphasize man's responsibility to determine his own destiny seemingly without regard to God's overarching designs. After his elder son Lycurgus was promoted to sergeant, James Remley challenged him and George to "push *yourselves* a *little* forward" and seek to become captains. Nevertheless, regardless of their final rank, they had volunteered to preserve the Union, and at the very least this sacrifice would cause "Heaven and your country...[to] smile upon you" at war's end.[29]

When applied to the nation itself, God's sovereign control over human history enabled a theological interpretation of the war to flourish. By affirming God's sovereign power to shape the outcome of events in accordance with his divine will, some fathers viewed the war as a sacred undertaking directed by God and urged their sons to comply with his plan. Caleb Mills revealed his millenarian leanings when he claimed that God was purifying the American people through the "fiery trial" of war in order to make the United States "the glory of all nations." He charged Benjamin to "be a worthy actor" in the noble undertaking by following "Him who controls & guides the destinies of individuals & nations." In February 1865, John Ketcham emphatically asserted that God would bring the war to a favorable conclusion, for he perceived "His hand...in the struggle." He encouraged Willie to trust that God would lead and use him to accomplish the divine purposes. "What a sublime thought that we are Gods agents to carry out His plans," he marveled. An antislavery advocate, Ketcham claimed that God intended the war to bring about the eradication of slavery. "God will deliver the poor & oppressed," he maintained, and "who ever resists will be found fighting against God."[30]

To be sure, some religious Northerners disagreed with the notion that God intended the war to effect the destruction of slavery. At the beginning of 1862, Joseph Beebe, a merchant and Republican officeholder in Michigan, espoused his hope that "God the disposer of all things" would intervene and impart discernment to the nation's leaders so that the war could be terminated swiftly. However, by year's end, he had concluded that Radical Republicans had taken over the party and duped Lincoln into issuing the

Emancipation Proclamation in order to make slavery "extinct." Since the war's new objective superseded the Constitution, he urged his sons to resign from the army as quickly as possible. Although he opposed slavery personally, he firmly believed that the government lacked authority to compel its citizens to leave home and fight for emancipation while "nigars lay in the shade and look on." Other men contended that God absolutely abhorred war, and any Christian who fought violated the very essence of his religion. Jerome Brown attempted to convince his nephew Darius, whose father was deceased, to resign from the 12th Michigan rather than dishonor himself by participating in "an Abolition War." He regarded Christianity as intrinsically peaceful and God as entirely benign and loving. The God he worshiped knew nothing of "hell fire or murder or malice or...retribution." Indeed, Christ had taught his disciples to love their enemies and had commanded Peter to sheath his sword, saying "he that uses the sword shall perish by it." An extreme pacifist, Brown approved diplomatic compromise as the only proper means of resolving the conflict with the South, and he yanked scriptural phrases from their contexts to justify his position, in the process fashioning a spineless and effeminate god that no soldier reared in the principles of Christian manhood would dare embrace.[31]

Political differences, especially when centered on abolition, strained family relationships, often to the breaking point. Raised in a family of dyed-in-the-wool Democrats, Joseph Vannest went to war to preserve the old Constitution. After enlisting with the 120th Ohio in the summer of 1862, he shortly felt betrayed by the Emancipation Proclamation, and evidently his dissatisfaction became known throughout the community. One minister even claimed that Joseph, if given the opportunity, would be willing to shoot the president if he did not retract the edict. As would be expected, Joseph's father John took offense at this slanderous statement, for he had seen the letter in question and knew that his son had expressed no such sentiment. John personally confronted "the Abolition Preacher," who "in order to dodge the matter claimed that he had *misunderstood* his wife." The offended father, however, did not buy this lame excuse but continued to regard the Republican cleric as "a Liar & Mischiefmaker" unworthy to fill the office of a man of the cloth. Undoubtedly grateful for his father's willingness to defend his name, Joseph, though no assassin, nevertheless despised the new war aim and seriously contemplated desertion rather than continuing to fight for a cause he opposed. Several family members even encouraged him to resign or do anything possible to extract himself from participating in the "abolition war." John considered desertion an entirely appropriate option, for in his opinion "Negro lovers" should be the ones dying for black freedom instead of Democratic soldiers.[32]

Yet before he could pursue such a rash course of action, Joseph was promoted to orderly sergeant, and this new position seemed to make his service more bearable. However, the fall election revealed deep family divisions regarding the Ohio gubernatorial race. In late September 1863, Joseph's wife Mary informed him that she supported Republican candidate John Brough while all of his family favored the notorious Peace Democrat Clement Vallandigham. Mary urged her husband to write his parents "and let them know what you think of the old traiter." Fearing that she had been too forward in stating her political views, Mary stressed that she had not presumed "to tell you who to vote for." Nevertheless, she made clear her wish for him to vote for Brough. Evidently, the relationship between Mary and her Democratic in-laws deteriorated over the next two months to the degree that Joseph learned of the political squabble. Lecturing his wife for meddling in politics, a sphere "that women in my opinion have no business to dabble in at all," Joseph lamented that Mary had treated his father in an "unbecoming" manner. Forced to take sides, Joseph felt compelled to side with his father. "I cannot...believe that as good and kind a woman as you...could ridecule *my* father, whom I love and respect as only a dutiful son can," Joseph wondered in amazement. Mary's dishonorable behavior toward his father cut to his heart and even made him reconsider submitting his application for a furlough, for he had no interest in returning home in the midst of familial discord.[33]

Even when minor troubles disrupted domestic harmony, most soldiers thought of home fondly. Receiving letters and packages with clothing or food from home brightened any soldier's day, but preoccupation with thoughts of home, in contrast, could prove demoralizing. When some three-year men who had declined reenlistment bid farewell to their comrades in the 13th Indiana, they asked Willie Ketcham if he had any messages for home. Envisioning "the pleasures, comforts, & the loved ones" at home, Willie admitted to his father that he became "completely unmanned" and was struck speechless "for fear I should begin crying right there." At the first opportunity, he removed himself to a nearby swamp and "took a good cry." Although life in the army had proven to be better than he had anticipated, it nevertheless seemed "very uninviting" when compared to home. In particular, Willie complained that the army lacked the loving environment that caring family members provided at home. In his opinion, most soldiers were essentially "heartless," for they quickly forgot a fallen friend and envied the wounded for having the good fortune to escape combat for a few months. Willie recognized that displaying an emotional attachment to home before such battle-hardened veterans would bring him only ridicule and possibly elicit charges of effeminacy. However, soldiers could show emotion at the proper time and still retain their manliness. When Warren Alford's brother-in-law Charles Donaldson enlisted in late August 1862 and joined him in Virginia after more than sixteen months of separation from his family at home, a joyous reunion could be expected to follow. Franklin Alford envisioned "the tear[s] of affection stealing down" Warren's "care worn yet manly cheeks" as the two relatives embraced.³⁴

While home often evoked deep longings for the restoration of familial bonds broken by war, it also served as a place of economic stability. With the breadwinner gone to war, wives and children frequently boarded with their extended family. This scenario presented potential difficulties if a father exerted greater authority over those domiciled in his home than an absent husband thought necessary. Henry Ankeny's wife and infant son Josie left their home in Iowa and lodged with Henry's father Joseph in Ohio. When his wife desired to return to Iowa before the winter of 1862, Henry permitted her to do as she thought best. However, he underscored how difficult and "lonesome" it would be keeping house by herself. In the end, though, Joseph Ankeny intervened and made the decision for her. When Henry learned "that Father will not let Josey go west this winter," he made no argument on his wife's behalf. Furthermore, Henry placed his father in charge of important financial matters during his absence. Although he sent his wife money for immediate expenses, he forwarded a portion of his salary to his father to invest and earn interest. While married soldiers might have considered it appropriate to rely on their fathers to help provide for their wife and children during the war, unmarried soldiers often sought to alleviate the increased workload of family members remaining at home. With three sons in the service, the Alford family lost three farm laborers, and Warren feared that his father might overwork himself. Demonstrating genuine filial concern, he offered to send money in case the family might be struggling financially and assured his father that asking for assistance was no disgrace. Indeed, Christian duty demanded that they not only encourage each other spiritually but help meet their physical needs as well.³⁵

Even after acquitting themselves like men in battle, unmarried soldiers often found themselves struggling to establish their own independence upon reentering civilian life. Returning to Wabash College in the autumn of 1864, Ransom Hawley discovered how little his relationship with his father had changed. Almost immediately, the elder Hawley reasserted his fatherly authority, especially regarding his son's finances and activities. Somewhat perturbed that Ransom had spent thirty-three dollars in two weeks, father Hawley wondered if he needed to journey to Crawfordsville to check on his son. "I presume you can & will give us an explanation," he admonished gently. Although he sincerely desired for Ransom to have the things he needed to be comfortable while away from home, he stipulated that the family's finances "require strict economy." From all appearances, Ransom convincingly justified his expenditures, possibly reminding his father that he had earned his own pay in the army. In less than three weeks, the elder Hawley practically gave his son carte blanche to secure "as much [money] as you need" from a family friend in Crawfordsville providing that he kept receipts and notified him of the sums. By effectively explaining his actions, Ransom secured a measure of personal autonomy without usurping his father's patriarchal prerogatives.[36]

Notwithstanding this small victory, Ransom still hesitated to spurn his father's personal advice. After learning that his son desired to travel to Indianapolis to view the body of Lincoln when the presidential funeral procession stopped in the state capital, father Hawley made clear his reservations without strictly forbidding such a trip. First, he doubted that the casket would be open for rank-and-file citizens to see the corpse, and, more seriously, he feared that the throng of people gathered for the occasion likely would include a criminal element, making it dangerous to "life, limbs, morals, [and] money." Furthermore, he completely opposed journeying on Sunday. Even if the trip could be made on Saturday, subsequent events might "hardly comport with the proper observance of the Lords day." While he ultimately gave Ransom the freedom to do as he pleased, the elder Hawley plainly revealed his displeasure over a seemingly harmless, patriotic outing to pay respects to the fallen president. In case his fatherly advice might prove less than compelling, he closed by appealing to his son's sympathy for his mother by adding, "Your Ma does not wish you to go."[37] Although the evidence is inconclusive, it seems most likely that Ransom stayed at Wabash.

A father's counsel might have seemed overbearing to some sons and sometimes crossed the line between appropriate instruction and meddling. But in the end, such patriarchs merely sought to fulfill their responsibility to guide sons into the ranks of Christian manhood. Knowing that the task was complete proved immeasurably gratifying. An acquaintance of Franklin Alford informed him that a member of the 14th Indiana home on furlough had testified that Warren was "more respected" than any other soldier in the regiment because he always strived to help his fellow man and spoke graciously to all persons he met. "You cannot over estimate the satisfaction...[this report] gives me," Franklin commended his eldest son. Yet more important than becoming well-respected among peers and receiving worldly praise, youths embarking on their own course in life needed to demonstrate Christian virtues in order to complete the transition to manhood. Shortly after his son arrived in Virginia in the summer of 1861, Franklin expressed his delight in learning that Warren was endeavoring to live as a Christian while in the army. "There is nothing that you could have done that would have given us half the comfort tha[n] did your remarks relative to your spiritual health," he related.[38] Although he would have refused any personal credit for his son's maturation into Christian manhood and given all praise to God, Franklin Alford knew he had performed his fatherly duties by raising a soldier for God and country.

6

"Discord Sown among Brethren"

The Appropriation of Scripture, Politicized Religion, and Church Division

The euphoria elicited by battlefield successes in late summer 1863 could not resolve the theological disputes that the war had intensified. The Bible, regarded by many Americans as the authoritative book of God's words and will whose plain message could be understood by even the most unsophisticated observer, remained at the center of the controversy. Despite this purported simplicity and transparency of interpretation, Scripture served as a means both to defend and condemn slavery, and disagreements over the meaning of Christ's teachings and a Christian's relationship to government resulted in the Bible's exploitation as a divisive political weapon. Few religionists, however, seemed to recognize that the politicization of Scripture undermined its spiritual authority. Even fewer mourned the attenuation of Christian unity that led to new church movements in Ohio and Illinois beginning in late 1863. Because the majority of Northerners held firmly to their belief in the sacred nature of the Union and the divine mission that awaited a United States cleansed of slavery, they could never interpret the war as anything but a religious contest. This inability to overcome the traditions of common sense moral reasoning inherited from the Enlightenment, the covenantal basis of American society passed down from the Puritans, and postmillennial expectations fueled by nineteenth-century revivalism sealed the alliance between religion and politics for the duration of the war.

A handful of religious leaders discerned that the church was suffering from some malady yet felt powerless to diagnose the cause of the affliction or to prescribe a suitable remedy. At its annual meeting in late August, the New School Presbytery of Crawfordsville, Indiana, admitted that "the past year has not been one of marked religious interest in any of our churches." Although attendance had remained steady, "no general awakenings, nor excessive outpourings of the Holy Spirit" had revitalized believers. The presbyters realized that war had occupied the people's attention to a great degree, yet they did not feel comfortable blaming citizens for fulfilling their "specific duty of patriotism to the country." Yet at the same time, the unusual interest in current events detracted from the "more active vital spirituality" that elders yearned to see in their members. Despite their inkling that this observable spiritual apathy related in some way to the military contest and the associated preoccupation with politics, the delegates, in keeping with custom, selected a committee to analyze the state of the country. This body asserted that the war to preserve the Union was "a righteous cause" and condemned church members who complained about political sermons when ministers discoursed on loyalty to the government. Unable to refrain from commenting on political matters themselves, these ruling elders contributed to their predicament by sanctifying the war.[1]

In September 1863, Old School Presbyterians in Vincennes, Indiana, addressed a similar plight at their annual meeting. The previous year, they had resolved to "disown and reprobate" the vote of their lay delegate to the General Assembly because he had opposed the declaration on the state of the country that, among other things, had denounced the rebellion as sinful and urged the suppression of any dissent within the church. Furthermore, denominational leaders had blacklisted Stuart Robinson's *True Presbyterian*, the Louisville publication that contended for the spirituality of the church. Asserting that the paper merely tried to hide behind this claim of neutrality while in reality promoting a pro-southern agenda, the assembled ministers affirmed their responsibility "to teach christian patriotism." Having established this precedent of outspoken Unionism in 1862, the elders now questioned the wisdom of encouraging such unbridled patriotism, for it seemed to detract from more weighty matters of spiritual import. These Presbyterians in southwestern Indiana now sought to avoid both extreme positions by recovering the middle ground on which church members would support the government but devote their primary attention to the gospel and pursuit of Christ's kingdom.[2]

In some cases, church leaders had due cause to fret over diminished interest in religious matters, but evidence also confirms that some laypersons continued to use the Bible to make sense of the war. Rather than finding satisfactory answers in public speeches or editorial opinions, these individuals appropriated scriptural phrases and principles to help explain a mixed-up world that seemed unendurable without the aid of Holy Writ. Complaining to soldier Edward Ingraham about vocal Copperhead cowards near her home in Princeville, Illinois, Mary Robinson was mystified that this "synagogue of satan" could spout off its venomous calumnies against the government for which her own son had given his life to preserve. Nevertheless, like the Apostle Paul when opposed by the wicked schemes of Alexander the coppersmith as recorded in 2 Timothy 4:14, she could wait for the future judgment when "the lord will reward them according to their deeds." In the meantime, national prospects looked bleak from her vantage point. The spark of slavery that the Founders had ignored in order to get the southern states to join the Union had grown into a raging inferno that had caused the war. This harmful influence of slavery reminded her of the incalculable power of the tongue to do evil, something that James described in the third chapter of his epistle with the phrase, "Behold what a great matter a little fire kindleth." Sounding like a Jewish prophet herself, Robinson lamented, "Wickedness sits in high places, [and] abomination is spread all over the land." God, however, had promised to "receive" those repentant wanderers who forsook their iniquities. Turning to God, as Isaiah had stipulated in the fifty-eighth chapter of his prophecy, encompassed more than putting on an insincere, superficial show of devotion through fasts and religious observances. God required genuine repentance that manifested itself in changed actions, specifically "that ye break the bands of the oppressed and let them go free." She doubted that the nation could overcome its hypocritical past and heed this divine instruction. "I believe that slavery will exist until the end of time, when the savior will come the second time without sin unto salvation." Christ's incarnation had enabled him to pay the penalty for sin through his death, the writer of Hebrews pointed out in the last verse of the ninth chapter, but his second coming would complete the work of salvation by eradicating the presence of sin entirely. Robinson anticipated that Christ would not only exterminate slavery at his next appearance but also take "vengence on them that obey not the gospel of our lord jesus Christ." This phrase from 2 Thessalonians 1:8 somewhat eased her frustration over the seeming prosperity of the degenerate during their sojourn on earth, for eventually they would receive their due recompense, not because they had rejected the gospel as the text stipulated, but because they had opposed the war and black freedom. Despite her overall pessimism regarding the prospects for improved conditions on earth before the millennium, she encouraged Ingraham to keep himself unpolluted by separating from evil. "Touch not, taste not, handle not," she quoted from Paul's letter to the Colossians, completely disregarding the circumstances that prompted the apostle to deprecate this erroneous philosophy of ascetics who were attempting to measure a person's spirituality by outward conformity to man-made rules. Altogether, Robinson cited six different verses in one letter, creatively manipulating most of them to apply to the war, slavery, and Copperhead agitation. Weighed down by grief and disconcerted by the injustices of life, she looked to Scripture to provide hope that all things eventually would be made right.³

In addition to possessing principles and promises that, when extracted from their context, could be twisted to bear upon the war, the Bible also served as an authoritative source that families divided over the war's meaning could cite when attempting to substantiate contested viewpoints. Forty-eight-year-old David Demaree, the eldest of eight brothers raised in Kentucky, had lived in Indiana and Illinois since the late 1830s, and this long residency in the North caused his brother George Whitefield Demaree to hesitate writing for fear that David had become "a deciple of 'blood and thunder.'" Far from being a radical abolitionist, the lifelong Democrat nevertheless remained supportive of the government. When he found reason to doubt his brother's loyalty, David pointed him to Romans 13:1, which enjoined Christians to submit to civil authorities as established by God. George Whitefield had suggested that those who governed in Washington might be "the powers of Satan" and therefore undeserving of a Christian's allegiance. David countered by appealing to the context of the times in which Paul had written his epistle, for the apostle had commanded obedience to none other than the bloodthirsty Nero, who later had him martyred. Obeying laws enacted by corrupt rulers in no way implied personal consent to their policies, David reminded his brother, for in the end God would punish all evildoers.⁴ David Demaree ultimately hoped to avoid familial discord and appealed to the Bible to discredit rebellion and promote loyalty rather than basing his argument on a weaker foundation.

Regardless of the validity of their exegesis, laypersons who cited Scripture in private correspondence demonstrated their sincere belief that the Bible could make the war more comprehensible. Public invocation of the Word, in contrast, typically resulted in Scripture being bandied about for the primary purpose of making political grist. Dr. Edson Olds illustrated the latter case when he withdrew from the Methodist church in Lancaster, Ohio, over the preaching and publication of a political sermon by C. A. Van Anda. In a letter published by the *Newark Advocate*, the disgruntled state representative marshaled scriptural evidence in an effort to disprove his former minister's assertion that he had discussed political matters in accordance with "'the example and...command of Christ and his apostles.'" Flabbergasted by this claim, Olds responded that he had read the Gospels several times and found no such injunction. On the contrary, Matthew had recorded the Great Commission as Christ's final earthly directive to his disciples: "'*Go into all the world and preach the GOSPEL to every creature.*'" Although he began on solid biblical footing, Olds quickly yielded to the temptation to interject his own interpretation on what that gospel entailed. Quoting Luke's account of Jesus' birth, he emphasized the angel's announcement to the shepherds of "'*good tidings of great joy*'" and the subsequent chanting of the heavenly host with the sublime refrain, "'Glory to God in the highest, and on earth *Peace and good will* towards men.'" According to Olds, the gospel that Christ commanded to be preached throughout the world was the simple message of peace in contradistinction to the abolitionist gospel of war. The doctor, however, failed to see the meaninglessness of the message of peace apart from the person and work of the Messiah, who had come to earth to provide spiritual peace through the forgiveness of sins.

Convinced that he had accurately defined the gospel and exposed Van Anda's neglect of the Great Commission, Olds tackled the cleric's scriptural argument for bringing politics into the pulpit, which the parson had justified with Christ's enigmatic saying, "'Render unto Caesar the things that are Caesar's, and unto God the things that are God's.'" Like a sound biblical exegete, the politician examined the statement within its context, correctly noting that Jewish religious leaders had sought to trick Christ into making a treasonous remark against Rome so that he could be put to death. Far from endorsing political preaching, he frustrated their scheme and refrained from criticizing the Roman regime despised by most Jews. Having interpreted the passage better than his former pastor, Olds made a blatantly political application by comparing the incident to the arrest of Clement Vallandigham. "The Burnsides of that day surrounded our Lord with spies and provost marshals" who, in the words of Luke, sought to "deliver him unto the power and authority of the Governor." But when Pilate questioned him about his kingly claims, Christ explained that he had not come to establish an earthly kingdom at that time. Likewise, Olds insisted, true followers of the Savior would imitate this example and refrain from meddling in politics. Either Van Anda should "wear the image of Abraham Lincoln" and leave the ministry or "wear the image of Christ...[and] eschew political preaching," for Jesus plainly taught that "no man can serve two masters."[5] Yet when invoking this phrase from the Sermon on the Mount, Olds failed to see the blatant incongruity of his position. According to his arbitrary standard, Democratic politicians could interpret Scripture publicly without betraying a conflict of interests, but ministers who commented on political matters in church served the Republican party rather than God.

The mingling of religion and politics was so ubiquitous by the fall of 1863 that a ludicrous caricature of an uneducated Democrat who took up political preaching was about to become a favorite political satire read by Republicans throughout the North and enjoyed especially by Lincoln. Petroleum Vesuvius Nasby, the creation of Ohio newspaper editor David Ross Locke, first appeared in the *Hancock Jeffersonian* on April 25, 1862, and went on to gain national prominence with the publication of *The Nasby Papers* in pamphlet form in 1864. In one of his earliest appearances, the oft-inebriated loafer made himself pastor of "the first Dimekratic Church uv Ohio" in order to counteract the dangerous influences of Republican institutions in the fictitious community of Wingert's Corner. The church's political philosophy came out clearly in Nasby's limited sermon material, which comprised Genesis 9, "the cussin ov Canaan, provin that niggers is Skriptoorally slaves, and the chapters about Hayger and Onesimus, which proves the Fugitive Slave Law to be skriptooral." Nasby's admission that he regarded the remainder of Scripture to be "figgerative" and therefore extraneous enabled Locke to portray Democratic supporters as spiritual frauds who only used religion to justify slavery. By the summer of 1863, the partisan assembly had been christened the "Church ov St. Vanlandigum," and Nasby discoursed passionately on the violation of his "martered" hero's rights by the "tyrant Linkin." When eighteen young men, none of whom could write their names, came forward to join the church, they affirmed its confession of faith, which included the gospel message "that Vallandigum wuz sent in2 the world to save the Dimocratic party; that in doin it he wuz arestid at Dayton, tride afore Ponteus Burnside, and sent sowth; that after 3 months he riz agen in Canydy, whense he shel cum ez soon ez hese electid." Even after Vallandigham's defeat at the polls in October 1863, Nasby continued to find biblical justifications for ending the war by pacifying the South. Expounding on the parable of "the prodygal sun" in early 1864, he equated the forgiving father with "Uncle Samyooel," the prodigal with southern Democrats, and the elder son with spiteful "Abolishnists." As the loving father joyfully received his wayward son and celebrated his return home despite protestations by his firstborn, so the government needed to embrace the rebellious southern states, ignore the ravings of abolitionists, and let the South rule once more. Only then would loyal members of the Democracy be rewarded again with cushy post office jobs and escape "the cuss uv labor." Nasby's career spanned several decades of entertaining political satire, but his early role as a Democratic political preacher highlighted the politicization of the church and the Bible that plagued the North during the Civil War.[6]

Hancock County's religious disputes were real enough, and without Nasby's outrageous persona and outlandish sermons to provide comic relief, the cutting allegations and palpable animosity in that area demonstrated a lamentable lack of brotherly love among church members of differing political persuasions. Shortly after the fast observance on August 6, 1863, the Democratic *Hancock Courier*, a weekly publication edited by Lewis Glessner and his son Will, reported that the service at the Methodist church in Findlay on that occasion smacked of a political rally, for the minister gave "a violent partisan harangue" that the congregation greeted with exuberant shouts of approval. Although Glessner directed this barb at Presbyterian J. A. Meeks, the speaker at this interdenominational gathering, fellow minister John S. Kalb took umbrage at what he regarded as a malicious misrepresentation of the incident at his church and fired off a letter to the *Courier* on August 17. When the next edition of the paper came out without printing his rebuttal, he contacted Glessner's rival David Ross Locke, who, in the midst of running a six-part series of letters by an anonymous clergyman defending political preaching, placed it in the *Jeffersonian* without editorial comment the following week. For whatever reason, Will Glessner, as editor of local matters, decided to reproduce the letter with a refutation of its arguments that same week, so Kalb's epistle appeared in both city papers on August 28. In his letter, the irritated Methodist pastor asserted that "more than nine-tenths" of those in attendance at the fast day meeting would vouch that the sermon had nothing to do with politics, for no specific party had been commended or berated. Only one of Meeks's comments had drawn a noticeable response, which consisted of nothing more than "a few persons stamping their canes on the floor" in an appropriate display of agreement. Furthermore, Kalb accused Glessner of making blanket allegations against so-called "political priests" despite having never personally heard these men preach. He therefore challenged the young newspaperman to identify the name, date, and location when any local pastor had supported a specific party or candidate in church.[7]

Without yielding an inch of ground, Will Glessner defended his earlier rendering of the meeting at the Methodist church. He had based his report on reputable witnesses who held membership in Kalb's assembly, evidently that insignificant fraction of listeners whom the pastor brushed off as unreliable observers. Furthermore, Glessner defended himself from the charge of religious indifference, for he regularly attended a local church and would not leave his preferred house of worship to verify personally the political pronouncements of other ministers. Finally, since Kalb had insisted that Glessner specifically identify those preachers guilty of besmirching the pulpit with politics, the obliging editor unabashedly indicted Kalb as the chief offender. At the Union prayer meeting held in late July at the Lutheran church, he had lambasted all citizens who disapproved of Republican war policy, slandering them as "infidels and frequenters of beer shops." He then followed up this reprehensible effort with a sermon at his own church entitled "National Affairs." Glessner claimed that only a sense of public duty motivated him to expose "clerical demagogues" such as Kalb, and he hoped that the removal of such "excresences upon the religious body" would lead to a genuine revival throughout the churches. In order to strengthen his position, he closed by quoting Edmund Burke, whose opinion had become a favorite of Democratic editors. "Politics and the pulpit are terms that have little agreement," the English political theorist had written nearly a century earlier. "*No sound ought to be heard in the church but the voice of healing charity*.... Surely the church is a place where one days truce ought to be allowed to the dissensions and animosities of mankind."⁸

Infuriated further by Glessner's attack on the legitimacy of his ministry, Kalb fired back another letter to the editor, who refused to print this rejoinder verbatim, citing lack of space. Nevertheless, Glessner devoted over a column to discrediting Kalb's position. As was often the case in public disputes over the proper relationship between religion and politics, both men invoked Scripture to disarm their critics. The pastor cited the three primary New Testament passages about obedience to civil authorities—Romans 13:1–7, Titus 3:1–2, and 1 Peter 2:13–14—as defense for his preaching on topics that Glessner alleged to be political in nature. The editor countered with two biblical selections culled to condemn Kalb for promulgating his personal preferences rather than the gospel. In 1 Corinthians 2:1–5, Paul reminded the church at Corinth that he had not employed "enticing words of man's wisdom" but had proclaimed nothing but the unadulterated message of the crucified Christ. Then in 1 Timothy 6:1–5, the apostle added that any person who contradicted Christ's teachings was "proud, knowing nothing." Having done his best to use Scripture to portray Kalb as a clerical fraud, Glessner affirmed his willingness to end the dispute. However, the fruitless exchange continued for two more weeks without either party admitting that the other might have raised a valid point concerning the proper duties of ministers in relation to contemporary matters of political importance.⁹

Unlike other newspaper editors who were more interested in exploiting religious-related squabbles for political advantage, the Glessners, from all appearances, exhibited a genuine desire to see the cause of Christianity furthered. In the midst of the controversy with Kalb, one of them authored a brief piece entitled "A Sermon to Preachers" imploring them to remain true to their spiritual callings. Reminding ministers that support of a political party had no eternal significance when compared to the worth of a soul, the writer urged them to "seek to save" the lost, including Democrats. Even if the Republican party represented righteousness and all Democrats were no better than rank sinners, clerics needed to remember that Christ had come to bring sinners to repentance. The Glessners' genuine interest in the souls of men, however, led them to a position similar to that of many Southerners who used the Bible to defend slavery. Indeed, in employing 1 Timothy 6 to denounce Kalb, Will Glessner had extracted a phrase from a passage in which Paul had enjoined believing servants to honor their masters. Since the apostle had not required Christian masters to emancipate their slave brethren, some commentators capitalized on Paul's silence by claiming that slavery was a spiritually beneficial institution when both parties followed the scriptural injunctions regulating its practice. Only two weeks after the verbal hostilities with Kalb had ceased, the *Courier* lambasted Presbyterian J. A. Meeks for a Sunday sermon that condemned slavery and justified the administration's emancipation policy. The minister had described slavery as a barrier to the gospel, but Glessner asserted that more blacks had been converted as slaves in America than through missionary endeavors in Africa, demonstrating to his satisfaction that Christians should support the institution because of this potential for evangelism.[10] The Glessners, like many proslavery southern Christians, did not conclude that any good that might have resulted from the institution of slavery came about in spite of the inherent evils of the system. They and other well-meaning but misguided observers credited the merits of slavery instead of positing that an omnipotent God could overrule man's sinful actions in enslaving other human beings by giving spiritual freedom to some who lived in physical bondage.

Most antislavery Christians failed to exploit this theological weakness in the armor of proslavery thought. In fact, historians have been hard pressed to find evidence of abolitionists who could demonstrate conclusively that Scripture condemned slavery as sinful. Lacking such authoritative backing, they could never convince proslavery apologists, who had a well-developed biblical justification for slavery, to abandon their position. When Christians appealed to the spirit of Christianity rather than Scripture itself as their primary rationale for opposing slavery, they became vulnerable to the charge that the Bible no longer mattered as the sole basis for faith and practice. Even the secular press recognized this as a compromise that undermined the authority of the Word and rebuked those abolitionists who had distorted the Bible or ignored it altogether in order to support an antislavery position. After the *Western Christian Advocate* argued that God's sanctioning slavery in the Jewish dispensation did not automatically mean that it had gained divine approval throughout the rest of history, the editor of the *Cincinnati Enquirer* grilled the denominational weekly for presumptuously assuming that God had altered his will regarding slavery without specifically revealing such a modification in the New Testament.[11] As a Democrat, the editor of the *Enquirer* may have been motivated in part by political considerations, but he nonetheless exposed a glaring weakness of those Christians who could not reconcile emancipation with a literal reading of the Bible.

Since no honest interpreter of Scripture could deny that God had allowed slavery to exist, the burden fell on antislavery Christians to show how the specific conditions of southern slavery violated the Bible, thereby rendering the institution worthy of eradication. R. H. Bolton of Findlay, Ohio, an itinerant pastor who ministered to Church of God assemblies throughout the western part of Ohio and southern Michigan, decided to outline a scriptural argument against slavery because of his frustration at finding a sizable number of "misled brethren and sisters" in his denomination who believed slavery to be ordained of God. Hoping to persuade the uninformed and unenlightened, he dashed off a letter to the denomination's weekly paper that admittedly contained "some thoughts promiscuously [thrown] together." At times this haste showed in his lack of thorough analysis, for he cited a few favorable Old Testament passages where the prophets prohibited the taking of war captives but ignored problematic verses that described the Mosaic system of servitude. Furthermore, he claimed that Christ never encountered a slave during his life in Roman-controlled Palestine, an embarrassingly inaccurate statement, and therefore had no reason to condemn it. Weaknesses aside, Bolton referenced the verse that probably did more to discredit slavery than any other. When speaking to Athenians on Mars' Hill, Paul had asserted that God "made of one blood all nations of men for to dwell on all the face of the earth" (Acts 17:26). The unity of the human race completely undermined racial slavery as practiced in the American South, for race never figured into the equation as a justification for servitude in Old Testament times. Although he did not directly emphasize black equality, possibly for fear of alienating too many readers, Bolton marshaled scriptural evidence that undercut the idea of racial superiority that served as the basis for southern slavery.[12]

Unfortunately, many religious Northerners were still unwilling to stomach the idea of racial equality and embrace blacks as their neighbors and coreligionists. Cincinnati's *Catholic Telegraph* made this position entirely clear in a series of editorials intended to reassure its readers that the emancipation of African-Americans ultimately would benefit the Catholic laboring class. Editor Edward Purcell underscored that slavery limited the opportunities of working-class whites and the growth of Catholicism in the South. The paper's support of emancipation, therefore, was both qualified and conditioned by ulterior motives. "Our hostility to the restoration of slavery is not so much for the emancipation of the blacks as for the social elevation and independence of our white brethren," Purcell frankly maintained. Repeating arguments made by his counterpart at the *Western Christian Advocate* in October 1862, the Catholic editor claimed that freedmen would remain in the South rather than compete with white laborers for jobs in the North. Although personally favoring the separation of the races, he had no qualms about blacks and whites laboring side by side, for the interaction would demonstrate "the natural superiority of the white race." In sum, eliminating slavery and breaking up southern plantations would elevate working-class whites by leveling the social and economic playing fields. To be sure, Purcell conceded, all men regardless of skin color "are equal in the sight of God," but the unity of the human race did not presuppose intellectual or political equality. Nearly 55,000 in number, Cincinnati Catholics could embrace emancipation, confident that the eradication of a moral evil would not produce unwanted social and economic ills.[13]

Oftentimes, even well-meaning gestures of sympathy toward blacks, while likely beneficial and appreciated, lacked a genuine sense of empathy for needy people. At their annual meeting in late September 1863, Methodists in northwestern Indiana pledged to assist the state's Freedmen's Aid Commission and affirmed their intention to send a missionary to work among freedmen in the South while simultaneously supporting colonization in Liberia. Lending aid to blacks who remained down South or left for distant Africa may have left a warm feeling inside, but reaching out to black refugees who lived nearby would have demonstrated genuine care by forging a relationship with disadvantaged persons in the community. Most freedmen, born and raised in America, had no desire to leave its shores and sought nothing more than the opportunity to start a new life in their native land. At Camp Delaware in Ohio, where African-American troops trained for combat, a correspondent for an eastern religious periodical overheard a black female delivering a rousing speech to the soldiers. Exhorting them to demonstrate their manhood by fighting bravely for the preservation of the Union and the destruction of slavery, she praised God "that, at last, I can say I have a country, and brothers able and willing to defend it!"[14]

In the autumn of 1863, most white Northerners cared more about the outcome of state and local elections than addressing problems of race. Clement Vallandigham was arguably the most polarizing figure in the North, and his success or failure as a gubernatorial candidate in Ohio would indicate how citizens felt about continuing to prosecute the war through 1864. After the former congressman's arrest in Dayton in May and conviction before a military tribunal for uttering treasonous statements, President Lincoln banished him to the South, only to have Jefferson Davis refuse to grant him asylum. A man without a country, Vallandigham nonetheless gained enough sympathy from Peace Democrats to earn the party's nomination for governor. Running his campaign from Canada, the political lightning rod was ably represented on the stump by George E. Pugh, a fine public speaker and candidate for lieutenant governor, and was heartily defended by a host of Democratic editors. His supporters unabashedly sang his praises and risked the derision of their peers, his detractors took every opportunity to denigrate his name, and numerous families suffered strained relations because of his candidacy. A woman in Painesville, Ohio, showed "the most perfect contempt" for her uncle because he was "a *know nothing Vallandingham Copperhead*," and she anticipated the day when she could witness "some soldier tackle him." Although a few enlisted men wrote approving letters to their local papers, most Union soldiers utterly loathed the man and anyone who dared vote for him. A letter to the *Hardin County (Ohio) Republican* contained a resolution signed by fifty-nine members of the 54th Ohio that threatened Vallandigham supporters with future judgment if they persisted in their error. "There is not a man in the army—except...perhaps one in a hundred, black-hearted traitors like yourselves—but hates your course as he does Satan, and is ready to sweep you from the face of the earth as soon as we get through [with] your more honorable allies." Echoing a latter-day Jewish prophet, the soldiers urged the county's Copperheads "to repent while it is called today" or suffer "the vengeance of an abused and offended army."[15]

Not to be outdone by soldiers, many ministers and churches matched or exceeded them in directing virulent rhetoric against Vallandigham and his followers. At a statewide gathering of the United Brethren in Christ, denominational leaders resolved that anyone who voted for the exiled Democrat had forfeited the right to be called a patriot, a Christian, and even a man. After exhorting his brethren to exercise their God-given right to the franchise in an enlightened nation that did not discriminate based on religious affiliation, a member of the Church of God insisted that those who supported "a condemned and banished rebel" would "bear the mark of Cain and share the character and fate of Judas." In contrast, men who backed a loyal candidate discharged their civic duty in a way that glorified God. Preferring action to verbal intimidation, delegates to the presbytery of the United Presbyterian church hinted that church members who cast a ballot for Vallandigham might find themselves removed from fellowship. After reading about the dubious proceedings, one unruffled Presbyterian felt confident that several members would vote a straight Democratic ticket and dare the ruling elders to make good on their threat. While some churches attempted to regulate the political leanings of laymen, others clamped down on ministers suspected of holding Democratic sympathies. At least one preacher who had labored faithfully for twenty-five years in the United Brethren church had his license revoked for endorsing Vallandigham, and several other United Brethren ministers from western Ohio were defrocked for allegedly supporting slavery and the rebellion. Methodist leaders in Auglaize County, Ohio, likewise confiscated the licenses of several pastors after questioning revealed their intention to vote for Vallandigham.[16] The vehement persecution of Peace Democrats in the months prior to the Ohio gubernatorial campaign proved that many churches had come to regard outspoken support for the war as a test for fellowship. By making Unionism and abolitionism essential tenets of religious orthodoxy, Republican ministers intentionally ostracized church members who questioned the wisdom of fusing religion and politics or who invoked the right of freedom of conscience in matters not essential to biblical doctrine.

After the ballots had been tallied, Republican John Brough carried Ohio by more than one hundred thousand votes and would have won handily even without adding the soldier vote. Although some observers might claim that the ecclesiastical campaign against Vallandigham had proven extremely effective in contributing to Democratic defeat, it is more likely that ministers needlessly alienated a portion of their congregations by making much ado about a candidate who had little chance of winning. Nevertheless, Unionists throughout the North interpreted the result as an indication of providential favor that a significant political setback had been avoided. "It is something to rejoice over and thank God for," Iowan Mary Vermilion affirmed with much relief, for "a more terrible calamity could scarcely befall our country than Vallandigham's election." The *Milwaukee Daily Sentinel* called for "a general Jubilee of thanksgiving" throughout the North because Ohio Unionists had crushed Copperhead traitors who sought to derail the war. William Patrick believed that the merciful "interposition of... providence" demonstrated by "the unexpected strength of the citizens vote" had prevented Ohio from erupting in "civil revolution." According to one undocumented story, even President Lincoln could not hide his elation upon learning of the crucial Republican victory. "Glory to God in the highest; Ohio has saved the Union," he reportedly wired Ohio governor David Tod. The day after the election, a chaplain in Columbus led a throng gathered outside the offices of the *Ohio State Journal* in a spontaneous rendition of the doxology, a poignant scene which one witness viewed as proof that the grateful electorate "recognize[d] the hand of God" in the propitious outcome. In addition to paeans of thanksgiving, at least one malicious editor called for permanent ostracism of all Democratic leaders who influenced Ohioans to vote for Vallandigham. Just as Scripture spoke of the unpardonable sin, a transgression against the Holy Ghost, likewise treason should be considered the unforgiveable political offense. The editor called for a veritable mark of Cain to be stamped on the heads of these "northern traitors," a stigma representing "the blood of our murdered soldiers" that would extend even to several generations of innocent offspring so that posterity would cringe at the heinous sight of treason.[17]

As to be expected, most Democrats reluctantly swallowed this bitter pill of electoral defeat. One disappointed Iowan concluded that Vallandigham's trouncing signaled that the war would continue "until we have been much more severely punished *for our sins.*" The resourceful editor of the *Cincinnati Enquirer*, in contrast, attempted to soften the blow and rally the party faithful by labeling the Republican victory "an immaterial and fleeting triumph." Intentionally ignoring present realities in order to indulge his political fantasies, the editor received consolation from his belief that "a just and beneficent Providence" would not always permit the forces of tyranny to prevail against "the friends of civil liberty" but would someday enable the Democracy to rise again. One Democratic editor in Holmes County sought to insult Republicans by likening his party's defeat to the biblical parable of the beggar

Lazarus, who survived the ignominy of being *"licked* by the dogs." Seemingly more familiar with the story than his Democratic counterpart, the quick-witted editor of the *Toledo Blade* wondered if defeated Copperheads, like the dying Lazarus, would find refuge "in ABRAHAM's bosom."[18]

While many of these religious responses come as little surprise, it is especially noteworthy that the fallout after Vallandigham's defeat engulfed even the Catholic leadership of Cincinnati. Because the Catholic church had not divided geographically over slavery or the war like the major Protestant denominations had, it gained a reputation for institutional silence concerning matters that could prove politically entangling. Although this description is generally true, many individuals within the church demonstrated their personal Unionism through public speeches at secular venues or by volunteering with organizations that supported the war. As religious, cultural, and, oftentimes, ethnic outsiders, many Catholics viewed the conflict as an opportunity to prove that they were as American as their Protestant counterparts. In the days after the election, Archbishop John Purcell and Bishop Sylvester Rosencrans, brother of General William S. Rosencrans, received numerous complaints from local Catholics and drew the ire of the *Chicago Times* and *Dubuque Herald* for voting for Brough and severing the Catholic church's traditional ties with the Democratic party. According to one rumor which Purcell denied, the two men had disgraced their offices by working the polls on Election Day in an effort to convince Catholic Democrats to reject Vallandigham. The editor of the *Cincinnati Enquirer* did not quibble over their right to vote according to the dictates of conscience, but he charged the prelates with converting the archdiocese's periodical, the *Catholic Telegraph*, into an abolitionist organ and jeopardizing ecclesiastical unity for a political dalliance. In a speech at Cincinnati's Mozart Hall nearly three weeks after the election, Archbishop Purcell vigorously defended himself and Bishop Rosencrans and contended that they were accountable to God alone for how they had discharged their civic duties. Furthermore, he claimed that the Catholic church had always stood for freedom, and his longing to see all men possess physical liberty paralleled Christ's mission to make man free spiritually.[19] Like the Protestant majority, Purcell believed that spiritual principles underlay the political issues of the day; therefore, his open support of a Republican candidate and public opposition to slavery in no way compromised his religious authority.

While concerned citizens devoted their energies to influencing the outcome of state and local elections, their thoughts often remained with the armies in the field. In September, fierce fighting at Chickamauga, Tennessee, had resulted in over sixteen thousand Federal casualties and the retreat of the defeated Army of the Cumberland to Chattanooga. In Charleston Harbor, Union guns rained shells on Fort Sumter for several consecutive days in late

October and again in mid-November, yet the Confederate stronghold stood firm. The ubiquity of death prompted W. S. Lankford, an African-American from Lafayette, Indiana, to recall the biblical description of Herod's murdering the male children around Bethlehem shortly after the birth of Christ. Quoting the prophet Jeremiah, Matthew had written, "'In Rama was there a voice heard, lamentations and great mourning. Rachel weeping for her children, and would not be comforted, because they were not.'" Lankford's sympathy went out to the many Rachels throughout the country who had lost sons, fathers, and husbands "upon the bloody field of carnage" so that his fellow men might have liberty. Indeed, the northern populace directed its attention to memorializing the dead as the National Cemetery at Gettysburg was consecrated on November 19. Thousands of citizens descended upon the sleepy Pennsylvania town, and scores of dignitaries came to honor the fallen from their states. At least one Ohio editor accused Governor Tod of flagrant prodigality for attending the ceremonies and contended that taxpayers' money would have been better spent by dividing the expense among the state's widows and orphans. Most observers, in contrast, thought it highly fitting that Union troops who fell in that decisive battle should receive a proper burial and due recognition for their noble sacrifice.[20]

The keynote speaker at the dedication, the eminent orator Edward Everett, recounted the battle in meticulous detail, speaking for two hours. A correspondent for the *Daily Cleveland Herald* lauded the discourse as "an invaluable contribution to history" that originated "in the store house mind of a scholar, a historian, a statesman and a patriot." After much applause and the singing of an ode composed for the occasion, President Lincoln delivered a three-minute speech, much of which "carried the rhythms of the Bible." Although few present realized the magnitude of his brief remarks, the president outlined his version of "the American Gospel," the belief that the nation could undergo a spiritual rebirth by implementing the revolutionary idea "that all men are created equal." Future generations would come to consider the Gettysburg Address "the sacred scripture of the Civil War's innermost spiritual meaning," but many contemporaries regarded it as little more than an admirable but unspectacular offering. In the weeks following the ceremony, scores of newspapers published Everett's complete address, and glowing editorials followed from most Republican organs. Lincoln's comments generally garnered less attention. A correspondent for the *Milwaukee Daily Sentinel* reported that Everett had recited a "beautiful" speech "which I have not words to describe," yet the president's utterance was merely "short and very appropriate." Some Democratic editors tore into both men with scathing fury. The *Cincinnati Enquirer* derided Everett's oration as "a collection of disjointed drivel and platitudes; barren in sentiment, poor in argument, and weak in delivery." Lincoln's effort, the editor maintained, had been even worse. He especially took umbrage at the *Western Christian Advocate* for praising the "'perfect gem'" presented by Lincoln. In his opinion, his "clerico-journalistic brethren" at the religious weekly had made the president into an idol and, in their "insanity of dotage," had stooped to the lowest levels of sycophancy in order to gain his attention and approval. Caring neither for Lincoln nor his political supporters, the Democratic paper asserted that the foolish commendation of the president's appalling speech at Gettysburg demonstrated "an abjectness of worship proportioned to the meanness of the divinity."[21]

Although Lincoln avoided overt religious references in the Gettysburg Address, except for the impromptu addition of the phrase "under God," he continued to encourage northern citizens to praise God for blessing the country even in the midst of war's desolation. A proclamation that nationalized the traditional observance of Thanksgiving Day as the last Thursday in November listed several reasons for rejoicing. Peace with European powers had been preserved, population had increased despite battlefield casualties, industry and agriculture had flourished, and, rather disingenuously, domestic relations had remained harmonious "everywhere" except the seat of war. These "gracious gifts of the Most High God" demonstrated his kindness and mercy even while the nation endured chastening for its sins. Newspapers throughout the North devoted much space to reprinting the Thanksgiving Proclamation and editorializing upon it, and pundits lavished more praise on it than Lincoln's short and allegedly unmemorable speech at Gettysburg. Unbeknownst to the public, Secretary of State William Seward had written the Thanksgiving Proclamation, but Lincoln received credit or blame for the sentiments expressed therein. At the annual meeting of the Presbyterian Synod of Michigan, delegates interpreted the proclamation as evidence that "the President of the United States clearly recognizes the national dependence on the will of God" and suggested that churches hold special prayer services. Most civilians appreciated the announcement and encouraged soldiers or absent loved ones to observe the day as best as possible. With the exception of a few disgruntled Democratic editors, the press likewise approved of the opportunity to express gratitude to God and reported that many citizens complied with the spirit and purpose of the holiday. Not surprisingly, the *Cincinnati Enquirer* quibbled with the proclamation and attempted to put a damper on the spirit of solemnity and gratitude. The editor discerned no specific reason for another day of thanksgiving because the army had not won a significant battle since the last special observance in early August. The absence of victory convinced him that a fast would be more appropriate than consuming "turkeys with oyster trimming." Evidently, the editor had not read the proclamation closely, for he incorrectly asserted that it had summoned citizens to assemble in the nation's churches, where political preachers, he derisively assumed, would instruct skeptics like himself concerning the things for which they should give thanks. However, when neither the *Commercial* nor the *Gazette* reported on messages delivered in the Queen City's churches on Thanksgiving Day, he took the liberty to suggest that ministers had lectured on the beatitude, "'Blessed are the peacemakers.'" Listing several applications that clerics might have made from this text, the editor's burlesque of Thanksgiving sermons allowed him to promulgate his antiwar opinions and belittle Cincinnati's ministers, most of whom he considered to be Republican dupes.[22]

Of course, most Thanksgiving Day sermons contained little that the *Enquirer* would endorse. For instance, in his address *God Doing Wonderful Things in Behalf of the Nation*, Illinois Presbyterian Isaac Carey pointed out that the Thanksgiving Proclamation had enumerated only material blessings graciously showered by God, and he contended that none of these benefits was worth the sacrifice of a single soldier's life. Only "the marked *moral* progress of the nation," convincingly demonstrated by emancipation, made the terrible loss of life worthwhile. God alone had been the moving force that enabled "justice and humanity" to triumph through the military might of the Union armies and navies. While Peace Democrats deplored weapons of destruction, Carey exulted in "our gleaming swords and bayonets,... our revolvers,... our seven-shooting rifles,... [and] our cannon" because they were instruments of liberation. With slavery removed, blacks finally could share in the blessings of freedom. "Now the country is the black man's country," Carey reached the climax of his oration. "Henceforth the black man is a man and a brother and a fellow citizen." God had "raised up" the United States to further the causes of liberty and humanity, and it would someday be the agent in ushering in the millennial reign of Christ on earth. In his zeal to sanctify the war as a God-ordained conflict to break the shackles of slavery, Carey portrayed "the principles of justice and liberty" as "living, indestructible powers" that not "even the gates of hell can prevail against."[23] Scripture, however, never recorded such a promise, for Christ had spoken this phrase in reference to the church. By equating the Union war effort with the progress of humanity and making this a religious endeavor, Carey and other prowar ministers ignored the Bible's clear teaching that Christ would accomplish his purposes through the institution of the church and not a particular nation or political party.

Fed up with what they regarded to be the complete politicization of the church, disgruntled clerics and laymen finally took action in the latter months of 1863. The day before Thanksgiving, the *Crisis* of Columbus, Ohio, carried an article about the formation of an "Independent Methodist Church" in Carthage, Illinois. The leader of the movement, Reverend S. A. Hall, envisioned houses of worship that resounded once again with the message of the gospel rather than political manifestos. Within a month of organizing his new church, Hall reported that people were coming forward to join his assembly fifteen to twenty-five at a time. In mid-December, four preachers met in Putnam County, Ohio, and drafted a formal resignation from the United Brethren in Christ denomination. Tired of being "persecuted" by their former ministerial brethren and disgusted by resolutions passed at the last annual meeting withholding fellowship from supporters of Vallandigham, the offended ministers established a separate religious body called the Reformed United Brethren in Christ. Three weeks later, with their ranks increased by three, they created seven circuits in western Ohio where nothing but "Christ and Him crucified" would be preached.[24]

These separations initiated by ministers garnered little attention from the press outside of their immediate vicinities, but a gathering of approximately 125 people at the courthouse in Lancaster, Ohio, on January 14, 1864, demonstrated that the new church movement was gaining notice. Maintaining that the majority of existing churches had lost all spiritual credibility because of rampant political preaching and as a result had diffused "infidelity and atheism" throughout the country, the meeting's organizers invited delegates from across the state to convene in Columbus to discuss the formation of new religious assemblies undefiled by politics. With prominent local Democrats such as state representative Edson Olds and Judge Virgil Shaw leading the proceedings, the meeting had a conspicuous political flavor. One unsympathetic observer considered it a telling sign that a group purportedly interested in starting a church never bothered to offer a prayer or sing a hymn. He concluded that the omission of such traditional religious practices stemmed from the absence of any minister sympathetic to their cause. Even more damning evidence against the true motives of these lay leaders of the new church movement emerged when Judge Shaw confessed that he had not attended church for three years because of the prevalence of political preaching. Of course, one keen spectator pounced on this incriminating admission and asked the judge how he could make such an accusation without having firsthand knowledge of the condition of the churches. With Shaw unable to provide a convincing answer, the crowd became restless, and afterward a correspondent to the *Western Christian Advocate* quipped that the judge's public ramblings were unparalleled in that vicinity "for downright balderdash and silly nonsense." Although it brought attention to the movement, the convocation at Lancaster, with its "malignant, spiteful animus" toward existing churches and ministers, gave most Republicans the impression that a few peevish Democrats merely wanted a church that would cater to their political preferences.[25]

Despite being maligned by the opposition press, the gathering of dissident religionists inspired other disaffected churchgoers around Ohio. In rural Allen County, members of several denominations met in late January, resolved to leave their churches and unite with an assembly undefiled by politics, and selected delegates to attend the convention in Columbus. When that body amassed on February 3, representatives from seventeen counties formed the Christian Union, a new denomination composed of congregations that banned political matters from the church. Prospective members needed only to accept "the received Scriptures of the Old and New Testament as the word of God," the lone doctrinal provision intentionally made broad enough to attract adherents of all Protestant denominations. Almost three years into the war, the creation of the Christian Union offered Ohio Democrats a safe haven from preachers whose open support of the war and forceful condemnations of slavery and Copperheads offended them deeply. As expected, denunciations of the Christian Union abounded, and at least one critic satirized the new sect as possessing demonic endorsement. The editor of the *Cincinnati Daily Commercial* offered the most penetrating critique by noting that organizing a new church proved that either the Democratic party or the northern churches erred on the day's most important issue. If the church had become nothing more than another political club, then Democratic church members acted properly in leaving it and beginning anew. However, if the church had a duty to speak out against the nation's moral deficiencies, even when such transgressions spilled over into politics, then clerics could not remain silent concerning slavery as Democrats insisted. Rather than demonstrating spiritual discernment, those individuals who willfully departed from an institution that endeavored to follow biblical principles by denouncing a moral evil like slavery instead revealed spiritual blindness. Furthermore, the editor contended that no minister could preach the Bible, the Christian Union's only authority for faith and practice, and avoid topics with political bearing unless he limited the sermon "to discussions of antediluvian subjects."[26] Although Ohio's Christian Union, at least in name, sought to bring together believers from all Protestant denominations, it clearly exposed the utter disunity of some northern churches and the inability of church members to tolerate brothers and sisters who differed over politics.

Yet at the same time that ecclesiastical divisions rent some communities, other areas and individual churches reported religious revivals. During the early months of 1864, the pages of the *Church Advocate*, the weekly paper of the Church of God, contained several accounts of conversions and accessions to both established assemblies and pioneer works throughout Ohio and Michigan. One Church of God pastor marveled at the interdenominational unity that was manifested during meetings in Reedsburg, Ohio, as the United Brethren and Lutheran ministers joined in services that produced forty-three professions of faith, twelve baptisms, and twenty-five new members. "The party spirit and sectarian bickering that once prevailed here, thank God has given way to a more generous charity," J. S. McKee reported with great satisfaction. After several weeks of nightly meetings throughout January, the George Street Methodist Protestant Church in Cincinnati had increased its membership by one hundred. The African Methodist Episcopal Church especially experienced growth as contrabands from the South moved north. A majority of members of the A.M.E. congregation in Galesburg, Illinois, had recently come from Missouri and, though economically impoverished and often illiterate, had earned their pastor's respect because of their "willing[ness] to do all they can for the cause of Christ." Feelings of Christian unity and brotherhood prevailed so completely in Terre Haute, Indiana, that white clerics from the local ministerial association invited the pastor of the A.M.E. church to join their weekly fellowship.[27]

Congregational harmony provided an ideal environment for fostering zeal for domestic missions. Churches with financial means often supported missionary preachers to go out and establish new assemblies as westward settlement continued to advance. Newly arrived in Minnesota, a preacher's wife described herself and her husband as being *"truly missionaries"* whom "God has placed...here to work in his vineyard...[so] that we may see sinners brought into the church." Black Christians focused their efforts on ministering to former slaves. An A.M.E. pastor from Chester, Illinois, traveled about fifty miles south to Cape Girardeau, Missouri, and organized a church of forty enthusiastic African-American believers who, prior to this meeting, were not cognizant that blacks had their own denomination. No longer fearful of being "prison-bound by the cruel hands of slaveholders" when setting foot in Missouri, the grateful minister praised God for opening the door to "preach his Gospel to every creature." Many more Northerners looked at the South as a region needing Union-loving ministers to go and teach biblical truths to a people whom disloyal southern divines had led astray. Three orders issued by the War Department in late 1863 had authorized Union generals throughout the South to allow northern bishops to take control of all Methodist Episcopal churches that lacked a loyal pastor. Subsequent directives in early 1864 gave northern Baptists and Presbyterians similar prerogatives over their wayward southern brethren. After arriving in New Orleans in late January and being unceremoniously snubbed by "the secession pastor" of the McGhee Methodist Church, Bishop Edward Ames of Indianapolis took swift action and placed a northern chaplain in the pulpit of each Methodist church in the city. The outraged partisan press accused the Lincoln administration of violating the separation of church and state and alleged that Secretary of War Edwin Stanton would likely become a Protestant pope who would reign over the churches and enforce compliance to his creed that consisted of nothing more than loyalty to the government.[28]

Stanton's orders indeed raised legitimate questions regarding the propriety, prudence, and constitutionality of interfering with southern churches. More than a year earlier, Presbyterian Samuel McPheeters had appealed to President Lincoln after being removed from his St. Louis church because of his alleged Rebel sympathies. After reviewing the case, Lincoln found no conclusive evidence that McPheeters had done anything seditious, but he allowed local authorities, presuming that they possessed superior knowledge of the situation, to decide the preacher's fate. However, he underscored in no uncertain terms that "the United States Government must not...undertake to run the churches" by selecting leaders for specific assemblies. Learning on February 11 of Stanton's independent action granting Bishop Ames control over Methodist churches in the South, Lincoln expressed his "embarrassment" at having his well-documented position on the relationship between church and state contradicted by this decree and asked the secretary of war what he intended to do about it. The latter lost little time in explaining that his circular letter did not apply to churches in loyal states, and the president informed concerned Methodist minister John Hogan of St. Louis that Stanton merely had hoped to revive support for the Union among people who lived in places where the war had disrupted their regular meetings. Countermanding Stanton's ill-conceived mandate with an endorsement given to Hogan, Lincoln admitted that some damage had likely been done already and speculated that further "abuses" would result. Two weeks later, a confused General William S. Rosencrans, commander of the Department of Missouri, still wondered if Stanton's edict remained in force. Then in early March, members of St. Paul's Church in New Orleans, invoking Lincoln's response to the McPheeters case, petitioned the president to overturn the provost marshal's order commanding them to deliver over the church property to federal authorities. Once again, Lincoln repeated his conviction that the government should not become entangled in ecclesiastical affairs by confiscating a church building unless the army required it for a specific military use. Traitorous church members within a particular assembly could be prosecuted as any other citizen without interfering with organized religion.[29]

The possibility that provost marshals and other military authorities could remove preachers whom they considered disloyal understandably caught the attention of Episcopal bishop Charles McIlvaine. Having read in the *National Intelligencer* about the recent controversy over church-state relations, McIlvaine took "entire satisfaction" that Lincoln had comprehended the issue thoroughly and settled it properly. If a military officer could remove and replace a minister based on his subjective definition of what constituted loyal preaching, then no clergyman was safe. The bishop of Ohio perceptively recognized that political preaching lay at the heart of the conflict. Some parishioners desired a political sermon every week and would question a minister's patriotism if he did not oblige them, and even loyal ministers disagreed over how often "they should turn aside from the direct preaching of the Gospel to introduce matters of political character." Indeed, McIlvaine wondered if some casual observers might consider him disloyal simply because he rarely inserted political themes into his messages. In his opinion, too many preachers dwelled excessively on political subjects and thereby damaged the cause of religion without producing any tangible advantage to the country.[30] As a staunch Unionist who questioned the necessity of political preaching, McIlvaine held a minority position that, if followed, might have done much to foster unity within the church.

Instead, controversies over trivial matters continued to distract the leadership of some denominations from focusing on the church's spiritual mission. In some instances, a willingness to relinquish personal preferences and swallow the majority opinion allowed a spirit of unity to be maintained. At the opening session of the general assembly of the Cumberland Presbyterian Church in Lebanon, Ohio, in May 1864, the speaker discussed John 18:36, "My kingdom is not of this world," and 1 Corinthians 13:13, "The greatest of these is charity," in an attempt to set a tone of brotherly kindness, harmony, and spiritual mindedness. By the afternoon of the second day, a resolution had been introduced calling for the American flag to be flown from the church steeple for the remainder of the meeting. Some delegates immediately greeted this proposal with "warm opposition" and argued that "the interest of Christ's kingdom" had nothing to do with public demonstrations of fidelity to the government. One opponent contended that the mere hoisting of a flag in no way proved anyone's loyalty and only risked dividing the assembly over a dispute that dishonored God. After the resolution passed by a three-to-one majority, the dissenters held their peace, and although both parties had defended their positions fervently, the debate, according to one participant, had been conducted in a manner characterized by "much brotherly feeling." At other times, church leaders took positions that aroused animosities and led to unnecessary divisions. As late as May 1864, controversy still stirred in western Ohio regarding Church of God ministers who had voted for Vallandigham in the past election. In particular, members of the examining board refused to renew the preaching license of pastors who had supported the Democrat unless they publicly acknowledged their error and repented of it. When one elder refused to reveal the content of his ballot, he had his license suspended based on "strong circumstantial evidence" that he had shouted for Vallandigham at a political rally and subscribed to the *Cincinnati Enquirer*. Rather than admit wrongdoing, the offended cleric accused the examining board of being tyrants "worse than Jeff. Davis." Militant Unionist R. H. Bolton ardently defended his role in defrocking the erring brother and claimed that a vote for Vallandigham clearly violated scriptural teaching concerning a Christian's responsibility to civil government. One preacher, overtaxed from the added duty of filling another man's circuit, questioned the necessity of removing a capable minister on such dubious grounds when several churches lacked regular ministers. "Zion in our country is bleeding at every pore," he lamented, deeply troubled by what he perceived to be the declining state of the churches.[31]

Even the simple act of prayer could sometimes become tainted with political overtones or could be perceived as having a partisan thrust. Although several factors prompted a discouraged Edward Meyer to relinquish his Episcopal pulpit in Lansing, Michigan, his growing uneasiness with the behavior of "the leading men in the vestry" played a primary role. According to Meyer, these "palpably disloyal" laymen prayed publicly for peace and prosperity but privately "sympathized with the Rebellion." While hypocritical prayers rankled some listeners, others took insult over petitions offered with heartfelt sincerity. As a pastor in Oxford, Ohio, entreated God for the protection and speedy return of a regiment of soldiers about to leave for the field, one offended man "got up off of his knees and walked out of church." Finding no fault in such an innocuous prayer, a female observer quipped that an irritable "butternut [was] prayed out of church." References to prayer occasionally appeared on the pages of the secular press, sometimes for strictly partisan purposes. A Republican wag satirized the new church movement and its alleged opposition to the politicization of religion with the prayer of a devout Butternut.

> Oh Lord, if thou art an abolitionist and in favor of freeing the niggers, please make it known to us, so that at our next church meeting,... we may appoint a new Lord, and make some arrangements about a new Heaven, for we have resolved not to have an abolition God, nor go to a Heaven where abolitionists and niggers are.... Oh Lord, restore the Democratic party to power, and the niggers to their masters; oh Lord, don't let the niggers come up North lest they become our equals;... and now, oh Lord, save our pure church from politics and niggers; may these things never be referred to in our sermons or prayers.

Not to be outdone, a Democrat parodied the Lord's Prayer in order to portray Republicans as brainwashed dupes who followed Lincoln with religious zeal.

> Father Abraham, thou art in Washington, of glorious memory—since the date of thy proclamation to free the negroes. Thy kingdom come, and overthrow the republic; thy will be done, and

the laws perish. Give us this day our daily supply of greenbacks. Forgive us our plunders, but destroy the Copperheads. Lead us into fat pastures, but deliver us from the eye of the detectives; and make us the equal of the negro, for such shall be our kingdom, and the glory of thy administration.[32]

While some Democratic editors found that this caustic revision of the Lord's Prayer accurately conveyed their disillusionment with the president and his policies, several people testified that Lincoln regarded prayer seriously and had relied on it to cope with the sometimes unbearable strain of the war. His response in early May to yet another military setback confirms this. After General Ulysses S. Grant began his push toward Richmond during the first week of May, Lincoln anxiously awaited reports of the army's progress. Hints of initial success proved untrue, and the Federals suffered an unsettling 17,666 casualties at the Battle of the Wilderness, more than twice that of Confederate losses. Despite an effort to maintain an appearance of calm, signs of sleepless nights betrayed his anxiety. Yet in a telegram issued on May 9, the president inexplicably called on "the Friends of Union and Liberty" to offer "gratitude to God" for the army's movements over the last five days. Imploring patriotic citizens "to unite in common thanksgiving and prayer to Almighty God" after such a tragic slaughter seemed like desperation to the skeptical editor of the *Cincinnati Enquirer*. Lincoln, however, firmly believed in the efficacy of prayer, and in his dispatch he underscored the futility of man's endeavors when undertaken without relying on God. Making this religious appeal after a significant military reverse demonstrated his high regard for prayer and deep confidence in divine sovereignty, two scriptural concepts that served as a comforting refuge of hope when striving through one's own strength proved unavailing.[33]

To be sure, many devout Northerners had been praying for the success of Union arms, and others made a concerted effort to comply with the president's request. The day before Lincoln circulated his plea for prayer, members of a church in Indiana who often supplicated God on behalf of the nation enjoyed an especially moving time of communion in prayer. Fully cognizant that the battle was then raging in Virginia, they drew ineffable comfort from the assurance that God still reigned and promised to renew the strength of those who waited on him. The following Sunday at Roberts Chapel in Indianapolis, Calvin Fletcher heard a compelling message from Luke 18:1, "Men ought always to pray & not to faint." The May 15 services at Vine Street Congregational and Trinity Methodist Episcopal in Cincinnati both accentuated the optimistic tone of Lincoln's pronouncement by focusing on the theme of thanksgiving, a notable irony considering that the Army of the Potomac had taken more total casualties from May 5–12 than the entire

Federal army had tallied during any week since war commenced. Despite the unsurpassed carnage that caused some observers to label Grant the "Butcher," heavy-hearted citizens rarely contemplated whether or not the enormity of the slaughter was appropriate. A spiritual understanding of the war theoretically made it easier to downplay the loss of life, for God, according to Indiana resident Levi Lough, would eventually "vindicate the right." While Lough placed much confidence in Grant's abilities, he nonetheless trusted God "above all" and supposed that the "thousands on thousands of fervent appeals...made in behalf of the sol[d]iers" had not been asked for naught. In a public speech delivered as the incoming president of the American Tract Society, Bishop Charles McIlvaine reiterated Lincoln's sentiments expressed almost three weeks earlier and emphasized the vital role of kneeling saints at home whose prayers "reinforce our armies in the field." At their general conference in Philadelphia, northern Methodists assured the president that "millions of Christians" prayed daily for him and the country. More importantly, "many thousands" of Methodist laymen and ministers had "rushed to arms" to defend the country. Lincoln expressed his sincere appreciation for the willingness of the churches in general and the exemplary record of Methodists in particular in supporting the government throughout the war. "God bless the Methodist Church—bless all the churches," he exclaimed, "and blessed be God, Who, in this our great trial, giveth us the churches."[34]

By the middle of 1864, vocal patriotism displayed by most churchgoers since the outset of war had precipitated an ecclesiastical crisis of immense proportions. While some churches exhibited signs of spiritual vibrancy and grew numerically, others saw their ranks thinned by divisions that often pertained to politics. Methodist churches in two conferences located in southern Indiana decreased by more than nine thousand members over the course of the war. Although some of these losses resulted from relocation, death by natural causes, or battlefield casualties, a majority of them doubtlessly resulted from political divisions. When describing the condition of the state's Methodist churches for an eastern religious periodical, W. R. Goodwin of Brookville, Indiana, reported that a preoccupation with national issues had rendered church affairs little more than an afterthought for many people. Considering the extraordinary circumstances of the times, he seemed entirely satisfied with this situation, especially since the church as a whole had distinguished itself for loyalty. In Goodwin's opinion, those individuals who left the fold over political differences never belonged to the spiritual flock in the first place. Their withdrawal signified that they had cast their lot with "the original secessionists, who were tired of heaven, and who found a warmer climate." Like chaff blown by the wind, they would feel "the breath of God's anger in the day of wrath." Far from weakening the church, the removal of "men who love party more than they love their country, church, or God" purified the church from all taints of slavery and disloyalty. A Baptist in Iowa concurred with Goodwin's assessment that the exodus of religious imposters strengthened the true church. A "troubler of Israel" who demanded that blacks and abolitionists be barred from attending services found himself pressured out of the church instead. The Iowa Unionist regarded the man's "unrelenting persecution" of African-Americans as conclusive demonstration that he merely professed Christianity without genuinely possessing it.[35]

Most Unionist church members interpreted the removal of politically offensive members as vital for the preservation of the purity of the church rather than an indication of the absence of Christian unity and brotherhood. In some instances, political tensions may have played only a secondary role in the circumstances that led to the falling out and expulsion of members, but they nonetheless tipped the scales in favor of mutual separation. After a two-year conflict that began over accusations of duplicity concerning the trading of a horse, J. G. Honnell, a respected physician and elder of the Rockport Presbyterian Church in Allen County, Ohio, was found guilty of failing to attend meetings and committing "the sin of immorality." Regarding the first charge, one witness testified that Honnell had admitted to neglecting the Lord's house and "intended raising his own [church]." Two other witnesses produced evidence that substantiated the accusation of immorality, which had nothing to do with sexual misconduct but merely consisted of Honnell denigrating the church. In October 1863 he allegedly had claimed that the assembly was "in league with hell and had made a covenant with the Devil," and on another occasion he reportedly quipped that he would visit "the Republican prayer meeting at Rockport...if they would give him the privilege of standing off and laughing at them." Having produced a favorable witness in his case regarding the livestock transaction, Honnell likely felt railroaded by the session's ruling against him, and this perceived injustice, combined with his political support for the Democracy, led him to denounce his former associates whom he blamed for politicizing the meetings. From the church's standpoint, Honnell's defiant attitude demanded his excommunication in order to vindicate "the glory of God and [maintain] the *purity* of the church." In extreme cases, some churches even made political issues a test for continued fellowship. At Providence United Presbyterian Church in Johnson County, Indiana, John Clendenning had his church membership temporarily suspended in June 1864 "until he could acknowledge slavery to be a sin."[36]

Although sympathetic believers viewed the dismissal of erring members as a beneficial purging, outsiders sometimes thought twice about joining an institution that possessed significant control over its members. A congregation that from all outward appearances looked to be riven by infighting over politically sensitive issues had even less appeal for believers seeking a place to worship or sinners needing to be evangelized. Pleasant Run Baptist Church in Rush County, Indiana, illustrated such a negative example, for the congregation suffered through a prolonged period of ineffectiveness because of its decision to make a political statement. In August 1863, layman Huston Morris, a staunch Republican, submitted three resolutions supporting the war effort. In particular, the motion equated failure to pray for governmental authorities with treason and exhorted church members to refrain from any behavior that might be construed as sympathetic to the rebellion. In October the church initially voted against the resolutions but for some unstated reason reversed its decision and adopted them in November. At the request of Morris, the clerk even recorded members' names and their respective votes in the church minutes, which revealed a tie at ten votes apiece. Because the incident was so divisive, the congregation agreed to summon a council involving seven other Baptist churches so that members could express their views before impartial arbiters. After deliberation, mediators determined that the resolutions were "of the world and ought not to com[e] in the Church." Despite this verdict, only one resolution was repealed. In the process of all this hullabaloo, moderator Harvey Wright, a Democrat and ordained minister who pastored the church, became extremely offended. At the February 1864 meeting, "Brother Harvey Wright came forward" and expressed sorrow "that he had left the Church in a disorde[r]ly manner." Wright had opposed the resolutions but evidently decided after further consideration that he could overlook the partisanship and continue to serve at Pleasant Run. However, Wright's unease with the church's political stance persisted, and by April 1865, he and his wife, two other men who voted against the resolution, and at least four other individuals had asked for "letters of dismission" from the church. The surrounding community must have noticed the division and rancor within Pleasant Run Baptist Church, for not a single person sought membership throughout the entire war. A summary of each monthly business meeting during the war records the telling phrase, "Opened a door for the reception of members and none received."[37]

The incident at Pleasant Run is undoubtedly an extreme case, but it superbly demonstrates the potential pitfalls for churches that insisted on making political statements that could be construed as falling outside the spiritual realm. However, since the denominations had already set a precedent for schism by splitting along sectional lines years before the war, it is little wonder that individual churches across the North followed suit once open hostilities made it impossible for citizens to remain neutral. A pacifist such as Mennonite bishop John M. Brenneman maintained that religious divisions sparked by war served a beneficial purpose, "sift[ing]...the truly concientious from the worldly minded" and "striking a line between the kingdom of Christ, and the kingdom of this world." In his opinion, the sacred and the secular had become "too much blended & mingled together," a common complaint of pacifist denominations and antiwar Democrats. By the summer of 1864, at least one Democratic editor insisted that the merging of church and state had become "an accomplished fact" through the deliberate "usurpation and lawlessness...of Mr. Lincoln and his favored 'churches.'" Unionist believers accurately responded that the Bible made no distinction between a secular and sacred sphere in a Christian's daily activities, for Paul had written that "whether we eat or drink, or whatsoever we do, we should do all to the glory of God."[38]

The sticking point, then, revolved around what exactly glorified God and constituted the accomplishment of his will. Instead of viewing the church as the means through which God intended to achieve his sovereign purposes in the world, many Christians looked to the nation as the primary vehicle for establishing his earthly kingdom. Ellen Woodworth anticipated the day when America would become a *"purified nation...* purged from the sin into which it has fallen." To be sure, numerous Christians regarded slavery to be that foremost sin, a heinous iniquity harbored since the nation's birth upon which God was finally emptying the storehouse of his wrath through the war's terrible slaughter. David Lough called attention to the Founders' inconsistency in laying a foundation of liberty, a gift "given by *God* for the use of man unrestricted," that intentionally excluded an entire group of people. Now Americans were "reaping the bitter fruits of their error," suffering like the Egyptians at the hand of the death angel. Louisa Semple asserted that even if "hundreds of thousands of heroes perish" to prove that man is "capable of self-government," it still would be "worth the cost." She regarded republicanism as the guiding force of progress, and nothing less than a "divine necessity" compelled loyal Northerners to "put forth our highest efforts to sustain the right." The final result of such a noble endeavor would produce "a full revelation of the will of Heaven." Only antiwar partisans questioned the creed that God sanctioned and directed the war for some sacred design. Decrying warmongering ministers whose politically themed resolutions and sermons had converted the church into the handmaiden of the government, the disillusioned editor of the *Cincinnati Enquirer* defied all who claimed to "see the hand of an Allwise Providence in the conduct of the war." Unwilling to accept the notion that God's will included death and destruction, the editor wondered how self-deceived clerics could claim to be "doing God service" by supporting the war when even their prayers for the triumph of Union arms remained unanswered, a telling sign of their degeneracy. A resident of Dearborn County, Indiana, similarly censured what he regarded as the hypocrisy of local clergymen who polluted the church. These two-faced rabble-rousers, who prayed for victory and the end of hostilities while at the same time insisting that the bloodletting must continue for the nation to be redeemed, violated the sanctity of the church by brazenly condemning peace-loving citizens as traitors deserving death.[39]

Yet for all their disagreement over the exact nature of God's will, both prowar and antiwar apologists looked to Scripture to substantiate their views. In the summer of 1864, a reader of the *Scioto Gazette* systematically outlined the primary New Testament texts about a Christian's duty to civil authorities in an effort to justify prosecution of the war. According to Romans 13:1–4, God had commanded all men to obey magistrates and invested them with the power to punish evildoers. Again in Titus 3:1, Paul had exhorted his pastoral protégé on Crete to remind his flock to submit to authorities. Since Abraham Lincoln was the duly elected leader of the government and Jefferson Davis was a usurper and violator of the nation's laws, citizens had a divine directive to follow Lincoln only. Furthermore, 1 Timothy 2:1–2 instructed Christians to pray for rulers, confirming that ministers were acting within biblical bounds in praying for the president and the success of Union arms in putting down a sinful rebellion against the legitimate government. Although no specific verse required Christians to aid a magistrate in punishing lawbreakers, the implication of these principles, the writer insisted, allowed a Christian to fight "if need be." Arguing for the antiwar position, the editor of the *Cincinnati Enquirer* emphasized verses like Luke 2:14 and Isaiah 2:4 that referred to earthly peace and the cessation of war. He condemned hypocritical ministers who vocally entreated God on behalf of Lincoln and the army yet allegedly ignored the latter part of 1 Timothy 2:1–2 by refusing to "lead a *quiet* and *peaceable* life in *all godliness* and *honesty*." But because few interpreters of Scripture paid careful attention to the context of a passage, they often applied verses to matters that had nothing to do with the meaning of the text. The result pitted two groups who both claimed to be true to the Word, yet their frequent disregard for following proper hermeneutical practice undercut the authority of Scripture by making it a means of division rather than unity. An extended debate waged on the pages of the newspapers of Chillicothe, Ohio, that began when a drafted minister thanked his friends and parishioners who had raised money for him to buy an exemption from service culminated when a Republican noted how supporters of the Democracy cited the Bible to prove that Christians should not hate any man. He countered with Psalm 139:21–22, where David declared that he had "perfect hatred" for the enemies of God. As resisters of authority and despisers of blacks whom God had created, Copperheads, the writer maintained, clearly fit the bill of a divine foe. Three years into the war, it had become almost customary for professed Christians and religious individuals to wield the Sword of the Spirit to combat each other. More significant than revealing the political fissures of northern society, this common practice of discounting believers of a different political persuasion harmed the testimony of the church before a watching world. After commending his preacher son for always making practical applications from the text, Nathaniel Wright reminded him that "the Bible[,] candidly studied, always leads to what is useful & good." In a perfect world, Wright's advice contained much wisdom. But in a nation divided by war where passing familiarity with Holy Writ seemed to outweigh methodical and unbiased investigation of the Word, the outcome rarely proved edifying.[40]

7

"Earth Has No Sorrow That Heaven Cannot Cure"

Civilian Perspectives on Death and Eternity

Although the death angel severely afflicted the Alfords of Daviess County in southwestern Indiana during the Civil War, it could not have chosen a family as well-grounded in their religious beliefs or as confident in their future reunion beyond the grave. In the mid-1840s, Franklin Alford had helped found the Christian church in the town of Alfordsville, and he and his wife Mary devotedly reared their seven children in the faith. They also instilled an intense patriotism in their sons, and the oldest, twenty-two-year-old Warren, enlisted with the 14th Indiana in the spring of 1861. In his letters, Franklin frequently emphasized God's protective care for his son, and Warren responded by acknowledging his submissiveness to the sovereignty of God over his life. "We have reason to believe that our life and our health is peceous [precious] in the sight of our heavenly Father," Warren professed from Cheat Mountain in western Virginia, "and we do not dout for one moment but he will bring us back home safe if it is for the best." However, if God saw fit for him to perish, he expected to meet his family in heaven. "Let us live so that if we neaver meat on eart[h,]...we may be prepared to live togethe[r] aroun[d] the throne of God where parting and crying will be no more."[1]

As the spring of 1862 approached, Franklin remained hopeful that his separated family, which now included the absence of twenty-year-old Wayne and eighteen-year-old Lafayette serving with the 6th Indiana, would someday be reunited at home. "I feel asshured that if it is the Lords will," he related to Warren, "we...[will] all meet again in the family circle with the propper use of our bodys and minds." If parental pride happened to well up in his heart it could be forgiven, for his sons not only conducted themselves as courageous soldiers but consciously strived to live as Christians in the army. The past winter, Wayne and Lafayette, while affirming their intent to maintain a godly testimony, also expressed a readiness to die if necessary. "Our desire is that we may be soldiers and Christians while it is ours to live," Wayne wrote for the two of them on January 30, "and if we never meat on earth let us live so that we may meat in heaven." Their days were numbered indeed, for that spring Lafayette contracted a camp disease and died at home in May. Still fighting in the Shenandoah Valley, Warren took the news in stride, insisting to Wayne on June 13 that "we sorrow not as those that have no hope." Wayne, however, never received the letter, for he died of typhoid fever the next day. Unbeknownst to Warren, he had been confined to a field hospital at Corinth, Mississippi, since the beginning of June, too ill to be transported back to Evansville where his parents might have visited him. Warren tried to remain optimistic and consoled his parents with the thought that God had permitted the deaths of his brothers. "We are brought to see the powerful hand of god upon our family," he maintained, "but I hope we will bair the trials as best we can." The promise of an eternal home, he reminded them, gave consolation and hope that their family would be reunited again. "If this earthly house of our tabernacle is desolved... [and] we have done our heavenly fathers will," a stipulation they knew Lafayette and Wayne had attempted to fulfill, "we [have a] house high up in the Heavens not made with hands their to dwell for eaver and ever."[2]

Forever arrived all too soon for Warren, for in September he was counted among the victims of the bloodiest single day of the war, suffering a mortal wound at Antietam and dying two days later. After receiving the awful tidings, Franklin journeyed east to retrieve the body of his eldest son, a trip on which he must have carried a burden of unspeakable grief. Unfortunately, only one letter from home was preserved beginning with the death of Lafayette, a missive dated two days after Warren's passing in which Franklin lamented the outbreak of a controversy at church. This lone piece of evidence seems to indicate that he had remained faithful in performing his Christian duties, inevitably saddened over his loss but not despairing. In all likelihood, he still might have affirmed the outlook he expressed at the close of a letter to Warren in late January. "In hope that God in his abundant mercy may bless us all in time and save us in eternity for the sake of Christ is the prair of your humble father."[3] Time, at least during a five-month period in 1862, had been incomprehensibly brutal, snatching away three sons in the prime of their lives. Eternity, however, offered the prospect of a glorious future and the complete restoration of familial bonds.

Several historians have identified the Civil War as marking a transition from a primarily religious understanding of death to a more secular approach to dying. According to the standard interpretation, the Puritans represented the apogee of a sacred emphasis on death. However, because most Puritans believed that they could never know with complete assurance whether or not God had elected them to salvation, they confronted death with great fear regarding their eternal status. By the antebellum era, Puritanical dread of death for spiritual reasons had degenerated into out-and-out fatalism. While some individuals continued to affirm their religious convictions in their last earthly moments in order to leave evidence of dying in the faith, most merely desired to die happy and face the end with stoic dignity. Accordingly, most antebellum Americans simply regarded death as the termination of worldly troubles. Furthermore, the few souls who clung to a religious conception of death seldom spoke of heaven with any specificity but satisfied themselves with the thought that family members would never be parted there. James J. Farrell concludes that the gradual acceptance of Darwinism and the rise of liberal Christianity in the postwar period not only caused Americans to contemplate death less frequently but nearly rendered obsolete any tendencies to speak of it as having spiritual meaning. Because scientific naturalism had placed death within the normal patterns of nature and theological liberalism had quenched the fires of hell, few people had any reason to fear death. Indeed, by the end of the nineteenth century, it seemed evident that death had lost its cultural dominance, prompting one writer to trumpet "the dying of death." At the same time, heaven gained in popularity because of the work of fiction writers, whose depiction of it as a place that preserved the best aspects of earthly life led to widespread acceptance that heaven resembled the Victorian home. Coincidentally, the theology of liberal Protestantism emboldened some individuals to claim that all men would go to heaven at death. Nevertheless, few people had taken time to develop a systematic approach to eschatology, thereby allowing numerous conceptions of eternity to flourish in the popular imagination.[4]

Because countless families directly experienced the effects of war's devastating slaughter, death dominated the thoughts of many Americans. While some Northerners might have regarded death as having little value for religious instruction or embraced other secular frameworks for dealing with it, numerous northern civilians continued to find spiritual meaning in death. Furthermore, the success of the Second Great Awakening in undermining the Calvinistic doctrine of predestination and elevating the believer's role in securing salvation enabled religious Northerners to approach death with greater confidence in their attainment of a heavenly home. To be sure, individuals often held conflicting visions of heaven and emphasized different conditions that had to be fulfilled to gain it, but this lack of consensus did not diminish their enthusiasm for describing it. Far from dwindling in importance, a spiritual attitude toward death enabled religious citizens to deal with the staggering loss of life brought about by the war. After four years of unprecedented carnage, northern civilians had left a substantial documentary record permeated with death, grief, and, oftentimes, steadfast hope in a joyous, eternal reunion.

For many nineteenth-century Americans, death represented the end of a person's time on earth and the beginning of an eternal existence. Man needed time to mark the passage of hours, days, and years, but ultimately it belonged to God, who, though timeless in nature and unbounded by its constraints, determined its duration. Many Americans from the Puritans through the antebellum period viewed time as a gift from God to be used productively in light of a coming judgment when man would give account of his use of time. Time, therefore, was both cyclical and linear, for man observed its seasonal patterns during life while anticipating a future period when physical time would give way to an infinite eternity. Throughout the antebellum period and continuing into the war, northern civilians typically used the occasions of New Year's, birthdays, anniversaries, and the last day of December to reflect on their past achievements and future prospects. As 1863 commenced, Samuel Hibbard affirmed that God alone knew "what joys, what griefs, what lives & deaths" the new year held in store. On December 31, he solemnly recorded that 1863 had "gone into eternity," and all actions and events could never be changed, including sins committed and missed opportunities to serve God. Most time-conscious religionists could agree that engaging in reflection and introspection for the purpose of drawing one's thoughts to God were appropriate uses of time. After perusing some of his earlier diaries on successive birthdays in 1863 and 1864, Calvin Fletcher described his life as a "Journy" through which God had providentially directed him, contemplated his spiritual progress along the way, and affirmed his hope of obtaining "a better future." Almost inevitably, the ubiquitous subject of death found its way into moments of personal retrospection about time on earth. When Emily Beeler Fletcher, Calvin's daughter-in-law, began keeping a journal in May 1863, she opened with a brief reminiscence about her wedding nearly fourteen years before, marveling that time had "passed so swiftly away...like a dream that has fled." After recalling this blissful memory, she abruptly yet almost intuitively transitioned into a listing of all her relatives who had died in the interim, including her father, mother-in-law, a son, and three siblings by marriage.[5]

Without doubt, most northern civilians understood and accepted the reality that death predominated while earthly time existed, and they underscored the necessity of using their limited time on earth to prepare for the next world. "Time is passing on & we are all rushing on to eternity," Drusilla Dean of Silver Creek, Iowa, reminded her former neighbors in Steuben County, Indiana. "We may pass the thoughts of death & eternity from our mind for a few days," she admitted, "but then we will have to mourn for unimproved time for all Eternity." Most Christian denominations attempted to inculcate its members with the recognition of life's brevity, so it is not surprising that a line from the Methodist burial service became something of a cliché during the war. "Truly in the midst of life we are in death," Eunice Brown mused in March 1864 after several unexpected deaths in Connersville, Indiana. "None of us can count on the morrow as we know not what a day may bring forth," she added, paraphrasing Proverbs 27:1. She regarded these sudden losses as both a sobering warning and an instructive reminder to take stock of her spiritual condition. "I fear that we do not let such realities impress our minds as much as they are intended. They should by [be] leading us into the narrow path which leads to eternal life." After a spooked horse kicked a neighbor in the head, crushing his skull, Mollie McPheeters observed, "O, how quick can the brittle thread of life be broken and the soul ushered into eternity. How true the saying That in the midst of life we are in the midst of death." Since death inevitably encompassed life, according to the aphorism, McPheeters understood the seriousness of making preparation while time remained. "Knowing that life is so uncertain and death sure, how very important that we prepare, while in health, for this change, so that whether it comes sooner or later we may be ready."[6]

Although many nineteenth-century Americans maintained a belief in fatalism and referred to death as some impersonal force that chose victims at random, religious individuals, in contrast, rejected the concept of fate because they believed that a personal, sovereign God determined each person's day of death. As she struggled to raise her family while her husband Taylor served with the 22nd Iowa, Catharine Peirce maintained that her many trials would make it easier "to leave this world when God sees fit to call us off." On another occasion, she sought to understand why God selected certain individuals for death but permitted others to live. It bewildered her that "so stout and health[y] a girl" as her friend Kate should "be taken and such delicate creatures as I be left. Seemes quere but we do not know the ways nor the will of the lord and therefore must abide our time." Virginia Alford, cousin of the Alford brothers, affirmed "that it is the Lord that gives us theas friends that we love so dear and...[it] is the Lord that takes them away." In July 1864, the entire North lamented the loss of one of its heroes, General James B. McPherson, who was shot in the back attempting to return to his lines after refusing to surrender to a group of Rebels during the battle of Atlanta. Mary Vermilion considered McPherson's death a hefty price to pay for the capture of that city. "We could not well spare such a leader at this time," she claimed. "I wish he could have lived to finish his work. But it is right as it is, or God would not have taken him."[7]

Other Northerners favored the use of a metaphor for the second coming of Christ to convey the idea that God, rather than the grim reaper, decided the time of man's passing. Since no human could forecast when either one would occur, the expression "the Son of Man cometh" became a frequently used figure of speech to describe the unexpected nature of death's arrival.[8] In April 1863, Cincinnati resident Josephine Foster referred to the passing of an aunt as a reminder for her brother, Brigadier General William Haynes Lytle, to be prepared for death at any moment. "'*Be ye* also *ready* for ye *know not* the day, neither the hour, when the Son of Man cometh.'" Less than six months later, Lytle was killed at Chickamauga during an unsuccessful counterattack that he ordered in an effort to arrest a panicked Federal retreat. At least one individual took this metaphor for death literally and claimed that Christ actually came for his own at their departure from life. Following the death of a soldier from their hometown, Alexander McPheeters apprised his son John that it mattered little "where and when" a man died so long as he was "prepared to meet God in peace." "This lesson should be improved by us all," he resolved, "for we know not the day or the hour when the son of man cometh but he cometh to the christian at his death." Despite the popular prevalence of this expression to denote death, a careful reading of Scripture clearly demonstrates its erroneous application. In an 1862 article in the *Indianapolis Witness*, an unidentified author carefully examined the context of all passages in the Gospels that contained the phrase "the coming of the Son of Man." According to the writer, the verses under consideration never equated death with a metaphor for Christ's second coming, and the context proved that the disciples never understood Jesus to apply this figure to a person's death. Nevertheless, the figure of speech suited the purposes of Northerners who wished to convey the suddenness of death and the great need to be prepared to enter eternity at any moment.[9]

It would be fallacious to claim that the aforementioned individuals who contemplated the reality of death suffered from a morbid fascination with dying. On the contrary, Christians could face death without fear because Christ had conquered death and the grave through his resurrection. Convinced that she was nearing the end of her earthly days, Margaret Ross forewarned her sister not to mourn when she received word of her death. "Be asured my robe is washed white in the blood of the lam," she professed. "I have nothing to do but gather up my feet like Jacob of old and go in peace." With his health declining, seventy-year-old J. W. Osborn of Terre Haute, Indiana, likewise thought that death would summon him shortly, and he expectantly anticipated "the glories that await the finally faithful." "Having submitted myself to His keeping," he testified, "I know that there is none that can wrest me out of the hand of my Almighty Father." Echoing the Apostle Paul, he asserted, "I am content whether I live a few months or a few years longer, or whether I depart, all is well." Elderly Christians who referred to death without trepidation might elicit little surprise, but young people who espoused the sentiment is noteworthy indeed. Already a wife of three years in 1863, seventeen-year-old Viana White informed her husband George, a soldier with the 19th Michigan, that although she hoped to witness the war's conclusion, it mattered little whether or not she outlived the fighting. "When the lord sees fit to call me away from this troblesom world," she affirmed, "I am redy to go."[10]

Because God providentially controlled all things, including the timing of a person's death, he most certainly could protect his children from harm if he so desired. As sovereign Creator of the universe, God cared for the material world even to the minutest detail. Franklin Alford recalled from the Sermon on the Mount that God cultivated the "tender grass" and kept his watchful eye on the fowls of the air so that not even a sparrow could "fall to the ground" without his knowledge. Since God showed such concern for his physical creation, surely he would take even greater interest in humans who possess an eternal soul. For this reason, many civilians recognized that God could providentially protect their loved ones in battle. Therefore, in order to avoid the appearance of presumption, some individuals qualified their requests to ensure that they conformed to the will of God. "I hope and pray that it may be gods will to spare your life and all the rest of the poor solgers," an Ohio resident informed a soldier with the 67th Ohio. The author clearly understood that God's will trumped any human contrivances to preserve life, for even the most extreme precautions would prove futile if they failed to coincide with divine decrees. "If your life is saved it is through gods kind will," the person continued, "for thousands of men could not save your life...[apart from] the lords will." In contrast to those who only hoped for God's protection, other individuals possessed faith that God would shield their loved ones from injury. "I have sutch confidence...[that] you will be permitted to come home safe that I feel like praseing God in advanse," Henry Tutewiler exclaimed to his son in March 1865. John L. Ketcham expressed a similar sentiment but cautioned his son Willie to avoid risking his life needlessly by "attempting desperate things." "Trust all to God and be hopeful, cheerful, brave, but not rash," he counseled. "Dont throw away a precious life." Alexander McPheeters likewise warned John that having the hedge of God's protection should not entice him to recklessness. "You are immortal until your work is done," he insisted, "but this will not justify unnecessary exposure." Family members of soldiers who narrowly escaped scrapes with death had every reason for thanksgiving. After Mary Logan was presented with the bullet that grazed her husband John's uniform, she expressed gratitude "to God who so mercifully saved you."[11]

Individuals who suffered the loss of a family member had their faith in God's sovereignty tested. Although coping with the death of a loved one was never an easy task, believing that a person could die only if God permitted it provided a measure of consolation. After his son Lycurgus died at a field hospital near Vicksburg in June 1863, James Remley was "deeply afflicted" but purposed to "bear it as [a] Christian." Expounding a theodicy based on Romans 8:28 that befitted his station as a Baptist minister, he professed, "We console ourselves with the reflection that God does all things right, that he is too wise to err, and too good to do wrong, that he will cause all things to work together for the good of them that love him and are called according to his purpose." Michigan lawyer and Sunday school teacher George Woodruff also endured an extremely trying period during the summer of 1863. In June his wife succumbed to illness after a five-year battle, and less than a month later his son George suffered a mortal wound on the third day at Gettysburg and died July 4. Woodruff recorded in his journal that news of his son's death "went to my heart with a crushing weight. Was not my affliction in the death of his mother enough," he sorrowed. Despite the emotional depths to which his spirit had fallen, Woodruff was relieved when he learned that the letter bearing the unpleasant tidings of his wife's passing had not reached his son before the battle, and the boy had gone to his grave untouched by that added grief. Contemplating this remarkable providence, he reflected on God's kindness to his son and consoled himself that "such a mercy [would only] be extended to one who was...an object of his...aid." By Thanksgiving Day, the passage of time and God's grace had helped heal his broken heart, and Woodruff regarded his trial as spiritually beneficial. "I am thankful that the Lord has done to me what seemed to Him good," he testified. "If the bitter load of grief shall make me walk more humbly do justice & love mercy—& make me holy," he added, then "I will rejoice in the remembrance of my tribulations."[12]

Probably few people handled the anguish caused by the death of a loved one as well as James Remley or George Woodruff. Oftentimes, the ability to give intellectual consent to God's sovereignty did not provide immediate comfort or completely ease the pain of a loss. "It is hard...to part with him," the parents of George Covington admitted after his death in 1864. "But it is the will of our Heavenly Father who knows what is best, and He always does right. We believe this and it consoles us in some measure," they acknowledged. Although an individual might have possessed a sincere desire to submit to God's will, sometimes an afflicted heart needed time to mend before it could align with a person's mental wishes. Nearly a year after the deaths of a son and son-in-law in the war, Eleanor Bereman of Mt. Pleasant, Iowa, still struggled to come to terms with her loss. "Oh that I could say the will of the Lord be done more fully than I do," she confessed. Other persons seemed almost powerless to master their grief and remained disconsolate, unable to find relief in the doctrine of God's sovereignty. "I know it is my duty to resign to the will of God," Jane van den Tak of Holland, Michigan, conceded in May 1863 after obtaining her fallen brother's personal effects from Claude Buchanan. "The Lord reigns as well on earth as he does in heaven," she willingly asserted, and though some might consider her brother's death "an accident," she recognized that the attributes of "the Almighty ruler" rendered such an explanation infeasible. Despite understanding and affirming the actuality of God's sovereignty, she struggled to find solace and confessed, "It is very hard for me to have comfort from that [doctrine]."[13]

Since death might visit soldiers sooner rather than later, civilians often stressed the urgency for them to prepare while time remained. Elvira Aplin yearned "to hear that the soldiers begin to care for their souls" because they might "exchange worlds at any moment." After her son Arthur died in the summer of 1864, she counseled her son George to make "his peace with God" while time remained. "Do not wait till you are wounded, or on a sick bed, before you attend to these things," she advised, "for you may never have such an oportunity." When her brother George Howell became discouraged shortly after enlisting, Almira Dart directed his attention away from earthly matters. "Live so you will be prepared to die," she admonished, "for you know not how sudenly you may be called into eternity." Receiving word that a soldier had examined his spiritual condition and settled his eternal state made the prospect of parting in this life more bearable. "If our friends fall in this war we know they die in a glorious cause," Sarah Dooley maintained, "and if we only had the asurence they was prepared for a better world we could give them up."[14]

The deathbed was a prominent facet of mid-nineteenth-century American social culture, both in the North and South. Indeed, many people of all denominations and religious backgrounds considered dying to be an art and sought to leave this world in a way that exemplified the "Good Death." Since the fifteenth century, religious manuals outlining the *Ars Moriendi*, or art of dying, had instructed people how to meet death without fear. In the ideal scenario, a person would die at home surrounded by family and friends, who offered encouragement and watched to see that their loved one did not tremble at death but exhibited "Christian fortitude and resignation" to the very end. According to Drew Gilpin Faust, firsthand observation of these last moments on earth allowed family to glimpse the person's "spiritual condition" at the point of death and gauge the prospects of heavenly reunion. Obituaries in religious newspapers helped promote the model Christian death, serving both to honor the deceased for having left a commendable testimony while challenging the living to emulate such saintly examples. After noting her church membership and consistent "daily walk and conversation," the obituary for thirty-five-year-old Martha Shanks of Indiana recounted her final earthly hours. "To the last, she was entirely composed, giving charges to her family and counseling and biding farewell to her friends until she fell asleep in Jesus." Far from being limited to middle-class white culture, the *Ars Moriendi* tradition had even transcended racial boundaries. According to the *Christian Recorder*, the official organ of the African Methodist Episcopal church, the death of eighty-five-year-old Mary Bass, a Methodist church member for over forty years and faithful congregant of Terre Haute's A.M.E. church for more than twenty, epitomized the Good Death archetype. "Up to the day of her death she maintained the religion which she professed," her obituary read. "The nearer she drew to the grave, the stronger became her faith in the Saviour. She died as she prayed she might, surrounded by her children and grand children." This testimony of persevering faith gave her family confidence that she had gone "to join the company of those who walk in white, being found worthy."[15]

Unlike these ideal examples, many soldiers perished far from home, thereby disrupting this standard ritual of death. To be sure, a few individuals dismissed social conventions altogether and stressed that preparation for eternity was all that counted. "If you are ready to go," Almira Dart claimed, "it will not...matter how nor where you die." Most families, however, sought a detailed account of how their loved ones had died. Although local newspapers listed names of the dead and wounded after a battle, they sometimes contained errors, so letters from soldiers were prized highly for their greater accuracy. Ethan Brown informed his brother Darius of the 12th Michigan that the community depended on his eyewitness reports for authenticated "facts" concerning who had perished in the fighting. According to Ethan, one local housewife was becoming "almost crazy" to learn where her husband had received his mortal wound, and he matter-of-factly warned Darius that his "popularity" at home hinged on his "promptness in writing and giving full particulars."[16]

Over the course of the war, the composition of condolence letters to family at home became something of a stock-in-trade for some soldiers. Typically, condolence letters penned by soldiers included references to the deceased's love for country, family, and God. After Clement Webb of the 13th Michigan died at Murfreesboro in February 1863, a sergeant in his company assured Clement's wife Clarissa that "the captain fought the good fight, both of a soldier of the cross and a[n] officer [of the Union]." Before dying, Webb expressed his wish "to see his famely," especially his "little ones." As the two soldiers conversed about religion, Webb acknowledged that "he loved his Christ," and although the rigors of army life had made it difficult for him to be as faithful as he would have liked, he fully expected to reach "that shining shore." Besides soldiers, chaplains and hospital workers also helped meet the demand for descriptions of the Good Death. After her husband Simeon expired at a St. Louis hospital in January 1863, Elizabeth Stevens received word from a stranger, possibly a U.S. Sanitary Commission worker, that Simeon had been "prepared" to die, "for in all conversation his thoughts were of his family and his God." By emphasizing the patriotism, familial devotion, and religious piety of the dying soldier, condolence letters fit the expectations of grieving relatives rather than depict the horrible suffering of the battlefield. However sanitized, condolence letters allowed family members at home to participate vicariously in their loved one's final moments.[17]

The privilege of being present to hear the final words of the dying had always been a central component of the deathbed. Family members cherished last words for their heartfelt truthfulness and edifying qualities. This concluding utterance afforded the living a meaningful memory that not only characterized the life of the deceased but also provided valuable instruction and application for the remainder of life's journey. Families made every possible effort to discover final remarks made by soldiers, and, once ascertained, they willingly shared them with all concerned relatives. When Lycurgus Remley passed away, he had his brother George at his side to record his dying words. Lycurgus "requested me to tell you that 'he died in hope of a blissful immortality,'" George dutifully notified his mother Jane. "All along through his illness he expressed complete resignation to the will of God knowing full well that whatever He did would be for the best," George assured her. Knowing that Lycurgus had died well encouraged his friends and helped them cope with his passing. "The consciousness of having done his duty together with a well founded hope in Christ doubtless made his deathbed pleasant even though far from home," a classmate from the University of Iowa assumed. The multiple losses suffered by the Lough family allowed them to exchange last word accounts for the consolation of all. After the death of his nephew James in late 1864, David Lough recounted the passing of his son Albert, a sergeant with the 3rd Iowa who had been sent home and died of disease in January 1862. Upon realizing that he would die shortly, Albert, his father narrated, claimed to "see angels reaching out their...hands to receive my spirit" and affirmed "his confidence in Jesus as his Redeemer." Likewise, David had learned, James had invoked publicly "our Heavenly Father the God of Battles" to succor him during his final moments, and this display of devotion confirmed his preparation for death and left his family a comforting remembrance.[18]

Many soldiers, in contrast, died anonymously on the battlefield with no comrade there to note the details of their passing. Sarah Dooley wished that her son Rufus had been present to hear the dying words of his older brother Atellus, who fell at Baton Rouge in the summer of 1864. She hoped Rufus would be able to ascertain whether or not Atellus had thought of his family in his final moments and "appeared willing to die." Lacking these particulars, Sarah conjectured about what might have occurred, and she assured herself that if Atellus had retained full command of his faculties he would have "reflect[ed] and prepare[d] to meet his God." Sarah Chapin lamented that her son George had died unattended by his family but trusted that "unseen...angels wachd" over his body and "escorted his soul" to heaven. Indeed, the absence of a definitive account about a soldier's final moments on earth seemed to encourage wild conjecturing. If Martha John wondered what might have transpired when her son Samuel was shot on a scouting mission in July 1861, her friend A. D. Lynch of Indianapolis filled in every conceivable gap. Lynch imagined that Samuel had thought of God, his family, and his country during his final moments. Although no family member was present at Samuel's side, Lynch envisioned that angels, Samuel's guardian spirit, or possibly even his "sainted father" had noted his last words and carried them to "the throne of God." Unsatisfied by such otherworldly speculations about anonymous deaths, some families searched for tangible signs that pointed to a soldier's noble ending. After his son was killed at the battle of South Mountain in September 1862, Edward Meyer discovered that the Bible found on his son's body had been marked at 2 Kings 22:19–20. The text read, "Because thine heart was tender, and thou hast humbled thyself before the LORD,...I will gather thee unto thy fathers, and thou shalt be gathered into thy grave in peace." Meyer regarded this passage to be "so strikingly true" of his son's "character, course & ending to seem sent providentially for our consolation."[19]

Most soldiers were buried where they fell, but families with economic means sometimes had the body of a slain soldier brought home for burial. The relatively new practice of embalming facilitated the shipment of cadavers to grieving families who desired to observe traditional mourning practices that battlefield deaths had denied them. The opportunity to pay last respects by having a public funeral gave great satisfaction to those who regarded the death of a soldier as having redemptive significance for the nation. Indeed, scores of Northerners flocked to the funerals of Union officers, and such public ceremonies enabled ministers to memorialize individuals while reinforcing the necessity of dying for a righteous cause. At the December 1863 funeral of Colonel William Creighton and Lieutenant Colonel O. J. Crane of the 7th Ohio, both of whom fell at the battle of Ringgold, Georgia, patriotic applications far outnumbered references to religious devotion. Although Methodist preacher Adam Crooks mentioned Creighton's childhood baptism, he focused on the colonel's patriotic sacrifice and comforted his family with the thought that he fell "covered with glory," and now future generations could visit his grave and remember the noble cause for which he had died. Reverend C. C. Foot did not hide from citizens of Cleveland that Crane "had never made a public profession of faith in Jesus," yet he chose to admonish his listeners to pay their debt of gratitude to the widows and orphans of soldiers who had sacrificed their lives for the nation's freedom rather than warn them to prepare their souls for death. According to Susan-Mary Grant, some Northerners considered the gravestones of soldiers and the cemeteries that housed their remains to be holy places, for these burial grounds were visible reminders that helped validate the enormous sacrifice in human life while also providing the living with a basis for an American national identity.[20]

While not immune to the influences of patriotism or indifferent about the location of their loved one's body, family members of Christian soldiers seemed to place less importance on these temporal issues, for their belief that the departed had gained entrance into heaven enabled them to focus on eternal priorities. "I have no doubt but Lycurgus has gone to heaven," his mother Jane Remley maintained. "I always believed him to be a devoted christian." Armed with this assurance, Christian civilians often seemed to accept more willingly the termination of earthly bonds. Upon receiving word that her brother McLeod Mumford had perished from complications caused by an arm amputation in June 1864, Jane Mauck of Mt. Carmel, Illinois, mourned his passing but "not as those who have no hope." "We have every reason to believe that he was God's own," she affirmed, and "god has taken him Home." Several members of the Chapin family accepted with Christian fortitude the deaths of three of their own during the war. John Chapin, a minister in Plymouth, Indiana, regarded the sermon entitled "'Blessed are the dead who die in the Lord'" to be entirely fitting for his brother Coy's funeral in April 1863. "It is not terrible to die when we can leave such a heritage behind us as our brother has left," he professed. When John Blinn perished at a field hospital, his mother Dorothy did not despond but confidently asserted that "*God has taken him to himself.*" Alice Chapin estimated that her cousin John's funeral was the largest she had ever attended and inferred that those who had come to pay their last respects took "comfort...to know he died a happy Christian rejoicing in the Savior." Helen Kemper anticipated that George Chapin would survive the war because he modeled "the religion of the glorious Savior" by displaying a consistent Christian testimony. When her hunch proved false, the remembrance of his godly reputation and certainty of his admittance into heaven assuaged her grief. "Oh with what joy immeasurable can his friends resign him, when compared with those who have to give up their friends in despair."[21]

In addition to possessing hope that their departed loved ones had been ushered into heaven, religious civilians often received encouragement and consolation from fellow believers. The godly counsel of like-minded friends helped them maintain a proper outlook concerning death and reinforced right thinking should they find themselves tempted to second-guess God or question his sovereign purposes. The outpouring of support showered on

Calvin Fletcher after the tragic death of his son Miles superbly illustrates this point. In May 1862, Indiana governor Oliver P. Morton invited Fletcher to accompany him to Pittsburg Landing to speak with General Henry Halleck concerning Morton's desire to deliver sanitary stores for the exclusive benefit of Hoosier troops. The elder Fletcher declined the mission, citing farm work and business affairs that required his time, but his son Miles, state superintendent of public instruction and professor at Indiana Asbury University, went in his stead. While journeying in the middle of the night, their train struck a freight car that had partially blocked the tracks in the town of Sullivan, Indiana. Awakened by the noise, Miles Fletcher peeked his head out the window and immediately suffered a fatal blow from the protruding car. Severely shocked by this unexpected news, Calvin nevertheless responded in typical fashion by focusing his attention on God's numerous blessings and sovereign acts. In the past, God always had protected his children, causing him to marvel "at his forbearance." Although he had prayed for Miles's safety as was his habit, he deemed that God in his wisdom had "seen proper to permit this sad dispensation." Even with such a terrible loss, he could offer only praise to God. "He ruleth; let the earth rejoice.... He is perfect & knows what is best. Blessed be his holy name."[22]

Despite his seemingly stoic acceptance of his son's death, Calvin Fletcher struggled to come to terms with such a profound loss. After the burial, he abandoned his diary keeping for almost two full weeks, a remarkable negligence considering the daily regularity of this decades-long routine. Furthermore, he left space in the diary to attach newspaper clippings about his son, but he lacked "the courage to insert them" until September, nearly four months later. Although Fletcher's thoughts and emotions during this self-imposed silence are irretrievable, the consoling counsel of his friends directed his attention to the providential nature of all God's doings. Andrew Ingram had confidence that Fletcher would not lose faith but would endure his affliction with "a right spirit" and overcome it through grace and strength supplied by God. "I know...the high christian standpoint upon which you look upon the dispensations of Divine Providence," he asserted. You "will be sustained in this hour of trial, by Him who is able to 'bind up the broken heart.'" Methodist minister J. W. T. McMullen of Delphi, Indiana, envisioned that Fletcher would develop a more eternal perspective since Miles had been ushered into heaven. "God took the noble son to himself, that the fathers 'Heart' and 'affections' might be 'set' 'on things above.'" None of Fletcher's well-wishers captured more clearly the inscrutable nature of God's actions than Willis Revels. "The providences of god my friend strangely strewen in our path way are at times dificult to be under stood." Only in eternity, he maintained, would God reveal "the mystery" of his will. Revels compared man's inability to understand the ways of God to the disciples in John 13 who wondered why Jesus stooped to wash their feet. "Jesus said to his disciples What I do thou knowest not now—but thou shalt know hereafter." Offering a deeper perspective that looked beyond the death of Miles as an isolated incident, Revels placed his friend's individual circumstance within the context of God's purposes for the nation through the war. "It may be that some of the most precious and valuable lives in this country have been required of god to fully arouse the people to see and under stand the enormity of the curse of this rebellion."[23]

During the war, scores of Northerners revealed their expectant longing for heaven. Although only a few volumes on the afterlife were published in

Willis R. Revels (1810–79) was born a free black in North Carolina. Ordained to the ministry, he helped found the Indiana Conference of the African Methodist Episcopal church. He also served as the chief recruiting officer for the 28th U.S. Colored Troops, Indiana's only black regiment, which trained on land owned by Calvin Fletcher. During Reconstruction, his younger brother Hiram Revels became the first African-American elected to the U.S. Senate. A first cousin, Lewis Leary, was killed during John Brown's raid on Harper's Ferry. *Indiana Historical Society*

the years preceding the war and throughout its duration, these scant numbers do not reflect accurately the interest in heaven exhibited by many religious individuals, a trend that accounts for the subsequent surge in the popularity and publication of books on heaven during the 1870s. According to Colleen McDannell and Bernhard Lang, the modern vision of heaven became ascendant during the middle decades of the century. However, the traditional image based on ideas of the Protestant Reformers endured nonetheless. The latter proposed a theocentric model of heaven that presented God receiving praise from the redeemed for all eternity. With no sorrow, sickness, or dying, heaven was the antithesis of earth, and even familial relationships ceased to matter. God was the focus of heaven and the reason for its existence, and the thought of enjoying eternal communion with him stimulated the believer to seek its shores. In contrast, the modern representation of heaven mirrored the best of life on earth, and reunion with family replaced devotion to God as the primary objective of heaven. This anthropocentric conception narrowed the distance between heaven and earth because it envisioned the saints lovingly nurturing their families and engaging in the same activities that characterized everyday life. In essence, the modern view of heaven made earthly bonds sacred. Heaven resembled the Victorian home on a grander scale, and the family, not God, "served as the foundation of heavenly life."[24]

Despite the prevalence of the modern image of heaven during the war, the traditional vision that emphasized man enjoying endless fellowship with God occasionally appeared. Although adherents of this view looked forward to rejoining family, they recognized that heaven existed for the primary purpose of worshiping the God of the universe for all eternity. According to the New Testament, those who died in the Lord went immediately to be with him, and this promise provided consolation to grieving family members and offered security in the knowledge that death could not separate believers from the love of Christ. After the death of George Chapin, Helen Kemper confidently asserted that he had departed to be "forever present with the Lord." Sarah Chapin assured her nephew Amory Blinn that his father's preparation for death had enabled him to live "with his savior." To be sure, the blessings of earthly communion with Christ, no matter how inspiring, paled in comparison to the joys of heaven. Although "Jesus communicates with his friends by his word" and "sympathizes" with a believer's infirmities during the earthly sojourn, Ohioan Eliza Fanning noted, this fellowship could not approach the rapturous delight "that await[s] the christian in heaven where he shall see the redeemer face to face and enjoy his presants forever." Indeed, being with Christ would elicit praise from the saints, and David Lough expected to "join in songs of everlasting praise to Jesus who has redeemed us." Emily

Eliot perceptively comprehended how the traditional interpretation envisioned a proper balance between family and God. After the death of her husband Denton, a lieutenant colonel with the 103rd Ohio, she expressed hope of "see[ing] him in heaven" but fully expected that "Christ will occupy my thoughts there."[25]

The modern depiction of heaven, in contrast, primarily emphasized that parting from family members would cease in heaven, and many individuals expressed an intense desire to go there for the primary purpose of reuniting with loved ones. Civilians often conveyed their wish to see soldiers return home safely, but if prevented from doing so, they intended to greet each other in heaven. "May God grant that we may meet again...in this world," Lizzie Bowler prayed, "and above all prepare us both for the future world that we may not be separated there." Those left behind to mourn often assumed that their dearly departed were eagerly anticipating the time when they would be brought together again. Lizzie Griffith of Chicago asserted that those who "have gone first...are only waiting for us on the other shore." Because of their difficulty in comprehending the intangible nature of heaven, some civilians found that the prospect of joining loved ones made going there more appealing. "Heaven look[s] much brighter to me," Amanda Hudelson of New Castle, Indiana, admitted after the death of her mother, "and more interest have I to live so as to gain that bright shore to meet my dear father and mother there." Likening herself to the disciple Thomas, who had to see and touch the risen Christ before he could believe in the resurrection, Alice Chapin needed a personal connection to make heaven's existence seem more concrete. "I never had so tender a yearning for *heaven* until I had a *link* to...what had been *earthy*," she confessed after the death of her infant son. "I can realize there is a *heaven* much more since I have friends...there."[26]

Besides rejoining adult family members in heaven, parents expected to reunite with their children who had died in infancy or early childhood. By the early nineteenth century, the decline of Calvinism had enabled many northern civilians to conclude that God, because of his love, would permit children who died before they developed a consciousness of sin or reached an age to differentiate between right and wrong to enter heaven. In February 1863, Hoosier J. R. Jones tried to comfort some Quaker friends with the thought that their baby "has gone to a better world." Some parents attempted to convince themselves that it advantaged their children to escape the troubles and trials of life. Anna Starr consoled herself that her two deceased infants had "been removed in mercy ere *one blot* of *sin*, had stained their infant purity." "*Their* eternal gain," she reckoned, should cause "*our* loss...[to] loose its sharpest stings." A female friend of Schuyler and Lucia Hendryx regarded the death of their infant daughter as a "solemn admonition" to draw "nearer to the Saviour" by dwelling on their heavenly "treasures," for the child, she believed, was now an angel in heaven. In the mid-nineteenth century, writers of popular serials such as *Godey's Lady's Book* and novelists such as Harriet Beecher Stowe promoted the idea that deceased infants became angels in heaven who helped rescue and purify the souls of family members on earth. Convinced that her daughter Eva had "gone to sing songs around the throne of god in heaven," a mother in Flint, Michigan, determined "to live in such a way" that she could "meet that little angel in heaven" when she died.[27]

Although many people seemed content to accept that heaven was a better world for the simple reason that it afforded familial reunions, others specifically delineated some of its additional advantages. In particular, individuals often alluded to the absence of earthly conditions that stemmed from man's fall, particularly the eradication of sin, sorrow, and sickness. If Kelsey Adams of the 21st Wisconsin fell in battle, his sister Lucretia hoped to meet him "in Heaven where sin & sorrow are not known & partings never come." Helen Kemper contrasted earth's "mortal scenes of turmoil and strife" with the heavenly abode, "free from sin and sorrow." After his brother Jesse died from measles that he had contracted while in the army, Charles Hamilton of Ripley County, Indiana, vowed to "strike glad hands with him on the sunny banks of deliverance where sicness sorrow pain & death are felt & feared no more." Untainted by sorrow and death, heaven inevitably eliminated war from its confines. Eliza Porter consoled herself that her departed friends "have gone to a land where its sons goeth not forth to war" because "eternal peace and joy prevail" there.[28]

In addition to its perfect conditions untouched by sin or war, heaven was described by Christ as a place filled with mansions outfitted for the saints. James Remley asserted that his son Lycurgus had "no doubt gone home to his Heavenly father to those mansions which Jesus has prepared." Catharine Peirce hoped that good behavior and the steadfast endurance of earthly cares would merit her own heavenly home. Prior to the war, her husband Taylor had moved the family so frequently that in almost twenty years of marriage she had not lived in the same home for more than three years. His service during the war even necessitated that she and her three children board with her brother's family. "We never have had a permanant home on this earth," she reflected pensively, "and if we never have I hope we will live so that we can enjoy our rest after this life is done." Implicit in that "rest" was the possession of a heavenly home. "I think if I bare my share [of trials] with patiance that maybe I may get my reward," she alleged. In order to gain that desired end, she concluded to "try to make peace with God and man ... so that I may grow rich in kingdom come." Rather than being completely finished, some of the mansions in heaven, according to Franklin Thorpe, were still under construction, and he imagined that his departed family members lent a hand in "preparing places for us." His outlook typified the modern depiction of heaven as an active, bustling city where citizens engaged in constructive service rather than relaxed in restful repose.[29]

Evidence confirms that a person's understanding of salvation shaped his or her notion of heaven. Northerners who ascribed to a God-centered view of salvation were more apt to picture God as the focal point of heaven since he alone enabled them to enter heaven's gates, but people who believed that salvation could be earned by good works had little reason to think that God should predominate there. In fact, few individuals examined in this study explicitly linked their admission to heaven with salvation by grace alone through faith. Alice Chapin confessed, "I feel *indeed* that if I am *ever* permitted to join the hosts of the redeemed in heaven it will be *all* of *Grace*." Her mother-in-law Sarah Chapin hoped to be "reunited" with "those who have gone before" exclusively "through [the] riches of free grace." David Lough stressed that only "a living faith upon Jesus...will sustain us when we come to die" and enable a person to reach "the blissful shores of a never ending eternity." An Illinois resident emphasized the atoning death of Christ and implored a Hoosier soldier whose believing mother had died to seek "an interest in the blood of Christ" so that he could "gain admittance into the kingdom of Heaven."[30]

More civilians, in contrast, emphasized the necessity of virtuous living in order to gain entrance into heaven. Although some of this number, if asked to clarify their opinion, might have disavowed the idea that moralism alone could provide access to heaven, their correspondence nevertheless gives the impression that human endeavor, rather than the imputed righteousness of Christ, was sufficient grounds for securing their residence in heaven. From the context of their letters, reaching heaven seemed contingent on manifesting faithfulness on earth. However, lacking specific instructions on what exactly faithfulness entailed, these exhortations resembled little more than platitudes. For instance, Mary Chittenden counseled her son George to "strive to live in the enjoyment of vital piety...[so] that if you should never return we may have an assurance if faithful that we shall meat beyond the reach of war." Helen Sharp of Kirkwood, Iowa, admonished her husband John of the 2nd Iowa to "live right so that if you do fall you will fall Zionward and we will try to meet you in heaven." Although the prescription for procuring heaven seldom advanced beyond the admonition to live faithfully on earth, individuals sometimes specified, still without adequate detail, that obeying God's decrees mattered most. "I want you...to observe all that the Lord has commanded," Franklin Alford charged Warren in October 1861, "so that if you should fall we may be in possession of a well grounded hope of your title [to] a ma[n]sion in the spirit land."[31]

Because of the prevalent belief that God would welcome into heaven all who strived to live faithfully, it is not surprising that some Northerners claimed that fallen soldiers had earned their ticket to heaven and would receive special recognition there. A female resident of Oskaloosa, Iowa, wondered why the community paid special tribute to a slain soldier who had been a prominent lawyer before the war. In her estimation, all patriotic soldiers, regardless of their social status, would receive equal honor in heaven. "In the great hearafter their will be written with that shining list those that loved their country and liberty better than life." Rhoda Eggleston assured her son Hubert that he would earn eternal rewards for giving his life for his country. "If you fall in this contest you can lay by the soldiers garb for a crown of glory at Christs right hand." Harrison Kellar supposed that his son John needed only to live an exemplary life to merit his heavenly recognition. "Surely my boy if you maintain your integrity Greatness is before you," he claimed, "for if not in this world God will honor you with a seat near by the Throne." Such a presumptuous assertion bordered on the blasphemous for some individuals, especially those disinclined to support the war. In the summer of 1864, Emeline Ritner of Mt. Pleasant, Iowa, concluded that a "very good neighbor" was a Copperhead. "I heard the other day that Mrs. Morley said she didn't believe *one* of the soldiers would ever go to heaven," she prated. "If she was not my nearest neighbor and I knew it was so [that soldiers could enter heaven], I would never have anything to do with her again."[32] Even heaven, at times, was not too hallowed to escape being politicized by war.

Although a few individuals conjectured that self-sacrificing patriotism had guaranteed soldiers their reward in heaven, other Northerners did not disregard the Scripture's injunction that all men would stand before God as Judge of the universe. Margaret Denny of Charlestown, Indiana, reminded her brother John that the dead would be resurrected at Christ's second coming and "be called to account for all the deeds done in the body whether good or bad." Some civilians emphasized that this certainty of future judgment should influence people's actions and cause them to modify their behavior in order to avoid divine punishment. Appalled by the deportment of some members of the 10th Michigan who acquired a reputation "for drunkenness and disorderly conduct" while home on furlough in the spring of 1864, Elvira Aplin hoped the offenders would "retrieve their carachter...and repent of their evil deeds" before returning to the field and facing Rebel bullets that might "send them to their last *acct*." Because Christ had paid the penalty for sins and placated God's wrath through his death on the cross, those who trusted in him had no reason to dread the approaching judgment. Instead, the righteous could anticipate receiving rewards for their faithful service. Anna Seawright promised her brother James Rizer that by giving his "soul, and body to God" in the present life, his "sentence" in eternity would be "joyful" and his "rewards...glorious." The wicked, in contrast, had every reason to tremble. Citing a proverb of Solomon, Frances Ely observed, "The 'Good Book' assures me that...'the wicked shall not go unpunished,' and I have faith to believe it will be *even so*."[33]

Most people regarded the existence of a separate place of eternal punishment for the wicked as a serious matter. Many soldiers even refrained from referring to hell by name and instead hinted at it euphemistically. Northern civilians likewise handled such a grisly topic with utmost delicacy, revealing the initial stages of what James Moorhead identified as "a growing silence on the subject" of hell that characterized the pulpit during the last quarter of the nineteenth century. For staunch Unionists especially, disloyalty to the government certainly deserved everlasting punishment, though God alone would determine when he would mete out his justice on traitors, whether through the course of the war as many northern ministers claimed or in eternity. Whatever the case, man should not seek to perform God's duties as Judge. When George Aplin threatened to shoot any "northern Rebels" he encountered while home on furlough, his mother Elvira reminded him that it mattered little whether or not Copperheads received the hanging she felt they deserved. "We shall have to let them work out their own distruction, which they will do in Eternity if not in Time." She compared Copperheads to tares in a parable of Christ's and confidently assumed that hell awaited northern traitors after the Judgment. "Our Savior said let the wheat and tears grow together in this world, [for] the harvest time would come when the tares should be bound in bundles and be burned with unquenchable fire." A resident of Kokomo, Indiana, made clear his opinion concerning the eternal abode of those who refused to support the Union. "The true soldiers that die or are killed in this war will go to heaven," he averred, "but the copperhead that dies on a feather bed will surely go to *hell*."[34]

While most northerners generally referred to eternity with great reverence, on occasion flippant attitudes surfaced. For some wives, prolonged separation from their husbands became overwhelming, and during a moment of acute loneliness they expressed sentiments that they might have regretted later. For example, Mary Logan admitted to her husband John, "I have been wicked enough to say in my heart that I would rather be with you than in heaven." Anxiously awaiting news that her husband William had survived the Confederate attack on Helena, Arkansas, in early July 1863, Mary Vermilion frankly revealed her innermost feelings. "I love you too much. I have loved you more than I love all on earth besides, or all in heaven." Immediately recognizing her transgression in placing her affections for him above her devotion to God, she confessed, "I am afraid I have sinned in my wild idolatry, and God has punished me." It was only natural that some women cherished the companionship of marriage more than a distant heavenly home, but their openness paled in comparison to the shockingly blunt behavior of some gung ho volunteers shortly after the fall of Fort Sumter. According to an anecdote recounted by Lizzie Little, a Methodist minister stressed to a company of soldiers their need to repent and prepare for death before facing enemy bullets. Presuming that he had made a "deep impression" on the men, he closed his sermon with the sobering thought that some of them might be in hell in three weeks. To his bewilderment, the soldiers spontaneously erupted by giving three cheers for hell. When the consternated minister asked their captain to explain the reason for such an inappropriate outburst, the quick-thinking officer replied that his men "were not used to scripture Language and supposed Hell was some where near the Confederate Capital." In May 1861, some soldiers may have scoffed at the idea that death and even hell might be lurking around the corner, but mounting casualties quickly drove this misapprehension from their minds. Henry Cobb offered a more accurate synopsis of the situation in the fall of 1862. "Thousands upon thousands of our brothers have mingled their blood with each other in deadly strife, & the '*great* Hereafter' has received their unprepared spirits long before they ought to have gone."[35]

Although many Northerners pondered eternity throughout the war, the diversity of opinions that characterized descriptions of the afterlife and the heavenly abode reveal a topic that was anything but orderly. Since the systematic study of eschatology did not gain widespread appeal until the last quarter of the nineteenth century, the exact sequence and precise details of what transpired after death remained open to interpretation. Margaret Denny looked for the unheralded return of Christ, who would "come as a thief in the night" to resurrect the dead and immediately summon them to the Judgment. Mary Mumford, in comparison, specified that only those who "sleep in Jesus will Christ bring with him" at the resurrection, implying that the unregenerate dead would not be raised at the Second Coming. In addition to questions over the scope of the resurrection, some individuals differed over the nature of the saints in eternity. A female resident of Fremont, Ohio, suffering from ill health possessed "the consolation of knowing that I shall be like him" at death.[36] She presumably expected to receive a glorified, physical body in heaven just as Christ's post-resurrection body exhibited corporeal attributes. Since sickness and pain could not exist in heaven, the earthly body with its many infirmities had to be made new, a process that awaited the resurrection of the dead. In the interim, a Christian's soul resided in heaven, though Northerners, as the evidence has shown, disagreed over the specific activities there.

Spiritualism, however, as popularized by eighteenth-century Swedish mystic Emanuel Swedenborg, deviated from the biblical view that the spirits of deceased saints resided strictly in heaven. Spiritualism maintained that a person's spirit could pass between heaven and earth with great ease because only a short distance separated the spirit world from the terrestrial realm. A November 1862 editorial in *The Crisis*, a spiritualist newspaper published in LaPorte, Indiana, attempted to convince mourners that the intervention of the spirit world could cause heaven to be nearer and ease the pains of earthly loss. "The only way to bring heaven down to earth is to bring the employments of the angels to our doors. Where...would be our sorrows, if we could but feel that the Lord and His holy angels were near us inspiring every good thought and action." Those who embraced spiritualism, the writer asserted, could gain "peace within, and a quiet sphere of peace flowing out" from them. This purported ability of the spirit of a dead loved one to leave heaven periodically and observe family at home provided encouragement and consolation to devotees of the spiritualist philosophy. Despite her orthodox views concerning salvation and the Christian life, Alice Chapin apparently imbibed deeply from the fountain of spiritualism as well. As she gazed upon the grave of her infant son while writing to her husband, she wondered if his spirit might be nearby. "I almost feel as though his dear little spirit was hovering round me trying to draw his mother upward...to that happy resting place his unfettered soul is now so delightfully enjoying." By regarding the nature of man as tripartite, she envisioned her son's body lying cold in the grave, his soul experiencing the joys of heaven, and his spirit lingering close beside her, actively drawing her mind to heavenly things. On another occasion, spent in George Chapin's old bedroom, she speculated about the present location of his spirit. "Perhaps his spirit may be hovering round the home where his friends still so fondly cherish his memory," she divulged to Lucius, "or maybe with *you* his lonely brother who still mourn[s] his loss."[37]

In the end, knowing and understanding every particular facet of eternal life was not the primary goal for most northern civilians. Heaven was the prize, and taking the necessary steps to get there mattered most. Many people recognized that the process began by first coming to terms with the reality of death and accepting that God determined the hour of each person's departure from this world. Since no one could predict the arrival of that final day, advance preparation had to be made. During the war, most Northerners still agreed that only Christians could enter heaven,[38] but they often differed over how a person became one. Individuals who maintained an eternal perspective anticipated the day when the trials and struggles of earthly life would pass away and they would experience the ecstasies of heaven, particularly the blessed occasion of a blissful reunion with departed loved ones. But until that day arrived, family members had to press on through difficult times, trusting in God's sovereignty and satisfied that the deceased had completed life's course and been prepared for eternity. For patriotic Northerners like S. F. and Mary Covington of Cincinnati, who sacrificed their son George on the altar of the nation, this knowledge alone was sufficient. "He died for his country and died a Christian," they related to John Wilder, George's commanding officer who had shown him kindness in the moments before he passed away. "After all, dear Colonel, could we ask for more. Life is fleeting, uncertain, unsatisfying. To die in the service of one's country and to die a Christian is all that in life is worth striving for."[39]

8

"God Be Thanked the Nation and Humanity Were Saved"

Retribution against Traitors, the Reelection of Lincoln, and the Termination of War

In late May 1864, a delegate to the Republican state convention in Springfield, Illinois, reportedly asserted that the "great man, old Abe Lincoln, is a special gift from God Almighty, and if we reject him in this Convention, we reject God Almighty." Although few civilians were audacious enough to draw such an explicit connection in public, many nonetheless concurred with this general sentiment. Despite the previously unimaginable carnage that was becoming almost commonplace since Ulysses S. Grant had taken command of the Army of the Potomac, numerous religious Northerners still clung to their belief that God would preserve the sacred Union. According to this outlook, Lincoln, as commander in chief, served as God's instrument on earth, a primary means through which he accomplished his will. Therefore the president's reelection loomed large for the nation's future. His defeat at the polls might not have signaled that God had forsaken his chosen American people completely, but it definitely would have indicated that further chastening could be expected. Although many believers had interpreted the war as proof that the Father's disciplining hand was falling heavily on wayward sons in both sections of the country, some devout Northerners began to wonder if their erring southern brothers really deserved forgiveness. Rumors of Rebel atrocities committed against Union prisoners caused some observers to clamor for vengeance against southern leaders and, in some cases, civilians too. Northern Copperheads increasingly became the target of even greater hostilities, and more churchgoers demanded an "eye for an eye" retribution against opponents rather than display a willingness to turn the other cheek. Lincoln, however, doubted that God had made his providential purposes as transparent as most religionists claimed, and he humbly offered mercy to repentant Southerners. Yet victory confirmed in the minds of many believers that God had "restore[d] to us the light of His favor." But as one black Hoosier keenly observed the day after Lee's surrender, the triumph of northern arms was only half the battle. "The tug of moral war" still had to be decided. Unfortunately, the failure of Reconstruction demonstrated that significantly fewer religious Northerners cared about the outcome of that contest.[1]

The drift toward meting out strict punishment against Rebel soldiers who violated the unwritten laws of war grew slowly at first among devout Northerners. Although the press had furnished detailed descriptions of the barbarous massacre of black and white soldiers attempting to surrender at Fort Pillow in April 1864 and in some cases called for reprisals against Rebel prisoners, these reports failed to elicit demands of retribution from most members of the Christian community. To be sure, a group of Congregationalists meeting in Chicago maintained that the government should punish crimes committed against black soldiers in the same manner as it would treat offenses against whites. However, after congressional investigation, the government took no direct action against any Rebel soldier who participated in the slaughter and wisely carried out no reprisals against imprisoned Confederates. In fact, most churchgoers seemed content to let an omniscient God deal with the perpetrators as he saw fit rather than allow fallible men dispense judgment. Caleb Mills affirmed that "God's hand may be seen in permitting that fiendish act," for the Rebel "madness" on display at Fort Pillow would inspire black troops to fight to the death in future contests. Southern desperation and northern perseverance would contribute much to bringing about the Confederacy's overthrow, Mills suggested, but ultimately God alone "will deliver us in his own good time & manner." Even an African-American woman in Ohio dismissed any notion of seeking revenge for the three hundred black soldiers murdered in cold blood at Fort Pillow but conceded that "some of the best blood of the nation must be spilt" to subdue rebellion. Instead of becoming discouraged over such base savagery, she encouraged black soldiers and members of the African Methodist Episcopal church to take comfort "that a just God...saw those dark crimes that were committed, and the recording angel was not an idle spectator." Her belief that only divine retribution could satisfy fully the injustice that prevailed at Fort Pillow caused her to trust that God would punish the wicked more thoroughly and appropriately than man.[2]

Even if reports of the butchering of Union soldiers at Fort Pillow did not produce demands for vengeance among the majority of religious northerners, the massive number of casualties suffered by Federal forces during the summer of 1864 fostered the growth of war weariness and propelled some frustrated civilians to vent their ire against their enemies. After three days of fighting at Cold Harbor on June 1–3 that culminated with a determined but foolish frontal assault and the loss of 3,500 men in one hour, Grant reluctantly accepted that his Army of the Potomac could not break through Lee's entrenched lines and forge a path to Richmond. The needless sacrifice of men at Cold Harbor brought the number of total casualties to over 55,000 since the Overland Campaign had begun one month earlier. Such unprecedented carnage weighed heavily on the minds of many citizens, some of whom fervently yearned to see Confederate forces bear the brunt of the killing. After Grant moved his army across the James River and began his assault on Petersburg in mid-June, Milwaukee resident Valentine Nicholson expressed his hope "that God through Grant, may speedily destroy Lees army." However, recent reverses underscored the certainty that "many precious lives" would be required in order to remove "the Rascaly Southern Scoundrils off from the earth," an elimination that Nicholson deemed necessary. Of course, not all civilians possessed the same resolution to have additional Union soldiers die simply to annihilate Rebels. By the summer of 1864, Ann Cotton was tired of hearing about the carnage of war and ready to reunite with her husband Dexter. She could not fathom how he, an army surgeon, could tolerate the recurrent sight of "so much suffering, & inflict so much pain...[by] amputating limbs." Yet her unease with the brutal realities of war did not prevent her from wishing that her Copperhead neighbors might be drafted and "killed off instead of our best men." Not all women shared Ann Cotton's squeamishness over the thought of bloodied and agonizing soldiers, for three years of war had hardened their feminine sensibilities to the point that they might relish or at least claim to take delight in the macabre. After affirming that "the rebels...ought to be strung up by the neck," a Chicagoan matter-of-factly claimed that she could view such public executions without batting an eye. Indeed, she and other patriotic girls sometimes affirmed that if they had been born male they "would be after the rebels" to ensure that they received their just recompense.[3]

Without doubt, the president would play a central role in determining the degree of harshness or leniency that would be applied to erring Southerners. In December 1863, Lincoln's Proclamation of Amnesty and Reconstruction had offered complete pardon to all Southerners who pledged their loyalty to the Union and accepted the dissolution of slavery. Furthermore, once reconstructed citizens within each state equaled ten percent of the total voters in 1860, this loyal minority could create a new state government. From the outset, Lincoln never intended his Ten Percent Plan to become an exclusive or rigid model of reconstruction, for he merely sought a program for shortening the war and convincing Southerners to consent to emancipation before Union armies forced them to adopt it. But Radical Republicans feared that the master class would remain ascendant under Lincoln's policy, and they quickly abandoned presidential reconstruction and sought stricter measures governing the reintegration of Southerners into the body politic. A handful of Radicals who hoped to unseat Lincoln in the upcoming presidential election met in Cleveland on May 31 and nominated the president's former antagonist General John C. Frémont. Dubbing themselves the Radical Democracy, approximately four hundred delegates adopted a plank that, among other things, demanded the redistribution of Confederate landholdings among Union soldiers. Far from alarmed by this third-party bid, Lincoln displayed his keen wit and vast familiarity with Scripture after learning the convention's attendance figures. Turning to 1 Samuel 22:2, he compared the description of those who rallied around David at the cave of Adullam to the Cleveland delegation. "And every one that was in distress, and every one that was in debt, and every one that was discontented, gathered themselves unto him; and he became a captain over them; and there were with him about four hundred men." In reality, Frémont's candidacy was dead in the water from the outset, but his nomination demonstrated how desperately some Northerners wanted Lincoln out of office.[4]

When delegates to the National Union Convention met in Baltimore one week after the Cleveland travesty, they rallied around Lincoln and renominated him with ease. However, northern civilians received news of the president's renomination with mixed feelings. Loyal Unionists such as Cincinnatian David Este believed that Lincoln's reelection by a wide margin would betoken the providential salvation of the Union and secure the final destruction of slavery. Other patriotic civilians preferred a military man such as Ulysses S. Grant or Benjamin Butler but acquiesced to letting the incumbent try to finish his task. Dyed-in-the-wool Democrats like Cyrus McCormick longed for a change at the top and presumed that only a Democratic victory could "save the country from ruin." A few loose-tongued malcontents like one Hoosier Butternut even declared that Jeff Davis would make a better president than Lincoln. The general excitement surrounding such a pivotal election and wild speculation over who else, in addition to Frémont, might oppose Lincoln caused J. W. Osborn to doubt if most people, apart from "unconditional Unionists," possessed enough common sense to choose a suitable candidate. "The masses seem somewhat like flocks of geese...which have lost their leaders," he quipped. While Osborn assumed that a portion of the electorate lacked political acumen, other religious citizens had lost faith in the government altogether. Eleanor Bereman likened the government to Sodom, for she wondered if there could be found in its ranks "enough righteous to save it." Thinking it unlikely that God would again rain down fire and brimstone as he had done to punish that wicked city, she contented herself with wishing that "Fremont and all our last Congress were... [removed to the other] side of the sea."[5]

Bereman may have been pleasantly surprised to learn that some members of Congress indeed acknowledged a dependence on God, for on July 2 both houses approved a resolution asking Lincoln to set apart another day for prayer and fasting. The language of their petition recognized God as the primary agent at work in the world whose sovereign power alone could direct man's actions and bring the war to a favorable conclusion. After underscoring the necessity for citizens and soldiers alike to confess "their manifold sins," the proclamation then urged penitent patriots to offer a fivefold supplication entreating God to accomplish purposes that he alone could effect. If God so willed, he could demonstrate his bountiful "compassion and forgiveness" by quickly ending the rebellion and sustaining the Constitution. As "Supreme Ruler of the World," he governed the rise and fall of nations and could prevent the American people from being destroyed by his own hand, by foreign nations, or by self-destruction through a stubborn devotion to human wisdom that contradicted the divine plan. Moreover, he could "enlighten the mind of the Nation to know and do His will," which, though unknown at present, presumably included the continued existence of the United States. If the preservation of the nation were indeed destined, then God could supply the necessary determination and fortitude to northern armies and civilians to persevere until victory could be secured. Finally, he could transform the minds, will, and emotions of Rebels and convince them to give up the battle so that union, brotherhood, and peace might prevail once again throughout the land.[6]

Although President Lincoln willingly obliged this congressional request and selected August 4 as a day for supplicating God on behalf of the nation, he took issue with their attempt to take control of reconstructing the South. The Wade-Davis bill, which had passed Congress in early July, required fifty percent of voters within a southern state to swear loyalty to the Union in order to form a provisional government, something unlikely to happen until well after the war. Knowing that this legislation would undermine the governments already reconstituted in Louisiana and Arkansas under the Ten Percent Plan, Lincoln pocket vetoed the bill. In an attempt to restore party unity, the president issued an explanatory proclamation clarifying his reasons for rejecting the Wade-Davis proposal. Nevertheless, some offended Radicals refused to toe the party line, creating an internecine divide that attempted to weaken Lincoln's prospects in the upcoming election.[7]

Further compounding Lincoln's problems, the army's enormous loss of manpower through death and the expiration of the terms of three-year enlistees compelled him in July 1864 to call for an additional 500,000 men to fill the ranks. If the states did not meet their enlistment quotas by

September 5, the draft would be reinstituted at a time that fell precariously close to state elections in Ohio and Indiana. Many Copperheads who may have only simmered with discontent beforehand now blazed with indignation, but Lincoln willingly jeopardized his chances of reelection in order to swell the ranks and win the war. In some communities, bands of Copperhead ruffians threatened to resist the draft with violence if necessary. In Allen County, Indiana, James Weiler reported that many members of the secret Copperhead society that he had infiltrated in the spring of 1863 were now "armed to the teeth," probably, in his estimation, awaiting orders from Clement Vallandigham. Although Tory leaders held their tongues for the present, some of the underlings, who had "as much brains as a Babboon," openly threatened "to exterminate the Union Party" and fight off any enrollment officers who attempted to enforce the draft. Lincoln surely anticipated that Copperheads would be alienated by the possibility of conscription, but he might have been more surprised to learn that many Union-loving citizens had tired of bloodshed and were averse to having their family members become cannon fodder in a war with no perceptible end. One woman in Anderson, Indiana, expressed as much but added that she beseeched God to let her loved ones be spared from the draft and instead "take a butternut evertime." A girl in Fairland, Indiana, dreaded the thought of seeing her brothers taken in the draft and entreated God to "restrain the wrath of man, and soon bring about an honorable peace."[8]

An honorable peace was exactly what Lincoln desired, and on July 18 he composed an open memorandum that laid out the unalterable conditions necessary to end hostilities. He would accept only a peace that kept the Union intact and free from slavery.[9] While this brief declaration revealed that Lincoln's commitment to emancipation had not wavered, other Northerners made perfectly clear their willingness to abandon freedmen if doing so would stop the killing and bring their loved ones home. Emilie Gleichmann worried that her husband John would not be released at the end of his one hundred-days term. Frustrated and lonesome, she complained that Evansville, Indiana, was being overrun by black refugees with "bold and proud appearance[s]." Convinced that the war was being waged to secure black freedom, she wondered why her husband should have to leave family and home to fight for "those transient people." After realizing that she had become "too upset" over the thought of whites dying on behalf of African-Americans, she abruptly closed her letter, convicted in her heart that "man's scorn is not right before God." Even with African-Americans volunteering to fight and die for their own freedom, some Northerners feared what the Rebels might do to their white officers if captured. "My prayer to God is that you will never be permitted to lead that Regt of negrows into battle," Lizzie Bowler emphatically asserted to her husband Madison, "for I feel well assured what your fate will be if you should." Her reservations might have been well placed, for even after Fort Pillow, black troops were sent into battle under the most unfavorable circumstances. After successfully tunneling more than five hundred feet under the southern defenses at Petersburg and detonating eight thousand pounds of gunpowder that left a huge breach in the Rebel earthworks, Union commanders squandered their advantage by plunging soldiers headlong into the gigantic crater created by the explosion instead of fanning out and attacking around the perimeter as Grant had ordered. As had been planned, black units led the charge and inevitably bore the brunt of the slaughter. Upon learning of the debacle, Ann Cotton claimed that the loss of nearly four thousand men after such a promising opening "cast a gloom over the whole country." Knowing only "that the poor negroes had the worst of it" at the Crater, she assumed that the defeat had resulted from their lack of martial prowess rather than the incompetence of General Ambrose Burnside, and she wondered why unseasoned blacks had been given "such an important position."[10]

Regardless of their views on the prudence of employing African-American soldiers, civilians looking for explanations about the link between the war and slavery, emancipation, or the future of blacks in America could survey a sampling of clerical and editorial opinions on the fast day of August 4. Two main themes emerged from the pens and tongues of both secular and religious pundits, none of whom followed the congressional recommendation to beseech a sovereign God to intercede on the nation's behalf. On the day of the fast, Joseph Medill's editorial in the *Chicago Tribune* succinctly summarized the two issues that had defined the war by its fourth summer. "This [war] is in its profoundest aspect, a religious contest. It grows out of the conflict between the Christian law of love and the barbarism of slavery.... This is a war for Christian civilization, for God's pure truth and man's universal brotherhood, against ignorance, depravity, and slavery allied."[11] In sum, America was a Christian nation involved in a death struggle against slavery. Either the Union would survive intact, opening the way for liberty, equality, Christianity, and civilization to spread throughout the world, or the savage system of human servitude would prevail, prolonging the oppressive practices of a less enlightened age and dealing a crippling blow to human progress. With so much at stake, ministers had every obligation to support the war and publicly address issues of moral import. Yet while many Northerners accepted this basic premise, a minority questioned its validity. Positing that many clerics, in their zeal to promote the war and preach about political matters, had neglected the gospel, these naysayers challenged the very underpinnings of the idea of a Christian nation by calling attention to the historic mission of the church. On fast day, both positions received ample coverage.

As had been the case throughout the war, preachers who insisted that America was a Christian nation and possessed a special relationship with God latched on to any piece of evidence that might be construed to support their argument. A Methodist in Jeffersonville, Indiana, simply pointed to the prevalence of the Bible throughout the land and the scriptural basis for many principles of common law as proof of the country's Christian status. Annoyed at critics who condemned ministers for supporting the government lockstep in the war, he defended the right of Christian civilians to publicize their views and preserve the political sphere from becoming the dominion of godless politicians. In Fort Wayne, Indiana, Presbyterian George Little directly emphasized the U.S. government's divine mission to spread freedom and equality around the world. Slavery, of course, jeopardized the fulfillment of this sacred calling, and nothing short of war would destroy it. However, merely justifying its removal as a "military necessity" was not enough, Little asserted, for rampant racism gave freedmen few opportunities for advancement. Only full equality, together with the necessary corollary of suffrage, would satisfy the ideals of the Declaration of Independence and set the nation back on track to meet its destiny.[12]

Some Northerners disagreed and doubted that such a clearly planned national course existed. Scathing denunciations of the fasts dripped from the pens of Democratic editors such as one in Iowa City who attended a Methodist service fully anticipating a discourse on slavery. Not disappointing his cynical visitor, the minister discussed the plagues against the Egyptians and asserted that God reserved "only *wrath*" for all who enslaved their fellow men. In the typical fashion of proslavery apologists, the editor pointed out that, after the Exodus, God had allowed and regulated the practice of servitude by the Israelites. Likewise, Christ had not condemned Roman slavery, but his modern-day self-professed disciples had ignored the Master's example and filled their pulpits with antislavery rhetoric. Appealing for a return to preaching that emphasized the message of "'peace on earth and good will to men,'" the editor did his best to appear like a sincere saint seeking sustenance for his soul. However, his vicious tirade against the majority of northern preachers, whose iniquitous "crimson stains" of warmongering would allegedly obscure the lily-white "faults" of slaveholders at the Judgment, betrayed any real concern for the spiritual vitality of the church.[13]

In contrast to the majority of Democratic editorials on political preaching which were devoid of Christian charity and made no pretense at restoring an erring brother to fellowship, a piece reprinted in the *Cincinnati Enquirer* deserved notice because of the author's humility and restraint in critiquing abolitionist churches. The writer observed that prayers offered during previous fasts, at least those for Union victory, had failed to produce the desired end. He speculated that the absence of genuine contrition before

God had rendered the former fasts practically useless, for God would only hear and answer the requests of the truly penitent, who would recognize that the divine purpose in the war might be different from the one espoused by the majority of northern clerics, particularly in their insistence that the present conflict was "a holy war waged under the approval of the Almighty" in order to exterminate slavery. In fact, since "all the combatants are sinners," it might be possible that God intended to make desolate the entire country in order to humble the proud. Instead of confidently believing that America had a special relationship with God and thus merited his favor, discerning citizens should understand that all nations would receive a sentence similar to Sodom and Gomorrah if God always dealt out justice instead of mercy. With unfeigned concern for the preservation of the nation and the building up of the church, the author urged humbled Northerners who would embrace this countercultural view to fill their fast day prayers with the simple petition for God "to save the American Union in his own way."[14]

From all appearances, the appeal for public humility and restraint in deciphering the will of God fell mostly on deaf ears. Three days after the fast, Methodist J. W. T. McMullen unleashed a partisan diatribe against northern Copperheads during a Sunday service at his church in Lafayette, Indiana. More suited for a raucous political rally than a reverent religious gathering, the former chaplain's "War Sermon" classified all but the most zealous patriots as abettors of the Sons of Liberty, those "fallen angels of the great, red dragon,... the Devil." Boasting that he already had purged his congregation of Copperheads, who took asylum in a crosstown assembly where the minister denied that slavery had anything to do with the war, McMullen at least offered forgiveness to repentant northern prodigals who returned to the "loyal church." However, he clearly wanted no mercy shown to southern traitors, and even a pretense of spiritual humility could not mask the unchristian nature of his malice. "I say it with reverence. The rebel confederacy must go to hell and be damned." It seems puzzling and disturbing that a minister would display publicly such intense enmity in violation of several biblical principles regarding harboring hatred, seeking vengeance, and having a proper attitude toward enemies. Although completely unjustified, McMullen's unscriptural statements appear less surprising when considered in light of the almost total absence of biblical content in his sermon, which contained only two overtly religious references. The first, a quotation of Isaiah 8:12,[15] fulfilled the homiletic custom of basing a sermon on Scripture and conveniently served as a rallying point for fainthearted patriots who might believe the lies of northern traitors. The other occurred when McMullen asserted the similarity between the purposes of the war and the gospel. In essence, both sought to secure equality. The war sought to preserve equal personal rights outlined in the Declaration of Independence. The gospel,

McMullen claimed, focused on "equal love" first transferred from God to man, then reciprocated by man to God, and finally shared from man to man. Not only did his definition fall far short of resembling the historic, doctrinally orthodox understanding of the Christian gospel, its emphasis on loving mankind flew in the face of his vehement condemnation of Copperheads and Rebels. To be sure, McMullen's "War Sermon" confirmed the Democratic complaint that some ministers had politicized the pulpit and recklessly deviated from preaching scriptural truths.[16]

Rather than deplore the ecclesiastical disunity caused by political differences, by the latter part of 1864 many churchgoers had come to accept and in some cases heartily approve of the division within their assemblies. Some laypersons decided to endure preaching that they found objectionable without raising a ruckus. Describing to a soldier the Sunday services at Roberts Chapel in Indianapolis, Louisa Dunn recalled that Reverend H. N. Barnes had lectured on "some thing about exceeding great promises." Her lasting impression, however, was of a partisan meeting centered around "a political harangue" that concluded "with a hot abolition prayer." This combination left her "tired nearly to death when they got through." Congregants unwilling to tolerate sentiments that they opposed hastily left their unpleasant environment, sometimes seeking to coax away other dissatisfied souls and instigate a church split. In Plymouth, Indiana, Presbyterian minister John Chapin reported in September that one disgruntled member "rallied about him the Copperhead element," presumably intending to form a new assembly. Untroubled by this development, he claimed that his remaining congregation, now completely unified behind him, had been strengthened through subtraction. Two months later, a female observer still agreed with Chapin's assessment. "The tares are out to some extent & therefore as a church they are stronger," she explained, implying that Copperheads were false professors of Christianity mixed among true believers, hence their removal left a pure church. Too few Democratic churchgoers followed the advice of Ohioan William Burke, who asserted that any layman whose "ultra [political] notions" alienated him from the majority of the brethren should "conform his views" or find a different congregation that agreed with him without "sow[ing] discord among his former associates." Instead, proponents of each political persuasion almost seemed to enjoy the atmosphere of mutual animosity that had infected many churches. A woman from Dover, Indiana, welcomed the tidings that Mr. Thomas would fill the pulpit the following Sunday, for she knew that "the rebels hates him so bad that they wont go to hear him preach." Revealing her true feelings to soldier Rufus Dooley, she admitted, "I am glad they stay a way for I hate to se[e] them."[17] Because too many religious Northerners placed greater emphasis on political cohesion than the unity of believers in Christ, they often turned their sanctuaries into battlefields, producing spiritual casualties numbered only by God.

Yet as the body count continued to mount in all theaters of war and stalemates around Petersburg and Atlanta dragged into August with no end in sight, the upcoming election took on even greater significance, for its outcome would determine if the North would prosecute the war until Confederate defeat or settle for an ignominious compromise that would keep the Union divided. In early August, Mollie McPheeters, who had followed politics closely ever since her husband John's enlistment, freely conversed with him about the magnitude of voting responsibly. While he speculated that Grant might make a good president, she emphatically asserted her preference for the status quo. "If I were allowed to cast a vote I would not hesitate to give it in favor of 'Abe' even if Grant were a candidate too. I am willing to try him another term even if he has done some things I disapprove of. We must make allowances for him as we do for other people, knowing that he is a mere man and liable to err. I believe he has done the best that he knew, and I dont know of any one that would have done better." The knowledge of McPheeters's simple faith in him and confidence that he had competently guided the nation through its most trying hour would have warmed the president's heart, but he instead received only dire predictions of his political demise from several pessimistic friends. Indeed, some acquaintances thought that Lincoln's careworn visage manifested the crushing weight of uncertainty that he bore regarding the election. Nevertheless, he remained true to his convictions that the Union must be preserved and slavery destroyed. A Democratic victory at the polls, he told a former governor of Wisconsin and a circuit court judge on August 19, would lead to a policy of conciliation toward the South. The ultimate result for blacks, who had made such significant gains over the past two years, would be reenslavement at the hands of their former masters, a betrayal for which he "should be damned in time & in eternity." Even under such enormous stress, Lincoln could appear larger than life, and he rekindled his guest's faith "that he was Heavens instrument to conduct his people thro this red sea of blood to a Canaan of peace & freedom."[18]

Lincoln, however, did not share this optimism at present, and he decided to take preparatory action in anticipation of his defeat at the polls. On August 23, he passed around a sealed note and enigmatically asked each of his cabinet members to sign the back. Little did they know that their signatures indicated a pledge to work with the president-elect in a last-ditch effort "to save the Union" in the four months between the election and inauguration, for Lincoln knew that the Democratic platform would hinder the new president from uniting the sections after taking office. Six days later, Democrats held their national convention in Chicago and, as expected, nominated George

B. McClellan, the often sluggish but indubitably loyal former general. However, the arch-Copperhead Clement Vallandigham succeeded in inserting a peace plank into the platform that called for the "immediate...cessation of hostilities." Not having sought the nomination in the first place, McClellan found himself between a rock and a hard place and dawdled for time, a move that did not surprise his former boss in the least. "Oh, he's intrenching," Lincoln quipped, but other Northerners did not wait so patiently for the general's decision. While War Democrats counseled him to stand firm in his views and Peace Democrats tried to lure him into their ranks, some Unionists lost no time in denouncing the Chicago proceedings. John Ketcham was ready to include McClellan with the "collection of conspirators" who nominated him if he accepted the ticket that endorsed little more than "the establishment of the Southern Confederacy." With his son in the army and his wife having served a stint in Tennessee as a Union nurse, the Indianapolis lawyer could not understand why God allowed Vallandigham and other Copperheads to live and hatch "blatant treason" with their peace schemes that would "peril the life of the nation." When McClellan finally announced his decision more than one week after receiving the nomination, he underscored that the Union must be preserved at all costs and repudiated the peace plank in no uncertain terms. Despite this resounding affirmation that the war would not be abandoned prematurely, the very act of contesting Lincoln's reelection earned McClellan criticism from civilians like Mollie McPheeters, who thought that he might be "mean enough to give the Rebels all they desire."[19]

But instead of Southerners realizing the fulfillment of their wishes with the nomination of a strong antiwar candidate, they instead found that one of their worst nightmares had come true. Sandwiched between the time of McClellan's nomination and publication of his acceptance letter, General William T. Sherman's army drove the Confederate defenders from Atlanta and marched into the city uncontested on September 2. This notable breakthrough clearly shifted the political momentum back to Lincoln and gave hope to some Northerners that an end to war was near. The president responded to news of Sherman's success by issuing a proclamation of thanksgiving for divine aid on the nation's behalf and encouraging prayer for continued preservation of Federal soldiers. In typical fashion, ministers often used these special occasions to expound on the millennial implications of America's sacred mission rather than dwell on present realities such as the plight of "the sick, wounded, and prisoners" and the care of "orphans and widows" as the proclamation encouraged them to do. For example, Milwaukee Congregationalist J. T. Mathews compared America to Old Testament Israel, appropriating Isaiah 43:21, "This people have I formed for myself; they shall show forth my praise," as a verse that conveyed God's special relationship with his new Israel. Mathews considered it "unquestionably true that Eternal Providence had a great design in calling this nation into existence," specifically "the complete physical, mental, and spiritual emancipation of the race." These otherworldly abstractions seemed too remote from the everyday experiences or modest expectations of many members of the laity, who saw only the devastation and brutality of war. An Ohio housewife whose husband made it safely to Atlanta expressed her hope that he had complet[ed] his last "dangerous, desperate, slavish discouraging and tedious campaign" and would no longer have to witness the gruesome sight of "brave comrads mutilated & suffering by the hands of the enemy." Ann Cotton even contemplated the hardships of many of Atlanta's civilian population, who were forced to leave their homes, if they survived the Union bombardment, and flee further south at their own risk or be herded north under military protection. Her sympathy for their affliction had limits, though, for she believed that "the rebs certainly deserve" to be punished, "for they have been the cause of so much sufferings."[20]

Blame for the country's troubles, of course, was cast in many directions. Despite McClellan's disavowal of their peace principles, Copperheads stepped up the attack against the perceived source of their ills. According to the Republican press, one Butternut speaker at a meeting in Allen County, Ohio, accused Lincoln of being more vengeful than God. The president wanted to "exterminate the whole Southern people," the orator claimed, but God at least "had some little compassion, as he let one man live at the time that he *drowned Noah!*" A local judge followed this confused elocution with another allegation regarding the relative kindness of the aforementioned parties. Lincoln, he declared, was so unfeeling that he ignored the petitions of Democrats urging him to seek peace and discontinue the draft, while God condescended to "listen to the prayers of a *'Damned dirty Dog!'*" Regardless of the accuracy of the quotations scribbled down by the partisan reporter or the intentional word-doctoring of a less than scrupulous editor, the story conveyed two truths: Copperheads despised Lincoln, and Republicans assumed them to be irreligious traitors. Not known for taking slights meekly, the Democratic press responded tit for tat with accusations of hypocrisy and warmongering against the majority of northern clergy, who were charged repeatedly with advocating and exulting in war. After learning that Methodist bishop Matthew Simpson's spirited peroration and emotional presentation of the 73rd Ohio's tattered battle flag at a church conference in Chillicothe had roused his audience into a frenzied, patriotic outburst, the editor of the *Cincinnati Enquirer* called the scene a "humiliating reflection upon Christianity" when Ohio's leading churchmen "bow[ed] before an idol of war and blood." Any discerning observer would recognize that the participants' faith was a sham, he asserted, for they used religion merely to further political ends.[21]

Whether tormented by the Scylla of politicized religion or threatened by the Charybdis of the draft, many antiwar Democrats felt battered and abused at every turn. Because several counties fell short of their quotas for volunteers, some unlucky winners of Uncle Sam's lottery scrambled to find a way out of serving. Since Congress had rescinded the $300 commutation fee in July, the price of securing a substitute increased dramatically. "The Butternuts that are drafted are nearly breaking thare necks to get substituts and offering some say one thousand dollars," Sarah Dooley noted with satisfaction. "I hope they will get nary one and will have to go them selves," she added with a hint of ill will. Taking the opposite tack, Jacob Thorna commended some "young democrats" who disappeared shortly after being drafted in St. Clair County, Illinois. Rather than submit to the "cruel invention of abolitionists" and report for duty to be "slaughtered like beasts," they had demonstrated discretion beyond their years, and he hoped they would find nothing but "success in life whereever they may be." However, not all draftees who sought to escape the service based their opposition solely on political differences. John Poucher, who as an eighteen-year-old student at Indiana Asbury University became caught up in the war fervor in April 1861, had since lost all interest in political and military developments. But after being drafted in Floyd County, Indiana, on September 28, the ministerial student could only trust that God would make it possible for him to avoid the army and finish his training. Unlike the majority of northern clergy who championed the war without reservation, Poucher preferred to devote all his energies to the gospel ministry. Because of high bounties, Poucher's township secured enough volunteers to cover the draftees, and his parents contributed only $110 to the till. These circumstances appeared to him as God's working on his behalf, and in January he earned his preaching license and delivered his first sermon a month later.[22]

While Poucher believed he could "discern the finger of God" manipulating the circumstances of life for his personal well-being, other religious Northerners expected to detect the imprint of God's hand on national events such as the all-important state elections in Pennsylvania, Ohio, and Indiana. Since the outcome of these contests in mid-October would portend the likely result of the presidential race in November, citizens eagerly anticipated the ballot. On the eve of the election, Calvin Fletcher supposed that Democrats, the party of "ignorence and catholicism," would carry Indiana. Convinced that the Democracy would "destroy the union & oppose all [Protestant] religion & morals," the elderly banker could only pray that God would "turn the hearts of the people to judgment equity & wisdom" and thereby preserve the country from ruin. After encountering a Copperhead at the polls and giving him a stern lecture, Fletcher went about his daily business and awaited the returns. His worst fears never materialized, for Union candidates won by large majorities in all three states. Celebrations ensued, and Republican victories filled J. W. T. McMullen with jubilation. "The kingdom of heaven, and the Republic forever!" he gushed, hardly able to contain his excitement when writing a Hoosier chaplain a week later. Anticipating another more significant triumph, he added a climactic flourish that confirmed his penchant for taking Scripture out of context, even in private correspondence. "Once more, and Abraham Lincoln, and Andrew Johnson, servants of the Most High, 'elect according to the foreknowledge of God' and the will of the loyal American people, shall wield... power in this great land of ours."[23]

Energized by successes in the field and at the polls, loyal Northerners directed their swelling indignation at Copperheads. Catharine Peirce asserted that all civilians who failed to "come forward on the right side now... are not deserving the chance of American citizen ship and a place on the face of Gods earth." In her opinion, only noble and courageous individuals should be allowed to inhabit the land, and if the war did not "exterminate all cowards and cops," then God would be compelled to "send another flood" or some other cataclysm to destroy the wicked. Admitting to her soldier-husband that she had become carried away with her patriotic reverie, she nonetheless hoped that Union momentum would overwhelm "all kinds of reptiles that are inclined to wag thier venimous tongues in trying to destroy this glorious Union" and leave them confounded and confined to their holes on Election Day. Flushed with confidence after Governor Oliver P. Morton's reelection, Sarah Dooley thought she could decipher the handwriting on the wall for the insolent and irritating Copperheads who lived nearby. Envisioning their fate once the soldiers finally returned to restore order at home, she imagined that they would "crall in thare holes from whence they can never return." Although some might continue to "howl and spout" against the government and the war for a few short days, they would learn soon enough that "thare doom is sealed and they will reap thare reward." In the meantime, she would no longer "countnance them nor... neighbor with them." Even in the "awful copperhead hole" of Quincy, Illinois, the promising prospect of Lincoln's reelection gave Augustus Frey hope that the "home traitors will be burried out of sight." While Dooley and Frey merely insinuated what they wished would befall Copperheads, a Republican newspaper in Delaware County, Indiana, carried a clever obituary two days after the election that perfectly captured the mounting resentment of many religious northerners. "Died—On last Tuesday, the Copperhead party, of chronic negrophobia.... But the saddest reflection is that the deceased had lived an ungodly life, and died unrepentant; and it is written that whosoever dieth in his sins shall be damned." Yet before Unionists permanently interred them in the lake of fire, antiwar Democrats made every effort to salvage some victories in November. Unable to deny their opponents the freedom to assemble and speak publicly, a few "good folks" in Canton, Illinois, implored God to send a downpour on a local Democratic rally. Although the rain came, the electioneering continued, and Ellen Plattenburg, one of the prayer warriors, ventured out to see the spectacle. As she expected, the crowd was composed of the "ugliest big mouthed glaze eyed ignorant looking bushwhackery set of scamps" that she had ever seen. While insults may not have had any bearing on the election results, Plattenburg's colorful description of McClellan's likely supporters more than matched his previous put-downs of Lincoln as "the original gorilla" and "a well meaning baboon."[24]

In the days and weeks leading up to the election, religious Unionists underscored the national, spiritual, and historical significance of the outcome. After discoursing on the political duties of Christians, the *Western Christian Advocate* delineated the millennial implications of the election when it admonished believers to determine "which is God's side" and to cast a vote for "the interests of Christ's kingdom" and "the progress of the race." If some dull-witted reader failed to see that this eliminated the Democratic party, the editor framed the choice in more comprehensible terms. "In a word, we think we know how Jeff. Davis would like to have us vote, and we shall take care to vote precisely the opposite, and we think every loyal, patriotic Christian man ought to do the same." Some Methodist ministers may have taken this cue from the influential denominational weekly and attempted to publicly expose the political and moral shortcomings of the Democracy. On the last Sunday of October, an Illinois Methodist preached to a packed house on the Christian's duties to civil government and exhorted his congregation to defeat McClellan at the polls in order to avert "the greatest calamity" imaginable. In Miami County, Ohio, clergyman William Jackson agreed that a Democratic triumph would not only humiliate and ruin the country politically but, even worse, would "displease the God of heaven." Practically proclaiming a divine endorsement of the ticket, Jackson asserted that any true "lover of God" had no choice but to vote for "honest Abe & Andy." Franklin Thorpe likewise found religious meaning in the election and perceived that it would decide a momentous spiritual struggle for the nation's soul. In his opinion, the loyal electorate could "over throw the powers of wickedness that have infested this country" by voting the Union ticket. With slavery already dying, Lincoln's reelection would cause the Confederate States of America to "expire" in short order, and Thorpe felt inclined "to shout to see salvation of the Lord" in such propitious developments. Ovid Butler, antislavery advocate and active member in the Disciples of Christ denomination, chided his son Scot for doubting that he, a long-time radical on race relations, would vote for Lincoln. Fully aware that the upcoming election might be his last presidential contest, he praised God for the opportunity "to cast a vote of higher significance & deeper import," one that represented "National Universal Freedom." Besides ensuring freedom for all Americans, Lincoln's victory would preserve "the Integrity of the Union" by confirming that northern civilians wanted to prosecute the war until "the Serpents vitality" was enervated and the rebellion crushed. In Butler's opinion, God intended the war to produce a free and unified America, and by reelecting the president, the "National will" would conform at last to the divine will.[25]

On Election Day, Calvin Fletcher prayed for God to strengthen him, departed home, and headed to the polls for "one of the most important events" of his long and noteworthy life. To his satisfaction, "a McClellan vote could scarcly be found," but he managed to procure tickets from both parties to paste in his diary for posterity's sake. According to one allegedly true story, a Copperhead deacon in southeastern Wisconsin with a reputation for stomping out of church whenever the pastor delivered a political sermon received a leaflet announcing a Christian Commission meeting while heading to the polls shortly before closing time. Putting the circular in his pocket, he inadvertently deposited it into the ballot box instead of the Democratic ticket and did not catch his mistake until too late. His blunder mattered little, for Lincoln won handily, receiving over 400,000 more votes than McClellan and romping his opponent in the electoral count 212 to 21. Lincoln spent election night at the telegraph office and, showing no signs of apprehension while awaiting returns, thoroughly enjoyed himself by reading David Ross Locke's humorous stories about Petroleum Nasby, a subject matter that an irritated Edwin Stanton considered both senseless and inappropriate for the president to be indulging in at such a critical time. Yet when a moment for serious and forthright reflection presented itself, Lincoln did not disappoint. Greeting a group of serenaders before retiring to bed, he offered thanks to God that the American people had determined with their ballots "to stand by free government and the rights of humanity."[26]

Loyal Northerners celebrated Lincoln's victory, confident that it would help lead to a speedy termination of war. "Did you shout when you heard that Old Abe was reelected?" Mollie McPheeters inquired of her husband John. "I did, ... [and] *Papa almost danced when the news came*," she reported playfully, knowing how amused he would be trying to picture his devout Presbyterian father rejoicing so heartily that he would engage in a carnal practice condemned by the church. "*I say almost understand*," she added, careful to make sure he did not misconstrue her little jest. Milton Buswell joked at the expense of the defeated party and its hapless standard bearer. "That bogus convention called by them 'the great National Democratic Convention' have heard the loud peals of the death knell of their candidates as they fell and were crushed by that thing of a platform, but they say '(Be) little(d) Mac' aint buried so but his feet stick up. Be that as it may I think it will be more than three days, perhaps four years before his resurrection." Although Buswell gloated over the demise of the peace wing of the Democratic party, he thanked God that some "old veterans of Democracy" possessed the good sense to break ranks and vote for the party that would finish the task of destroying rebellion. At least one citizen who accused Lincoln of taking liberties with the Constitution even hailed his triumph. "We live in wonderful times," Mary Putnam asserted optimistically, for she considered the president's reelection a sign that "the Lord is leading us on," sovereignly working through Lincoln to end slavery while simultaneously using the war to chasten the nation for having tolerated the evil institution so long. Having consistently used its pages to support Lincoln and the war, the *Western Christian Advocate* took satisfaction in boasting, "The patriotism of the ministers and the Churches has saved the nation, and the triumph of the Union cause is a victory of conscience and religion over selfishness and sin."[27]

Still euphoric from election victory, many patriotic Northerners possessed a spirit of gratitude that dovetailed nicely with the observance of Thanksgiving Day only two weeks later. Few Americans had more to be thankful for than freedmen, and those who gathered with the members of the A.M.E. church in Indianapolis heard Willis Revels speak from Psalm 126:3, "The LORD hath done great things for us, whereof we are glad." They demonstrated their appreciation to God by giving back to others in need, collecting fifty dollars, a remarkable sum for a congregation still recovering from the fire that had destroyed its building the previous July, to be divided between impoverished families of soldiers and the Christian Commission. With prospects for Union military victory looking more favorable than ever, some ministers used the occasion to interpret the meaning of the war and chart America's future course. In Zanesville, Ohio, Presbyterian James Platt asserted that war had fostered a greater national awareness of the sovereignty of God. He regarded the nationalization of Thanksgiving and the addition of "In God We Trust" to the currency as evidence that the country was accepting its status as a Christian nation. Ohio Congregationalist C. Norris Grant agreed and maintained that the inscription on the coinage would testify to foreign nations of America's Christian position. At best, these examples represented only external tokens that lacked spiritual substance, mere trappings of civil religion that even the Confederacy manifested, and to a greater degree with its intentional inclusion of God in the southern constitution.[28]

On the Sunday after Thanksgiving, Indianapolis Baptist Henry Day, in contrast to some of his clerical counterparts, did not trifle with shallow expressions of religious sentiment but asserted that America, at its very core, possessed a providential destiny to accomplish God's will among the nations. Just as Palestine had been the hub of biblical history, so America would be the center of God's activity in the present and future. Firmly convinced of

American exceptionalism, Day maintained that the democratic nature of American religion, with its emphasis on every man reading and interpreting the Bible for himself, had enabled individual piety to flourish and surpass the devotion of the European masses. Furthermore, he claimed that the war was unifying the northern states and western territories, reforging the bond with the South, incorporating German and Irish immigrants into the fabric of society, and spurring all men to works of charity to help those who suffered. In Day's view, this growing national unity mirrored conditions that existed during the early church when the Roman Empire provided civil and linguistic homogeneity that allowed the gospel to spread throughout the known world. Similarly, the good news would take root from coast to coast, and the Christianized United States, a "monument of God's grace," would stand as a paragon of peace and brotherhood to the watching world. Over the ensuing centuries, first Europe, then Africa and Asia would embrace the American model as ambassadors, tourists, soldiers, and missionaries disseminated the gospel, "backed up by the power of a mighty nation." The war, according to Day, effectively prepared America for its divine mission to spread the "kingdom of Christ all over the world."[29]

Henry Day's millennial reverie might have tickled the ears of congregants in Indianapolis, but William T. Sherman had no intentions of letting Southerners experience anything that remotely resembled the halcyon conditions anticipated by the Baptist minister. Rather than play into the hand of John Bell Hood by pursuing his army north into Alabama and Tennessee, Sherman convinced Lincoln and Grant that a march through Georgia would demoralize Confederate civilians and hasten the end of the war. By living off the land and implementing a hard war policy, the captor of Atlanta would cause Southerners to withdraw their support from a government powerless to protect their homes from Yankee invaders. With only scattered Rebel opposition between Atlanta and Savannah, the Federals cut a wide swath through the middle of Georgia, foraging for food, slaughtering livestock, and more or less terrorizing the populace. Sherman condemned vandalism and the wanton destruction of civilian property, but his officers, because of uncontrollable circumstances or by intentional choice, did not always enforce strict discipline, and some private residences fell to the torch.[30]

Some Northerners reveled in the thought of southern civilians suffering because of the devastation unleashed by Sherman's army. In his Thanksgiving sermon, C. Norris Grant encouraged his listeners to exult over their countrymen's calamity, even going so far as to dispute Solomon's counsel in Proverbs 24:17, "Rejoice not when thine enemy falleth." Grant contended that exceptional circumstances required different responses and claimed that if the wisest of kings could see "Jeff Davis and the instigators of the cruel rebellion," then he would expunge the negative modifier from his proverb. Rather than quibble with Solomon, more northern laypersons focused on the prospect of Sherman bringing the war to a speedy conclusion. Anxious to follow the army's movements, civilians had to rely on reports from southern newspapers because Sherman lacked all means of communication. Mollie McPheeters figured that the Rebel press would publicize any Federal setback, so she assumed in late November that "the grandest [expedition] of the war" was progressing smoothly. Caleb Mills found it "amusing" how southern editors attempted to "conceal their fears" over how Sherman's juggernaut bulldozed through the Confederate heartland almost uncontested. He refused to believe their claims of Union "atrocities & barbarrities" but regarded them as propaganda pieces intended to convince an infuriated populace to keep resisting. Other Northerners expressed great concern for the safety of soldiers whom they had not heard from for several weeks. Reassuring herself as much as her son, the mother of a captain with the 100th Indiana reminded him that she had placed his life "in the hands of *God* who has thus far protected you." Elvira Aplin asserted that "all pious people are praying for them [Sherman's army,] and I hope the prayers of the righteous will avail much in their case." While she wanted soldiers to liberate Union prisoners and punish their captors, she manifested no ill will toward southern civilians at this time. "I do not wish all the southern people to be killed, but I hope they may be brot to their senses and return to the union while their lamp of life holds out."[31]

Bringing disobedient sons back into the Union was indeed one of Lincoln's primary goals, and in his annual message to Congress in December 1864 he reiterated that an extremely favorable policy had been offered to all Southerners who would pledge their loyalty to the government. Although "no voluntary application" for readmission had been denied to that point, he speculated that the people might demand "more rigourous measures" in the near future. At the same time, the nation needed to settle permanently the issue of slavery, and the president fervently urged the House to join the Senate in approving a constitutional amendment to abolish the institution. Public sentiment regarding the status of blacks in society was still mixed, however, and an A.M.E. minister in Springfield, Illinois, saw ample evidence of this during the Emancipation Day celebration on January 1, 1865. While exuberant blacks paraded through the city, "the copperheads, woodenheads, and all other kind of heads...opposed to negroes being any thing more than chattels, stood on the streets and gnashed their teeth." Nevertheless, the cleric took encouragement that some white citizens who favored "equity and justice" received them kindly, and positive change was afoot as support for abolishing the state's black codes continued to grow. A resident of southern Illinois deemed that "the negro question is becoming settled pretty fast," and he anticipated the day "when they all may be free before the law," which he defined as possessing "equal rights in all our courts." He drew the line, however, with black suffrage and even contended that some whites should be disfranchised. A fellow Illinoisan who believed in "the Universal Brotherhood of humanity" and eagerly awaited "a political millennium" maintained that an "intelligence test" should be used to determine voting privileges instead of a system based on "color and sex." While literate blacks would be able to cast a ballot, the ignorant majority of "Negros, Irish, [and] Copperheads" would be disqualified from tainting the electoral process. Although the issues of black equality and suffrage were far from being resolved, these opinions indicate that religious Northerners were thinking about how the country could move forward. Some, like Caleb Mills, knew that the transition period would not be easy, and after the House approved the Thirteenth Amendment on January 31, he predicted that "Rebeldom will find reconstruction on skin basis a hard road to travel." But if any people could accomplish the task of reunifying whites and incorporating blacks, "the Christian patriot," Mills believed, would form the vanguard and embrace the "glorious mission" of reconstructing the South.[32]

In fact, national developments and the trials of war had caused some of those Christian patriots to reexamine their assumptions and alter their opinions regarding God's purposes in the conflict. Two years earlier, the *Western Christian Advocate*, an antislavery organ from the war's outset, had defined equality in severely restricted terms and lobbied for the separation of whites and blacks. Yet near the end of 1864, the editor acknowledged the complicity of northern churches in helping to protect slavery during the antebellum era and censured the racial segregation that characterized most congregations. Indeed, God had been obliged to use "infidel philanthropists and sagacious statesmen" to humiliate the church and expose her moral deficiencies before making her a productive agent in the antislavery movement. To be sure, the church still had much room for improvement in the area of race relations, the editor conceded, but he was convinced that God would continue the war until all Americans "*recognize the essential manhood of the negro, and his entire equality, before the laws and in the sight of God.*" With this transformation completed, the United States, "purified and saved," would stand above all nations as "a glorious example of democratic invincibility and Constitutional freedom."[33]

Some less optimistic observers, in contrast, doubted that national redemption lay in the near future. Mennonite John M. Brenneman claimed that "Pride and forgetfulness of God" predominated throughout the land. America, like the "exalted" town of Capernaum, which Christ cursed for unbelief, "must be brought much Lower...before she can prosper as before." Even many "Christian Professors," the bishop alleged, cared for and conversed more "about worldly affairs, about Buying & Selling Land, or about the war, as if they were ashamed to talk about Christianity." This indifference to spiritual matters seemed more analogous to the days of Noah than to a religiously enlightened age. Methodist T. A. Goodwin was even harsher in his analysis and compared America to Pharaoh. At the end of 1862, the Indianapolis minister had reviewed in the *Western Christian Advocate* the numerous instances during the antebellum era when slavery expanded and the government, "assuming the character of Pharaoh," hardened its heart toward liberating African-Americans. Although the plague of war had prompted Lincoln to enact the Emancipation Proclamation, Goodwin regarded it as a military necessity rather than a "moral measure" stemming from a heart of true repentance and aversion to slavery. In the spring of 1864, he had cited the unequal pay of black soldiers and generally degraded conditions of black refugees as evidence that the American Pharaoh had only reluctantly let God's people go. As a nation, "we hate slavery more intensely than formerly," Goodwin had generalized, "but we hate it vindictively, because it has annoyed us." This offering of "a lame sacrifice, if sacrifice at all," in no way satisfied God or appeased his wrath but only invited more plagues. Yet even in mid-February 1865, when other religious citizens anticipated the war's end and claimed that the nation had forsaken the sin of slavery, Goodwin still insisted that more desolation awaited the country. To be sure, blacks were better off than before the war, but the government's policies had been driven by a desire for self-preservation. Even Pharaoh, "smarting from the latest plague," offered concessions and slowly progressed until he released the Israelites. However, he never experienced a genuine change of heart, but even after the death of the firstborns sent his army to recapture the children of Israel, only to have it destroyed in the Red Sea. Goodwin claimed that passage of the Thirteenth Amendment was no better than Pharaoh's empty promise to let the Jews worship in the wilderness but deny them the cattle necessary for sacrifice. "The mere abolition of slavery is downright mockery if the freedman has no power to protect himself [legally]," the Methodist alleged, citing black codes that still existed in Indiana. "There will be no peace till the manhood of the black man is acknowledged, and his rights to all that manhood implies are guaranteed." Knowing full well the unpopularity of such a gloomy assessment at a time when prospects for peace looked so promising, Goodwin concluded that more death and destruction, possibly even a disaster like that at the Red Sea, would be necessary to bring the nation to a place of real repentance where it would deal with African-Americans in a manner acceptable to God.[34]

Goodwin indeed erred in speculating that severe reverses lay on the horizon before the arrival of peace, and his blaming the government for the nation's moral failure rather than indicting the church and individual believers for failing to act as salt and light in the world revealed an implicit assumption that suitable legislation by secular authorities would shape society more than the words and deeds of Christians. Evidence indicates that some northern believers needed to show kindness and love to brothers and sisters within their midst before attempting to reconcile racial differences. As had been the case for the past two years, some laypersons continued to leave their congregations over political differences, like one Ohio woman who allegedly withdrew from her assembly because the minister was "such a good union man." Unionist member Jane Van Scyoc looked upon her departure as the church's gain. "I say let her go and the lord be with her," she expressed duplicitously before adding pointedly, "but I know the devle will be with her." Other individuals complained about the development of unhealthy rivalries among Christian denominations. A Methodist in Michigan lamented that approximately twenty ministers throughout the state had left the Methodist fold to preach for different denominations. Almost more disconcerting, many young people raised in Methodist homes were "learning the Calvinian dialect." While he called for a renewed emphasis on denominational distinctives, one man in Muncie, Indiana, lambasted local Methodists for emotional excesses displayed during a recent "'distracted' meeting." In a series of letters to the local newspaper, "Augustus" asserted that the histrionics at Methodist revival services masqueraded as piety but lacked "the genuine essence of godliness," which to him encompassed faith in Christ, obedience to God's commands, and humility before God. Convinced that true religion would affect the mind and will of man and manifest itself by permanently altering a believer's conduct, Augustus preferred a more intellectually based religion and blamed the frenzied outbursts associated with Methodist revivalism for producing shallow converts who quickly backslid once the emotional fires waned. Knowing that his outspoken opinion would subject him to intense criticism, Augustus stressed that he was no religious scoffer but an orthodox believer in Christ as the Savior who genuinely cared for the spiritual vitality of the church. Although well-meaning church reformers were unable to see into the hearts of individuals to determine whether they worshiped God out of pure motives or hypocritically used religion to gain the attention and praise of peers, northern church members could at least look on a person's outward appearance and prevent racial differences from disrupting the unity of believers in Christ. Some white Methodists in Lafayette, Indiana, clearly had done so, for they attended the revival services at the local A.M.E. church, "made themselves at home," and assisted in the work of winning souls. Sincerely grateful, the black pastor nonetheless recognized the necessity for "universal change in the churches," for unless believers could grasp what "brotherhood" entailed and model it in their own assemblies, it would be pointless to rhapsodize about millennial conditions and "harmonizing the world in one brotherhood."[35]

Instead of seeking ways to solve the everyday social and racial challenges that confronted them, some northern Christians simply trusted God to work out all difficulties that seemed beyond man's capabilities. In late January, Ovid Butler affirmed that God "holds in His own hand the issues of this conflict and He will dispose of them for the accomplishment of His own purpose." Drawing the same conclusion that Abraham Lincoln had reached over two years before when musing upon the divine will, Butler asserted that God's objective "has not hitherto been the purpose of *either* the North or of the South." The elderly Hoosier nevertheless felt confident that he had discerned the intentions of a sovereign God, specifically "the utter abolition" of the sinful practice of slavery as the sole condition for bringing the war to a conclusion. Attempting to decipher the will of God from current events had become common practice for many religious northerners, but the recent introduction of dispensationalism to American religion provided a systematic framework for interpreting history by dividing the Bible into seven distinct ages. Randie Cress of Clayton, Illinois, fully embraced the dispensationalist view and sought to convince soldier Rufus Dooley that it could unlock the secrets of the last days. "I learn from the Bible, that all Dispensations, since the world began, have closed up with a seven years war," she confidently maintained. With four years of fighting elapsed, three years remained to "wind [up] this Christian Dispensation." She conjectured that the Confederacy could hold out for only a few more months, but it seemed clear to her that European powers were preparing for a worldwide "death struggle" that would culminate with "the coming of Christ." According to Cress, evidence for the veracity of dispensationalism jumped off the pages of Scripture so intelligibly that no sincere Christian could disagree with its emphasis on the imminent return of Christ and the consummation of the present age. "It seems to me all who read and believe the Bible must come to this conclusion, [for] I think time will not be long till the appearance of the Judge of the living and the dead."[36]

When Sherman's army left Georgia and entered South Carolina on February 1, a temporal judgment came down hard on South Carolinians. Although destroying Confederate war matériel and pressuring Lee's army from the rear might have been the two official objectives outlined by the Federal brass, rank-and-file soldiers fervently desired to punish residents of the birthplace of secession. In contrast to the march through Georgia, the northward trek through the Palmetto State routinely featured the burning of homes and unwarranted destruction of civilian property. The nearly constant sight of flames and smoke on the horizon reminded one Ohio chaplain of the account of the Israelites during the Exodus. "We had the '*pillar of cloud* by day and *fire* by night,'" he informed his wife. Northern civilians correctly suspected that many soldiers would take satisfaction in making the arch-traitors of the South suffer intense pain and loss. Methodist minister Charles Cumings of Madison, Ohio, fully condoned Sherman's men taking vengeance on the state's populace. Borrowing apocalyptic terminology from the book of Revelation, he supposed that "the last vial of...wrath" would be emptied, and "South Carolina will feal that she is receiveing the reward of her innicuty [iniquity]." John Ketcham found it amusing that the Rebel papers seemed bewildered by Sherman's movements and listed a half dozen towns scattered across the state that he reportedly had decimated or was quickly approaching. "God grant that he may be not only marching on all these places but that he may utterly destroy them," the lawyer asserted bluntly. Reminded of Jesus' prophecy about the Roman demolition of Herod's Temple in Jerusalem, he wished that structures standing in the path of Sherman's army would meet a similar fate. "I hope that one stone may not be left upon another," he maintained with apparent vindictiveness. However, he attempted to check his vengeful emotions for fear he would "inculcate bitterness" in his son Willie and incite him to treat the enemy in ways he might regret later. Further clarifying his position, he affirmed that God was the primary actor involved in the military operations in South Carolina. "God is visiting this state for her great crimes" and "will make her to feel the consequences of her iniquity." Although Sherman's army as a whole might be serving as "His instruments...of wrath" by severely punishing traitors, each soldier was expected to fulfill his divine responsibilities in a manner above personal reproach, always demonstrating himself to be a "true, gentle, merciful, generous, & christian" warrior.[37]

Many men in the rifle pits might have wondered if it were even possible for a soldier to exhibit these qualities, for experience had taught them that war seldom brought out the best in human nature. The brutal conditions endured by Union prisoners especially demonstrated the depths of depravity to which man could stoop. In October 1864, a chaplain with the 12th Indiana informed readers of the *Indianapolis Daily Journal* about the thirty thousand starving prisoners at Andersonville, Georgia, who lacked proper medical treatment and sanitary living quarters. Approximately one hundred men had died there each day throughout the previous summer, yet the refusal of the Confederacy to exchange captured black soldiers on equal terms with whites prevented the prisoner exchange system from being reinstituted. Finally, in January 1865, when manpower shortages forced the Confederacy to take steps toward arming slaves, the Rebel government backed down and reopened the exchange. As the war drew to a close, some religious Northerners lashed out against the "Southern barbarians" who had treated Union prisoners so inhumanely. "It makes my blood boil, when I read of the cruelty towards, & starvation of our brave boys, while theirs are well fed, well sheltered, & have every consideration due to prisoners," John Ketcham grumbled, completely unaware that about twelve percent of all southern captives died in northern prisons. An article about Andersonville in the March 1865 issue of the *Atlantic Monthly* especially kindled the indignation of Lizzie Avery. "I did not believe Satan in his fury could have dared to torture mortal[s]...equal to this had he tried it in his inmost recesses of darkness," she expressed in utter shock. Yet "under the clear sunlight of Gods eye," these Rebel "demons" managed to "out do their father the *devil*" in the boldness of their "fiendish cruelty." She frankly confessed her failure to attain a level of "perfection in Christian faith" that rendered her "capable of praying" for such despicable enemies. Despite revealing a spiritual weakness, the account of Andersonville confirmed her theological conviction that all men would not be saved eternally, for universalism did not square with her need for a righteous "retribution."[38]

Inclined to make traitors bear the brunt of their merited punishment, most religious Northerners were unprepared for the theology of forgiveness proposed by Abraham Lincoln in his Second Inaugural. With this memorable oration, he ultimately questioned the foundational theological assumptions held by the majority of religious Northerners throughout the war. In the first place, he challenged the notion that God sided wholly with the North. "Both read the same Bible, and pray to the same God; and each invokes His aid against the other." Believers in each section had acted as if God was a partisan who cared only for one of the contestants, but Lincoln conceived of "an inclusive God" who was not a pawn of religionists with restrictive agendas. To be sure, some Northerners might think it "strange that any men should dare to ask a just God's assistance in wringing their bread from the sweat of other men's faces" as slaveholders had done. But before claiming the moral high ground, Northerners needed to remember Christ's words in the Sermon on the Mount, "Judge not, that ye be not judged." Here, Lincoln underscored the importance of humility, a quality oftentimes lacking in northern clergy and laity who mercilessly condemned Southerners, Copperheads, and Democratic editors who habitually returned "evil for evil" when criticizing ministers who vilified their constituents.[39]

After casting doubt on the belief that God favored the North, Lincoln took issue with the idea that man could easily discern God's providential intentions. Both northern and southern ministers frequently had spoken as if they knew the mind of God and could interpret the meaning of events authoritatively. However, Lincoln asserted that "the prayers of both could not be answered; that of neither has been answered fully." This observation paralleled the words of James the half brother of Jesus, who had written, "Ye ask, and receive not, because ye ask amiss, that ye may consume it upon your lusts." Both sides had failed to obtain the results that they desired because they often had petitioned God in a spirit of selfishness and pride. The manner in which the events of the war had played out therefore proved that "the Almighty has His own purposes." The war had lasted longer and cost more in money and lives than either side could have imagined, and "neither anticipated that the *cause* of the conflict might cease with, or even before, the conflict itself should cease." But if God "now wills to remove" the "offence" of "American Slavery" by giving "this terrible war" to the whole country, then man had no reason to second-guess the "Living God" who always acted in keeping with his "divine attributes." Indeed, even if God planned to prolong the war "until all the wealth piled by the bond-man's two hundred and fifty years of unrequited toil shall be sunk, and until every drop of blood drawn with the lash, shall be paid by another drawn with the sword," the scriptural truth remained that "'the judgments of the Lord, are true and righteous altogether.'" Although Lincoln joined with the majority of northern clerics in seeing the destruction of slavery as the central issue of God's providential plan in the war, he broke with many of them when he stressed man's inability to fully comprehend divine objectives or understand the timing of God's activities in human history. Only a man who possessed both a "confidence in providence along with humble agnosticism about its purposes" could conclude with a statement overflowing with mercy and humility.[40]

"With malice toward none; with charity for all; with firmness in the right, as God gives us to see the right, let us strive on to finish the work we are in; to bind up the nation's wounds; to care for him who shall have borne the battle; and for his widow, and his orphan—to do all which may achieve and cherish a just, and a lasting peace, among ourselves, and with all nations." Having undermined the theological assumptions that had fostered a self-righteous mind-set in so many religious Northerners, Lincoln positioned himself to offer forgiveness to the nation's erring sons. Love, rather than hatred, would heal national division and restore the Union. However, love had to be balanced with an insistence upon doing right, and only God could enable man to rise above his prejudices and shortsightedness to complete the task of reunion in a just and honorable way. With the fighting nearly over, Lincoln's Second Inaugural put a capstone on the theological understanding of the war. Balancing his healthy skepticism regarding the transparency of providential workings with a humble, yet resolute faith in the sovereignty of God, Lincoln offered a fresh alternative to the presumptuous certitude exhibited by many ministerial and lay interpreters of the war.[41]

In the weeks following the inauguration, it became evident that the president's admonition for Americans to reexamine their understanding of God's providential activity in the war largely fell on deaf ears. Several major northern newspapers and some local weeklies found little in the address worthy of compliment and regarded it as an oratorical flop. In southeastern Indiana, the Democratic editor of the *Decatur Eagle* alleged that the address was "perfectly borish" and rated it one of the worst inaugurals in American history. It is difficult to tell whether extreme partisanship or intellectual deficiency lay at the heart of his dissatisfaction, but he nevertheless concluded that the oration was "utterly void of reason and comprehension." Democratic editors who grasped the religious import of Lincoln's words especially denounced him for delivering what they viewed as a hypocritical preachment. Will Glessner of the *Hancock (Ohio) Courier* lumped the president with "fanatics in all ages of the world [who] have assumed the cloak of religion to carry out schemes entirely at variance with the Almighty's commandments." Still insistent that war was antithetical to Christianity, Glessner asserted that God had ignored the prayers of both sides because "war...is not acceptable in His sight." The editor of the *Allen County (Ohio) Democrat* completely missed the point about showing humility and claimed that Unionists' unanswered petitions proved that "'the prayers of the wicked availeth nothing.'" Any consistent reader of the *Cincinnati Enquirer* would not have been surprised that the editor tore into the "sermon on the Mount of the Capitol" delivered by "the head of the visible church" and classified it as the climax of "the prevailing politico-theology" that had held sway in the North throughout the war. He maliciously charged Lincoln with casting God as a "capricious and blood-thirsty tyrant" who encouraged men to sin by prospering slavery in America for two hundred fifty years but then impetuously inflicted them with devastating punishment in order to eradicate the means of his former blessing. Such a preposterous notion demonstrated to the editor's satisfaction that Lincoln had fashioned a god in his own image, "shallow, vindictive, cold, irresponsible, unreasonable and cruel."[42]

Lincoln seemed to expect that the speech, possibly his best ever in his opinion, would not be "immediately popular," and he understood the reason why. "Men are not flattered by being shown that there has been a difference of purpose between the Almighty and them," he explained to Thurlow Weed. "To deny it, however, in this case, is to deny that there is a God governing the world." After four years in the highest office of the land under the most difficult circumstances in the nation's history, Lincoln humbly admitted to having learned that the sovereignty of God superseded all human strength and wisdom. God's providence "is a truth which I thought needed to be told; and as whatever of humiliation there is in it, falls most directly on myself."[43]

The Second Inaugural Address allowed Americans to peer into a window of Lincoln's soul, and if they did not like his religious interpretation of the war, they could ignore it and be grateful for their constitutional right to disagree with him. However, some religious Hoosiers wanted to make Christianity a conspicuous part of the state constitution. A House committee controlled by Republicans approved a petition bearing the signatures of Calvin Fletcher and four hundred fifty-two other "christian gentlemen" to amend the preamble to read, "We, the people of the state of Indiana, humbly acknowledging Almighty God as the source of all power and authority in civil government, and Jesus Christ the ruler of all nations, and His revealed will of supreme authority, in order to constitute a Christian government,... do ordain and establish this constitution." The Republican majority argued that the proposed change should be adopted because it promoted "pure Christian patriotism" that all citizens should embrace; it would "secure the life and salvation of this nation" by giving God his due; and it anticipated millennial conditions when all the governments of the world would be "Christian republics." The dissenting minority pointed out that Indiana was no theocracy, for its constitution had several provisions that guaranteed freedom of worship and the separation of church and state. Most problematic, by making the "revealed will" into a "supreme authority" over man-made laws, the state invited immeasurable trouble, for even Christian denominations could not agree on all matters of biblical interpretation. Although the amendment failed to pass in the legislature, its broad support among religious Hoosiers demonstrated the eagerness of many churchgoers to make the government explicitly Christian.[44]

Instead of trying to require people to give lip service to religion by inserting God and Christ into public documents, other believers realized that a top-down approach to implementing change would not touch the inner man. William King of Marshall, Michigan, recognized that general social reform would be advanced by the removal of slavery, "one of Satan's strongholds," yet this alone would not transform the citizenry into "a holy people." "To cleanse a nation we must cleanse the individuals that compose it," he maintained, for only "if God is in the hearts of the people" could real spiritual vitality be generated. John Funk found ample evidence to confirm this sentiment after the North received news that Federal troops had entered Petersburg and Richmond on April 3. During celebrations in Chicago, "thousands got drunk, and oh, the cursing and swearing and all the wickedness that was carried on!" "We should reverently and devoutly have lifted our hearts in praise to God," he asserted, but instead "the whole city made a big fool of itself." Calvin Fletcher reported a more appropriate reaction in Indianapolis. "Some cried for joy & all blest God who felt that He ruled the nations of the earth." Perhaps few people were as jubilant as African-Americans in Richmond, and they flocked to see Lincoln as he toured the evacuated Confederate capital on April 4. Some were content to glimpse Father Abraham, but others rushed to touch their Great Emancipator and fell down before his feet. "Don't kneel to me," he allegedly admonished them. "You must kneel to God only, and thank Him for the liberty you will enjoy hereafter."[45]

After pulling out from Petersburg, Robert E. Lee hoped to rendezvous his Army of Northern Virginia with Joseph E. Johnston's troops in order to make one final stand. However, Federal cavalry in hot pursuit captured stragglers and eventually blocked his retreat near Appomattox Court House. Having been without rations for several days, his men nonetheless attempted one last offensive on April 9 but were quickly repulsed. Lee recognized the futility of further resistance and surrendered his army on Palm Sunday. In accordance with the wishes of the commander in chief, General Grant offered gracious terms to the vanquished foe. The Rebels would be paroled to return to their homes, and officers could retain their side arms and personal property, including mounts they owned in order to retain the means to begin spring planting. Greatly relieved by the favorable settlement, Lee remarked that the latter gesture "will do much toward conciliating our people."[46]

Northern civilians hailed Lee's surrender as the end of the war. An excited Mollie McPheeters informed her husband John, "O we had a happy time shouting, laughing, and 'cutting up.'" Having attended Baptist revival services, this Presbyterian housewife knew a fitting description for the mood at their home. "It was a camp meeting time fairly." George Tuthill welled up with praise "to God who alone giveth us...victory." Entirely confident that God had been directing the war for his purposes, specifically the overthrow of slavery, some religious Northerners were ready for him to usher the nation into an era of endless prosperity. An anonymous woman succinctly summarized this view the day after General Robert Anderson raised the Stars and Stripes over Fort Sumter. "Liberty with fresh wreaths leads forth three milion of new trophies from the last stronghold of bondage. We now lay aside the sins of the past and begin a new life with ardor & strong belief that he who led us victorious through this desolating war will at last crown us with bright Laurals of Peace forever." Other churchgoers were loath to forgive former transgressions so readily. Ellen Plattenburg deplored the surrender terms that allowed southern "scamps and outlaws who have been the cause of so much bloodshed and the desolation of so many homes" to return to their dwellings without punishment. She likened the injustice to thieves who broke into a house and killed some of the family members, yet the forgiving father pardoned them if they promised to behave properly thereafter. Her analogy made perfect sense—that is, until an assassin took the life of the father.[47]

9

"How Mysterious Are the Ways of Providence"

Civilian Attitudes toward the Assassination of Lincoln

On Good Friday 1865, four years to the day that the Rebels had opened fire on Fort Sumter, many religious Northerners gathered in their churches to celebrate the end of the war. Several local ministers spoke at Cincinnati's Second Presbyterian, but the church's pastor M. L. P. Thompson set the tone of the meeting by urging the packed assembly to renounce boasting and humbly thank God for his mercy in saving the nation from destruction. Over at Union Chapel, Alexander Clark spoke from Matthew 14 about Christ walking on the Sea of Galilee and calming the storm. Like the disciples' fishing boat, the ship of state had survived a purifying storm, for "the Master has not forsaken this little bark that set sail in '76." Indeed, the war had been "God's cause in the beginning," and he deserved all praise for bringing them safely to the harbor of peace. Clark commended the soldiers, generals, and especially the president for his willingness to pardon Rebels. By displaying the attribute of mercy, Lincoln mirrored "the suffering Christ of Calvary," who, while dying on the cross, cried, "'Father, forgive them, for they know not what they do.'" Little did Clark realize that his comparison shortly would become even more appropriate, for later that night, Abraham Lincoln was mortally wounded by an assassin's bullet.[1]

Upon receiving the awful tidings that Lincoln had died in the early morning hours of April 15, northern civilians displayed a range of emotions, including surprise, sorrow, anger, and revenge. Oftentimes, only the belief that a sovereign God had allowed the president's death enabled them to cope with the tragedy. By grounding in the doctrine of providence their understanding of a calamity that appeared entirely senseless and incomprehensible, civilians found deeper meaning in the nation's devastating loss. Some were content with the simple faith that God still controlled the universe and could bring good out of evil, but others presumed to know the mind of God in permitting the assassination. Ironically, this assurance in deciphering the ways of providence contradicted the opinion that Lincoln had offered nearly six weeks earlier in his Second Inaugural. By questioning the popular creed that God had sided with the North in the military contest, Lincoln positioned himself to offer "malice toward none" and "charity for all." Unfortunately, most contemporary observers had overlooked the theological depth of Lincoln's understanding of providence as articulated in the Second Inaugural. After John Wilkes Booth fired his fatal shot, many Northerners ignored Lincoln's plea for mercy and national healing. As forgiven people themselves, Christians might have been the most inclined to heed the president's wishes. However, in the weeks following the murder, devout civilians who ascribed to God's providential ordering of events and claimed to comprehend the assassination's meaning more often clamored for vengeance rather than charity. In the final analysis, religious interpretations of Lincoln's assassination reveal much about how Northerners envisioned the person and character of God.

Naturally, the initial shock of Lincoln's death produced profound sorrow throughout the North. The first impulse of some individuals was to despair. Elvira Aplin confessed, "I could not refrain from wringing my hands and exclaiming, All is lost! All is lost! Our country is ruined." Other grief-stricken people became almost paralyzed in their actions and thinking. Augustus Frey reported that he had become "completely unnerved" and could "scarcely do anything." Margaret Denny observed that her father was "as white as a sheet" when he came home with the ill tidings, and no one had an appetite for dinner. "Pa said he never shed a tear for any man's death out of the family until Lincoln was killed," she recounted to her brother. Indeed, Abraham Lincoln's humble beginnings, solid work ethic, and respected character had enabled him to become the everyman with whom many Northerners identified. "I almost feeal as though one of my derest friends had departed from this world of sorrow," Hoosier Jemima Potts expressed to her husband James. A native Illinoisan who had relocated to Kansas claimed to feel the loss even more deeply, almost as if her "own flesh and blood...had been called away." It was not just Lincoln's personal qualities that endeared him to citizens whom he had never met; his leadership during the war earned him high praise. As mourning led to reflection, some political supporters gushed adoration. "Thus falls the greatest and best man that ever stood at the head of our nation," Michigan farmer Henry Parker Smith claimed, for Lincoln, in his opinion, had guided the country "through the most critical savage relentless prodigious rebellion the world ever knew."[2]

Overstatement aside, Smith and a majority of Northerners recognized that the nation had suffered an irreplaceable loss. As the euphoria of victory instantly vanished with news of the unfathomable catastrophe, many individuals turned to their personal faith in God and his sovereign purposes as the only refuge to which they could flee for comfort and the hope of finding an explanation for the heinous crime. A few people satisfied themselves with the thought that God still reigned supreme, and although man did not comprehend his purposes, he had a beneficent design in mind. According to this view, God never intended for man to understand the inscrutable nature of his providence but merely to trust his omniscience. Augustus Frey grasped this theological concept better than most Northerners when he acknowledged, "How mysterious are the ways of Providence. God grant that this heavy affliction may prove a blessing in disguise to this nation." Nathaniel Wright similarly affirmed that "God rules...[and] will bring good out of it, certainly to those who trust in Him." Although some individuals emphasized the need to trust in a benevolent God as a necessary condition for receiving his favor, others focused on a different aspect of his character. Abiram Kidwell of Morgan County, Indiana, carried a heavy heart after learning of Lincoln's death, but he found consolation in the thought that "the lord has said all things work together for good to them that fear [him]." Even a transcendent God who inspired reverential awe in Kidwell would shower his goodness on "a god fearing people."[3]

Believers in God's omnipotence maintained that he could take man's sinful actions and malevolent schemes such as Booth's and cause them to glorify his name. Caleb Mills averred that God possessed the power and wisdom to "make the work of wicked men & devils to praise him, bring good out of evil, [and] light out of darkness." Despite Christian affirmations of divine omniscience and omnipotence, many other citizens failed to acknowledge the sovereignty of God in Lincoln's assassination. Religious individuals necessarily deplored such spiritual blindness. Lizzie Bowler lamented that "the people take too much in their own hands & do not look to *God* often enough in these hours of national affliction." She counseled her husband Madison to seek consolation through prayer, for God would "do all things right if we only ask in faith believing he will hear."[4]

Civilians who lacked cognizance of God's sovereignty over national affairs had the opportunity to be instructed in such doctrinal matters during Sunday services on April 16. In all likelihood, most ministers had nearly finished their Easter sermons when they received word of Lincoln's death sometime Saturday, but several hastily altered their addresses to include remarks relevant to the president's murder. From all accounts, mourners flocked to services throughout the North in greater numbers than on typical Sundays and packed pews in sanctuaries hastily decorated with "the national colors, shrouded in mourning." People had to be turned away from Roberts Chapel in Indianapolis, and a reporter for the *Indianapolis Daily Journal* could not find standing room within hearing range of Chaplain J. H. Lozier's sermon. In Cincinnati, Sixth Street Methodist Church was too small to hold the crowd that had assembled on Sunday evening, so the throng made its way to Pike Opera House where more than four thousand eager listeners packed the aisles to hear pastor Maxwell Gaddis's message. Although emotions raged high throughout many communities and the temptation to fan the flames of sectional animosity looked enticing, some ministers reined in their personal feelings. By emphasizing practical biblical application rather than recklessly speculating as to why the murder had occurred and confidently explaining

Interior of First Presbyterian Church, Kalamazoo, Michigan, displaying American flags hung in honor of Abraham Lincoln. Numerous churches throughout the nation decked out their sanctuaries with symbols of mourning for the slain president. *Peter J. Schmitt Collection, Western Michigan University Archives and Regional History Collections*

its meaning, a minority of preachers avoided grandiloquent panegyrics for the president that characterized later assassination sermons.[5]

In Detroit, Presbyterian minister G. Wendell Prime reminded his congregation of the importance of focusing completely on the steadfast truths of Scripture during the present trial. True to his word, Prime never specifically mentioned Lincoln by name throughout his entire message, for he had assembled to worship God, not "to pronounce a eulogy" for a man. Taking Psalm 39:4 as his text, Prime emphasized the mortality of man, his inability to control the circumstances of life, and his subsequent need to submit to God as the disposer of events. The certainty of death required that man prepare for eternity by placing his faith in Christ for salvation. Without intending to minimize the gravity of the hour, Prime felt compelled to "preach...the Gospel" of grace, for his consciousness of the suddenness of death and the reality of eternal judgment caused his heart to "overflow with desire" for the souls of his congregation.[6]

Although no other published sermon from April 16 went as far as Prime's in excluding direct references to Lincoln, several discourses underscored biblical principles and refrained from wildly conjecturing about the immediate meaning of the assassination. Ohio Presbyterian David Swing selected Psalm 97 to remind his congregation of the simple truth that God still reigned as sovereign over the earth even when adversity befell them. At First Presbyterian Church in Fort Wayne, Indiana, John Lowrie focused on the depravity of man, pointing out that man's natural disposition to evil often produced abominable deeds such as treason and murder. The reasons why God "allowed the wickedness of man" to prevail so flagrantly Lowrie did "not presum[e] to explain." M. L. P. Thompson admitted he had been "paralyzed with amazement and horror" by news of Lincoln's death, and nothing could explain the unsettling calamity apart from a belief in God's inscrutability, a truth the deceased ably had espoused. "I can find refuge only in a faith which asks no question of God, but simply trusts Him when He vails Himself more thickly in clouds and darkness," the Presbyterian humbly declared. Baptist minister Henry Northrop of Carthage, Illinois, concurred that man could not "see into His providences" in order to ascertain precise explanations for events. Nevertheless, Northrop trusted that God still intended to bless the nation and based this hope on his belief that the gospel would go forth from America into the uttermost parts of the earth, eventually culminating in "the conversion of the globe to christianity." By proclaiming the gospel to the nations of the world, America would remain a primary instrument in ushering in the millennial kingdom, so it could anticipate "a splendid future" and take comfort that "every calamity may purify and guide, but cannot destroy" the country. Combining millennial overtones with the Easter celebration of Christ's resurrection, an

Episcopal bishop in Toledo, Ohio, proclaimed that "a risen Saviour reigns over this Republic for the good of His Church" and would uphold a liberty-loving Union so that the Church could "prepare a people" for his second coming as the Prince of Peace.[7]

In contrast to the handful of ministers who exposited on biblical precepts or stressed spiritual applications such as personal salvation or worldwide evangelism, the majority of sermonizers on April 16 devoted their attention to aspects directly pertaining to Lincoln and the assassination. Some expounded upon Lincoln's exemplary character or delineated his political accomplishments. In many cases, the tension of the moment and lack of concrete details concerning the assassination plot contributed to a tendency to lay blame recklessly. At Detroit's First Presbyterian Church, George Duffield claimed that the Confederacy had attempted to engage in germ warfare by foisting on the North goods infected with yellow fever. Furthermore, he alleged that Rebel soldiers had been instructed "to sacrifice themselves by deeds of infamous daring and criminality," and the assassination represented the fruition of this "Satanically pursued" endeavor. Episcopal rector J. H. MacEl'rey of Wooster, Ohio, took aim at the "tens of thousands" of self-professed northern Christians who "know and love the 'U.S. Fugitive Slave Law,' better than they know or care to love the Higher Fugitive Slave Law of the Bible." According to MacEl'rey, these "enemies of Christ" and "incorrigible miscreant negro crucifiers" precipitated God's judgment on the nation. Detroit Unitarian A. G. Hibbard indicted "the system of American slavery" as the primary cause of the assassination but likewise accused northern Copperheads of complicity in the crime for joining secret societies, protesting the war, and publicly badmouthing Lincoln. These farfetched scenarios paled in comparison to the extreme view proposed by C. W. McCune of Cincinnati's Orchard Street Presbyterian Church. He contended that civil leaders had a duty to punish perpetrators of heinous crimes and especially disapproved of the "sympathy" shown to Robert E. Lee, whom he censured for breaking his oath to defend the Union. McCune cited the judgment of an unnamed prophet against Israel's wicked king Ahab after he had spared the life of his vanquished foe Ben-hadad, king of Syria, and compared this biblical example to Lincoln's treatment of Lee. 1 Kings 20:42 reads, "Thus saith the Lord, because thou hast let go out of thy hand this man whom I appointed to utter destruction, therefore thy life shall go for his life." Although the newspaper account of the service did not specify whether or not McCune offered detailed comment on the text, his very decision to quote it unmistakably revealed his personal feelings regarding the reason for Lincoln's death.[8]

Instead of Northerners being filled "with Christ-like feelings and desires" to love and forgive their enemies as Henry Northrop urged, the provocative innuendos and inflammatory rhetoric of some preachers stirred up vengeful passions. At Cincinnati's First Street Congregational Church, visiting minister N. A. Hyde of Indianapolis asserted that the assassination had awakened "popular indignation" against traitors, and the people's revived "sense of justice" would not be appeased until "everything belonging to the rebellion" was "crushed to earth." Although he defined this as justice rather than vengeance, his colorful word choices left little doubt as to what the fate of leading Rebels should be. With a captivated host that would inspire any preacher, Maxwell Gaddis made no effort to disguise his true sentiments. When he invoked the God of vengeance and clamored for the "death or expatriation of every leader of this foul rebellion," the audience erupted in cheers. He continued to incite the crowd with his vitriolic harangue and reiterated, "For every drop of blood that flowed from the veins of this great and good man, at least one leading Rebel must die, or be banished from this country forever." The boisterous multitude immediately stood, and thousands waved handkerchiefs, creating a spectacle that mirrored a gladiatorial contest more than a church service. During a Sunday afternoon meeting in Wesley Chapel, citizens of Indianapolis listened to speeches by several public officials. When one speaker claimed that he would like to see General William T. Sherman's army capture General Joseph E. Johnston's Confederate troops and immediately "people Hell with such Rebels," the bloodthirsty assembly, from "the most timid maiden...[to the] oldest Christian man," roared in approval.[9]

The frenzied atmosphere that characterized many northern communities too often proved dangerous for supporters of the Democratic party. "Let Copperheads be very careful to keep their mouths closed & utter no word in...exultation over this nefarious deed," Augustus Frey warned prophetically, *"for loyal men will not stand anything of the sort."* Perceptive Democrats rushed to denounce the murder and thereby remove themselves from possible harm. Hostility against Democrats ran so high that Republican governor Oliver P. Morton had to calm a partisan crowd in Indianapolis that initially had refused to listen to addresses by Democratic senator Thomas A. Hendricks and failed gubernatorial candidate Joseph E. McDonald. Individuals foolish enough to rejoice publicly at news of Lincoln's demise often fell victim to random acts of violence, and confrontations in Cincinnati and Chicago even resulted in fatal shootings. In Terre Haute, Indiana, a mob allegedly forced one woman accused of sympathizing with the Confederacy to parade around town waving the U.S. colors. Even the wife of a Methodist minister in Iowa joined in humiliating a disabled woman by making her carry a flag of mourning for supposedly celebrating the murder. When the victim's thirteen-year-old daughter proved too spirited in resisting, she was beaten. A Methodist minister in Dearborn County, Indiana, who attempted to convince his congregation that the assassination was "a good thing" found himself dragged out of the pulpit, forced to swear loyalty to the government, and given five minutes to leave town.[10]

At the same time that some vengeful Northerners were physically attacking vocal Copperheads, presumed southern sympathizers, and even innocent bystanders, others clamored for the government to be merciless in punishing Confederate leaders. The assassination silenced almost completely the calls for unity and forgiveness that had resounded in the days after Appomattox. Caleb Mills observed that the celebration of the long-anticipated peace had temporarily "blinded many people to the atrocities of the rebellion," and now those hasty and emotional endorsements of clemency had proven mere "folly." Mills even compared Southerners to Old Testament Canaanites whom God had commanded Israel to destroy completely before entering the Promised Land so that they would not lead his people into idolatry. Referencing 1 Samuel 15, which records the failure of Saul to exterminate the Amalekite king Agag and Samuel's fulfillment of God's decree, Mills expected the southern "Agags of rebellion" to "be hewed in pieces" by the new administration.[11]

To be sure, few people agreed with Nathaniel Wright's opinion that Rebel leaders, despite evidence of "cruelty, treachery, [and] base plotting for mischief, beyond the requirements of war," had not conceived or in any way condoned the president's murder. Most Northerners assumed that a grand scheme orchestrated by the Confederate brass had sought to topple the government by eliminating the entire cabinet but only succeeded in bumping off Lincoln and wounding Secretary of State William Seward. For instance, Sophia Buchanan, who described herself as typically inclined toward kindliness, deplored any notion of showing leniency to southern rulers and insisted that "this murderous act" could not have been the sole work of a "raving...maniac." She claimed that "a deep laid conspiracy" had planned the deaths of "Grant, Stanton, Johnston, & our best men" and maintained that only "the overruling hand of providence prevented" its diabolic consummation. After hearing the premature news of Booth's capture only three days after the assassination, Ohioan Kate Gary hoped that he would "suffer ten fold more" pain and misery than "he & his advisors" had brought upon the country. Immediately convicted in her conscience that such a vindictive mind-set violated the biblical injunction to forgive one's enemies, she more or less ignored her Christian sensibilities and jettisoned scriptural teaching in order to justify the prevalent belief that the exigency of the hour permitted harsh retribution. "This I know is a wrong spirit in *me*, for we are commanded to return good for *evil*, but I think this is one of the hardest to keep of any other Commandment, & after this I judge it will have *less attention* payed to it than before, for now we must have revenge & we have not good & honest *Abe* to...deal with *traitors*."[12]

Indeed, some devout Northerners asserted that God had removed Lincoln from the world because he would have been too merciful toward southern traitors. His deep longing for national healing might have prevented him from carrying out justice by punishing those who had caused the rebellion. According to Sophia Buchanan, Lincoln's overarching concern for "humanity" might have clouded his judgment, and future generations might allow treason to rear its ugly head once more if the perpetrators of disunion escaped prosecution. Nathaniel Wright agreed and speculated "that God, who knows better than we...what punishment they need, designs for them more of severity, than we were likely to give them" under Lincoln. Radical Republicans in Congress likewise considered Lincoln's death to be providentially intended so that the government could pursue a harsher course of Reconstruction. Michigan senator Zachariah Chandler, a Presbyterian layman, claimed that "the Almighty continued Mr. Lincoln in office as long as he was useful and then substituted a better man to finish the work." Caleb Mills even found a biblical parallel that prefigured the transfer of power from Lincoln to Vice President Andrew Johnson. "Moses has been called to die on Mount Nebo...in sight of the promised land of peace, & Joshua is commissioned to lead Israel to the conquest of the land."[13]

Lincoln's emancipation policies that led to the destruction of slavery might well have merited him a comparison to Moses' delivering Israel from Egyptian bondage, but Andrew Johnson was a far cry from Joshua. His deportment during the inaugural ceremonies did little to instill confidence in the American people. In his defense, he had been ill for several weeks, and he drank a glass of whiskey on his way to the Senate chamber in order to settle his stomach. The public, however, did not know about his sickness and only saw the results of his downing two more glasses. Because his muddled and rambling speech turned out to be the last impression that he made before his ascent to the presidency, many people questioned his qualifications to hold the land's highest office. Calling the Tennessean "a shame to himself and a disgrace to any people," Therese Elstine concluded that the country should "mourn to have...Andy Johnson take the reins of government in his hands." Mollie McPheeters considered it "very humiliating...to have a drunkard at the helm of this great ship of state." In her opinion, Johnson lacked all "sense of honor" to have allowed "his appetite to run away with his brain" on Inauguration Day. Although an opportunity now presented itself for Johnson "to redeem his character," McPheeters placed "little or no confidence" in his ability to recover his dignity or earn the people's respect.[14]

Other civilians, in contrast, were willing to overlook Johnson's embarrassing behavior at the inaugural because they anticipated that he would mete out justice to disunionists. Nathaniel Wright simply explained away

Johnson's recent "intemperance" as the result of nervousness and anxiety, and he fully expected the new president to prove competent enough in carrying out his duties and punishing Rebel leaders. Cognizant of Johnson's blatant public sin, Sophia Buchanan prayed "earnestly & fervently" for him to "be converted" so that he might be in a better position to "rule the land with a righteous hand." She considered Johnson to be a man of "iron nerve" who would enforce the law rigorously and demand the death penalty for Confederate leaders. Indeed, Augustus Frey placed "much faith in Old Andy" and anticipated the day when "Jeff [Davis] & Co... will under his administration swing between heaven & earth." In Frey's estimation, Southerners would come to rue the day that Lincoln died, for "the South... butchered it[s] best friend, in Abraham Lincoln." Although few Southerners seemed to express genuine grief at news of Lincoln's death, many of them viewed the accession of Johnson with horror and suspected that he would mete out retribution rather than mercy.[15]

Southerners who had reason to regard Lincoln as their friend may have shown little sorrow over his passing, but African-Americans sincerely mourned his loss. Black communities throughout the North, whether composed of free blacks or recent refugees from slavery, venerated Lincoln as the Great Emancipator and often linked their prospects for long-term success with the man himself. In New Albany, Indiana, a correspondent for the *Christian Recorder* reported that "the hope of our people is again stricken down." Other blacks, in contrast, rejected the urge to despair and instead focused on what God had accomplished for them through Lincoln. Some African-American citizens of Bloomington, Illinois, offered thanks to God for giving them a "GREAT DELIVERER" and pledged their continued support for the ideals for which he had died. Members of the A.M.E. Sabbath school in Scioto, Ohio, likewise reaffirmed their belief that God could "make... the wrath of man to praise Him" and would enable freedom and justice to prevail despite the loss of their "great Liberator."[16]

Similar sentiments echoed throughout northern churches on Wednesday April 19, the day of the public funeral in Washington, D.C., and again on Sunday April 23 as preachers extolled the slain president's character and celebrated his accomplishments. Oftentimes, these messages dripped with overstatement as they showered Lincoln in praise. Not surprisingly, several pastors asserted that his political success stemmed from his frontier upbringing. Unsoiled by the corruption of city life, Lincoln had descended from "the noble yeomanry" of the land and grown up "hearing the birds singing their sweet songs of liberty." According to Ohio Congregationalist E. E. Lamb, splitting rails as a youth had prepared the Prairie Statesman to "split in pieces the gigantic power of slavery." Even his characteristic humor derived from "the fertility of the prairies...[and] no doubt saved him from being crushed with anxiety" during the darkest days of war. Of course, several preachers regarded the Emancipation Proclamation as his greatest political achievement. One Ohio Methodist even predicted that September 22, 1862, the date of the edict's preliminary announcement, would take its place beside July 4, 1776, in popular memory as the most celebrated day in American history.[17]

Encomiums notwithstanding, a consensus emerged that Lincoln had fulfilled his task and exhausted his political usefulness. Indeed, many ministers claimed that postwar conditions required new leadership, and the president had been removed for the good of the country in order that harsher policies might be enacted against the South. As chief proponents of the war throughout its long duration, most northern clergymen sought stern penalties against the South in order to validate their impassioned calls for justice through the punishment of rebel sinners. Presbyterian Isaac Carey claimed that Lincoln underestimated "the depravity and malice animating the rebellion and its leaders," and this lone error combined with his tendency to forgive would exonerate unjustifiably those who deserved chastening. At First Presbyterian Church of Des Moines, Iowa, D. L. Hughes alluded to "the almost universal sentiment" that Lincoln had died "at the most auspicious time." With victory secured, the nation needed "a revenger to execute wrath" on traitors rather than a leader inclined by "the overflowing kindness and magnanimity of his heart" to give "amnesty to all the guilty." Even Walter Shelton, pastor of African Zion Baptist Church in Cincinnati, attempted to persuade his congregation that Andrew Johnson was better suited to deal with Rebels than "their best earthly friend." Lincoln had embodied God's "mercy and truth," but Johnson represented his "justice and judgment." Shelton admonished blacks to hold their tongues when whites harassed them or threatened reenslavement, for "God will make him [Johnson] the instrument of His vengeance." "In due time," he reassured his flock, Jeff Davis and other leading Rebels would receive their just retribution, which ultimately would result in their taking a permanent "abode in hell with that other traitor, Judas Iscariot."[18]

Since most ministers emphatically asserted that providence had elevated Andrew Johnson to the presidency, they consequently gave him their unqualified support, and several even attempted to excuse his behavior at the inauguration. One Indiana Presbyterian portrayed him as a friend of blacks, and a cleric in Michigan predicted that the American people eventually would come to love him "as purely and fondly as Abraham Lincoln." In sermons delivered the week after the assassination, preachers consistently hailed Johnson as the man "that God hath raised up and empowered...to do what President Lincoln could not." However, ministerial confidence in Johnson shortly proved misplaced, for on May 29 he gave amnesty to Southerners who swore allegiance to the Union and complied with emancipation. Over the remainder of his term, he pardoned 13,350 individuals, including top Confederate officials who had been excluded from the initial proclamation. Looking back on the high expectations he once had for the new president, Ohio Methodist Samuel Yourtee wrote in the margin of his published sermon that he had been "sadly disappointed" by both Johnson's Reconstruction policies and his personal character.[19]

The doctrine of providence furnished ministers a convenient framework through which to comprehend the assassination, and by April 23 many unambiguously interpreted the murder as necessary to ensure that traitors would be punished. However, Abraham Lincoln's spiritual condition at death proved more difficult to explain. His refusal to join a church throughout his adult life posed a potential problem for ministers who sought to demonstrate his Christian sympathies. Further troubling, his presence at a theater only heightened their challenge in establishing his religious character. Several preachers seized upon the opportunity to unequivocally denounce the demoralizing effects of the stage. D. L. Hughes maintained that the theater led to "immorality in all its forms," and Booth's atrocious deed convincingly confirmed this. Since actors were "trained for villainy or nurtured in vice," according to E. J. Goodspeed of Chicago's Second Baptist Church, Booth "was ripe for any crime," and Lincoln never should have entered such a corrupt environment. Presbyterian L. M. Glover, in contrast, took issue with ministers who claimed that the president "was out of God's jurisdiction and [had] forfeited the divine protection" by patronizing the theater. Providence had ordained Lincoln's hour of death, Samuel Yourtee asserted, so the location of his demise mattered little. Clergymen who carefully rationalized Lincoln's attendance without completely justifying it suggested that he had gone to relieve the tensions of office or to fulfill public expectations since newspapers had announced that both he and General Ulysses S. Grant would be present. Nevertheless, spiritual perception should have "prevailed against all such reasoning," in the opinion of D. L. Hughes, and thereby both Lincoln's "safety and honor" might have been preserved.[20]

Despite Lincoln's presence at the theater and his lack of church membership, he had left ample evidence of Christian leanings. In both public speeches and personal conversations, he had revealed his reliance on God, demonstrated his love of Scripture, and affirmed his belief in divine sovereignty and the efficacy of prayer. A few preachers simply noted Lincoln's overall Christian outlook and carefully pointed out his religious deficiencies without speculating on his eternal abode. However, many more expressed certainty that he had entered heaven. Universalists, who believed that all men would be saved eventually, had no problem envisioning Lincoln in heaven. Cincinnati Unitarian A. D. Mayo claimed not only that Lincoln had "gone up to his glorious inauguration in the heavens" but also implied that the president had shed his blood to redeem the nation just as Christ's death had provided salvation for mankind. Swedenborgian William Hayden of Cincinnati's New Jerusalem Church opened his sermon with the attention-grabbing declaration, "ABRAHAM LINCOLN *is not* DEAD. He is now even more alive than he was before the hand of the assassin had dismissed him from the mortal frame. He is not here,... he is risen,... welcomed by angels, and conducted by them into a higher, better, and more substantial world." In contrast to Universalists, most orthodox Protestant ministers reminded their congregations that salvation came only through Christ, and willingness to confess publicly one's commitment to the Savior helped substantiate the genuineness of faith. Since Lincoln had never united formally with a church and thus had not espoused a specific creed, no one knew with certainty his theological position on the deity or atonement of Christ. Despite lacking this crucial testimony, a few preachers, such as Ohio Presbyterian Henry Hitchcock, nevertheless expressed "confidence" that Lincoln had placed his personal trust in the Savior.[21] More commonly, though, ministers referred to an anecdote that related Lincoln's conversion after visiting Gettysburg in November 1863. According to the account, which had circulated in both religious periodicals and the secular press, Lincoln admitted to a White House visitor that he had not been a Christian when he became president. Even after the death of his son Willie in 1862, he stubbornly resisted the impulse to convert. Finally, upon seeing the graves at Gettysburg, he yielded to conviction and embraced Christ. According to various renderings of the story, he then freely confessed, "I love the Saviour," or, "I do love Jesus." Armed with such a forthright testimony as evidence, several ministers declared in good conscience that Lincoln had died a Christian and therefore had entered heaven because of his personal faith in Christ.[22]

Many civilians seemed eager to soak up the scores of sermons delivered in the eight days after Lincoln's death. To be sure, a few listeners might have returned home disappointed because a message lacked profundity. For instance, David Este complained that Episcopalian John McCarty's April 19 discourse was little more than "an animated off-hand address." Nevertheless, the laity, whether seeking solace for their grief or reassurance regarding God's sovereignty and continued relationship with his chosen American people, most often heard messages that coincided with their own views. In Sullivan, Illinois, Anna McPheeters found nothing amiss when the Methodist minister "preached Mr Lincoln and soldiers to heaven." At least one devout believer seemed to place more confidence in Lincoln's having gained heaven than in her own prospect of obtaining it. Regretting that she had never seen the president in person, Sophia Buchanan expressed hope that she would greet him "in heaven, if I ever get there, for I feel, that he was an earnest true christian." Besides appreciating the content of the messages they heard, other listeners were moved by the visual spectacle of crepe-covered churches filled with anguished citizens. A woman in Oskaloosa, Iowa, heartily approved of the unity displayed at an interdenominational convocation where clergymen lauded Lincoln as the "saviour" of the country. After attending services conducted by William Hayden in Cincinnati, Maria Carlisle envisioned how mourners across the nation had participated in similar meetings, and the belief that Americans had been united as "one heart" gave her great consolation.[23]

Aside from outward appearances, or at best a temporary sadness, the northern home front was far from unified. Divisions still existed that neither the war's termination nor the president's demise could mend. Some individuals questioned whether or not all Northerners truly had grieved at Lincoln's death. Living in a community known for its vocal Democratic opposition to the war, Anna McPheeters claimed that local Copperheads were merely "professing to lament" and felt no genuine sorrow over the loss of the president. Indeed, the Copperhead press, though careful to condemn the assassination, found little reason to memorialize Lincoln. Writing under the assumption that Seward also had died, the editor of the *Allen County (Ohio) Democrat* dismissed the social pressure to grieve. In his opinion, Lincoln and Seward had perished "in the happiest hour for their fame, [and] their very errors will be canonized in a million hearts and heads....As we did not praise them living, we shall not now indulge in useless laudation after they are in their grave[s]." In Iowa, outspoken Lincoln critic Dennis A. Mahoney, who as editor of the Democratic *Dubuque Herald* had been jailed temporarily in 1862 for his anti-administration diatribes, continued to sow discord. After momentarily celebrating Lee's surrender on April 12, Mahoney immediately reverted to his vitriolic manner and denigrated Lincoln as "a groveling Abolitionist" intent on "sacrificing the interests of a great and mighty nation and of millions of white men to an abstract question about a few niggers." News of the assassination three days later prompted a Dubuque storekeeper to consider leading a group of Union-loving residents to smash the paper's offices, but cooler heads prevailed and averted the violence. However, a group of incendiaries subsequently torched the barn of a Catholic bishop who dared to denounce the murder during Easter services. The *Herald*, in turn, ignored this villainy and brazenly censured "fanatical priests" who have forsaken "the work of their Master...[and] entered fully into the service of the devil." By pontificating against slavery "for the last fifteen years," these false teachers "preached the country into a revolution" and now sought to lead it "into anarchy."[24]

At least one minister devoted a portion of his eulogy to Lincoln to defend clerics from such reckless allegations. Affirming his pastoral duty to discuss issues of moral consequence from his pulpit, Presbyterian Samuel Baldridge of Wabash County, Illinois, branded those who denounced political preaching as unpatriotic and blamed them for attempting to remove God from the political arena. "The seeds of *political atheism* have been sown broadcast in this country by the violence of party strife," he charged in no uncertain terms. Maintaining that a restoration of the nation's Protestant heritage to the realm of politics would help eliminate partisan hostilities, Baldridge hoped that an emphasis on charity and moderation would heal divisions within the North.[25]

Several civilians agreed with Baldridge's premise that many Americans had placed greater trust in man's abilities to solve problems through the political process than in God's sovereignty and power to lead the nation. By staying the course and successfully guiding the country to victory through the prolonged ordeal of war, Lincoln had earned much admiration from his supporters. Some Northerners claimed that the public had bestowed excessive veneration upon him and in the process forgotten the goodness of God. The assassination therefore served to redirect people's allegiance to God. Elvira Aplin asserted that the tragedy should teach man "to trust more in God, and less in an arm of flesh" since the president "was but a finite being liable to be taken from us at any time." Although the leadership of Lincoln and military exploits of several Union generals had given the country much reason for thanksgiving, their accomplishments need not obscure the truth "that God only can save." Some Christian civilians even feared that the public had violated the first of the Ten Commandments by elevating Lincoln to a position higher than God. According to Sophia Buchanan, "Lincoln was rapidly becoming the idol of the American nation." Other observers even accused ministers of contributing to the sin of idolizing Lincoln through inordinately laudatory sermons that focused entirely on the man. After reading an excerpt of the eulogy by Henry Ward Beecher, the North's most prominent clergyman, Alfred Nisbet, a Methodist preacher in southern Illinois, indicted his illustrious counterpart for promoting idolatry. According to the mother of an Indiana soldier, the only antidote for such a misguided view was to "remember that the Lord reigns and ... is our King and our God." Consequently, he alone deserved people's trust.[26]

While many Northerners were looking to God and finding spiritual lessons in the assassination, the fugitive John Wilkes Booth engaged in his own soul-searching. Seeking to justify his action, Booth maintained that he had done no wrong in slaying a "tyrant," yet the nation regarded him "as a common cutthroat" and branded him with "the curse of Cain." Entirely impenitent, Booth remained defiant. "I do not repent the blow. I may before God but not to man." Convinced that only God could judge the morality of his deed, he placed his fate in God's hands. "I have too great a soul to die like

a criminal. O...may he spare me[, for]...its with him to damn or bless me."
Unbeknownst to Booth, few ministers even bothered to mention him by name in their sermons, for they regarded him as merely an insignificant agent who represented the culmination of the spirit of southern rebellion. Borrowing the scriptural designation for the Antichrist, Isaac Carey declared that "the guilty author of this dark and terrible crime is no other than 'that man of sin and son of perdition,'—American Slavery." Also without naming Booth, Michigan Baptist H. L. Morehouse laid collective blame on all Southerners, who, like the Jews who brought upon themselves "the curse of crucifying the Lord of Glory," deserved the "ineffaceable stigma" of being "a people of Cains" for their alleged complicity in the murder. In rare instances when ministers credited Booth as the sole assassin, they spewed malediction upon him with all their rhetorical might. With Booth still on the run, Illinois Methodist Thomas Eddy promised that "human justice" would avenge "the Lord's Anointed" and "follow the assassin, if need be, to the very gates of hell!" A preacher in Michigan likewise condemned Booth to the place of eternal torment where the actor, upon admission, would surpass all previous betrayers in vileness. According to Moses Hull, "Judas, who betrayed his Lord, was an *angel of light* compared with...the demon *damned* who robbed us of our more than immortal President."[27]

Although he wondered whether or not God would pardon him, Booth was in no hurry to face divine judgment. Having been on the lam for over a week, the hobbled fugitive had escaped into Virginia and taken refuge at the farm of Richard Garrett when Federal cavalry finally tracked him down. Trapped in a tobacco barn that was set aflame in order to smoke out the assassin, Booth reportedly made a move to shoot his way out. Carefully watching Booth through a gap between the boards, the eccentric Boston Corbett, who later claimed that God had "directed" his shot, fired his pistol, inflicting a neck wound from which the actor shortly died. After learning that Booth had been killed on April 26, northern civilians expressed relief. No one seemed to doubt that he would receive eternal punishment. "The people had no mercy on him," Margaret Denny remarked, "and I cannot think that God will[.] The blood stain of the Nation is on his soul." At least one individual even concluded that Booth had gotten off easy considering the heinous nature of his crime. An Illinois woman asserted that the assassin had "met with a sad fate but hardly as hard as he deserved." Nevertheless, she would be satisfied that "the Judge of all Earth doeth right."[28]

On April 21, the locomotive carrying Lincoln's body departed Washington, briefly stopping in some of the North's major cities on its way to the burial site in Springfield, Illinois. In Baltimore, Harrisburg, Philadelphia, New York City, Albany, and Buffalo, hundreds of thousands of mourners paid their last respects to the beloved president. In most cases, citizens waited in lines for hours to catch a brief glimpse of the body. In Cleveland, after Lincoln's friend Charles P. McIlvaine recited the Episcopal burial service, an estimated 120 people passed by on both sides of the casket each minute. Because of his position in the clerical honor guard, Congregationalist George Tuthill caught "a good view" of Lincoln's face—"dark, colored, leaden, & fallen away." In fact, the lengthiness of the public viewing obliged embalmers to periodically reapply "pigments and cosmetiques" to the face in order to make it more presentable. Nevertheless, at least one observer thought the president's visage looked unnatural, maybe even eerie. Randie Cress was appalled that the coffin had been kept open in Indianapolis, for she noticed "a purple mould setting all over his face." Even though she admired Lincoln, the whole idea of parading a corpse across the North had become "disgusting" to her. With the public giving inordinate attention to Lincoln's body, she was amazed that "his very bones do not cry out rest." Furthermore, the expense for such a lavish display seemed wasteful considering the costliness of war. She had heard that the state had forked out six thousand dollars for decorations, including ten arches across Washington Street draped with "the richest material" in the city. In her opinion, "dragging the body of a dead man through the country" created a popular spectacle that bordered on deification of a man. "If we would see heathens doing" the same, "we would call it idolitrary [idolatry] and want to send a minister to tell them there was a true and living God to worship." Henry Hawley remained at home in Terre Haute rather than journey to Indianapolis, for he likewise concluded that Lincoln's funeral train had degenerated into "a traveling show of his remains" that wasted both "time & money" that could have been used to rebuild and reunify the country. Presumably, few Northerners gave credence to such extreme interpretations. Instead, many more likely agreed with Thomas Bryan's assessment of the sight that he witnessed in Chicago where approximately 40,000 citizens flocked to the courthouse to behold the body of their native son and another 120,000 turned out to view the funeral procession. Bryan regarded that inspiring display as "a great tribute to his worth & a convincing evidence of his strong hold upon the affections of the people."[29]

Finally, on May 4, twenty days after the assassination, Lincoln's body was laid to rest in Springfield. Methodist Bishop Matthew Simpson delivered the funeral oration. Reiterating many of the themes that fellow ministers had discussed in previous weeks, Simpson underscored Lincoln's own belief that he had been an instrument used by God to save the Union and destroy slavery. Having completed his life's work, Lincoln "fell under the permissive hand of God," and in all likelihood angels transported him "to that high and glorious realm where the patriot and good shall live forever." During the trying weeks after the assassination, many religious Northerners found strength in their personal faith. Although they esteemed Lincoln greatly, they believed

Lincoln's funeral procession traveled through downtown Chicago on its way to Springfield and passed under this magnificent, thirty-foot-high arch erected in the center of Park Place. Placed on a platform inside the hearse, the coffin could be seen by spectators on both sides of the street. Thirty-six high school–aged girls arrayed in white accompanied the coffin to its public viewing place at the courthouse. The train that carried Lincoln's body and numerous dignitaries from Washington is visible in the background. *Wisconsin Historical Society*

that the nation's preservation and future success did not rest on one man alone. God had directed Lincoln in life, called him from the world at the appropriate time, and would continue to sustain his favored people. As one Ohio woman explained to a soldier friend nearly a week after the burial, "Though this blow was a terrible one it was inflicted by a loving Father's hand and it will certainly be blessed to the country's good."[30]

Although reaction to Lincoln's assassination reveals the preeminence of personal faith in the lives of many civilians, it more importantly confirms how theology had become the handmaiden of politics during the Civil War. The explanation that God allowed the murder of Lincoln in order to bring to power a more unforgiving president especially incensed Democrats. In early May, Joseph J. Bingham, embattled editor of the *Indianapolis Daily State Sentinel*, took offense at a sermon preached by Presbyterian M. L. P. Thompson on April 23 and published the following day in the *Cincinnati*

Daily Commercial. In Bingham's opinion, Thompson had spoken blasphemously in his providential interpretation of the assassination by practically making God the author of the evil deed in order that the merciful Lincoln would be replaced by the vindictive Johnson. Bingham conceived of God as a kind, beneficent Deity who could have demonstrated his providence just as clearly by allowing Lincoln to die in bed. To transform the God who on Mt. Sinai condemned murder into the initiator of a presidential assassination seemed utterly contrary to his divine character. Furthermore, he regarded the ministerial claim that Lincoln had been removed because of his "charitable" disposition as little more than a ploy to convince Johnson that God wanted him to be harsh toward Southerners. The contradictory assertions of such "artful dodgers in theology" amazed the Hoosier editor, and he wondered how Thompson and other preachers could denounce Lincoln's murder as abominable if God had willed it according to his providence. Even more alarming, the hypocrisy of this self-professed gospel minister who taught that a merciful God would forgive repentant sinners but then objected to the nation's leaders pardoning erring Southerners was inexcusable. In no uncertain terms, Bingham accused Thompson of recasting God to fit his partisan political purposes. By portraying God as "angry" with Lincoln because of his disposition to be compassionate, the Presbyterian cleric "attributes to God the passions of resentment, hate, vindictiveness and malice," iniquities that Bingham alleged issued from Thompson's "own unregenerate nature."[31]

Democrats might have regarded the providential interpretation of Lincoln's assassination as expounded by Thompson and other northern ministers to be completely one-sided, but their own understanding of God suffered from a similar bias. By emphasizing the forgiveness and mercy of God, they often ignored his demands for justice and punishment of sin. Both Republicans and Democrats appropriated the divine characteristics that best fit their political agendas and fashioned a god of their own making. Failing to heed Lincoln's admonition that God seldom revealed his intentions to man, Northerners accepted a simplistic understanding of God and his providence that confirmed their belief in America's status as a divinely chosen nation. Ohio Methodist Rolla Chubb laid out this millennial vision on June 1, the day of national humiliation called for by President Johnson that denoted the official conclusion to six weeks of mourning for Lincoln. Chubb placed the Civil War within the context of the end times described in Revelation, "the great battle of Gog and Magog...fought on the gory field of Armageddon, which is the American Republic." The war may have resulted in the triumph of liberty and freedom over slavery and oppression, but the American people had endured "the cup of Divine wrath" as "the vials of God's displeasure were poured out upon our devoted heads." In the cosmic morality play constructed by Chubb, Lincoln had represented the forces of freedom by emancipating the slaves, while Booth had embodied slavery and treason. Johnson symbolized justice and would mete out punishment to those who sought to destroy the government that God intended "to stand forth as a beacon of light to the world," disseminating "the seeds of Liberty" that eventually would "produce a plentiful harvest of millenial glory" when peace reigned on earth.[32]

While Chubb waxed eloquent about the apocalyptic meaning of Lincoln's assassination, at least one minister attempted to wrestle with the theological dilemma of the war. In Davenport, Iowa, Congregationalist William Windsor chose Micah 6:8 as his text in order to demonstrate the need for both justice and mercy. "He hath shewed thee, O man, what is good; and what doth the LORD require of thee, but to do justly, and to love mercy, and to walk humbly with thy God?" By placing justice at the beginning of the series of prescriptions, the verse made it clear to Windsor that treason first had to be punished in order to follow the biblical model. In his opinion, Rebel leaders had given little evidence of genuine repentance, and Johnson's amnesty policy seemed equitable since it excluded most Confederate officials. Justice would remain incomplete, however, if directed exclusively toward Southerners. African-Americans deserved just treatment as well, and Windsor asserted that blacks had earned the rights of citizenship and enfranchisement. Northerners who feared black equality before the law stood in opposition to justice. Only after Southerners and African-Americans had received an appropriate recompense for their deeds could mercy be given to those in need.[33]

Despite his commendable effort to find a scriptural formula that would solve the theological quandary of the war, Windsor failed to reconcile how two such contradictory attributes as justice and mercy could be applied simultaneously. The answer lay with the third directive to walk humbly before God. Individuals who first bowed in humility before an omniscient God and acknowledged their complete dependence on him would be equipped with the wisdom to know when to require justice and when to show mercy. Lincoln, it seems, recognized this principle and strived to live by it. The providential interpretation embraced by most northern civilians and preachers in the weeks after the assassination lacked the humility and uncertainty that characterized Lincoln's understanding of God throughout his presidency. Perhaps it should come as no surprise that most Northerners eulogized the man but rejected his view of God.

Epilogue

Throughout four long years of unprecedented national bloodshed, religious Northerners held firmly to their belief that God was the moving force behind the Civil War. As Ruler of nations, he used the war to prepare his chosen people for the fulfillment of their future mission in the world. In late May 1865, a Chicago resident perfectly summed up this outlook. "I thank God for what has been done for our country through His good providence. We have been terribly scourged, but not a whit more than we needed. We were like wayward children" needing a sound "whipping." As a result of the Father's loving discipline, the Union is "free of the curse of slavery," "the rebellion is crushed,...and the way is open for a career such as no nation ever had in prospect." Equally filled with hope, some clergymen fully expected that millennial conditions would become visible in America as godly principles refashioned society. Edward Beecher, pastor of First Congregational Church of Galesburg, Illinois, and older brother of Harriet Beecher Stowe and Henry Ward Beecher, confidently asserted, "Now that God has smitten slavery unto death, he has opened the way for the redemption and sanctification of our whole social system."[1]

That transformation never materialized, yet many religious citizens continued to strive to make it a reality. Indeed, the decades after the Civil War witnessed the growth and dominance of the Social Gospel in the North. Although no scholar has drawn an explicit connection between the war and the rise of the Social Gospel, James M. McPherson has posited that efforts by churches to improve the lives of freedmen through education and job training anticipated the social emphasis of liberal

Protestantism during the last quarter of the nineteenth century. But during the first few years of Reconstruction, the spiritual beliefs that flourished throughout the war remained prevalent. The problems that plagued northern religion did not disappear either. While the glaring evil of slavery had been destroyed, the insidious vice of racism was deeply ingrained in the North. As Radical Reconstruction crumbled under the determination to reunite the sections at the expense of blacks, many religious civilians abandoned the quest to secure racial equality. At the same time, most churchgoers continued to see the hand of God in political developments, and the partisanship that divided congregations during the war still endangered assemblies whose ministers persisted in interpreting the spiritual significance of political incidents. To be sure, genuine revivals of religion occurred in churches on the home front and in camps on the battlefield during the war, and they remained a prominent facet of postwar Christianity in the North due to the influence of popular evangelists like D. L. Moody and Billy Sunday. However, the effort to Christianize the Union ranks as the ultimate legacy of northern religion during the Civil War. The majority of ministers and laymen who fervently supported Federal armies and insisted that the preservation of the Union lay at the heart of God's divine plan for the ages effectively clothed patriotism in spiritual garb. In the process of trying to create a sacred nation, they trivialized religion by making it the handmaiden of politics. In the midst of the conflict, these well-meaning, patriotic religionists could not foresee the long-term consequences of their misplaced zeal. But as George Fredrickson keenly observed, "It is clear in retrospect that the secularizing of American Protestantism was a more fundamental process than the spiritualizing of American patriotism."[2]

Still seething with desires for vengeance during the months after Lincoln's assassination, many religious Northerners wholly supported a harsh policy against southern traitors. The capture of Jefferson Davis on May 10 elicited calls for execution from many civilians, and rumors that he was dressed in women's clothing when apprehended did not gain him sympathy. "Shame, shame on him and his confederacy," Mollie McPheeters reproached the disgraced Rebel. "He ought to be hung in [a] peticoat." A Methodist in Michigan informed a denominational weekly that citizens in his state demanded the deaths of southern leaders, the permanent disfranchisement of all men who participated in the rebellion, and the inclusion of blacks into the body politic as citizens with full legal rights. In reality, northern whites were far from unified regarding the proper course to pursue toward Southerners, and Nathaniel Wright recognized a growing division between adherents of "severity" and supporters of "clemency." He feared that "the old habits of party violence, recklessness & bitterness" would prevent the country from moving forward. In his eagerness to bring the South back into the national fold, Andrew Johnson opened the floodgates of political factionalism. On May 29, he offered amnesty to Southerners who pledged loyalty to the Union, excluding only high Confederate officials and wealthy landholders with more than $20,000 taxable property. Over the next few weeks, he also appointed provisional governors who reassured their constituents that accepting emancipation did not include black equality or civil rights. Southerners quickly realized that they had a friend in the White House, and northern Democrats likewise lauded these moves. However, by proceeding with his version of Presidential Reconstruction independent of Congress, Johnson completely alienated Radical Republicans.[3]

As early as June, several religious Northerners already had concluded that the commendations showered on the Tennessean in assassination sermons were entirely misplaced, and others began to wonder if he would squander all the gains that had been purchased at the cost of so much blood. John Ketcham thought that pardoning "unrepentant" Southerners and giving them the reins of state governments was a tragic mistake, and he feared that Johnson and "the combination of Southern Rebeldom and northern democrats" would ruin the country. "If God do[es] not help us," he lamented, "we are in a sad state." Religious radicals throughout the North denounced the president for pursuing a course that abandoned freedmen and empowered their former oppressors. On the last day of July, Granville Moody, outspoken Methodist minister who served as a colonel of the 74th Ohio until he was wounded at Murfreesboro, wrote a bizarre letter in which he warned Johnson that his life was in grave danger from the slave power. Now pastoring in Piqua, Ohio, Moody alleged that "desperate assassins" who supposed that God willed the continuation of slavery would stop at nothing to kill Johnson. It is unclear if he truly believed that this threat existed or if he simply wanted to unnerve Johnson and convince him to adopt a harsher policy against the South. In any event, Moody asserted that the war had revealed God's intention to destroy slavery and cited three scriptural passages to confirm that the Lord always had demanded liberty for captives. Furthermore, the "Fighting Parson" sought to persuade the president that giving impenitent Rebels "too easy or too early access to the Ballot Box" would devastate the country. In his opinion, many traitors had taken a loyalty oath "under duress," and he urged Johnson to use care and wise judgment when distinguishing between "true union" men and treacherous Southerners.[4]

Granville Moody likely had his brother in mind when referring to the reliable Unionists of the South. However, George Moody had some real convincing to do to prove his fidelity, for he had served as a captain of Rebel artillery during the war. Taken prisoner in early December 1863, he endured fifteen months in prison before being paroled and sent to Richmond in mid-March 1865. While traveling to his home in Mississippi, he encountered Varina Davis and her children in Georgia. He agreed to help protect them and accompany their escape to Florida when Jefferson Davis unexpectedly joined their party. Captured with the president of the Confederacy, George spent a month at Fort McHenry before Granville's appeal to Johnson led to his release. Familial ties undoubtedly put Granville Moody in a difficult position, and he had little choice but to retract his earlier admonition to deal sternly with traitors. It hardly mattered, for Johnson had already determined how he would treat Southerners. By fall he was granting pardons or paroles to generals and other high-ranking Confederates, including members of the Rebel cabinet. In addition, he ordered lands that had been distributed among freedmen returned to their former owners, further strengthening the hand of aristocratic whites. In a letter written in mid-November, Granville Moody essentially maintained that God had sanctioned Johnson's course. "We rejoice in the wisdom given you from on high," the preacher fawned. "Your just discriminations in the exercise of executive clemency command respect." To be sure, Moody still insisted that the president punish treason and defend the rule of law, but for all practical purposes his personal drift toward leniency undermined his bold rhetoric. Indeed, his shift to a more forgiving stance mirrored the trajectory that many Northerners would take over the next few years. Although Radicals gained the ascendancy for a brief interval and secured passage of the Fourteenth and Fifteenth Amendments, giving blacks citizenship and voting rights, by the mid-1870s a majority of religious Northerners ultimately forsook African-Americans in favor of national reunion with southern whites.[5]

Oftentimes, exonerating Southerners came easier than reestablishing brotherly ties with accused Copperheads because of lingering bitterness over political stances taken during the war. In late October 1865, Illinois minister Francis Laird detailed his religious trials, poor health, and financial plight in a plea for monetary assistance. During the war, he "suffered severe denunciation & persecution" because of his disagreement with Republican policies. Afflicted with severe neuralgia, which left him bedridden for eight weeks, he nevertheless attempted to continue with his ministerial duties, even being carried to church and preaching from a seated position. Finally in 1863, "a clamor arose" when his parishioners accused him of southern loyalties, even though he "never preached or *prayed politicks.*" He therefore resigned at the end of the quarter and asked for one-fourth of the promised subscription for the year, but lay leaders refused to pay him a cent. Compounding matters, three of his sons, who helped supplement his meager income, had enlisted against his will. Two were killed and one crippled, leaving him practically destitute. Even though two churches owed him $300, Laird refused to take legal action against them to secure his rightful remuneration. His only source of income, a bimonthly preaching appointment, earned him a meal and provender. In his estimation, all his troubles stemmed from political intolerance in the church. "I was a democrat, uncle to C. L. Vallandigham, [and] would not join the Union League." His religious ostracism because of his political views and blood ties to the most notorious northern Copperhead caused him to lash out against the partisanship that he blamed for corrupting religion. "Abolitionism has become the substitute of Christianity & the church a nursing mother to the world."[6]

The rabid Unionism that pervaded most northern churches during the war may have ruined the livelihoods of some Democratic clergymen like Laird, and consequently critics of politicized religion took every opportunity to denigrate alleged political preachers in order to discredit Unionist churches after the war. Marcus "Brick" Pomeroy, strident editor of the *La Crosse Democrat* who, in one fit of anti-Lincoln rage, suggested that someone should assassinate the president if reelected, reported the story of Henry Clannard in May 1866 to stoke the fires of Democratic hostility toward prowar clergymen. On his deathbed, Methodist minister Clannard confessed to Pomeroy that he had sold his soul to the Republican party. Preaching politics and promoting the equality of African-Americans endeared him to party leaders, and he had made money by using his office to convince Christians to vote Republican. Cognizant that "politics paid better than religion," he became a chaplain during the war and lived like a king, stealing from Southerners, plundering sanitary stores intended for wounded Union soldiers, and making a fortune speculating in cotton. However, he caught fever in Arkansas and now lay in the very jaws of death in a Chicago boardinghouse, friendless except for an illiterate freedwoman who clung to his side. Tormented with guilt, Clannard speculated that Christ no longer even heard his prayers for mercy. "I was unfaithful to my religion, and am forgotten. I was faithful to the negro; but alas! the negro...can't ease my guilty soul. I am going to hell, and I know it." Delivering his final earthly admonition, the disgraced minister warned, "I expect to meet many persons there who forgot religion for politics." When read in Democratic papers, the Methodist's melodramatic story may have aroused sympathy in a few kindhearted individuals but most likely evoked scorn from the Francis Lairds of the North. Whatever the response, Pomeroy invented the story, for no Henry Clannard served as a chaplain of a Wisconsin regiment.[7]

The deceitful editor's fabricating a rapacious, profane Republican clergyman in order to caricature and cast doubt upon the motives of scores of ministers who became chaplains or actively supported the war demonstrates the depths to which religion had been politicized. Yet no matter how despicable Pomeroy's publishing shenanigan, it ultimately paled in comparison to the blatant misapplication of Scripture for political advantage that persisted after the war. After Granville Moody learned about the upcoming National Union Convention in the summer of 1866, a meeting that Andrew Johnson hoped would enable him to forge a new political alliance and rally support for his policies, the Ohio Methodist cautioned the president to resist the influence of Copperheads and unreconstructed Rebels. Never known for humility, Moody boldly claimed, "I can see the end as with a Prophets eye." He feared that Johnson would become the pawn of traitorous Democrats and urged him to back Radical Republicans in supporting the Fourteenth Amendment. By making a few political compromises with Radicals, Johnson could avoid party strife and reunite the country. Moody applied portions of six verses from the fifty-eighth chapter of Isaiah that described Israel's restoration during the millennial kingdom to Johnson's opportunity to unify the country. "*You* have the peerless honor of 'Building the waste places—and raising up the foundations of many generations,'" the cleric apprised Johnson, and such an accomplishment would earn him the honorific designations "'repairer of the breach'" and "'restorer of paths to dwell in.'" Upon securing the maintenance of the Union, his fame would be broadcast throughout the land. "'Then shall thy light break forth as the morning and thine health shall spring forth speedily and thy *righteousness* shall go before thee—the glory of the Lord shall be thy rereward.'" If this were not incentive enough, Johnson could even gain the ear of God and receive untold blessings for himself and, according to the glosses that Moody inserted into the text, his countrymen. "Then shalt thou *call* and the Lord shall *answer*. Thou shalt cry and *He* shall say *Here I am*. And if thou draw out thy soul to the hungry (the freedman) and satisfy the afflicted soul, then shall thy Light rise in obscurity and thy darkness be as the noon day, and *the Lord shall guide thee* continually and thou shalt delight thyself in God and he will cause thee (*with thy people*) to ride upon the *high places* of the earth and feed thee with the heritage of thy fathers." After this sermonette, the Methodist preacher took even more liberties with the Bible and compared Johnson to Christ by citing Hebrews 8:6. "*You* above *any other man* can lay your right hand on the North—And your *left* hand on the South and be 'the Mediator of the New Covenant founded on better promises.'"[8]

Moody envisioned Johnson as the man who could reunite the nation that had been chastened through war and guide it to a more prosperous era, a future devoid of slavery where the Jeffersonian axiom that all men are created equal held true in its most inclusive sense. In the Old Testament, covenants were ratified by cutting an animal in half and having the parties walk between the pieces as a sign of good faith that they would honor the agreement or have their own blood spilled. In the New Testament, Christ sealed the New Covenant by shedding his blood on the cross. Northern soldiers gave their lives in the Civil War to preserve the Constitution, that American covenant drafted by the Founders and ratified by the people in order "to form a more perfect Union." Many Northerners believed it was a flawed document because it had protected slavery, but amendments outlawing the institution and securing equality before the law reestablished it on better promises. Religious Northerners sincerely affirmed this conviction throughout the war, and the support of the church proved invaluable to the Union. The politicization of northern religion during the conflict demonstrated that many churchgoers failed to understand that those better promises were spiritual ones that no government could give them. When he traveled to the capital for his first inauguration, Abraham Lincoln fittingly foreshadowed the nation's spiritual ascendancy over the church when he spoke to well-wishers in Indianapolis. The president-elect asserted, "When the people rise in masses in behalf of the Union and the liberties of their country, truly may it be said, 'That the gates of hell shall not prevail against them.'" Lincoln intentionally applied Christ's promise about his church to the American nation, a revealing indication that many Northerners believed the Union possessed a spiritual significance that transcended the church. In the early twentieth-century, Roman Catholic intellectual G. K. Chesterton called America "a nation with the soul of a church," a memorable phrase that informed subsequent debates about American civil religion. However, the words and actions of religious Northerners confirm that during the Civil War the church wholeheartedly gave its soul to the nation.[9]

Abbreviations

ALPL	Abraham Lincoln Presidential Library, Springfield, Illinois
Bentley	Bentley Historical Library, University of Michigan, Ann Arbor
BGSU	Bowling Green State University Archives, Ohio
BSU	Ball State University Archives, Muncie, Indiana
ChiHS	Chicago Historical Society
CinHS	Cincinnati Historical Society
Clarke	Clarke Historical Library, Central Michigan University, Mt. Pleasant
Clements	William L. Clements Library, University of Michigan, Ann Arbor
CW	*The Collected Works of Abraham Lincoln*
DCF	*Diary of Calvin Fletcher*
DePauw	DePauw University Archives, Greencastle, Indiana
Earlham	Earlham College Archives, Richmond, Indiana
FL	Firestone Library, Rare Books and Special Collections, Princeton University, New Jersey
Hanover	Hanover College Archives, Hanover, Indiana
IHS	Indiana Historical Society, Indianapolis
ILHS	Illinois Historical Survey, Urbana
ISL	Indiana State Library, Indianapolis
LC	Library of Congress, Washington, D.C.
Lilly	Lilly Library, Indiana University, Bloomington
MCA	Mennonite Church USA Archives, Goshen, Indiana
MHS	Minnesota Historical Society, St. Paul

Minnetrista	Minnetrista Cultural Center Archives, Muncie, Indiana
OHS	Ohio Historical Society, Columbus
RBH	Rutherford B. Hayes Presidential Library, Fremont, Ohio
TCHA	Tippecanoe County Historical Association, Lafayette, Indiana
USAMHI	U.S. Army Military History Institute, Carlisle, Pennsylvania
WHS	Wisconsin Historical Society, Madison
WMU	Western Michigan University Archives, Kalamazoo
WRHS	Western Reserve Historical Society, Cleveland, Ohio

Notes

INTRODUCTION

1. *Presbyter*, April 26, 1860.
2. Miller, Stout, and Wilson, *Religion and the American Civil War*; Woodworth, *While God Is Marching On*; Noll, *The Civil War as a Theological Crisis*; Stout, *Upon the Altar of the Nation*; Miller, *Both Prayed to the Same God*.
3. Smith, *Faith and the Presidency*, 91–127.
4. Cayton and Onuf, *The Midwest and the Nation*, 25–30; Hurt, *The Ohio Frontier*, 284–314; Nation, *At Home in the Hoosier Hills*, 13–76; Etcheson, *The Emerging Midwest*, 1–14; Simeone, *Democracy and Slavery in Frontier Illinois*.
5. "Message to Congress in Special Session," July 4, 1861, in *CW*, 4:438–39.
6. Anna Seawright to James Rizer, January 15, 1862, Military Collection, box 2, TCHA.

CHAPTER I

1. The title quotation comes from Henry Demaree to Samuel Demaree, April 18, 1861, Demaree Letters, BSU. Elisha Mills Huntington to Robert P. Huntington, November 8, 1860, Huntington Mss., Lilly; *Chicago Daily Times and Herald*, November 21, 1860, in Perkins, *Northern Editorials on Secession*, 1:96; Duffield, *A Thanksgiving Discourse*, 7–8, 19–20, 25–27, 31.
2. Guyatt, *Providence and the Invention of the United States*; Berens, *Providence & Patriotism in Early America*; Hay, "Providence and the American Past," 79–101; Nagel, *One Nation Indivisible*, 150–51, 157, 178–81; Nagel, *This Sacred Trust*, 53.

3. Smith, *Daniel Webster and the Oratory of Civil Religion*. Robert Linder defines civil religion as "a way of thinking which makes sacred a political arrangement or governmental system and provides a religious image of a political society for many, if not most, of its members.... It is a religious way of thinking about politics which provides a society with ultimate meaning." Although civil religion today, in order to accommodate pluralism, is little more than basic theism, nineteenth-century civil religion had a distinctly evangelical bent due to the far-reaching effects of the Second Great Awakening. With this in mind, Linder's definition of civil religion carries essentially the same meaning as Christian republicanism, a concept defined later and the term preferred throughout this work. See *Dictionary of Christianity in America*, 281–82. Saum, "Providence in the Popular Mind of Pre-Civil War America," 315–46; Saum, *The Popular Mood of Pre-Civil War America*, 3–26; Saum, *The Popular Mood of America*, 13–39.

4. Parish, "The Instruments of Providence," 315; Parish, "From Necessary Evil to National Blessing," 86–87; Noll, *The Civil War as a Theological Crisis*, 79–81, 93–94.

5. Potter, *The Impending Crisis*, 514–21; Stampp, *And the War Came*, 147–51; Farber, *Lincoln's Constitution*, 13.

6. *Indianapolis Daily Journal*, January 8, 1861; George Tuthill Diaries, January 4, 1861, Bentley; Smart, *National Fast*, 5; Hovey, *The National Fast*, 4–5.

7. McIlvaine, *The Necessity of Religion to the Prosperity of a Nation*, 9–10, 18; McCoskry, *Trust in God the Strength of a Nation*, 7–11; Corning, *Religion and Politics*, 9–13.

8. Wilson, *A Nation Nonplussed*, 10; Duffield, *Our National Sins to be Repented Of*, 8–11, 23–35; Smart, *National Fast*, 15–22; Hovey, *The National Fast*, 5–12; *Presbyter*, January 3, 1861; Glover, *The Character of Abraham Lincoln*, 3–4, 18. Moorhead, *American Apocalypse*, 24–35; Carwardine, *Evangelicals and Politics in Antebellum America*, 308–11.

9. Chesebrough, *"God Ordained This War,"* 9–10; E. M. Huntington to "Dear Smith," December 9, 1860; E. M. Huntington to Robert P. Huntington, December 15, 1860, Huntington Mss., Lilly; Fletcher diary, December 9, 1860, January 14, 1861, in *DCF*, 6:645, 7:16; Jane C. Merick to Nettie Fowler McCormick, January 12, 1861, Nettie Fowler McCormick Papers, McCormick Manuscripts 2B, box 6, WHS; Talbert diary, February 2, 1861, Martha White Talbert Collection, IHS.

10. Andrew Ingram to Calvin Fletcher, December 24, 1860, Calvin Fletcher Papers, box 9, IHS; George Woodruff Journal, April 7, 1861, Bentley.

11. E. M. Huntington to Hamilton Smith, December 24, 1860; E. M. Huntington to his sister, January 14, 1861; E. M. Huntington to Robert P. Huntington, January 15, 1861, Huntington Mss., Lilly; Andrew Ingram to Calvin Fletcher, December 24, 1860, Calvin Fletcher Papers, box 9, IHS; Fletcher diary, January 19, February 11, 1861, in *DCF*, 7:20–21, 44; John L. Ketcham to Bettie [Ketcham], February 21, 1861, John L. Ketcham Papers, box 2, IHS.

12. White, *Lincoln's Greatest Speech*, 133–38; Guelzo, *Abraham Lincoln*, 151–58; Smith, *Faith and the Presidency*, 94–98; Lincoln to William S. Speer, October 23, 1860, in *CW*, 4:130; William Sloane to Lincoln, December 5, 1860, Lincoln Papers;

"Farewell Address at Springfield, Illinois" (C. Version), February 11, 1861, in *CW*, 4:190–91; Harris, *Lincoln's Rise to the Presidency*, 316–18.

13. Unsigned letter to Hattie, March 4, 1861, Stanley Barney Smith Family Papers, box 2, WMU; "First Inaugural Address—Final Text," March 4, 1861, in *CW*, 4:262–71; White, *The Eloquent President*, 73, 81–86, 96–97.

14. Fletcher diary, December 15, 28, 1860, January 29, 1861, in *DCF*, 6:650, 657, 7:28; W. G. Johnson to "My dear children," February 19, 1861, Stanley Barney Smith Family Papers, box 2, WMU; E. M. Huntington to Hamilton Smith, December 24, 1860; E. M. Huntington to Robert P. Huntington, January 15, 1861, Huntington Mss., Lilly; Andrew Ingram to Calvin Fletcher, February 1, 1861, Calvin Fletcher Papers, box 9, IHS.

15. Noll, *America's God*, 73–92; Hatch, *The Sacred Cause of Liberty*, 3, 12–13; Carwardine, *Evangelicals and Politics in Antebellum America*, 17–30. Joseph Fornieri prefers the term "biblical republicanism" in *Abraham Lincoln's Political Faith*, 6. *Christian Times*, quoted in Dunham, *The Attitude of the Northern Clergy toward the South*, 40.

16. Hart, "The Spirituality of the Church, the Westminster Standards, and Nineteenth-Century American Presbyterianism." The doctrine of the spirituality of the church was primarily used by southern theologians such as James Henley Thornwell as a convenient excuse for southern churches turning a blind eye to slavery. Princeton's Charles Hodge also employed it to oppose the Spring Resolutions in the summer of 1861 when Old School Presbyterians officially gave support to the federal government. The border state pastor Stuart Robinson most consistently applied this doctrine during the war and used his position as editor of the *True Presbyterian* to denounce the politicization of churches. See Graham, *A Kingdom Not of This World*; Curran, *Soldiers of Peace*, xii–xiii, 6–8; *Indianapolis Daily Journal*, January 18, 1861; Thornbrough, *Indiana in the Civil War Era*, 98. According to fourth-century church historian Eusebius, Pilate committed suicide after being removed from office. First Baptist Church was destroyed in an early morning fire on Sunday, January 27, 1861. According to the *Indianapolis Daily Journal*, the blaze resulted after the sexton heated the furnace around six a.m., and the fire somehow escaped from the flue to the roof. In 1897, James Simmons alleged that the conflagration was not an accident, but arson. "*Our meeting-house was burned because the doctrine of emancipation was taught within its walls.*" However, the resolutions passed by church members three days after the fire do not insinuate the presence of foul play. See *Indianapolis Daily Journal*, January 28, February 1, 1861, and Hoffman and Briggs, *A Light in the Forest*, 34.

17. Funk diary, December 23, 1860, John F. Funk Papers, box 1, MCA; George Tuthill Diaries, January 4, 1861, Bentley; Perry Hall Diary, January 11, 13, 15, 17, February 5, 1861, IHS. Hall became a chaplain with the 79th Indiana and was killed in 1862 at the Battle of Perryville.

18. Carwardine, *Evangelicals and Politics in Antebellum America*, 308–10; Moorhead, *American Apocalypse*, 24–33; Goen, *Broken Churches, Broken Nation*, 156–57.

19. McPherson, *Battle Cry of Freedom*, 267–75; Long and Long, *The Civil War Day by Day*, 54–59.

20. Fletcher diary, April 13, 1861, in *DCF*, 7:87–88; Elijah Fletcher to Calvin Fletcher, April 16, 21, 1861, Calvin Fletcher Papers, box 9, IHS; Poucher diary, April 24, 29, 1861, John Poucher Papers, DePauw; Ann to "Sister Mollie," April 16, 1861, Rev. Abel Bingham Papers, box 10, Clarke; James Doolittle to Abraham Lincoln and Simon Cameron, April 23, 1861, Letters Received, Office of the Paymaster General, RG 99, Entry 7, National Archives, Washington, D.C.; Funk diary, April 21, 1861, John F. Funk Papers, box 1, MCA.

21. *Chicago Tribune*, April 22, 1861; S. W. Lynd quoted in Dunham, *The Attitude of the Northern Clergy toward the South*, 114; Goodrich, *A Sermon*, 14–15; Hovey, *Freedom's Banner*, 6–9; Paddock, *Our Cause, Our Confidence, and Our Consequent Duty*, 5–6, 10; Parish, "The Instruments of Providence," 292, 304.

22. *Presbyter*, May 9, 1861.

23. *Rockford Register*, April 13, 1861; *Niles Republican*, March 30, 1861, in Perkins, *Northern Editorials on Secession*, 1:499–500, 505–7.

24. *Daily Capital City Fact*, April 13, 1861; *St. Clairsville Gazette and Citizen*, April 18, 1861; *Evansville Daily Journal*, April 20, 1861; *Wisconsin Daily Patriot*, April 30, 1861, in Perkins, *Northern Editorials on Secession*, 2:727, 784, 811–12, 1072.

25. Fletcher diary, April 15, 19, 27, 1861, in *DCF*, 7:91, 97, 106; Poucher diary, April 15, 17, 1861, John Poucher Papers, DePauw; Henry Demaree to Samuel Demaree, April 18, 1861, Demaree Letters, BSU; Lizzie Little to George Smith Avery, May 10, 1861, George Smith Avery Papers, ChiHS; Andrew Ingram to Calvin Fletcher, April 20, 1861, Calvin Fletcher Papers, box 9, IHS.

26. Poucher diary, April 17, 1861, John Poucher Papers, DePauw; Fletcher diary, April 13, 19, 1861, in *DCF*, 7:87, 96; William Patrick to Calvin Fletcher, May 17, 1861, Calvin Fletcher Papers, box 9, IHS; Cyrus McCormick to Nettie Fowler McCormick, May 14, 1861, Nettie Fowler McCormick Papers, McCormick Manuscripts 2B, box 6, WHS.

27. Poucher diary, April 13, 1861, John Poucher Papers, DePauw; Thomas Barland to Betsy, June 5, 1861, Additional Thomas Barland Papers, microfilm reel 3, WHS; Therese Elstine to Helen L. Kemper, April 23, 1861, Blinn Papers, box 4, CinHS; Ann Conkling to Clinton Conkling, July 4, 1861, Clinton Levering Conkling Papers, box 2, ALPL.

28. Thomas Barland to Betsy, June 5, 1861, Additional Thomas Barland Papers, microfilm reel 3, WHS; E. M. Huntington to Hamilton Smith, July 7, 1861, Huntington Mss., Lilly. Compounding Fletcher's cares was his anxiety that "the church treasury is as empty as a whisky barrel at the close of an old fashioned election day." Elijah Fletcher to Calvin Fletcher, April 16, 1861, Calvin Fletcher Papers, box 9, IHS; John Maine to "Dear brother," April 28, 1861, Mary Rice Collection, ISL; McCormick diary, May 1, 1861, Nettie Fowler McCormick Papers, McCormick Manuscripts 4B, box 1, WHS; Talbert diary, April 22, 1861, Martha White Talbert Collection, IHS; Andrew Ingram to Calvin Fletcher, April 20, 1861, Calvin Fletcher Papers, box 9, IHS.

29. Thomas Barland to Betsy, June 5, 1861, Additional Thomas Barland Papers, microfilm reel 3, WHS; Lizzie Little to George Smith Avery, May 10, 1861, George Smith Avery Papers, ChiHS.

30. Thomas Bryan to his parents, May 31, June 15, 1861, Thomas Barbour Bryan Letters, ChiHS; Elijah Fletcher to Calvin Fletcher, April 23, 29, 1861, Calvin Fletcher Papers, box 9, IHS; Lizzie Little to George Smith Avery, May 10, 19, 29, 1861, George Smith Avery Papers, ChiHS.

31. Gallman, *The North Fights the Civil War*, 141–42; Lawson, *Patriot Fires*, 70–72, 83–84; A. H. Davidson to James Davidson, April 20, 1861; A. H. Davidson to his parents, June 28, 1861, James Davidson Letters, ISL; Henry K. Wilson to Hamet Helms, May 27, 1861, Hamet N. Helms Collection, ISL; Smith Jones to Allen Hamilton, June 30, 1861, Allen Hamilton Papers, box 7, ISL; Therese Elstine to Helen L. Kemper, April 23, 1861, Blinn Papers, box 4, CinHS.

32. Smith Jones to Allen Hamilton, June 30, 1861, Allen Hamilton Papers, box 7, ISL; A. H. Davidson to James Davidson, April 20, May 12, 1861, James Davidson Letters, ISL; Henry K. Wilson to Hamet Helms, May 27, 1861, Hamet N. Helms Collection, ISL.

33. *Franklin (Indiana) Democrat*, June 21, 28, 1861; *Cincinnati Enquirer*, June 26, 1861; *Norwalk (Ohio) Experiment*, July 15, 1861.

34. *Presbyter*, July 4, 1861; John Funk to "Dear Parents," December 28, 1860, John F. Funk Papers, box 129, MCA; Benjamin Webb to Edith Pusey, May 28, 1861, Edith Pusey Flint Papers, MHS; L. A. Young to Elizabeth Young Humphrey, June n.d., 1861, Noah Marcus Humphrey and Family Papers, MHS; William Patrick to Calvin Fletcher, May 17, 1861, Calvin Fletcher Papers, box 9, IHS.

35. McPherson, *Battle Cry of Freedom*, 335–50; Funk diary, August 10, 1861, John F. Funk Papers, box 1, MCA; E. M. Huntington to Hamilton Smith, August 25, 1861, Huntington Mss., Lilly; Fletcher diary, July 22, 31, 1861, in *DCF*, 7:158, 163.

36. Milton Marsh to Aaron Mead, August 1, 1861, Mead Family Papers, ChiHS.

CHAPTER 2

1. The title quotation comes from Rhoda Southworth to Eli Southworth, June 30, 1862, Newton Southworth and Family Papers, MHS. Gunderson, *The Old Gentlemen's Convention*; Goodwin, *Team of Rivals*, 147–48, 250–52, 317–19. Reuben Hitchcock to Sarah Hitchcock, February 19, 1861, Peter Hitchcock Family Papers, box 9a, WRHS.

2. Reuben Hitchcock to Sarah Hitchcock, August 18, 1861, Peter Hitchcock Family Papers, box 9a, WRHS.

3. William Cline to "Friend Quincy," September 12, 1861, Gadbury Auction, Minnetrista; E. M. Huntington to Robert P. Huntington, November 1, 1861, Huntington Mss., Lilly; Granville Moody to Abraham Lincoln, August 10, 1861, excerpted in *Christian Advocate and Journal*, August 29, 1861; Franklin Alford to Warren Alford, September 1, 1861, Alford Family Papers, IHS.

4. Elijah Fletcher to Calvin Fletcher, August 15, 1861, Calvin Fletcher Papers, box 9, IHS. The Old Testament refers to God providing "a large place" in 2 Samuel 22:20, Psalm 18:19 and 118:5, and Hosea 4:16. Fletcher diary, August 31, 1861, in *DCF*, 7:181; Mary Chittenden to George Chittenden, August 11, 1861, George F. Chittenden Papers, box 1, ISL.

5. Serena Wright to George Wright, August 28, 1861, George Burdick Wright and Family Papers, box 3, MHS; E. Edwards to "My dear friend," September 21, 1861, Corrie Family Papers, ILHS; Fletcher diary, August 17, 1861, in *DCF*, 7:173.

6. McPherson, *Battle Cry of Freedom*, 352–57; Syrett, "The Confiscation Acts," 287–92. Frémont's proclamation had little actual effect in Missouri, freeing only two slaves. See Volpe, "The Frémonts and Emancipation in Missouri," 339–54.

7. Fletcher diary, August 31, 1861, in *DCF*, 7:184; *Central Christian Advocate*, excerpted in *Christian Advocate and Journal*, October 3, 1861. Bishop Edward Ames informed Fletcher that four Methodist church conferences he had attended supported Frémont's action. See Fletcher diary, October 11, 1861, in *DCF*, 7:209; Alice Grierson to Ben Grierson, October 16, 1861, Benjamin H. Grierson Papers, box 1, ALPL; J. S. Scoland to "Dear Madam," October 27, [1861], Calvin Fletcher Papers, box 9, IHS; E. M. Huntington to Hamilton Smith, November 3, 1861, Huntington Mss., Lilly.

8. *Presbyter*, September 12, August 29, 1861; Illinois Conference of the Methodist Episcopal Church to Lincoln, September 13, 1861; United Presbyterian Synod to Lincoln, October 28, 1861, Abraham Lincoln Papers.

9. "Proclamation of a National Fast Day," August 12, 1861, in *CW*, 4:482; Morel, *Lincoln's Sacred Effort*, 108–10; Parrillo, "Lincoln's Calvinist Transformation," 238–40; Stout, *Upon the Altar of the Nation*, 77.

10. Bittinger, *A Sermon*, 13–20; Thompson, *Discourses*, 20–23; Moorhead, *American Apocalypse*, 47–48; *Chicago Tribune*, September 27, 1861, reported on William W. Patton's address. John Funk attended the service at First Congregational and accurately summarized Patton's message as "advocating that the war was brought upon us by our upholding the Great national sin of slavery even from the Birth day of our Independence and that the cause of our apparent failure in quelling the Rebellion was caused by the same sin and our only hope to succeed was to abolish slavery and let the oppressed go free." Funk diary, September 26, 1861, John F. Funk Papers, box 1, MCA. Simmons, *The Cause and Cure of the Rebellion*, 2–9. Thompson and Simmons explicitly denied being abolitionists, although the latter, in a tongue-in-cheek passage, confessed that an article in the *Southern Literary Messenger* had shown him his error and that he was an abolitionist. Indeed, according to that paper's inclusive definition, the entire northern population should be classified as abolitionists. Bittinger and Patton probably deserved to be designated as abolitionists, for they had preached sermons in December 1859 praising John Brown and upholding him as a martyr. While New York minister George Cheever's fast day sermon paid tribute to Brown and lauded abolitionists as ideal American patriots, Bittinger and Patton gave no hint of radical

abolitionism in their September addresses. See Dunham, *The Attitude of the Northern Clergy toward the South*, 63–64, and Stout, *Upon the Altar of the Nation*, 78–79.

11. Stout, *Upon the Altar of the Nation*, 76, 78; *Chicago Tribune*, September 27, 1861; M. Frash to William Cline, September 26, 1861, Gadbury Auction, Minnetrista; Alice Grierson to Ben Grierson, September 29, 1861, Benjamin H. Grierson Papers, box 1, ALPL; Franklin Alford to Warren Alford, October 29, 1861, Alford Family Papers, IHS; Fletcher diary, September 26, 1861, in *DCF*, 7:197.

12. Bittinger, *A Sermon*, 11; Simmons, *The Cause and Cure of the Rebellion*, ii.

13. *Minutes of the Tenth Session of the North-Western Indiana Conference of the Methodist Episcopal Church*, 28; Minutes of the Indiana Synod, October 1861, Synod of Indiana, box 1, Hanover; Lowrie, *Christian Loyalty*, 3–4, 11, 24–26.

14. J[ohn] Dunham circular letter, 1861, in Bethel Baptist Association Minutes, IHS; *Presbyter*, October 31, 1861; *Western Christian Advocate*, September 25, 1861, cited in Neace, "A Study of Methodism in Indiana during the Civil War," 19; Franklin Alford to Warren Alford, November 10, 1861, Alford Family Papers, IHS; P[eter] Demaree to George Demaree, November 13, 1861, Demaree Letters, BSU.

15. Amanda Wilson Diary, October 30, 1861, CinHS; Mary Logan to John Logan, December 31, 1861, John Logan Family Papers, box 33, LC; Fletcher diary, December 7, 19, 27, 28, 1861, in *DCF*, 7:254, 265–66, 272–74. Although Logan and Fletcher interpreted the release of Mason and Slidell as evidence of administrative bungling and cowardice, Lincoln's cabinet, following the prudent advice of Seward, made the proper decision, correctly realizing that the two emissaries posed a greater threat to the Union war effort as prisoners of war than as agents negotiating abroad. Furthermore, most civilians supported their management of this complicated and volatile incident. See McPherson, *Battle Cry of Freedom*, 289–91, Goodwin, *Team of Rivals*, 396–400, and Jones, *Union in Peril*, 80–99. Frances Ely letter, November 17, 1861, Mathias Van Pelt Family Papers, box 1, IHS.

16. Fletcher diary, September 23, October 3, November 1, 1861, in *DCF*, 7:196, 201, 222; McPherson, *Battle Cry of Freedom*, 348–50, 359–65; J. S. Scoland to Calvin Fletcher, December 1, 1861, Calvin Fletcher Papers, box 9, IHS.

17. Bailey, *The Moral Significance of War*, 19–20; McPherson, *Battle Cry of Freedom*, 323–24; John McCullough to Stephen Riggs, January 18, 1862, Stephen Return Riggs and Family Papers, box 1, MHS; Margaret Ross to "My Dear Sister," November 1, 1861, Cassady–Nelson Family Papers, BSU; Fletcher diary, October 23, December 20, 1861, in *DCF*, 7:215, 266–67.

18. William Patrick to Calvin Fletcher, December 25, 1861, Calvin Fletcher Papers, box 9, IHS; Reuben Hitchcock to Sarah Hitchcock, November 28, 1861, Peter Hitchcock Family Papers, box 9a, WRHS.

19. John Agenbroad, unpublished sermon, November 28, 1861, John P. Agenbroad Papers, box 3, WRHS; Reuben Hitchcock to Sarah Hitchcock, November 28, 1861, Peter Hitchcock Family Papers, box 9a, WRHS; Robinson, *Christianity and War*, 2–3, 7, 14, 16.

20. Joseph Beebe to "My Dear Boys," January 1, 1862, Joseph E. Beebe Collection, Bentley; Phebe Mount to Charles Mount, January 19, 1862, Charles Greene McChesney Mount Papers, OHS; Fletcher diary, January 5, 1862, in *DCF*, 7:289; Hannah Bingham diary, January 8, 1862, Bingham Family Papers, box 2, Bentley. In September 1814, the repulse of the British naval attack and subsequent retreat of its ground forces rendered Plattsburg a significant American victory. After the battle, American naval commander Thomas Macdonough reported, "The Almighty has been pleased to Grant us a Signal Victory on Lake Champlain," and it is possible that Hannah Bingham might have alluded to this specific engagement because of this declaration of divine assistance. See Hickey, *The War of 1812*, 190–93; Abel Bingham to Claude Buchanan, January 27, 1862, Bingham Family Papers, box 1, Bentley.

21. *Presbyter*, January 9, 1862; *Dayton Empire*, excerpted in *Darke County (Ohio) Democrat*, January 1, 1862.

22. McPherson, *Battle Cry of Freedom*, 396–403; Emma Ely to Edna Van Pelt, February 21, 1862, Mathias Van Pelt Family Papers, box 2, IHS; Elijah Fletcher to Calvin Fletcher, February 18, 1862, Calvin Fletcher Papers, box 10, IHS. Elijah's financial difficulties were improving as well, which encouraged him in his ministry and furnished an additional reason for jubilation. "There is a heap of preach in me yet," he affirmed. "Ft Donaldson is taken, and my people are paying me better." Ammi Williams to Henry Williams, February 23, 1862, Civil War Collection Miscellaneous Mss., RBH; Gurley, *Sermon on the Victory at Fort Donelson*, 15; Fletcher diary, February 22, 23, 1862, in *DCF*, 7:353–54.

23. Striner, *Father Abraham*, 147–50; Syrett, "The Confiscation Acts," 298–318; *Congressional Globe*, 37 Cong., 2d sess., 606; *Minutes of the Nineteenth Session of the North Indiana Conference of the Methodist Episcopal Church*, 32; *Minutes of the Twenty-Seventh Anniversary of the Washtenaw Baptist Association*.

24. "A Citizen" [Alonzo Hudson] to Abraham Lincoln, January 27, 1862, Abraham Lincoln Papers; C. M. Hatch to Abel Bingham, March 26, 1862, Rev. Abel Bingham Papers, box 10, Clarke; Fletcher diary, January 5, 23, 1862, in *DCF*, 7:289, 310.

25. Berwanger, *The Frontier against Slavery*, 44–51; Lizzie Little to George Avery, May 23, June 7, 1861; January 12, 16, 1862, George Smith Avery Papers, ChiHS.

26. George to Lizzie, January 26, February 25, 1862; Lizzie to George, February 24, 1862, George Smith Avery Papers, ChiHS. George Avery represents the typical Northerner who feared that an influx of blacks would prove economically and socially catastrophic for whites. See Voegeli, *Free but Not Equal*, 4–9.

27. Milton Buswell to Oliver Buswell, February 12, 1862, Milton Buswell and Family Papers, MHS; James Meharry to "Dear Brother & Sister H[ezekiah] Smith," March 23, 1862, Smith–Marsters Mss., Lilly.

28. Lizzie Caleff to Madison Bowler, March 2, 1862, James M. Bowler and Family Papers, box 1, MHS; Rice diary, June 1, 1862, Edwin Rice Papers, ILHS; Funk diary, March 23, 1862, John F. Funk Papers, box 2, MCA.

29. Letty Longnaker to Lizzie Longnaker, February 23, 1862, Adams Lee Ogg Papers, ISL; [Ann Cavins] to Elijah Cavins, n.d., Elijah H. C. Cavins Papers, box 1, IHS.

30. Ann Waldo to Morris Waldo, January 26, 1862, Waldo–Henderson Family Papers, box 2, University of Wisconsin Green Bay Archives; Jacob Thorna to "Dear Daughter," February 18, 1862, Barnett Family Papers, ISL; Muncie Presbytery Minutes, April 1, 1862, Hanover.

31. Minutes Book of the Deer Creek Regular Baptist Church, February 2, 15, 1862, October 17, 1863, IHS.

32. Alice Grierson to Ben Grierson, August 10, 1862, Benjamin H. Grierson Papers, box 1, ALPL; William Kennon to "Dear Lucy," July 5, 1862, William Kennon Sr. Collection, OHS; N. C. Burt to Henry Van Dyke, April 29, 1862, Henry Van Dyke Family Papers, FL. Van Dyke became a favorite of Southerners after denouncing abolitionists in a sermon preached in December 1860. See Moorhead, "Henry J. Van Dyke, Sr.," 24–25.

33. Ira Borton to Ezra Borton, January 29, 1862, Borton Family Papers, box 1, BGSU; Ann Conkling to Clinton Conkling, June 23, 1862, Clinton Levering Conkling Papers, box 2, ALPL; Perry Hall Diary, July 21, 1862, IHS.

34. Neely, *The Last Best Hope of Earth*, 97–106. On March 6, 1862, Lincoln presented Congress his recommendation for financial reimbursement to border state slaveholders, and it received congressional sanction on April 2. Guelzo, *Abraham Lincoln*, 334–35; Klingaman, *Abraham Lincoln and the Road to Emancipation*, 117–120; Guelzo, *Lincoln's Emancipation Proclamation*, 84–88; Voegeli, *Free but Not Equal*, 23–26; Moorhead, *American Apocalypse*, 104–109; Fredrickson, *The Black Image in the White Mind*, 148–59.

35. *Christian Recorder*, May 17, 1862. For Lincoln's attempt to sell his Central American colonization scheme to black leaders, see "Address on Colonization to a Deputation of Negroes," August 14, 1862, in *CW*, 5:370–75, and Guelzo, *Lincoln's Emancipation Proclamation*, 140–44. *Christian Recorder*, July 5, 1862. Unlike most blacks, Revels was not entirely opposed to colonization and once expressed hope of going to Liberia. See W. R. Revels to Calvin Fletcher, July 21, 1862, Calvin Fletcher Papers, box 10, IHS. A colonization project was launched in April 1863 when 453 contrabands from Fortress Monroe took up residence on Île de Vaches off the coast of Haiti, but it ended abruptly and ignominiously in March 1864 when Lincoln learned of the general unrest caused by the mismanagement of colony organizer Bernard Kock. This fiasco conclusively convinced Lincoln of the futility of colonization and terminated all congressional financial support for any subsequent attempts.

36. Cox, *Emancipation and Its Results*, 2–3, 7.

37. Lizzie Little to George Avery, June 3, 1862, George Smith Avery Papers, ChiHS.

38. McPherson, *Battle Cry of Freedom*, 454–60, 464–71; Foote, *The Civil War*, 1:516; Rhoda Southworth to Eli Southworth, June 30, 1862, Newton Southworth and

Family Papers, MHS; Aunt Catharine to Anna Starr, July 6, 1862, William C. Starr Papers, IHS; Fletcher diary, July 14, 1862, in *DCF*, 7:470.

39. Grimsley, *The Hard Hand of War*, 2–4, 68–70, 75, 78, 94–95; Syrett, "The Confiscation Acts," 320–25; Sherman quoted in Guelzo, *Lincoln's Emancipation Proclamation*, 65; *Western Christian Advocate*, August 6, 1862; W. R. Revels to Calvin Fletcher, July 21, 1862, Calvin Fletcher Papers, box 10, IHS; Franklin Thorpe to [Joseph Thorpe], July 20, 1862, Reuben Green Papers, IHS; Fletcher diary, July 19, 1862, in *DCF*, 7:475–76.

40. Carwardine, *Lincoln*, 191–93, 220–24; Guelzo, *Abraham Lincoln*, 312–14, 318–29; Parrillo, "Lincoln's Calvinist Transformation," 240–41. Browning reconstructed this conversation during an 1875 interview. See Burlingame, *An Oral History of Abraham Lincoln*, 5.

41. "Remarks to a Delegation of Progressive Friends," June 20, 1862; "Meditation on the Divine Will," [September 2, 1862?], in *CW*, 5:278–79, 403–04; Noll, "'Both... Pray to the Same God,'" 11–12; Stout, *Upon the Altar of the Nation*, 145–46.

42. "Reply to Emancipation Memorial Presented by Chicago Christians of All Denominations," September 13, 1862, in *CW*, 5:419–25. The Chicago memorialists insisted, "There can be no deliverance from Divine judgments *till slavery ceases in the land*. We cannot expect God to save a nation that clings to its sin. This is too fearful an hour to insult God." See "Memorial of the Public Meeting of the Christian Men of Chicago," September 8, 1862, Abraham Lincoln Papers.

43. Carwardine, *Lincoln*, 193, 207; Neely, *The Last Best Hope of Earth*, 106–110; Guelzo, *Lincoln's Emancipation Proclamation*, 112–23; Goodwin, *Team of Rivals*, 459–68.

44. Lizzie Little to George Avery, August 6, 17, 1862, George Smith Avery Papers, ChiHS; Sophia Buchanan to Claude Buchanan, August 25, 1862, Rev. Abel Bingham Papers, box 10, Clarke; Stout, *Upon the Altar of the Nation*, 143–44. Despite failing in the field, Pope's appointment marked the beginning of the administration's shift to a harsher prosecution of the war. See Grimsley, *The Hard Hand of War*, 85–92.

45. McPherson, *Battle Cry of Freedom*, 534–36; Serena Wright to George Wright, September 3, 1862, George Burdick Wright and Family Papers, box 3, MHS; Hannah Bingham diary, September 4, 1862, Bingham Family Papers, box 2, Bentley; Abel Bingham to Angie Bingham, September 5, 1862, Bingham Family Papers, box 1, Bentley.

46. Reuben Hitchcock to Sarah Hitchcock, August 31, September 7, 1862, Peter Hitchcock Family Papers, box 9a, WRHS; Sophia Buchanan to Claude Buchanan, September 12, 1862, Rev. Abel Bingham Papers, box 10, Clarke.

47. Fletcher diary, September 10, 20, 1862, in *DCF*, 7:527–28, 534.

48. Guelzo, *Lincoln's Emancipation Proclamation*, 130–37; Lincoln to Horace Greeley, August 22, 1862, in *CW*, 5:388–89.

49. Carwardine, *Lincoln*, 209; Orville Browning to Lincoln, September 10, 17, 1862; Herring Chrisman to Browning, September 12, 1862; Miami Conference of

the Wesleyan Methodist Convention to Lincoln, September 6, 1862; Cincinnati Conference of the Methodist Episcopal Church to Lincoln, September 8, 1862; Indiana Conference of Wesleyan Methodists to Lincoln, September 12, 1862; North Illinois Conference of the Methodist Protestant Church to Lincoln, September 14, 1862; Millburn, Lake County, Illinois Congregation to Lincoln, September 14, 1862; North Ohio Conference of the Methodist Episcopal Church to Lincoln, September 15, 1862; Christian residents of Lamoille, Bureau County, Illinois to Lincoln, September 14, 1862, Abraham Lincoln Papers.

50. Serena Wright to George Wright, August 25, 1862, George Burdick Wright and Family Papers, box 3, MHS; E. M. Huntington to Hamilton Smith, September 6, 1862, Huntington Mss., Lilly; Jennie to "Cousin Lizzie," September 1, 1862, Jeremiah B. and Elizabeth Taggart Mansfield Papers, WRHS; Rhoda Southworth to Eli Southworth [September] 9, 1862, September 16, 1862, Newton Southworth and Family Papers, MHS.

51. Stout, *Upon the Altar of the Nation*, 151–55; Welles, *Diary of Gideon Welles*, 1:143; "Preliminary Emancipation Proclamation," September 22, 1862; "Reply to Serenade in Honor of Emancipation Proclamation," September 24, 1862, in *CW*, 5:434, 438; Guelzo, *Lincoln's Emancipation Proclamation*, 153–56; Winger, *Lincoln, Religion, and Romantic Cultural Politics*, 162–64.

CHAPTER 3

1. The title quotation comes from Margaret Barland to John Barland, January 1, 1865, Additional Thomas Barland Papers, reel 3, WHS. Leckie and Leckie, *Unlikely Warriors*, 15–21, 24–33, 38–39, 44–45, 48–49, 51–52; Alice Grierson to Ben Grierson, July 22, August 28, 1861, Benjamin H. Grierson Papers, box 1, ALPL.

2. Attie, *Patriotic Toil*, 160; Cutter, *Domestic Devils, Battlefield Angels*, 7–8, 154–95; Richard, *Busy Hands*, 1–78; Silber, *Daughters of the Union*, 103–5; Gedge, *Without Benefit of Clergy*, 198–201.

3. Mary Ann Hobbs to William Hobbs, February 7, 1863, William P. Hobbs Papers, IHS; Cornelia Chase Diary, January 15, 18, February 2, 1863, Bentley; Margaret Smith to George Smith, March 9, 1863, George R. Smith Papers, IHS; Emilie Gleichmann to John Gleichmann, June 1, 26, 1864, Civil War Miscellaneous Collection, box 37, USAMHI.

4. Eliza Porter to John Porter, September 17, 1862, Core–Porter Letters, OHS; Rhoda Eggleston to Hubert Eggleston, August 28, [1863], Hubert N. Eggleston Papers, MHS; Louisa Semple to Ben Grierson, February 9, 1864, Benjamin H. Grierson Papers, box 2, ALPL; Sophia Buchanan to Claude Buchanan, June 13, 1863, Rev. Abel Bingham Papers, box 10, Clarke.

5. Corrigan, *Business of the Heart*, 207–8, 217–30; Alice Chapin to Lucius Chapin, July 31, 1863, Lucius Chapin Papers, box 1, IHS; Sophia Buchanan to Claude Buchanan, June 13, 1863, Rev. Abel Bingham Papers, box 10, Clarke.

6. Eliza Mears to her husband, November 2, 1862, Blinn Papers, box 4, CinHS; Emma Stevens to John Griffin, July 13, 1863, John A. Griffin Papers, ALPL; unsigned letter to James Hill, November 27, 1861, Hill Mss., Lilly; Therese Elstine to Helen Kemper, June n.d., [1864], Blinn Papers, box 4, CinHS; Margaret Bender to daughter Mary, May 31, 1863, Bender Family Papers, USAMHI.

7. Alice Chapin to Lucius Chapin, September 26, 28, October 7, 1862, and letter fragment, n.d.; Lucius to Alice, September 28, October 22, 26, 1862, Lucius Chapin Papers, boxes 1, 2, IHS.

8. Alice Chapin to Lucius Chapin, July 21, 1863, Lucius Chapin Papers, box 1, IHS; Alice to Cousin Nellie, March 2, April 6, 1864; Sarah Chapin to "My Dear Niece," June 19, 1864; Alice to Cousin Nellie, June 11, 1864, Blinn Papers, box 6, CinHS; Alice to Lucius, December 21, 1863; Lucius to Alice, October 30, 1864, Lucius Chapin Papers, box 1, IHS.

9. Hannah Bingham diary, July 17, 1864, Bingham Family Papers, box 2, Bentley. For Calvinism, see Holifield, *Theology in America*, 341–94, and Noll, *America's God*, 262–329.

10. Rabinowitz, *The Spiritual Self in Everyday Life*, xxviii–xxx, 83, 104, 111, 157, 217–18; A[ntoinette] Cobb to "Friend Esther, August 17, 1862, Schuyler V. R. Hendryx Papers, MHS.

11. Hattie Godfrey diary, April 19, July 19, 1863, Ard Godfrey and Family Papers, box 2, MHS.

12. Amanda Chittenden to George Chittenden, September 8, October 2, 20, 27, 1861, George F. Chittenden Papers, box 1, ISL.

13. Serena Wright to George Wright, December 14, 1862, November 6, 1863, April 4, 1864, George Burdick Wright and Family Papers, boxes 3, 4, MHS.

14. Ann Conkling to Clinton Conkling, November 17, 1861, Clinton Levering Conkling Papers, box 2, ALPL; Elizabeth Duncan to Mary Duncan Putnam, July 22, 1863, Duncan Family Papers, ILHS; A. H. Moss to Dr. McMeens, October 19, n.d., Lewis Leigh Collection, box 15, USAMHI; Mary Cheney to friend, August 1, 1864, March 4, 1865, Mary Cheney Hall Papers, ChiHS.

15. Sophia Buchanan to Claude Buchanan, July 12, 1862, Bingham Family Papers, box 1, Bentley; Ellen L. Woodworth Diary, July 12, 1864, Clarke; Rhoda Southworth to Eli Southworth, September 28, 1862, Newton Southworth and Family Papers, MHS; Sarah Dooley to Rufus Dooley, June 6, August 30, 1862, Rufus Dooley Papers, box 1, IHS.

16. Elvira Aplin to George Aplin, May 25, 1862, Aplin Family Papers, box 1, Clements; Madison Bowler to Lizzie Bowler, September 16, 1864; Lizzie to Madison, September 2, 18, 1864, James M. Bowler and Family Papers, box 1, MHS. The Bowler letters have since been published in Foroughi, *"Go If You Think It Your Duty."*

17. Ann Cotton to Dexter Cotton, December 28, 1862, January 1, February 20, June 15, 1863, March 13, 1864, Papers of Josiah Dexter Cotton, box 1, LC; Silber, *Daughters of the Union*, 14–15. Ann's letter of March 6, 1864, effectively captures her

divided loyalties. "If you once get out of the army I will never give my consent to your entering again. It is not very pleasant to live alone as I have done for so long a time; yet if I was sure that you would get back safe, even if it was a year or two I had to wait, I would try & bear it patiently."

18. Phebe Mount to Charles Mount, January 7, 11, 19, 23, February 6, March 29, 1862; Charles to Phebe, January 12, 22, 1862, Charles Greene McChesney Mount Papers, OHS. After seeing action at Fort Donelson and Shiloh, Charles Mount was discharged in August 1862 because of a disability and died at home of bilious fever on September 3, 1863.

19. Ann Cotton to Dexter Cotton, October 18, 1863, April 3, September 28, 1864, Papers of Josiah Dexter Cotton, boxes 1, 2, LC; Alice Chapin to Lucius Chapin, September 26, 1862, Lucius Chapin Papers, box 1, IHS; Sophia Buchanan to Claude Buchanan, November 2, 1862, Rev. Abel Bingham Papers, box 10, Clarke; Anna Starr to William Starr, March n.d., 1863, William C. Starr Papers, IHS.

20. Alice Grierson to Ben Grierson, July 28, 1861, Benjamin H. Grierson Papers, box 1, ALPL; Rhoda Southworth to Eli Southworth, July n.d., [1862], August 10, 1862, Newton Southworth and Family Papers, MHS; Mary Stork to James Hill, February 8, [1863], Hill Mss., Lilly; Ellen Woodworth to Sam Woodworth, March 18, September 3, October 2, 18, 1864; Sam to Ellen, August 21, 1864, pasted in Ellen L. Woodworth Diary, Clarke.

21. Almira Dart to George Howell, September 28, 1862, Howell Family Papers, Bentley; Anna Seawright to James Rizer, January 15, 1862, Military Collection, box 2, TCHA; Lizzie Bowler to Madison Bowler, March 7, 1863, James M. Bowler and Family Papers, box 1, MHS; Elvira Aplin to George Aplin, June 26, July 28, 1864, Aplin Family Papers, box 2, Clements.

22. Mary Collett to T. E. Smith, November 19, 1861, Thomas E. Smith Letters, box 6, CinHS.

23. Hannah Bingham diary, December 20, 1862, Bingham Family Papers, box 2, Bentley; Mercy Bates to George White, January 22, [1865], George M. White Collection, box 2, WMU; Alice Chapin to Lucius Chapin, January 18, March 18, September 13, 1863, Lucius Chapin Papers, box 1, IHS.

24. Rhoda Southworth to Eli Southworth, June 8, 1862, Newton Southworth and Family Papers, MHS; Elvira Aplin to George Aplin, May 21, 1863, Aplin Family Papers, box 2, Clements; Elizabeth Mendenhall to Jehiel Bond, November 2, 1863, Bond Family Papers, box 1, ILHS; Dorothy Blinn to Amory Blinn, July 29, 1863; Alice Chapin to "Cousin Nellie," September 7, 1863, Blinn Papers, box 5, CinHS.

25. Rhoda Southworth to Eli Southworth, July n.d., [1862], Newton Southworth and Family Papers, MHS; John Gleichmann to Emilie Gleichmann, June 13, 1864, Civil War Miscellaneous Collection, box 37, USAMHI; George Avery to Lizzie (Little) Avery, June 22, 1864, George Smith Avery Papers, ChiHS.

26. Anna Starr to William Starr, December 13, 1862, William C. Starr Papers, IHS; Sallie Pattison Van Sellar to Henry Van Sellar, July 19, October 21, December 26, 1863, November 27, 1864, Henry Van Sellar Correspondence, ILHS.

27. Elizabeth Stephens to Simeon Stephens, October 12, 1862, in Ellis, "The Civil War Letters of an Iowa Family," 575–76; Ann Cotton to Dexter Cotton, October 19, 1862, Papers of Josiah Dexter Cotton, box 1, LC; Rhoda Eggleston to Hubert Eggleston, June 7, [1864], Hubert N. Eggleston Papers, MHS; Mollie McPheeters to John McPheeters, June 21, 1863, John S. McPheeters Correspondence, IHS; Ellen Woodworth to Samuel Woodworth, September 24, October 20, November 10, December 22, 1863, pasted in Ellen L. Woodworth Diary, Clarke.

28. Sarah McLean to Edgar McLean, October 6, 1862, Edgar McLean Papers, Newberry Library, Chicago; Elvira Aplin to George Aplin, April 4, 1865, Aplin Family Papers, box 3, Clements; Aunath Bishop to Amory Blinn, August 6, 1863, Blinn Papers, box 5, CinHS; Lucy Bradford to William Bradford, January 23, 1862, William S. Bradford Letters, ISL; Mollie McPheeters to John McPheeters, July 27, 1863, John S. McPheeters Correspondence, IHS; Sarah Dooley to Rufus Dooley, February 26, 1863, Rufus Dooley Papers, box 1, IHS.

29. Ann Cotton to Dexter Cotton, February 9, 1863, Papers of Josiah Dexter Cotton, box 1, LC; Sarah Dooley to Rufus Dooley, December 11, 1863; Mary Stork to Rufus Dooley, July 14, 1861, Rufus Dooley Papers, box 1, IHS.

30. Elvira Aplin to George Aplin, January 7, March 16, April 27, 1863, Aplin Family Papers, box 1, Clements; Alice Grierson to Ben Grierson, May 19, 1861, Benjamin H. Grierson Papers, box 1, ALPL; Sarah Dooley to Rufus Dooley, June 3, 1864, Rufus Dooley Papers, box 1, IHS.

31. Alice Grierson to Ben Grierson, October 9, 16, 1861, August 31, 1862, Benjamin H. Grierson Papers, box 1, ALPL; Mary Stork to Rufus Dooley, July 14, 1861, Rufus Dooley Papers, box 1, IHS; Amanda Chittenden to George Chittenden, October 20, 1861, George F. Chittenden Papers, box 1, ISL; Hannah Bingham to Claude Buchanan, February 4, 1862, Bingham Family Papers, box 1, Bentley; Richard, *Busy Hands*, 56–57, 65–72.

32. Almira Dart to George Howell, September 28, 1862, Howell Family Papers, Bentley; Elvira Aplin to George Aplin, May 18, 1862, Aplin Family Papers, box 1, Clements; Alice Chapin to Lucius Chapin, June 10, December 21, 1863, Lucius Chapin Papers, box 1, IHS; Alice Grierson to Ben Grierson, March 22, 1863, Benjamin H. Grierson Papers, box 2, ALPL.

33. Alice Grierson to Ben Grierson, March 4, June 9, 1863, Benjamin H. Grierson Papers, box 2, ALPL; Leckie and Leckie, *Unlikely Warriors*, 135.

CHAPTER 4

1. The title is from Fairfield, *Christian Patriotism. Western Christian Advocate*, October 1, 1862.

2. Sophia Southworth to Eli Southworth, September 28, 1862, Newton Southworth and Family Papers, MHS; Milton Buswell to Oliver Buswell, November 9, 1862, Milton Buswell and Family Papers, MHS; *Church Advocate*, October 9, 1862.

3. *Minutes of the Indiana Conference of the Methodist Episcopal Church*, 19; *Christian Recorder*, November 8, 1862; Minutes of the Old School Logansport Presbytery, October 16, 1862, Logansport Presbytery Collection, box 1, Hanover; Howard, *Religion and the Radical Republican Movement*, 37.

4. Ethan Brown to Darius Brown, October 1, 1862; Jerome B. Brown to Darius Brown, October 22, 1862, Ethan A. Brown Letters, WMU; H[enry] Cobb to "Friends," October 10, 1862, Schuyler V. R. Hendryx Papers, MHS; Weber, *Copperheads*, 63–64.

5. As a result of congressional passage of the Militia Act the previous summer that enabled the War Department to call up militiamen for federal service, states had to enroll 300,000 men for nine-month terms. See McPherson, *Battle Cry of Freedom*, 492–93. A[ntoinette] Cobb to "Friend Esther," August 17, 1862; [Annis Cobb] to "Friend and sister Ett," September 14, 1862; [Nute Cobb] to "Bob & Et," September 14, 1862; H[enry] Cobb to "Friends," October 10, 1862, Schuyler V. R. Hendryx Papers, MHS; Weber, *Copperheads*, 67–68; *Cincinnati Enquirer*, excerpted in *Norwalk (Ohio) Experiment*, October 13, 1862.

6. Fletcher diary, October 14, 1862, in *DCF*, 7:551; Andreasen, "'As Good a Right to Pray,'" 37–45; *Cincinnati Daily Commercial*, December 31, 1862, January 16, 1863.

7. McPherson, *Political History*, 483–93. McIlvaine's pastoral letter won approval over John Henry Hopkins's traditional alternative. The quintessence of northern conservatism, the Vermont bishop's antiabolitionist tract *Scriptural, Ecclesiastical and Historical View of Slavery*, published in 1864, became an immediate favorite of Southerners because it argued that slavery was not inherently sinful or unscriptural.

8. Butler, *Standing against the Whirlwind*, 164–66. Butler claims that McIlvaine "identified the Union with righteousness and the Confederacy with sin," which signaled "the complete politicization of Evangelicalism" by bringing the Episcopal church into agreement with other northern Protestants regarding the war. As the following paragraphs explain, I do not believe McIlvaine crossed that line.

9. McPherson, *Political History*, 486–89.

10. *Cincinnati Enquirer*, October 29, 31, 1862; *Cincinnati Daily Commercial*, November 1, 1862; McPherson, *Political History*, 488.

11. Wert, *The Sword of Lincoln*, 175–79; Lizzie Little to George Avery, March 30, October 26, 1862, George Smith Avery Papers, ChiHS; Sophia Buchanan to Claude Buchanan, November 2, 1862, Rev. Abel Bingham Papers, box 10, Clarke; McPherson, *Battle Cry of Freedom*, 568–70; Robert H. Rice to Alfred Rice, November 27, [1862], Dr. and Mrs. Robert H. Rice Collection, box 1, RBH.

12. Sophia Buchanan to Claude Buchanan, November 22, 1862, Rev. Abel Bingham Papers, box 10, Clarke; Robert H. Rice to Alfred Rice, November 27, [1862], Dr. and Mrs. Robert H. Rice Collection, box 1, RBH; Mary Hall to Emery Hall, September 21, October 26, 1862, John Emery Hall Collection, WMU;

Charlotte Conner to Calvin Fletcher, November 5, 1862, Calvin Fletcher Papers, box 9, IHS.

13. Guelzo, *Abraham Lincoln*, 313–14; "Order for Sabbath Observance," November 15, 1862, in *CW*, 5:497–98; Morel, *Lincoln's Sacred Effort*, 92–96.

14. Psalm 79:8–9 reads, "O remember not against us former iniquities: let thy tender mercies speedily prevent us: for we are brought very low. Help us, O God of our salvation, for the glory of thy name: and deliver us, and purge away our sins, for thy name's sake." Duffield, *Humiliation and Hope*, 5–8, 12–23.

15. Duffield's text on repentance falls in the midst of a lamentation over the destruction of the temple by the Babylonian king Nebuchadnezzar in 586 B.C. The first three verses of Psalm 79 lay out the desolation of Israel. "O GOD, the heathen are come into thine inheritance; thy holy temple have they defiled; they have laid Jerusalem on heaps. The dead bodies of thy servants have they given to be meat unto the fowls of the heaven, the flesh of thy saints unto the beasts of the earth. Their blood have they shed like water round about Jerusalem; and there was none to bury them." Duffield certainly could have related these verses to the devastation of the current war. Following his text, he could have employed verses 10 and 12 to incite vengeance against Southerners. "Wherefore should the heathen say, Where is their God? let him be known among the heathen in our sight by the revenging of the blood of thy servants which is shed. And render unto our neighbors sevenfold into their bosom their reproach, wherewith they have reproached thee, O Lord."

16. Senour, *The Hand of God*, 3–4, 7. Furthermore, Senour's assertion that the Edomite derides the watchman with his query is far from conclusive. Several prominent expositors, including Matthew Henry and seventeenth-century British Baptist John Gill, view the Edomite as a Jewish proselyte concerned about the welfare of Jerusalem.

17. Permelia Gordon to Samuel Gordon, December 28, 1862, Samuel Gordon Papers, ALPL; Serena Wright to George Wright, December 21, 1862, George Burdick Wright and Family Papers, box 3, MHS; Catherine Ladley to Oscar Ladley, December 28, 1862, in Becker and Thomas, *Hearth and Knapsack*, 70; Fletcher diary, December 16, 17, 18, 29, 1862, in *DCF*, 7:592–93, 601.

18. Guelzo, *Lincoln's Emancipation Proclamation*, 179–80; John Ketcham to Jennie Ketcham, January 3, 1863, John L. Ketcham Papers, box 2, IHS; Fletcher diary, December 29, 1862, January 2, 1863, in *DCF*, 7:601, 8:6; Serena Wright to George Wright, January 4, 1863, George Burdick Wright and Family Papers, box 3, MHS; George Tuthill Diaries, January 1, 1863, Bentley; B. P. Douglass to Victoria, January 4, 1863, Boone–Douglass Family Papers, IHS; Ethan Brown to Darius Brown, January 4, 1863, Ethan A. Brown Letters, WMU.

19. White, *The Eloquent President*, 170–89; Sophia Buchanan to Claude Buchanan, January 1, 1863; Abel Bingham to Judson Bingham, January 20, 1863, Rev. Abel Bingham Papers, boxes 10, 11, Clarke.

20. Abel Bingham to Judson Bingham, January 20, 1863, Rev. Abel Bingham Papers, box 11, Clarke; Noll, *The Civil War as a Theological Crisis*, 92–94.

21. Christian Kohlsaat to parents, January 25, 1863, Reimer Kohlsaat and Family Papers, MHS; Nancy Mitchell to Frank P. Grove, November 12, 1862, quoted in Hall, *Appalachian Ohio and the Civil War*, 123.

22. *Putnam (Indiana) Republican Banner*, February 12, 1863; *Lima (Ohio) Weekly Gazette*, December 3, 1862; First Baptist Church, Canton, Ohio, Record Book, February 27, 1863, BGSU.

23. *New York Times*, October 4, 1862; Samuel Borton to James Elwood Borton, March 26, 1863, Borton Family Papers, box 1, BGSU; Lizzie Rice to John Rice, March 4, 1863, John B. Rice Collection, RBH; George Upfold to "My dear daughter," May 15, 1863, cited in Andreasen, "'As Good a Right to Pray,'" 555.

24. *Western Christian Advocate*, January 14, 1863; Sarah Kohlsaat to Christian Kohlsaat, February 22, 1863, Reimer Kohlsaat and Family Papers, MHS; Cornelia Chase Diary, February 1, 1863, Bentley; Mary Mowl to Samuel and Elisabeth McCreery, March 24, 1863, private collection of Sandra Price, copy in author's possession.

25. Mary Ann Hobbs to William Hobbs, March 3, 1863, William P. Hobbs Papers, IHS; W. G. Johnson to Henry and Hattie Smith, January 27, 1863, Stanley Barney Smith Family Papers, box 3, WMU; *Franklin (Indiana) Democrat*, January 30, February 6, 1863; Eliza Harrell to Nerva Harrell, January 25, 1863, Letters of Edmond Harrell, in Jack K. Carmichael Collection, ISL; *Christian Recorder*, March 14, 1863.

26. Thornbrough, *Indiana in the Civil War Era*, 628; Fletcher diary, February 18, 25, 28, March 9, 13, 15, April 2, 13, May 11, 1863, in DCF, 8:54–57, 61, 64, 74, 79–80, 82, 101, 111, 135.

27. Ann Cotton to Dexter Cotton, March 1, 3, 1863, Papers of Josiah Dexter Cotton, box 1, LC; Ella Johnston to Henry Cumings, March 7, 1863, Henry Harrison Cumings Papers, box 1, WRHS; Mary Ladley to Oscar Ladley, April 29, 1863; Alice Ladley to Oscar Ladley, April 29, 1863, in Becker and Thomas, *Hearth and Knapsack*, 117–18. After the *Cincinnati Enquirer* carried a letter that described the commotion and disruption of classes at Antioch due to the arrival of the black student, the school's acting president denied that any ruckus had erupted on campus and claimed that the girl was Native American rather than African-American. See *Cincinnati Enquirer*, April 30, May 9, 1863. Eliza Rice to Robert H. Rice, January 25, 1863, Dr. and Mrs. Robert H. Rice Collection, box 1, RBH; Escott, *"What Shall We Do with the Negro?"*

28. Sarah Shively to "Dear Cousin," April 5, 1863, Thomas Marshall Papers, IHS; Sarah Dooley to Rufus Dooley, March 28, June 4, 1863, Rufus Dooley Papers, box 1, IHS; George to Jacob Leidigh, January 4, March 11, 1863, Jacob M. Leidigh Collection, OHS; Henrietta Wheeler to William Wheeler, May 18, 1863, Brian Shumway Collection, WMU; M. L. P. Thompson to [illeg.], February 24, 1863, M. L. P. Thompson Letter, OHS.

29. Margaret Smith to George Smith, March 9, 1863, George R. Smith Papers, IHS; Klement, *The Copperheads in the Middle West*, 134–69, and *Dark Lanterns*, 7–33;

Weber, *Copperheads*, 25–26, 54, 78–82; *Putnam (Indiana) Republican Banner*, April 23, 1863; James Weiler to Joseph Vannest, April 19, 1863, Joseph P. Vannest Papers, IHS.

30. *Indianapolis Daily State Sentinel*, March 30, 1863; *Franklin (Indiana) Democrat*, May 8, 1863.

31. *Indianapolis Daily State Sentinel*, March 30, April 17, 1863.

32. Hawley, *The Fall of Sumter*, 3–4, 7–8, 14–18.

33. "Proclamation Appointing a National Fast Day," March 30, 1863, in *CW*, 6:156–57; Morel, *Lincoln's Sacred Effort*, 111–12.

34. Elvira Aplin to George Aplin, April 27, 1863, Aplin Family Papers, box 1, Clements; Ann Conkling to Clinton Conkling, April 27, 1863, Clinton Levering Conkling Papers, box 2, ALPL; *CW*, 6:156–57; *Indianapolis Daily State Sentinel*, April 30, 1863.

35. Richard Brown to John Blackwell, April 30, 1863, John Blackwell Collection, IHS; Giles, *The Problem of American Nationality*, 4–5, 8, 18, 22; Barr, *Fast-Day Sermon*, 5–6; Collins, *God and Our Country*, 2–6, 8–14, 16.

36. Charles P. McIlvaine to Abraham Lincoln, July 27, 1863, Abraham Lincoln Papers; Fletcher diary, April 30, 1863, in *DCF*, 8:124; Alice Ladley to Oscar Ladley, April 29, 1863, in Becker and Thomas, *Hearth and Knapsack*, 119; Samuel Hibbard diary, April 30, 1863, Robert C. Hibbard Collection, WMU; *Chicago Times*, excerpted in *Indianapolis Daily State Sentinel*, May 6, 1863.

37. Wert, *The Sword of Lincoln*, 231–52; Stout, *Upon the Altar of the Nation*, 223–26.

38. Stout, *Upon the Altar of the Nation*, 227; Mary Cheney to friend, June 6, 1863, Mary Cheney Hall Papers, ChiHS; *Cincinnati Enquirer*, May 13, 15, 1863.

39. McPherson, *Battle Cry of Freedom*, 577–79, 626–33.

40. L. A. L. Williams to Worthington Williams, May 30, 1863, Worthington B. Williams Family Papers, box 2, IHS; Fletcher diary, May 24, 1863, in *DCF*, 8:145–46; Mollie McPheeters to John McPheeters, May 28, June 4, 1863, John S. McPheeters Correspondence, IHS.

41. Hattie to William Kemper, May 31, 1863, G. W. H. Kemper Collection, box 4, BSU; S. B. to John Griffin, June 7, 1863, John A. Griffin Papers, ALPL; Alice Chapin to Lucius Chapin, March 29, 1863, Lucius Chapin Papers, box 1, IHS.

42. J. H. Stoneburner to James Hartley, May 3, 1863, Papers of James J. Hartley, LC; Asa Sutherland to Silas Dooley, May 3, 1863, Rufus Dooley Papers, box 1, IHS. Sutherland quotes 2 Timothy 4:6–8 verbatim.

43. More than twelve hundred Indiana Friends bore arms, about one quarter of all eligible Quaker men in the state. See Nelson, *Indiana Quakers Confront the Civil War*, 16–25. Cy [Lewis] to "Mell," May 17, 1863, Miriam Wilson Green Collection, IHS. Although Lewis believed that a Friend had appealed directly to the president in order to secure the release of these Quakers, no evidence exists to substantiate this. Most likely, the men paid the commutation fee. For the draft in general, see Geary, *We Need Men*, 32–38, 109–110.

44. "A Petition to Mr Abraham Lincoln," unsigned, August 19, 1862; John M. Brenneman to Jacob Nold, August 21, 1862, Nold/Yoder Collection, box 7, MCA; Schlabach, *Peace, Faith, Nation*, 178–85; Lehman and Nolt, *Mennonites, Amish, and the American Civil War*, 3, 101–2.

45. Brenneman, *Christianity and War* (1863), reprinted in Stoltzfus, *Mennonites of the Ohio and Eastern Conference*, 408–24; Lehman and Nolt, *Mennonites, Amish, and the American Civil War*, 178–79.

46. Funk diary, *passim*, John F. Funk Papers, boxes 1–2, MCA; Funk, *Warfare*, 7–9, 13–14; Lehman and Nolt, *Mennonites, Amish, and the American Civil War*, 174–78.

47. *Cleveland Leader*, June 1, 1863, excerpted in *Cincinnati Daily Commercial*, June 2, 1863; *Hancock (Ohio) Jeffersonian*, July 31, 1863; *Hancock (Ohio) Courier*, July 24, 1863.

48. Mary Sutton to Rufus Dooley, May 19, 1863, Rufus Dooley Papers, box 1, IHS; Andreasen, "'As Good a Right to Pray,'" 91; *Catholic Telegraph*, May 27, June 10, 17, 1863. The *Catholic Telegraph* took its lead from the editor's outspoken brother Archbishop John Purcell, who publicly had called for emancipation three weeks prior to the issuing of the Preliminary Emancipation Proclamation. See Endres, "Rectifying the Fatal Contrast."

49. *Newark (Ohio) Advocate*, May 1, 1863.

50. Fletcher diary, June 16, 25, 28–29, 1863, in *DCF*, 8:157, 164–66.

51. Wert, *The Sword of Lincoln*, 259–67; S. Emmitt Barr to John McPheeters, July 3, 1863, John S. McPheeters Correspondence, IHS.

52. "Announcement of News from Gettysburg," July 4, 1863, in *CW*, 6:314; Nancy Anderson to Princie Anderson, July 5, 1863, in Anderson, *Life and Letters of Judge Thomas J. Anderson and Wife*, 288–89; Sophia Buchanan to John C. Buchanan, July 7, 1863; Angie Bingham to Sophia Buchanan, July 27, 1863, Rev. Abel Bingham Papers, boxes 10, 11, Clarke; Serena Wright to George Wright, July 9, 1863, George Burdick Wright and Family Papers, box 3, MHS.

53. Talbert diary, July 25, 1863, Martha White Talbert Collection, IHS; Bernstein, *The New York City Draft Riots*, 3–5, 18–42; Schecter, *The Devil's Own Work*, 4, 236–38; Angie Bingham to Sophia Buchanan, July 15, 1863, Rev. Abel Bingham Papers, box 11, Clarke; Fletcher diary, July 15, 1863, in *DCF*, 8:178.

54. Foote, *The Civil War*, 2:671, 679–80; Benjamin Wible to John McPheeters, July 23, 1863; Mollie McPheeters to John McPheeters, July 16, 1863, John S. McPheeters Correspondence, IHS; Stampp, *Indiana Politics during the Civil War*, 205–10; Sarah Dooley to Rufus Dooley, July 17, 1863, Rufus Dooley Papers, IHS.

55. Foote, *The Civil War*, 2:680–81; William Jessup to "Dear Son," July 26, 1863, William Jessup Letter, CinHS.

56. Ella to "Ever Dear Cousin," July 19, 1863; [Cyrus Lewis] to "Mell," July 24, 27, 1863, Miriam Wilson Green Collection, IHS.

57. Foote, *The Civil War*, 2:681–683; Marilla Leggett diary, July 23–25, 1863, Marilla Wells Leggett Papers, WRHS; J. M. Shackelford to Lewis Richmond,

July 26, 1863, in *New York Evangelist*, July 30, 1863; Fletcher diary, July 27, 1863, in *DCF*, 8:184.

58. Ann Cotton to Dexter Cotton, July 5, 26, 1863, Papers of Josiah Dexter Cotton, LC; C. D. Helmer, "The War in Progress," in *Milwaukee Daily Sentinel*, July 17, 1863; Mary Vermilion to William Vermilion, July 24, 1863, in Elder, *Love amid the Turmoil*, 164; Ovid Butler to Scot Butler, July 22, 1863, in Davis, *Affectionately Yours*, 30–31.

59. "Proclamation of Thanksgiving," July 15, 1863, in *CW*, 6:333.

60. Charles P. McIlvaine to Abraham Lincoln, July 27, 1863, Abraham Lincoln Papers; Elizabeth Duncan to Mary Duncan Putnam, July 22, 1863, Duncan Family Papers, ILHS; Alice Chapin to Lucius Chapin, August 4, 1863, Lucius Chapin Papers, IHS; *New Castle (Indiana) Courier*, August 13, 1863; Daniel Brenneman to John Funk, August 6, 1863, John F. Funk Papers, box 6, MCA; A. Bishop to Amory Blinn, August 6, 1863, Blinn Papers, box 5, CinHS.

61. Ottman, *God Our Leader*, 6–14.

62. Gurley, *Man's Projects and God's Results*, 7–13, 15–16, 18; Hein, "A Sermon Lincoln Heard," 161–66; Dennett, *Lincoln and the Civil War in the Diaries and Letters of John Hay*, 74. On one occasion during the war Lincoln reportedly remarked, "I like Gurley. He don't preach politics. I get enough of that through the week, and when I go to church, I like to hear the Gospel." See White, *The Eloquent President*, 162–64.

63. H[enry] F. McPheeters to John McPheeters, August 17, 1863, John S. McPheeters Correspondence, IHS; Emma Stevens to John Griffin, August 31, 1863, John A. Griffin Papers, ALPL; Rhoda Eggleston to Hubert Eggleston, August 28, [1863], Hubert N. Eggleston Papers, MHS.

CHAPTER 5

1. The title quotation comes from Franklin Alford to Warren Alford, February 10, 1862, Alford Family Papers, IHS. Mitchell, *The Vacant Chair*, 3–18; Griffen, "Reconstructing Masculinity from the Evangelical Revival to the Waning of Progressivism," 185–88; Rotundo, *American Manhood*, 26–27, 172–74; Frank, *Life with Father*, 2, 24, 30–31.

2. Greenberg, *Manifest Manhood and the Antebellum American Empire*, 11–14.

3. Ransom E. Hawley to "Dear Parents and Sister," April 22, 1861, Ransom E. Hawley Papers, box 3, ISL.

4. Ransom E. Hawley to "Dear Parents," June 4, 1862, Ransom E. Hawley Papers, box 3, ISL.

5. Sarah Hawley to "Dear Brother and Sister," March 9, 1863; Ransom E. Hawley to "Dear Father, Mother, and Sisters," June 23, [1863], Ransom E. Hawley Papers, box 3, ISL.

6. Sarah Kohlsaat to Christian Kohlsaat, May 28, 1862; Reimer Kohlsaat to Christian, May 29, 1862; Christian to parents, May 31, 1862; Reimer to Christian, June 10, September 29, 1864, Reimer Kohlsaat and Family Papers, MHS.

7. Andrew Evans to Sam Evans, March 9, 1862; Amos Evans to Sam Evans, October 3, 1862, Evans Family Papers, OHS. These letters have since been published in Engs and Brooks, *Their Patriotic Duty*, 6–7, 67–68. Also see Glatthaar, "Duty, Country, Race, and Party," 332–57.

8. Sam Evans to Andrew Evans, May 10, June 1, 14, 1863; Andrew to Sam, June 7, 1863, February 5, May 7, July 9, 1865, in Engs and Brooks, *Their Patriotic Duty*, 139, 151–53, 158, 324, 347, 354–55.

9. J. L. French to John Blackwell, October 10, 1862, John Blackwell Collection, IHS; *Church Advocate*, September 4, 1862; Nathaniel Wright to William Wright, February 5, 1865, Nathaniel Wright Letters, CinHS.

10. *Christian Recorder*, September 27, 1862; *Western Christian Advocate*, June 26, August 28, 1861.

11. *Presbyter*, September 18, 1862; *Cincinnati Enquirer*, September 26, 1861; *Hancock (Ohio) Courier*, October 11, 1861.

12. Minutes of the Indiana Presbytery, September 1862, Indiana Presbytery Collection, Hanover; Herrick and Sweet, *A History of the North Indiana Conference of the Methodist Episcopal Church*, 73–77; *Western Christian Advocate*, September 10, 1862.

13. For instance, members of First Presbyterian Church of Greenfield, Indiana, paid tribute to the church's founder, sixty-five-year-old W. W. Woods, who died in October 1864 while serving as a chaplain at Camp Nelson in Kentucky. At their annual meeting of 1862, Hoosier delegates of the Salem Presbytery expressed their sorrow over the death of young Edward Bevan, a ministerial student at Wabash College who joined the 38th Indiana and died from illness at Nashville. A more tragic lot could not have befallen thirty-three-year-old John Eddy, Methodist pastor in Attica, Indiana, who reluctantly left his congregation in 1863 to become chaplain of the 72nd Indiana after several friends in the regiment persistently urged him to join them. Eddy united with his comrades in Murfreesboro on Wednesday, June 17, preached in camp the next Sunday, and was slain the following Wednesday when a six-pound shell struck him in the chest while he was helping wounded soldiers during a cavalry skirmish. In at least one case, short-term volunteer work with the Christian Commission contributed to the death of a clergyman. Thirty-five-year-old H. B. Collins, Methodist minister from Franklin, Indiana, returned in mid-April from a six-week stint in Tennessee "enfeebled" from "hard fare and exposure" and died of flux in September 1864. See First Presbyterian Church Records, Greenfield, Indiana, IHS; Minutes of the New School Presbytery, Salem, Indiana, October 4, 1862, Salem Presbytery Collection, box 2, Hanover; *Western Christian Advocate*, July 15, 29, 1863, October 12, 1864. For additional obituaries of ministers or lay exhorters who died in the war, see *Church Advocate*, January 29, October 15, 1863, November 24, 1864; *Western Christian Advocate*, February 26, July 2, 1862, June 3, September 9, December 16, 30, 1863, November 16, 1864.

14. Joseph Ankeny to Henry Ankeny, August 13, 1861, in Cox, *Kiss Josey for Me!*, 10; Caleb Mills to Benjamin Mills, May 10, 1864, Caleb Mills Family Papers,

box 3, IHS; Thomas J. Anderson to James H. Anderson, September 1, 1862, in Anderson, *Life and Letters of Judge Thomas J. Anderson and Wife*, 241; Joseph O. Noyes to "Dear John" [Ballard], June 2, 1861, Mary P. Ballard Letters, WRHS.

15. Franklin Alford to Warren Alford, August 29, 1861, Alford Family Papers, IHS; Silas Dooley to Rufus Dooley, July 13, 1861, Rufus Dooley Papers, box 1, IHS; Ransom Hawley to Ransom E. Hawley, December 30, 1863, Ransom E. Hawley Papers, box 3, ISL; Harrison Kellar to John Kellar, February 18, 1864, Kellar Family Papers, OHS.

16. George and Lycurgus Remley to James Remley, August 26, 1862, in Holcomb, *Southern Sons, Northern Soldiers*, 4–5; Wayne Alford to Franklin Alford, November 28, 1861; Warren Alford to Chester Camp, December 31, 1861, Alford Family Papers, IHS.

17. Silas Dooley to Rufus Dooley, July 13, 20, 1861, February 21, 1862, Rufus Dooley Papers, box 1, IHS; Harrison Kellar to John Kellar, February 24, 1864, Kellar Family Papers, OHS. In 1863, an estimated 7,000 prostitutes staffed 450 bordellos in Washington. See Robertson, *Soldiers Blue and Gray*, 118.

18. Benjamin Mills to Caleb Mills, April 19, June 3, September 6, 1864; Caleb to Benjamin, June 13, 1864, January 23, February 21, 1865; Benjamin Mills diary, January 7, 1865, Caleb Mills Family Papers, boxes 1, 3, IHS.

19. Caleb Mills to Benjamin Mills, January 15, 1865, Caleb Mills Family Papers, box 3, IHS; Warren Alford to Franklin Alford, July 20, 1861; Franklin to Warren, September 1, 1861, Alford Family Papers, IHS; Silas Dooley to Rufus Dooley, July 20, 1861, Rufus Dooley Papers, box 1, IHS.

20. Harrison Kellar to John Kellar, January 16, 1864, Kellar Family Papers, OHS; George Remley to James Remley, September 16, 1862; S. D. Price to James Remley, October 4, 1864, in Holcomb, *Southern Sons, Northern Soldiers*, 5, 162.

21. Budd, *Serving Two Masters*, 38–39, 58–61; James Remley to Lycurgus Remley, November 11, 1862; Lycurgus to James, November 18, 1862, April 11, 1863, in Holcomb, *Southern Sons, Northern Soldiers*, 14, 16, 55; Thomas Barland to Abraham Lincoln, June 25, 1864, Barland Family Papers, WHS. The Roster of Wisconsin Volunteers lists Lark S. Livermore as chaplain of the 16th Wisconsin, Companies F and S.

22. Caleb Mills to Benjamin Mills, May 27, December 3, 1864; Benjamin to Caleb, May 7, 21, 1864, March 15, 1865, Caleb Mills Family Papers, boxes 1, 3, IHS.

23. Lafayette Alford to Franklin Alford, October 31, 1861, Alford Family Papers, IHS.

24. Lycurgus Remley to his parents, September 21, 1862; James Remley to "My Dear Boys," October 22, 1862, in Holcomb, *Southern Sons, Northern Soldiers*, 6, 11; Harrison Kellar to John Kellar, February 6, 1864, Kellar Family Papers, OHS; Alexander McPheeters to John McPheeters, July 3, 1863, John S. McPheeters Correspondence, IHS.

25. Caleb Mills to Benjamin Mills, August 20, 1864, Caleb Mills Family Papers, box 3, IHS.

26. Caleb to Benjamin, November 24, 1864, Caleb Mills Family Papers, box 3, IHS. Caleb copied verbatim James 1:5, Luke 11:13, 2 Timothy 3:15, and Matthew 11:28–30 for Benjamin to contemplate.

27. Benjamin Mills to Caleb Mills, February 7, 1865; Caleb to Benjamin, February 22, 1865, Caleb Mills Family Papers, box 3, IHS.

28. Franklin Alford to Warren Alford, September 15, 1861, April 7, 1862, Alford Family Papers, IHS; Andrew Evans to Sam Evans, July 24, 1864, Evans Family Papers, OHS; D. A. Lough to James Lough, October 21, 1864, Lough Family Papers, box 2, CinHS.

29. Alexander McPheeters to John McPheeters, July 3, 1863, John S. McPheeters Correspondence, IHS; John Ketcham to Willie Ketcham, March 27, 1865, John L. Ketcham Papers, box 2, IHS; Harrison Kellar to John Kellar, January 24, February 13, 1864, Kellar Family Papers, OHS; James Remley to Lycurgus Remley, November 11, 25, 1862, in Holcomb, *Southern Sons, Northern Soldiers*, 14, 18.

30. Caleb Mills to Benjamin Mills, August 20, 1864, Caleb Mills Family Papers, box 3, IHS; John Ketcham to Willie Ketcham, February 26, May 28, 1865, John L. Ketcham Papers, box 2, IHS.

31. Joseph Beebe to "My Dear Boys," January 1, November 18, 1862, Joseph E. Beebe Collection, Bentley; Jerome Brown to Darius Brown, October 22, 1862, Ethan A. Brown Letters, WMU.

32. John Vannest to Joseph Vannest, June 15, February 3, 1863; Rose Vannest to Joseph Vannest, February 24, 1863; Joseph M. Ryder to Joseph Vannest, February 24, 1863, Joseph P. Vannest Papers, IHS.

33. Mary Vannest to Joseph Vannest, September 27, 1863; Joseph Vannest to Mary Vannest, November 26, 1863, Joseph P. Vannest Papers, IHS.

34. Willie Ketcham to John Ketcham, June 20, 1864, John L. Ketcham Papers, box 2, IHS; Franklin Alford to Warren Alford, September 21, 1862, Alford Family Papers, IHS.

35. Henry Ankeny to Tina Ankeny, October 7, 12, 1862, in Cox, *Kiss Josey for Me!*, 93–95; Warren Alford to Franklin Alford, July 26, 1862, Alford Family Papers, IHS.

36. Ransom Hawley to Ransom E. Hawley, October 3, 22, 1864, Ransom E. Hawley Papers, box 3, ISL.

37. Ransom Hawley to Ransom E. Hawley, April 26, 1865, Ransom E. Hawley Papers, box 3, ISL.

38. Franklin Alford to Warren Alford, March 31, 1862, August 19, 1861, Alford Family Papers, IHS.

CHAPTER 6

1. The title is taken from *New York Evangelist*, July 21, 1864, which contains a letter written by a pastor's wife residing in Three Rivers, Michigan, who longed to see "the golden chain of love uniting Christians of every name, and so filling their hearts with a pure patriotism and love for Christ and country that they shall forget

their different [denominational] names, and labor with united heart and purpose." Ironically, her initials were W. A. R. Minutes of the New School Presbytery, Crawfordsville, Indiana, August 29, 1863, Crawfordsville Presbytery Collection, box 1, Hanover.

2. Minutes of the Old School Presbytery, Vincennes, Indiana, September 12–13, 1862, September 12, 1863, Vincennes Presbytery Collection, box 1, Hanover.

3. Mary J. Robinson to E. H. Ingraham, September 10, 1863, Edward H. Ingraham and Duncan G. Ingraham Papers, ALPL.

4. David Demaree to George Whitefield Demaree, August 10, 1863, Demaree Letters, BSU.

5. *Newark (Ohio) Advocate*, September 25, 1863.

6. Austin, *Petroleum V. Nasby*, 32–34, 77–79, 95–96; Locke, *The Nasby Papers*, 26, 28, 36–37, 59–60.

7. *Hancock (Ohio) Courier*, August 14, 1863; *Hancock (Ohio) Jeffersonian*, August 28, 1863. The multipart letter on political preaching appeared in the *Jeffersonian* from August 14 through September 18.

8. *Hancock (Ohio) Courier*, August 28, 1863.

9. *Hancock (Ohio) Courier*, September 4, 18, 1863; *Hancock Jeffersonian*, September 11, 1863.

10. *Hancock (Ohio) Courier*, September 4, October 2, 1863.

11. Fox-Genovese and Genovese, *The Mind of the Master Class*, 505–21; *Cincinnati Enquirer*, October 21, 1863.

12. *Church Advocate*, September 24, 1863.

13. *Catholic Telegraph*, July 8, 15, September 9, 1863.

14. *Minutes of the Twelfth Annual Session of the North-Western Indiana Conference, of the Methodist Episcopal Church*, 23. A resolution passed two years later made this sentiment even more explicit when delegates declared their wish that "the freedmen of our land may become the heralds of freedom and Christianity to the millions of Africa." See *Minutes of the Fourteenth Annual Session of the North-Western Indiana Conference, of the Methodist Church*, 39; *Christian Advocate and Journal*, September 17, 1863.

15. Klement, *The Limits of Dissent*. Civilian support for Vallandigham can be found in Clopper, "Country Life during the Civil War," 183, 186. Jennie E. Plimpton to Henry Cumings, August 24, 1863, Henry Harrison Cumings Papers, box 1, WRHS. For letters of two soldiers who favored Vallandigham, see *Hancock (Ohio) Courier*, September 18, October 2, 1863. *Hardin County Republican*, August 28, 1863, cited in Dee, *Ohio's War*, 151–52; Manning, *What This Cruel War Was Over*, 99–100.

16. Ohio Conference of the United Brethren in Christ to Abraham Lincoln, October 3, 1863, Abraham Lincoln Papers; *Church Advocate*, October 15, 1863; *Cincinnati Enquirer*, September 29, October 7, 1863; *Hancock (Ohio) Courier*, September 25, 1863; Andreasen, "'As Good a Right to Pray,'" 398–400; *Newark (Ohio) Advocate*, September 18, 1863.

17. Mary Vermilion to William Vermilion, October 27, 1863, in Elder, *Love amid the Turmoil*, 254; *Milwaukee Daily Sentinel*, October 15, 1863; William Patrick to Calvin Fletcher, October 15, 1863, Calvin Fletcher Papers, box 10, IHS; Klement, *The Limits of Dissent*, 252; *New York Evangelist*, October 22, 1863; *Jackson (Ohio) Standard*, excerpted in *Putman (Indiana) Republican Banner*, November 12, 1863.

18. Weber, *Copperheads*, 122; *Cincinnati Enquirer*, October 14, 1863; *Toledo Blade*, October 31, 1863.

19. *Catholic Telegraph*, October 21, 28, 1863; *Cincinnati Gazette*, October 23, 29, 1863; *Cincinnati Enquirer*, October 30, 1863; *Cincinnati Daily Commercial*, November 2, 1863.

20. *Christian Recorder*, November 14, 1863; *Mt. Vernon (Ohio) Democratic Banner*, excerpted in *Newark (Ohio) Advocate*, November 20, 1863.

21. *Daily Cleveland Herald*, November 27, 1863; Boritt, *The Gettysburg Gospel*, 3, 112, 120, 131–34, 138–43; Stout, *Upon the Altar of the Nation*, 268–70; *Milwaukee Daily Sentinel*, November 28, 1863. In addition to this eyewitness description, the *Sentinel* contained a brief editorial on November 25 commending Everett, printed his entire speech the following day, and even reproduced the prayer of chaplain Thomas Stockton on December 3 yet never saw fit to publish Lincoln's address. *Cincinnati Enquirer*, December 3, 1863.

22. "Proclamation of Thanksgiving," October 3, 1863, in *CW*, 6:496–97; Boritt, *The Gettysburg Gospel*, 165–67; *New York Evangelist*, October 29, 1863. For civilian comments on Thanksgiving, see Serena Wright to George Wright, October 18, 1863, George Burdick Wright and Family Papers, box 4, MHS; E. Anne Butler to Scot Butler, November 26, 1863, in Davis, *Affectionately Yours*, 52–53. Favorable opinions can be found in the *Milwaukee Daily Sentinel*, October 6, November 28, 1863, and *Toledo Blade*, November 27, 1863. Negative commentary appeared in the *Hancock (Ohio) Courier*, October 30, 1863, and *Newark (Ohio) Advocate*, November 20, 1863. *Cincinnati Enquirer*, November 26, 30, 1863.

23. Carey, *God Doing Wonderful Things in Behalf of the Nation*, 3–16.

24. Andreasen, "'As Good a Right to Pray,'" 385–94; *Cincinnati Enquirer*, January 22, 1864; *North-West*, February 3, 1864.

25. *Cincinnati Enquirer*, January 22, 1864; *Allen County (Ohio) Democrat*, January 27, 1864; *Western Christian Advocate*, January 27, 1864; *Cincinnati Gazette*, January 26, 1864; Andreasen, "'As Good a Right to Pray,'" 420–25.

26. *Allen County (Ohio) Democrat*, January 27, 1864; *Newark (Ohio) Advocate*, February 19, 1864; Andreasen, "'As Good a Right to Pray,'" 432–35; *Cincinnati Gazette*, February 5, 1864; *Cincinnati Daily Commercial*, February 18, 1864.

27. *Church Advocate*, January 7, February 11, 18, March 3, 1864; *Cincinnati Gazette*, January 29, 1864; *Christian Recorder*, January 23, March 12, 26, 1864.

28. Mary to Juliet and Helen, January 11, 1864, Blinn Papers, box 6, CinHS; *Christian Recorder*, March 26, 1864; Stowell, *Rebuilding Zion*, 29–30; *Daily Cleveland Herald*, February 1, 1864; *Chicago Times*, excerpted in *Newark (Ohio) Advocate*, February 19, 1864.

29. Vander Velde, *The Presbyterian Churches and the Federal Union*, 307–25; Abraham Lincoln to Edwin M. Stanton, February 11, 1864; "Endorsement to John Hogan," February 13, 1864, in *CW*, 7:178–180, 182–83; Sweet, *The Methodist Episcopal Church and the Civil War*, 106–7; John B. Morison et al. to Lincoln, March 5, 1864; Lincoln Endorsement, March 15, 1864, Abraham Lincoln Papers.

30. Charles P. McIlvaine to Lincoln, March 4, 1864, Abraham Lincoln Papers; *National Intelligencer*, February 25, 1864.

31. *Cincinnati Daily Commercial*, May 26, 1864; *Church Advocate*, May 19, June 16, 1864.

32. Edward Meyer to M. T. Reynolds, March 12, 1864, Edward Meyer Collection, Bentley; Martha Stork to Toby Dooley, April 24, 1864, Rufus Dooley Papers, box 1, IHS; *Putnam (Indiana) Republican Banner*, August 18, 1864; *Allen County (Ohio) Democrat*, April 27, 1864.

33. Reck, "Mr. Lincoln's Growth in Faith," 10; Donald, *Lincoln*, 500; "To the Friends of Union and Liberty," May 9, 1864, in *CW*, 7:333; *Cincinnati Enquirer*, May 12, 1864.

34. *New York Evangelist*, May 19, 1864; Fletcher diary, May 15, 1864, in *DCF*, 8:397; *Cincinnati Gazette*, May 14, 1864; McPherson, *Battle Cry of Freedom*, 732; Stout, *Upon the Altar of the Nation*, 338; Levi Lough to James Lough, May 18, 1864, Lough Family Papers, box 2, CinHS; *Daily Cleveland Herald*, May 28, 1864; General Conference of Methodist Episcopal Church to Abraham Lincoln, May 14, 1864, Abraham Lincoln Papers; "Response to Methodists," May 18, 1864, in *CW*, 7:350–51; Sweet, *The Methodist Episcopal Church and the Civil War*, 87–91.

35. Neace, "A Study of Methodism in Indiana during the Civil War," 40–42; *Christian Advocate and Journal*, July 28, 1864; *Zion's Herald and Wesleyan Journal*, July 20, 1864; *Indianapolis Witness*, July 20, 1864.

36. Rockport Presbyterian Church Session Minutes, February 17, 21, 1862; January 12, 22, 1863; February 26, March 17, August 29, 1864, BGSU. Although no further mention of Honnell's name ever appears in the church records after his expulsion from Rockport, his controversy with the church somehow escaped the notice of county historians, who referred to him as a forty-year member of the church. See Miller, *History of Allen County, Ohio and Representative Citizens*, 516; Mt. Pleasant United Presbyterian Church Records, June 16, 1864, IHS.

37. Records of the Church at Pleasant Run (Baptist), IHS. Indeed, the church's politicization cast a cloud over the congregation that lingered for over a decade. In 1866 Pleasant Run withdrew from the Whitewater Baptist Association after the latter censured the church and refused to listen to protests from the congregation's delegation led by Morris. Following Wright's abrupt departure, the church struggled to find a preacher and evidently failed to meet from August 1867 to February 1869 and again from January 1873 until August 1875. In April 1870, one of the few instances when the church gathered during this period of strained relations, Morris responded to allegations that the church had "erd" [erred] and defiantly challenged sister churches to give evidence of specific offenses. Finally in

June 1878, Stanley Cooper, the clerk and a supporter of the 1863 resolutions, offered a motion that acknowledged wrongdoing regarding "the difficulty that existed in this Church years ago." The rift had occurred "in times of high excitement" produced by the war, and now the church desired to "rescind everything which gave offence" and obtain forgiveness from all offended parties. That confession mended the breach, for Harvey Wright returned as moderator in December 1878 and later accepted the church's call to be its regular pastor, serving from 1880 until 1886 when Pleasant Run Church united with Little Salt Creek Church. *History of Rush County, Indiana*, 395–96; Barrows, *History of Fayette County, Indiana*, 416; *Atlas of Rush County, Indiana*, 64.

38. John M. Brenneman to Peter Nissley, August 17, 1864, Peter Nissley Collection, MCA; *North-West*, August 4, 1864; *Western Christian Advocate*, July 13, 1864, cited in Andreasen, "'As Good a Right to Pray,'" 442.

39. Ellen L. Woodworth Diary, June 14, 1864, Clarke; D. A. Lough to James Lough, June 28, 1864, Lough Family Papers, CinHS; Louisa Semple to Ben Grierson, August 12, 1864, Benjamin H. Grierson Papers, ALPL; *Cincinnati Enquirer*, July 28, 1864; *Lawrenceburg (Indiana) Democratic Register*, May 27, 1864.

40. *Scioto (Ohio) Gazette*, June 14, 1864; *Cincinnati Enquirer*, July 28, 1864; *Scioto (Ohio) Gazette*, July 12, 1864; Nathaniel Wright to William Wright, July 10, 1864, Nathaniel Wright Letters, CinHS.

CHAPTER 7

1. The title quotation comes from "Mother S[arah] Chapin" to "My Dear son," June 5, 1864, Lucius Chapin Papers, box 2, IHS. Franklin Alford to Warren Alford, August 5, 1861; Warren to parents, September 25, 1861, Alford Family Papers, IHS.

2. Franklin Alford to Warren Alford, March 2, 1862; Wayne and Lafayette Alford to Mary Alford, January 30, 1862; Warren to "Dear Brother," June 13, 1862, Alford Family Papers, IHS.

3. Franklin to Warren, September 21, 1862, January 27, 1862, Alford Family Papers, IHS.

4. Stannard, *The Puritan Way of Death*, 72–95; Saum, *The Popular Mood of Pre-Civil War America*, 78–104; Farrell, *Inventing the American Way of Death*, 4–7, 44–98; Moorhead, *World without End*, 17, 58–61.

5. O'Malley, *Keeping Watch*, 8–23; Smith, *Mastered by the Clock*, 41–43, 57–59; Wells, *Civil War Time*; Samuel Hibbard diary, January 1, December 31, 1863, Robert C. Hibbard Collection, WMU; Fletcher diary, February 4, 1863, February 4, 1864, in *DCF*, 8:42, 323–24; Journal of Emily Beeler Fletcher, May 11, 1863, IHS.

6. Drusilla Dean to [George and Elmina Lounsbury], August 14, 1861, George W. Lounsbury Collection, IHS. James Farrell traced the adage, "In the midst of life we are in death," to the Methodist "Order of the Burial of the Dead" published in 1836, and Steven Woodworth discovered it in *The Soldier's Prayer Book* distributed by the Episcopal church. See Farrell, *Inventing the American Way of Death*, 40–41,

and Woodworth, *While God Is Marching On*, 47–48; Eunice Brown to "Dear Brother," March 28, 1864, Eunice A. Brown Letters, IHS; Mollie McPheeters to John McPheeters, May 31, 1864, John S. McPheeters Correspondence, IHS.

7. Catharine Peirce to Taylor Peirce, August 2, 1863, November n.d., 1864, in Kiper, *Dear Catharine, Dear Taylor*, 136, 294; Virginia Alford to Warren Alford, January 26, 1862, Alford Family Papers, IHS; Mary Vermilion to William Vermilion, July 27, 1864, in Elder, *Love amid the Turmoil*, 288.

8. It is difficult to tell how and when people became accustomed to employing this phrase to describe death. The rise of Adventism during the antebellum period may have returned the expression to the popular vernacular. However, its usage to designate death goes back at least to the fifteenth century. Thomas à Kempis applied Matthew 24:44 to death in book one, chapter 23 of his classic devotional *The Imitation of Christ*. See Sherley-Price, *The Imitation of Christ*, 58. During the Civil War, Southerners also used "the coming of the Son of Man" to connote death, especially when admonishing Confederate soldiers to consider their mortality. See "Documenting the American South" from the University of North Carolina's Rare Book Collection, accessible at http://docsouth.unc.edu.

9. Josephine Foster to William Haynes Lytle, April 3, [1863], Lytle Papers, box 32, CinHS; Foote, *The Civil War*, 2:739–40; Alexander McPheeters to John McPheeters, July 3, 1863, John S. McPheeters Correspondence, IHS; *Indianapolis Witness*, March 5, 1862.

10. Margaret Ross to "My Dear Sister," November 1, 1861, Cassady–Nelson Family Papers, BSU; J. W. Osborn addendum to letter from Alice Chapin to Nellie, July 4–5, 1864, Blinn Papers, box 6, CinHS; Viana White to George White, April 30, 1863, George M. White Collection, box 1, WMU.

11. Franklin Alford to Warren Alford, January 12, 1862, Alford Family Papers, IHS; unsigned letter to Silas Borton, November 16, [1862], Borton Family Papers, box 1, BGSU; Henry Tutewiler to Henry W. Tutewiler, March 3, 1865, Henry W. Tutewiler Papers, IHS; John Ketcham to Willie Ketcham, February 15, March 27, 1865, John L. Ketcham Papers, box 2, IHS; Alexander McPheeters to John McPheeters, June 10, 1863, John S. McPheeters Correspondence, IHS; Mary Logan to John Logan, June 28, 1863, John Logan Family Papers, LC.

12. James Remley to George Remley, July 4, 1863, in Holcomb, *Southern Sons, Northern Soldiers*, 82; George Woodruff Journal, August 28, November 26, 1863, Bentley.

13. S. F. and Mary Covington to "Dear Friend," June 19, 1864, John T. Wilder Collection, ISL; [Eleanor Bereman] to [Samuel Bereman], June 5, 1864, in Larimer, *Love and Valor*, 283; Jane van den Tak to Sophia Buchanan, May 13, 1863, Rev. Abel Bingham Papers, box 11, Clarke.

14. Elvira Aplin to George Aplin, July 28, August 14, 1864, Aplin Family Papers, box 3, Clements; Almira Dart to George Howell, September 28, 1862, Howell Family Papers, Bentley; Sarah Dooley to Rufus Dooley, August 30, 1862, Rufus Dooley Papers, box 1, IHS.

15. Saum, *The Popular Mood of Pre-Civil War America*, 94–103; Mitchell, *The Vacant Chair*, 142–43; Faust, "The Civil War Soldier and the Art of Dying," 6–8, 12–13; *Indianapolis Witness*, July 20, 1864; *Christian Recorder*, December 12, 1863. The 1860 census lists Mary Bass, mulatto, as only seventy-five years old.

16. Almira Dart to George Howell, September 28, 1862, Howell Family Papers, Bentley; Ethan Brown to Darius Brown, April 17, 1862, Ethan A. Brown Letters, WMU.

17. Faust, "The Civil War Soldier and the Art of Dying," 16–17, 19; Lathan B. Byron to "Mrs. C. C. [Clarissa] Webb," February 22, March 4, 1863, Phyllis Burnham Collection, WMU; Henry Glover to Elizabeth Stevens, January 23, 1863, in Ellis, "The Civil War Letters of an Iowa Family," 578–79.

18. Faust, "The Civil War Soldier and the Art of Dying," 13; George Remley to Jane Remley, June 16, 1863, Charles Borland to George Remley, June 29, 1863, in Holcomb, *Southern Sons, Northern Soldiers*, 74, 80; D. A. Lough to William Lough, November 30, 1864, Lough Family Papers, box 2, CinHS.

19. Sarah Dooley to Rufus Dooley, August 9, 1864, Rufus Dooley Papers, box 1, IHS; Sarah Chapin to [Lucius Chapin], June 5, 1864, Lucius Chapin Papers, box 2, IHS; A. D. Lynch to Martha John, July 19, 1861, John Price Durbin John Papers, DePauw. Unbeknownst to Lynch, John W. Falconer had observed the passing of Samuel John, and his firsthand description related to his father somehow found its way into Samuel's hometown paper a week after Lynch had written her imaginative narrative intended to comfort Martha John. Falconer reported that Samuel "was standing at my right side, his shoulder touching mine, and he was shot through the body. He called 'John, John, I am killed, I am killed!' I laid him on his side, saw his eyes turn glassy; his face grow pale and his lips blue and the blood gush from his mouth. He whispered not to leave him—these were the last words he spoke.... He went into the fight with the full expectation of coming out safely. In five minutes he was a corpse." See *Franklin (Indiana) Democrat*, July 26, 1861. Edward Meyer to M. T. Reynolds, March 12, 1864, Edward Meyer Collection, Bentley.

20. Laderman, *The Sacred Remains*, 98–99, 109–16, 127–30; *Daily Cleveland Herald*, December 9, 1863. Lacking a Scripture text or religious application, the sermons delivered on behalf of Creighton and Crane demonstrate the shift toward memorial biographies focusing on worldly achievements rather than spiritual preparation. However, not all funeral sermons gave priority to patriotism. For instance, J. B. Bachman's tribute to J. M. Springer, chaplain or the 3rd Wisconsin who died in the battle of Resaca while attempting to rally a faltering company after the captain and two lieutenants had been killed, primarily emphasized the necessity of preparing to meet their former pastor in heaven. See *Wisconsin State Register*, July 9, 1864. At the funeral of Charles McGlone, 3rd Ohio Cavalry, the Episcopal rector C. F. Lewis of Wakeman, Ohio, completely repudiated the patriotic funeral discourses that predominated during the war. He insisted that "the virtues proclaimed from the lips of many a *Protestant* minister in eulogy over the dead, is but too frequently highly imaginative, purely fictitious, in one word false." Mentioning

McGlone only once in the entire address, Lewis maintained that hypocritical paeans to the dead rendered no spiritual benefit to the living, who needed to hear sermons that would cause them to focus on their soul's salvation and heed the scriptural command to prepare for the coming judgment. See *Norwalk (Ohio) Experiment*, June 30, 1862. Faust, *This Republic of Suffering*, 163–66; Grant, "Patriot Graves," 93–97.

21. Jane Remley to James Remley, June 29, 1863, in Holcomb, *Southern Sons, Northern Soldiers*, 79–80; Jane Mauck addendum to letter from William Mumford to Samuel Mumford, June 15, 1864, Samuel Mumford Papers, IHS; John Chapin to Lucius Chapin, April 19, 1863, Lucius Chapin Papers, box 1, IHS; Dorothy Blinn to Amory Blinn, July 29, 1863; Alice Chapin to Cousin Nellie, September 7, 1863, Blinn Papers, box 5, CinHS; Helen Kemper to Lucius Chapin, July 26, 1864, Lucius Chapin Papers, box 2, IHS.

22. Fletcher diary, May 9, 11, 1862, in *DCF*, 7:421, 423; O. P. Morton to Fletcher, [May 11, 1862], in *DCF*, 7:425–26.

23. *DCF*, 7:429n; Andrew Ingram to Calvin Fletcher, May 12, 1862; J. W. T. McMullen to Fletcher, May 13, 1862; W. R. Revels to Fletcher, May 16, 1862, Calvin Fletcher Papers, box 10, IHS.

24. Paludan, *"A People's Contest,"* 367; McDannell and Lang, *Heaven*, 178–80, 228–29, 272–75, 287.

25. Helen Kemper to Lucius Chapin, June 26, 1864, Lucius Chapin Papers, box 2, IHS; Sarah [Chapin] to Amory Blinn, February 28, 1864, Blinn Papers, box 6, CinHS; Eliza Fanning writings, n.d., [1863], Eliza Fanning Correspondence, RBH; D. A. Lough to William Lough, November 30, 1864, Lough Family Papers, box 2, CinHS; Emily Elliot diary, October 31, 1864, quoted in Woodworth, *While God Is Marching On*, 45.

26. Lizzie Bowler to Madison Bowler, October 23, 1864, James M. Bowler and Family Papers, box 1, MHS; Lizzie Griffith to Amory Blinn, March 27, 1864, Blinn Papers, box 6, CinHS; Amanda Hudelson to Jane Hudelson, January 10, 1865, Hill–Hudelson Family Papers, box 2, Earlham; Alice Chapin to Lucius Chapin, May [illeg.], 1863, Lucius Chapin Papers, box 1, IHS.

27. Moorhead, "'As Though Nothing at All Had Happened,'" 455; Hoffert, "'A Very Peculiar Sorrow,'" 605–7, 610–13, and *Private Matters*, 177–80, 183–87; J. R. Jones to "Dear Brother & Sister," February 22, 1863, Susan B. Unthink Papers, ISL; Anna Starr to William Starr, October 5, 1861, William C. Starr Papers, IHS; M. Buffington to Schuyler and Lucia Hendryx, January 25, 1865, Schuyler V. R. Hendryx Papers, MHS; N. Lounsbury to George and Elmina Lounsbury, February 16, 1864, George W. Lounsbury Papers, IHS.

28. Lucretia to Kelsey Adams, April 3, 1863, Kelsey M. Adams Civil War Letters, WHS; Helen Kemper to Lucius Chapin, June 26, 1864, Lucius Chapin Papers, Box 2, IHS; Charles Hamilton to James and Agnes Crandall, April 5, 1863, John Watts Hamilton Collection, IHS; Eliza Porter to Caleb Core, November 15, 1864, addendum to November 8 letter, Core–Porter Letters, OHS.

29. James Remley to George Remley, July 4, 1863, in Holcomb, *Southern Sons, Northern Soldiers*, 82; Kiper, *Dear Catherine, Dear Taylor*, 3–4; Catharine Peirce to Taylor Peirce, March 15, 1864, October 25, 1863, in Kiper, *Dear Catherine, Dear Taylor*, 186–87, 145–46; Franklin Thorpe to "Dear Brother," November 6, 1864, Reuben Green Papers, IHS; McDannell and Lang, *Heaven*, 287.

30. Alice Chapin to [Lucius Chapin], letter fragment, n.d., Lucius Chapin Papers, box 2, IHS; Sarah Chapin to "My Dear Niece," June 19, 1864, Blinn Papers, box 6, CinHS; D. A. Lough to James Lough, October 21, 1864; D. A. Lough to William Lough, November 30, 1864, Lough Family Papers, box 2, CinHS; A. J. Reiley to Jasper Kidwell, January 7, February 23, 1865, Kephart–Kidwell Family Papers, IHS.

31. Mary Chittenden to George Chittenden, August 11, 1861, George F. Chittenden Papers, box 1, ISL; Helen Sharp to John Sharp, April 23, 1862, in Mills, "The Sharp Family Civil War Letters," 495; Franklin Alford to Warren Alford, October 29, 1861, Alford Family Papers, IHS.

32. Hattie to William Kemper, July 11, 1864, G. W. H. Kemper Collection, box 4, BSU; Rhoda Eggleston to Hubert Eggleston, August 28, [1863], Hubert N. Eggleston Papers, MHS; Harrison Kellar to John Kellar, December 17, 1864, Kellar Family Papers, OHS; Emeline Ritner to Jacob Ritner, June 26, 1864, in Larimer, *Love and Valor*, 295.

33. Margaret Denny to John Denny, March 20, [1865], James M. Van Hook Papers, box 1, ISL; Elvira Aplin to George Aplin, May 1, 1864, Aplin Family Papers, box 2, Clements; Anna Searight to James Rizer, January 15, 1862, Military Collection, box 2, TCHA; Frances Ely to Edna Van Pelt, March 21, 1862, Mathias Van Pelt Family Papers, box 2, IHS.

34. Woodworth, *While God Is Marching On*, 46–47; Moorhead, "'As Though Nothing at All Had Happened,'" 457; Elvira Aplin to George Aplin, n.d., [1863], Aplin Family Papers, box 1, Clements; unsigned letter to John [Griffin], October 10, 1864, John Griffin Papers, ALPL.

35. Mary Logan to John Logan, July 27, 1864, John Logan Family Papers, box 33, LC; Mary Vermilion to William Vermilion, July 12, 1863, in Elder, *Love amid the Turmoil*, 159–60; Lizzie Little to George Avery, May 23, 1861, George Smith Avery Papers, ChiHS; H[enry] Cobb to "Friends," October 10, 1862, Schuyler V. R. Hendryx Papers, MHS.

36. Margaret Denny to John Denny, March 20, [1865], James M. Van Hook Papers, box 1, ISL; Mary Mumford addendum to letter from William Mumford to Samuel Mumford, June 15, 1864, Samuel Mumford Papers, IHS; E. A. Rice to Robert H. Rice, January 25, 1863, Dr. and Mrs. Robert H. Rice Collection, box 1, RBH.

37. In the preface to *Heaven and Hell* (1758), Swedenborg claimed that he had personally visited the spirit world. See McDannell and Lang, *Heaven*, 186–89. *The Crisis*, November 1, 1862, in John H. Armstrong Family Papers, box 3, IHS; Alice Chapin to Lucius Chapin, May [illeg.], 1863, Lucius Chapin Papers, box 1, IHS; Alice to Lucius, n.d., Lucius Chapin Papers, box 2, IHS.

38. Universalism had made inroads further west by the Civil War. For example, the Universalist newspaper *Star in the West*, published in Cincinnati, carried an article that argued against the "eternal death" of the soul in a place of physical torment. By interpreting Ezekiel 18:20, "The soul that sinneth, it shall die," to mean that any person living in a "state of sin" was simply morally blind and therefore already enduring punishment by having to exist in a "state of death" on earth, Universalists dismissed the need for any future, eternal damnation. See *Star in the West*, January 12, 1861.

39. S. F. and Mary Covington to "Dear Friend," June 19, 1864, John T. Wilder Collection, ISL.

CHAPTER 8

1. The title quotation is taken from Edward and Sarah Hall to William and Sarah Hall, January 22, 1865, Collet–Hall Families, box 1, Clarke. *Cincinnati Enquirer*, June 8, 1864; *Hancock (Ohio) Courier*, June 17, 1864; John Ketcham to Willie Ketcham, John L. Ketcham Papers, IHS; *Christian Recorder*, April 22, 1865.

2. *Ripley (Ohio) Bee*, May 12, 1864; *Chicago Tribune*, excerpted in *Liberator*, May 13, 1864; *Independent*, May 12, 1864; Caleb Mills to Benjamin Mills, May 10, 1864, Caleb Mills Family Papers, box 3, IHS; *Christian Recorder*, May 28, 1864.

3. Wert, *The Sword of Lincoln*, 361–67; Valentine Nicholson to Martha McKay, June 16, 1864, Valentine Nicholson Papers, box 1, IHS; Ann Cotton to Dexter Cotton, June 2, 1864, Papers of Josiah Dexter Cotton, box 1, LC; Julia to Lucie King, July 3, 1864, King Family Papers, ALPL; Mary C. Gookins to "My Dear Friend," July 15, 1864, Blinn Papers, box 6, CinHS.

4. Guelzo, *Abraham Lincoln*, 390–92; Waugh, *Reelecting Lincoln*, 177–81.

5. Este diary, August 14, 1864, David K. Este Family Letters and Miscellaneous Papers, CinHS; Valentine Nicholson to Martha McKay, June 16, 1864, Valentine Nicholson Papers, box 1, IHS; Cyrus McCormick to Nettie McCormick, July 9, 1864, Nettie Fowler McCormick Papers, McCormick Manuscripts 2B, box 6, WHS; Mollie McPheeters to John McPheeters, July 21, 1864, John S. McPheeters Correspondence, IHS; J. W. Osborn to Lucius Chapin, June 7, 1864, Blinn Papers, box 6, CinHS; Eleanor H. Bereman to Samuel Bereman, June 28, 1864, in Larimer, *Love and Valor*, 296.

6. "Proclamation of a Day of Prayer," July 7, 1864, in *CW*, 7:431–32.

7. Harris, *With Charity for All*, 186–90.

8. Weber, *Copperheads*, 151–54; James Weiler to Joseph Vannest, August 23, 1864, Joseph P. Vannest Papers, IHS; unsigned to "cousin," August 25, 1864, Davis Civil War Papers, box 10, Moore–Youse Museum Archives, Muncie, Ind.; Sarah to Lucretia, August 11, 1864, Blinn Papers, box 6, CinHS.

9. "To Whom It May Concern," July 18, 1864, in *CW*, 7:451. This document followed shortly on the heels of Horace Greeley's repeated pestering of Lincoln about a mission to parley with self-styled Confederate peace agents at Niagara Falls,

a rendezvous that proved both futile in terms of negotiations and personally humiliating to Greeley. See Weber, *Copperheads*, 154–56.

10. Emilie Gleichmann to John Gleichmann, August 5, 1864, Civil War Miscellaneous Collection, box 37, USAMHI; Lizzie Bowler to Madison Bowler, September 2, 1864, James M. Bowler and Family Papers, box 1, MHS; Stout, *Upon the Altar of the Nation*, 358–59; Wert, *The Sword of Lincoln*, 382–85; Ann Cotton to Dexter Cotton, August 4, 1864, Papers of Josiah Dexter Cotton, box 2, LC.

11. *Chicago Tribune*, August 4, 1864.

12. Curran, *A Sermon*, 4, 9–11; Little, *The Mission of Our Government*, 4–12.

13. *Iowa City Press*, excerpted in *Newark (Ohio) Advocate*, August 26, 1864.

14. *New York Journal of Commerce*, excerpted in *Cincinnati Enquirer*, August 11, 1864.

15. Isaiah 8:12 reads, "Say ye not, A confederacy, to all them to whom this people shall say, A confederacy; neither fear ye their fear, nor be afraid." This verse, one of two in the entire Bible that contains the English word "confederacy," records God's message to Isaiah about resisting the fear of man, in this specific case an alliance between Assyria and the northern kingdom of Israel against the southern kingdom of Judah. Interestingly enough, had McMullen considered the context of the passage and extended his analysis to verse 13, he would have seen that God then commanded his people to fear his holy name in reverence and humility, a fitting parallel to the emphasis of the piece in the *Enquirer*.

16. "A War Sermon," John William Thomas McMullen Papers, DePauw; also excerpted in *Ripley (Ohio) Bee*, September 22, 1864.

17. Louisa Dunn to Henry W. Tutewiler, September 11, 1864, Henry W. Tutewiler Papers, IHS; J. E. Chapin to Helen, September 22, 1864; Leide to "Dear Uncle," November 20, 1864, Blinn Papers, box 6, CinHS; William H. Burke to Dr. H. Stidger, October 7, 1864, Thomas B. Searight Collection, box 1, BGSU; Mollie to Rufus Dooley, September 28, 1864, Rufus Dooley Papers, box 1, IHS.

18. Mollie McPheeters to John McPheeters, August 4, 1864, John S. McPheeters Correspondence, IHS; Waugh, *Reelecting Lincoln*, 263–67; "Interview with Alexander W. Randall and Joseph T. Mills, August 19, 1864, in *CW*, 506–7.

19. "Memorandum Concerning His Probable Failure of Re-election," August 23, 1864, in *CW*, 514; Waugh, *Reelecting Lincoln*, 285–86, 298–301; John Ketcham to Willie Ketcham, September 4, 1864, John L. Ketcham Papers, box 2, IHS; Mollie McPheeters to John McPheeters, September 8, 1864, John S. McPheeters Correspondence, IHS.

20. "Proclamation of Thanksgiving and Prayer," September 3, 1864, in *CW*, 533; *Milwaukee Daily Sentinel*, September 22, 1864; Elizabeth Jane Jackson to Benjamin Jackson, September 20, 1864, Benjamin Basil Jackson Family Papers, BGSU; Ann Cotton to Dexter Cotton, September 25, 1864, Papers of Josiah Dexter Cotton, box 2, LC.

21. *Lima (Ohio) Weekly Gazette*, September 21, 1864; *Cincinnati Daily Commercial*, September 16, 1864; *Cincinnati Enquirer*, October 5, 1864.

22. Geary, *We Need Men*, 134–39; Sarah Dooley to Rufus Dooley, September 29, 1864, Rufus Dooley Papers, box 1, IHS; Jacob Thorna to "Dear Son & Daughter," October 31, 1864, Barnett Family Papers, ISL; Poucher diary, n.d. [written between September 28, 1864, and January 1865], March 12, 1865, John Poucher Papers, DePauw.

23. Poucher diary, March 12, 1865, John Poucher Papers, DePauw; Fletcher diary, October 10, 11, 1864, in *DCF*, 8:448; J. W. T. McMullen to G. W. Stafford, October 18, 1864, George Washington Stafford Papers, box 1, IHS.

24. Catharine Peirce to Taylor Peirce, October 22, 1864, in Kiper, *Dear Catharine, Dear Taylor*, 285; Sarah Dooley to Rufus Dooley, October 15, 1864, Rufus Dooley Papers, box 1, IHS; Augustus Frey to his mother, October 30, 1864, Augustus Frey Papers, ALPL; *Delaware County (Indiana) Free Press*, October 13, 1864; Ellen Plattenburg to Philip Dodson Plattenburg, October 31, 1864, Ellen D. Plattenburg Letters, ALPL; Wert, *The Sword of Lincoln*, 44.

25. *Western Christian Advocate*, October 12, 1864; Ellen Plattenburg to Philip Dodson Plattenburg, October 31, 1864, Ellen D. Plattenburg Letters, ALPL; William Jackson to Benjamin Jackson, November 4, 1864, Benjamin Basil Jackson Family Papers, box 1, BGSU; Franklin Thorpe to "Dear Brother," November 6, 1864, Reuben Green Papers, IHS; Ovid Butler to Scot Butler, November 6, 1864, in Davis, *Affectionately Yours*, 130–31.

26. Fletcher diary, November 8, 1864, in *DCF*, 8:465; *Milwaukee Daily Sentinel*, November 24, 1864; Waugh, 352–55; "Response to a Serenade," November 8, 1864, in *CW*, 8:96.

27. Mollie McPheeters to John McPheeters, November 18, 1864, John S. McPheeters Correspondence, IHS; Milton Buswell to Oliver Buswell, November 20, 1864, Milton Buswell and Family Papers, MHS; Mary Putnam to Elizabeth Duncan, November 14, 1864, Duncan Family Papers, ILHS; *Western Christian Advocate*, November 23, 1864.

28. *Indianapolis Daily Journal*, November 26, 1864; *Christian Recorder*, December 17, 1864; Platt, *Light in the Darkness*, 12–14; Grant, *"Praise Ye the Lord"—David*, 13.

29. *Indianapolis Daily Journal*, November 30, 1864.

30. Glatthaar, *The March to the Sea and Beyond*, 119–55; Grimsley, *The Hard Hand of War*, 190–200.

31. Grant, *"Praise Ye the Lord"—David*, 10; Mollie McPheeters to John McPheeters, November 28, 1864, John S. McPheeters Correspondence, IHS; Caleb Mills to Benjamin Mills, December 17, 1864, Caleb Mills Family Papers, box 3, IHS; "Mother" Sabin to Mardin Sabin, December 18, 1864, Brainard and Carla Sabin Collection, WMU; Elvira Aplin to George Aplin, December 4, 1864, January 26, 1865, Aplin Family Papers, box 3, Clements.

32. "Annual Message to Congress," December 6, 1864, in *CW*, 149, 151–52; *Christian Recorder*, February 25, 1865; T. A. Young to Mary [illeg.], January 16, 1865, T. A. Young Letter, ALPL; J. P. Charles to William Lough, January 15, 1865, Lough

Family Papers, box 2, CinHS; Caleb Mills to Benjamin Mills, January 12, February 2, 1865, Caleb Mills Family Papers, box 3, IHS.

33. *Western Christian Advocate*, December 14, 1864.

34. John M. Brenneman to Peter Nissley, November 9, 1864, March 10, 1865, Peter Nissley Collection, MCA; *Western Christian Advocate*, December 31, 1862, March 30, 1864, February 15, 1865.

35. [Jane Van Scyoc] to John W. Van Scyoc, February 19, 1985, Ralph Shackelford Papers, box 1, ISL; *Christian Advocate and Journal*, February 16, 1865; *Delaware County (Indiana) Free Press*, January 19, 26, February 2, March 2, 1865; *Christian Recorder*, February 11, 1865.

36. Ovid Butler to Scot Butler, January 22, 1865, in Davis, *Affectionately Yours*, 141; Randie Cress to Rufus Dooley, February 22, 1865, Rufus Dooley Papers, box 1, IHS.

37. McPherson, *Battle Cry of Freedom*, 825–27; Grimsley, *The Hard Hand of War*, 202–3; Charles Cumings to Henry Cumings, February 12, March 12, 1865, Henry Harrison Cumings Papers, box 1, WRHS; John Ketcham to Willie Ketcham, February 19, 1865, John L. Ketcham Papers, box 2, IHS.

38. *Indianapolis Daily Journal*, October 10, 1864; McPherson, *Battle Cry of Freedom*, 796–802; John Ketcham to Willie Ketcham, February 19, 1865, John L. Ketcham Papers, box 2, IHS; Lizzie (Little) Avery to George Smith Avery, March 20, 1863 [1865], George Smith Avery Papers, ChiHS.

39. "Second Inaugural Address," March 4, 1865, in *CW*, 8:332–33; White, *Lincoln's Greatest Speech*, 112–13, 119–20.

40. *CW*, 8:332–33; Noll, *America's God*, 431–35.

41. *CW*, 8:332–33; White, *Lincoln's Greatest Speech*, 171–73.

42. *Decatur (Indiana) Eagle*, March 10, 1865; *Hancock (Ohio) Courier*, March 9, 1865; *Allen County (Ohio) Democrat*, March 15, 1865; *Cincinnati Enquirer*, March 7, 1865.

43. Lincoln to Thurlow Weed, March 15, 1865, in *CW*, 8:356; White, *Lincoln's Greatest Speech*, 189–92, 197–98.

44. *Indianapolis Daily State Sentinel*, March 2, 1865. On a national level, a movement to amend the preamble of the Constitution to recognize God and Christ had begun in February 1863, and the National Reform Association, which at one time boasted 34,000 supporters, continued to lobby for the revision until 1876. See Borden, "The Christian Amendment," 156–67, and Jacoby, "Of Nationalism and Nativism," 143–61.

45. William King to "Dear Brother Amos," April 3, 1865, Henry Harrison Cumings Papers, box 1, WRHS; Funk diary, April 3, 1865, John F. Funk Papers, box 2, MHA; Fletcher diary, April 3, 1865, in *DCF*, 9:61; Foote, *The Civil War*, 3:897.

46. Wert, *The Sword of Lincoln*, 404–9; Foote, *The Civil War*, 3:946–48.

47. Mollie McPheeters to John McPheeters, April 12, 1865, John S. McPheeters Correspondence, IHS; George Tuthill Diaries, April 10, 1865, Bentley; unsigned to Nellie, April 15, 1865, Blinn Papers, box 7, CinHS; Ellen Plattenburg to Philip Dodson Plattenburg, April 11, 1865, Ellen D. Plattenburg Letters, ALPL.

CHAPTER 9

1. *Cincinnati Gazette*, April 14, 1865.
2. Elvira Aplin to George Aplin, April 18, 1865, Aplin Family Papers, box 3, Clements; Augustus Frey to mother, April 16, 1865, Augustus Frey Papers, ALPL; Margaret Denny to John Denny, April 18, 1865, James M. Van Hook Papers, box 1, ISL; Jemima Potts to James Potts, April 16, 1865, James Potts Collection, IHS; Addie to "My Darling Brother" [John Griffin], April 27, 1865, John A. Griffin Papers, ALPL; Henry Parker Smith Diary, April 15, 1865, Bentley.
3. Augustus Frey to mother, April 16, 1865, Augustus Frey Papers, ALPL; Nathaniel Wright to William Wright, April 16, 1865, Nathaniel Wright Letters, CinHS; A. G. Kidwell to Jasper Kidwell, April 16, 1865, Kephart–Kidwell Family Papers, IHS. Kidwell most likely had in mind Romans 8:28, which asserts that "all things work together for good to them that love God."
4. Caleb Mills to Benjamin Mills, April 17, 1865, Caleb Mills Family Papers, box 3, IHS; Lizzie Bowler to Madison Bowler, April 15, 1865, James M. Bowler and Family Papers, MHS.
5. *Putnam (Indiana) Republican Banner*, April 20, 1865; *Indianapolis Daily Journal*, April 17, 1865; Gaddis, *Sermon upon the Assassination of Abraham Lincoln*, 4–5. For a topical survey of assassination sermons, see Chesebrough, *"No Sorrow like Our Sorrow."*
6. Psalm 39:4 reads, "Lord, make me know mine end, and the measure of my days, what it is; that I may know how frail I am." Prime, *A Sermon*, 3–4, 10–13.
7. Swing, *The Death of the President*; Lowrie, *The Lessons of Our National Sorrow*, 6, 9, 12, 14–15; *Cincinnati Gazette*, April 17, 1865; Northrop, *A Sermon in Commemoration of the Assassination of Lincoln*, 6, 8; *Toledo Commercial*, April 18, 1865.
8. Duffield, *The Nation's Wail*, 11–12; MacEl'rey, *The Substance of Two Discourses*, 7–8; Hibbard, *In Memory of Abraham Lincoln*, 9–10; *Cincinnati Gazette*, April 17, 1865.
9. Northrop, *A Sermon in Commemoration of the Assassination of Lincoln*, 6; *Cincinnati Gazette*, April 17, 1865; Gaddis, *Sermon upon the Assassination of Abraham Lincoln*, 7, 11; Fletcher diary, April 16, 1865, in *DCF*, 9:70.
10. Augustus Frey to mother, April 16, 1865, Augustus Frey Papers, ALPL; Fletcher diary, April 15, 1865, in *DCF*, 9:69; Goodrich, 134–39; *Indianapolis Daily Journal*, April 17, 1865.
11. Caleb Mills to Benjamin Mills, April 17, 1865, Caleb Mills Family Papers, box 3, IHS. Mills regarded 1 Samuel 15:32–33 as especially applicable in proving that Southerners who had caused the war deserved harsh punishment. The verses read, "Then Samuel said, Bring ye hither to me Agag the king of the Amalekites. And Agag came unto him delicately. And Agag said, Surely the bitterness of death is past. And Samuel said, As thy sword hath made women childless, so shall thy mother be childless among women. And Samuel hewed Agag in pieces before the LORD in Gilgal."

12. Nathaniel Wright to William Wright, April 16, 1865, Nathaniel Wright Letters, CinHS; Sophia Buchanan to Claude Buchanan, April 18, 1865, Rev. Abel Bingham Papers, box 11, Clarke; Kate Gary to Rufus Dooley, [April 16, 1865], Rufus Dooley Papers, box 1, IHS.

13. Sophia Buchanan to Claude Buchanan, April 18, 1865, Rev. Abel Bingham Papers, box 11, Clarke; Nathaniel Wright to William Wright, April 16, 1865, Nathaniel Wright Letters, CinHS; Zachariah Chandler quoted in Howard, *Religion and the Radical Republican Movement*, 94; Caleb Mills to Benjamin Mills, April 17, 1865, Caleb Mills Family Papers, box 3, IHS.

14. Means, *The Avenger Takes His Place*, 87–91; Therese Elstine to "My Dear Friend," April 17, 1865, Blinn Papers, box 7, CinHS; Mollie McPheeters to John McPheeters, April 17, 1865, John S. McPheeters Correspondence, IHS.

15. Nathaniel Wright to William Wright, April 16, 1865, Nathaniel Wright Letters, CinHS; Sophia Buchanan to Claude Buchanan, April 18, 1865, Rev. Abel Bingham Papers, box 11, Clarke; Augustus Frey to mother, April 16, 1865, Augustus Frey Papers, ALPL; Harrell, *When the Bells Tolled for Lincoln*.

16. *Christian Recorder*, April 29, 1865; *Scioto (Ohio) Gazette*, May 2, 1865. In addition to passing resolutions, African-Americans, especially freedmen, demonstrated affection for their Moses by donating money to erect a statue to their Emancipator. The idea for the Freedman's Monument, dedicated in Washington, D.C., in 1876, originated with Charlotte Scott, a recently liberated slave who lived in Marietta, Ohio. See Peterson, *Lincoln in American Memory*, 55–59.

17. Lamb, *Sermon on the Death of President Lincoln*, 3, 7–8; Powell, *Sermon*, 5–6; Mather, *National Greatness*, 13.

18. Carey, *Discourse*, 5; Hughes, *President Lincoln's Death*, 117; *Cincinnati Daily Commercial*, April 20, 1865.

19. Rice, *The President's Death—Its Import*, 7; Powell, *Sermon*, 11; Hughes, *President Lincoln's Death*, 117; Foner, *Reconstruction*, 176–84; Trefousse, *Andrew Johnson*, 214–33, 346–47; Yourtee, *A Sermon*, 9–10. A copy of Yourtee's sermon with "Kind regards of the Author" inscribed on the front cover is housed in the Rutherford B. Hayes Presidential Library. A marginal comment inserted next to his attempt to downplay Johnson's intoxication at the inaugural reads, "I fear he is both a drunkard & a blasphemer."

20. Hughes, *President Lincoln's Death*, 113–14; Goodspeed, *Funeral Discourse on the Death of Abraham Lincoln*, 11–12; Glover, *The Character of Abraham Lincoln*, 19; Yourtee, *A Sermon*, 6, 11; Chesebrough, *"No Sorrow like Our Sorrow,"* 32–35.

21. Mayo, *The Nation's Sacrifice*, 12–13; Hayden, *A Brief Abstract of Remarks*, 1; Hitchcock, *God Acknowledged, in the Nation's Bereavement*, 15.

22. Indiana Presbyterian Thomas Hopkins, Ohio Methodist D. D. Mather, Ohio Presbyterian C. W. McCune, Illinois Presbyterian Andrew McGibbon, Illinois Baptist Henry Northrop, and Illinois Methodist Hiram Sears all recounted the conversion story in detail. Iowa Presbyterian D. L. Hughes, Michigan Baptist H. L. Morehouse, and Michigan Congregationalist E. P. Powell simply quoted the phrase

"I do love Jesus" as proof of the president's spiritual birth and certainty of heaven. The account of Lincoln's salvation appeared in religious papers sometime in the fall, for Iowan Benjamin Talbot personally expressed his gratitude that the president had become a Christian in a letter written November 21, 1864. See Abraham Lincoln Papers. Besides being given credence by the clergy, the narrative continued to run in newspapers after the assassination. See *Putman (Indiana) Republican Banner*, May 4, 1865 (copying the *St. Louis Dispatch*), and *Toledo Blade*, May 12, 1865. In the postwar period, Phineas D. Gurley vouched for the veracity of the Gettysburg incident to Reverend James Reed, who recounted it in his famous lecture as evidence against Ward Hill Lamon's 1872 biography based on William Herndon's research and personal insistence that Lincoln was a religious infidel. See Barton, *The Soul of Abraham Lincoln*. The best recent interpretations of Lincoln's religion are Guelzo, *Abraham Lincoln*, 312–29, 440–48, and Carwardine, *Lincoln*, 220–31. The fact of the matter remains, Lincoln almost never spoke of Christ. In the end, like similar unsubstantiated anecdotes offered by James Jacquess, Newton Bateman, and Noah Brooks, the Gettysburg episode remains dubious.

23. Este diary, April 19, 1865, David K. Este Family Letters and Miscellaneous Papers, CinHS; Anna McPheeters to Rankin McPheeters, April 23, 1865, McPheeters Family Papers, USAMHI; Sophia Buchanan to Claude Buchanan, April 18, 1865, Rev. Abel Bingham Papers, box 11, Clarke; Hattie to William Kemper, April 26, 1865, G. W. H. Kemper Collection, box 4, BSU; Maria Carlisle to Mrs. Edward Hooker, April 18, 1865, Maria Carlisle Letter, OHS.

24. Anna McPheeters to Rankin McPheeters, April 23, 1865, McPheeters Family Papers, USAMHI; *Allen County (Ohio) Democrat*, April 19, 1865; *Dubuque Herald*, April 12, 22, 1865, cited in Means, *The Avenger Takes His Place*, 109; *Catholic Telegraph*, excerpted in *Cincinnati Gazette*, May 19, 1865.

25. Baldridge, *The Martyr Prince*, 16–18.

26. Elvira Aplin to George Aplin, April 18, 1865, Aplin Family Papers, box 3, Clements; Sophia Buchanan to Claude Buchanan, April 18, 1865, Rev. Abel Bingham Papers, box 11, Clarke; commonplace book, Alfred Berry Nisbet Collection, DePauw; [Sarah Hawley] to Ransom Hawley, April 15, 1865, Ransom E. Hawley Papers, box 3, ISL.

27. Swanson, *Manhunt*, 250–51; Chesebrough, *"No Sorrow like Our Sorrow,"* 41; Carey, *Discourse*, 2; Morehouse, *Evil Its Own Destroyer*, 12; Eddy, *Abraham Lincoln*, 21; Hull, *Death of President Lincoln*, 17–18.

28. Swanson, *Manhunt*, 308–43; Margaret Denny to John Denny, April 29, 1865, James M. Van Hook Papers, box 1, ISL; Lena Linn to "My Darling Coz" [John Griffin], May 4, 1865, John A. Griffin Papers, ALPL.

29. *Toledo Blade*, April 29, 1865; Temple, *Abraham Lincoln*, 336–38; George Tuthill Diaries, April 28, 1865, Bentley; *Toledo Commercial*, April 29, 1865; Randie Cress to Rufus Dooley, April 30, 1865, Rufus Dooley Papers, box 1, IHS. William Coggeshall confirms the unique and "superior display" along Washington Street in *Lincoln Memorial*, 261, 278, 280. Henry Hawley to Ransom E. Hawley, May 1, 1865,

Ransom E. Hawley Papers, box 3, ISL; Thomas Bryan to parents, May 2, 1865, Thomas Barbour Bryan Letters, ChiHS.

30. Chesebrough, *"No Sorrow like Our Sorrow,"* 130, 134–36; Fannie Ford to soldier, May 10, 1865, Fannie E. Ford Letter, OHS.

31. *Indianapolis Daily State Sentinel*, May 2, 1865. Bingham charged, "This man is willing to transfer the responsibilities of this great transgression from the creature to the Creator." In reality, Thompson carefully worded his message to make it clear that God used a wicked deed without being the author of the sin. "We shrank from ascribing to the Divine will any agency in the crime of his death. But God used crime to further His own purposes.... Yes, we should attribute the death of Mr. Lincoln to the Divine agency, yet not relieve the guilty of the crime." See *Cincinnati Daily Commercial*, April 24, 1865. Bingham had been arrested and briefly imprisoned in late 1864 for his alleged involvement in the Sons of Liberty conspiracy. See Churchill, "Liberty, Conscription, and a Party Divided," 295–303.

32. Noll, *The Civil War as a Theological Crisis*, 81, 92–94; Chubb, *A Discourse*, 6–7, 11–13, 15–16, 18.

33. Windsor, *Justice and Mercy*, 4–5, 7–12.

EPILOGUE

1. S. B. Gookins to "My dear friend," May 27, 1865, Blinn Papers, box 7, CinHS; Hopkins, *The Rise of the Social Gospel in American Protestantism*, 9.

2. McPherson, "Afterword," 411; Fredrickson, "The Coming of the Lord," 124.

3. Mollie McPheeters to John McPheeters, May 15, 1865, John S. McPheeters Correspondence, IHS; *Christian Advocate and Journal*, May 4, 1865; Nathaniel Wright to William Wright, May 14, 1865, Nathaniel Wright Letters, CinHS; Trefousse, *Andrew Johnson*, 216–22; Foner, *Reconstruction*, 183–89.

4. John Ketcham to Willie Ketcham, June 25, August 27, 1865, John L. Ketcham Papers, IHS; Howard, *Religion and the Radical Republican Movement*, 96–99; Granville Moody to Andrew Johnson, July 31, 1865, Andrew Johnson Papers. While serving in Tennessee, Moody met Johnson, whom Lincoln had appointed military governor of the state in February 1862. Not known as a religious man, Johnson asked Moody to pray with him during an anxious moment in late 1862 when he feared that Nashville might fall. See Trefousse, *Andrew Johnson*, 160–61, for an interesting anecdote.

5. George V. Moody to Andrew Johnson, August 20, 1865, in Bergeron et al., *The Papers of Andrew Johnson*, 8:623–25; Moody, *A Life's Retrospect*, 361–62; Trefousse, *Andrew Johnson*, 226–27; Granville Moody to Andrew Johnson, November 17, 1865, in Bergeron et al., *The Papers of Andrew Johnson*, 9:398–99; Blum, *Reforging the White Republic*; Brodrecht, "'Our Country.'"

6. Francis H. L. Laird to Henry Van Dyke, October 23, 1865, Henry Van Dyke Family Papers, box 21, FL.

7. *Rushville (Indiana) Jacksonian*, May 30, 1866. The Roster of Wisconsin Volunteers, which also includes chaplains, has no record of Henry Clannard. For details on Brick Pomeroy, see Klement, *Copperheads in the Middle West*, 84–87, 236–37.

8. Foner, *Reconstruction*, 260, 264, 266; Granville Moody to Andrew Johnson, July 12, 1866, in Bergeron et al., *The Papers of Andrew Johnson*, 10:679–83.

9. "Reply to Oliver P. Morton at Indianapolis, Indiana," February 11, 1861, in *CW*, 4:193–94; Mead, "The 'Nation with the Soul of a Church,'" 262–63, 280–81.

Bibliography

MANUSCRIPT COLLECTIONS

Andrew Johnson Papers
Abraham Lincoln Papers

Ball State University Archives, Muncie, Indiana

Cassady–Nelson Family Papers
Demaree Letters
G. W. H. Kemper Collection

Bentley Historical Library, University of Michigan, Ann Arbor

Joseph E. Beebe Collection
Bingham Family Papers
Cornelia Chase Diary
Howell Family Papers
Edward Meyer Collection
Henry Parker Smith Diary
George Tuthill Diaries
George Woodruff Journal

Bowling Green State University Archives, Ohio

Borton Family Papers
First Baptist Church of Canton, Ohio, Record Book
Benjamin Basil Jackson Family Papers

Rockport Presbyterian Church Session Minutes
Thomas B. Searight Collection

Chicago Historical Society

George Smith Avery Papers
Thomas Barbour Bryan Letters
Mary Cheney Hall Papers
Mead Family Papers

Cincinnati Historical Society

Blinn Papers
David K. Este Family Letters and Miscellaneous Papers
William Jessup Letter
Lough Family Papers
Lytle Papers
Thomas E. Smith Letters
Amanda Wilson Diary
Nathaniel Wright Letters

Clarke Historical Library, Central Michigan University, Mt. Pleasant

Rev. Abel Bingham Papers
Collet–Hall Families
Ellen L. Woodworth Diary

William L. Clements Library, University of Michigan, Ann Arbor

Aplin Family Papers

DePauw University Archives, Greencastle, Indiana

John Price Durbin John Papers
John William Thomas McMullen Papers
Alfred Berry Nisbet Collection
John Poucher Papers

Earlham College Archives, Richmond, Indiana

Hill–Huddelson Family Papers

Firestone Library, Rare Books and Special Collections, Princeton University, New Jersey

Henry Van Dyke Family Papers

Hanover College Archives, Indiana

Crawfordsville Presbytery Collection
Indiana Presbytery Collection

Logansport Presbytery Collection
Muncie Presbytery Collection
Salem Presbytery Collection
Synod of Indiana Collection
Vincennes Presbytery Collection

Rutherford B. Hayes Presidential Library, Fremont, Ohio

Civil War Collection Miscellaneous Mss.
Eliza Fanning Correspondence
John B. Rice Collection
Dr. and Mrs. Robert H. Rice Collection

Illinois Historical Survey, Urbana

Bond Family Papers
Corrie Family Papers
Duncan Family Papers
Edwin Rice Papers
Henry Van Sellar Correspondence

Indiana Historical Society, Indianapolis

Alford Family Papers
John H. Armstrong Family Papers
Bethel Baptist Association Minutes
John Blackwell Collection
Boone–Douglass Family Papers
Eunice A. Brown Letters
Elijah H. C. Cavins Papers
Lucius Chapin Papers
Deer Creek Regular Baptist Church Minutes Book
Rufus Dooley Papers
First Presbyterian Church Records, Greenfield, Indiana
Calvin Fletcher Papers
Journal of Emily Beeler Fletcher
Miriam Wilson Green Collection
Reuben Green Papers
Perry Hall Diary
John Watts Hamilton Collection
William P. Hobbs Papers
Kephart–Kidwell Family Papers
John L. Ketcham Papers
George W. Lounsbury Collection
Thomas Marshall Papers

John S. McPheeters Correspondence
Caleb Mills Family Papers
Mt. Pleasant United Presbyterian Church Records
Samuel Mumford Papers
Valentine Nicholson Papers
Records of the Church at Pleasant Run (Baptist)
James Potts Collection
George R. Smith Papers
George Washington Stafford Papers
William C. Starr Papers
Martha White Talbert Collection
Henry W. Tutewiler Papers
Mathias Van Pelt Family Papers
Joseph P. Vannest Papers
Worthington B. Williams Family Papers

Indiana State Library, Indianapolis

Barnett Family Papers
William S. Bradford Letters
Jack K. Carmichael Collection
George F. Chittenden Papers
James Davidson Letters
Allen Hamilton Papers
Ransom E. Hawley Papers
Hamet N. Helms Collection
Adams Lee Ogg Papers
Mary Rice Collection
Ralph Shackelford Papers
Susan B. Unthink Papers
James M. Van Hook Papers
John T. Wilder Collection

Library of Congress, Washington, D.C.

Papers of Josiah Dexter Cotton
Papers of James J. Hartley
John Logan Family Papers

Lilly Library, Indiana University, Bloomington

Hill Mss.
Huntington Mss.
Smith–Marsters Mss.

Abraham Lincoln Presidential Library, Springfield, Illinois

Clinton Levering Conkling Papers
Augustus Frey Papers
Samuel Gordon Papers
Benjamin H. Grierson Papers
John A. Griffin Papers
Edward H. Ingraham and Duncan G. Ingraham Papers
King Family Papers
Ellen D. Plattenburg Letters
T. A. Young Letter

Mennonite Church U.S.A. Archives, Goshen, Indiana

John F. Funk Papers
Peter Nissley Collection
Nold/Yoder Collection

Minnesota Historical Society, St. Paul

James M. Bowler and Family Papers
Milton Buswell and Family Papers
Hubert N. Eggleston Papers
Edith Pusey Flint Papers
Ard Godfrey and Family Papers
Schuyler V. R. Hendryx Papers
Noah Marcus Humphrey and Family Papers
Reimer Kohlsaat and Family Papers
Stephen Return Riggs and Family Paper
Newton Southworth and Family Papers
George Burdick Wright and Family Papers

Minnetrista Cultural Center Archives, Muncie, Indiana

Gadbury Auction

Moore–Youse Museum Archives, Muncie, Indiana

Davis Civil War Papers

National Archives, Washington, D.C.

Letters Received, Office of the Paymaster General, RG 99, Entry 7

Newberry Library, Chicago

Edgar McLean Papers

320 BIBLIOGRAPHY

Ohio Historical Society, Columbus

Maria Carlisle Letter
Core–Porter Letters
Evans Family Papers
Fannie E. Ford Letter
Kellar Family Papers
William Kennon Sr. Collection
Jacob M. Leidigh Collection
Charles Greene McChesney Mount Papers
M. L. P. Thompson Letter

Tippecanoe County Historical Association Archives, Lafayette, Indiana

Military Collection

University of Wisconsin Green Bay Archives

Waldo–Henderson Family Papers

United States Army Military History Institute, Carlisle, Pennsylvania

Bender Family Papers
Civil War Miscellaneous Collection
Lewis Leigh Collection
McPheeters Family Papers

Western Michigan University Archives and Regional History Collections, Kalamazoo

Ethan A. Brown Letters
Phyllis Burnham Collection
John Emery Hall Collection
Robert C. Hibbard Collection
Brainard and Carla Sabin Collection
Brian Shumway Collection
Stanley Barney Smith Family Papers
George M. White Collection

Western Reserve Historical Society, Cleveland

John P. Agenbroad Papers
Mary P. Ballard Letters
Henry Harrison Cumings Papers
Peter Hitchcock Family Papers
Marilla Wells Leggett Papers
Jeremiah B. and Elizabeth Taggart Mansfield Papers

Wisconsin Historical Society, Madison

Kelsey M. Adams Letters
Barland Family Papers
Nettie Fowler McCormick Papers

NEWSPAPERS

Allen County (Ohio) Democrat
Catholic Telegraph (Cincinnati)
Chicago Tribune
Christian Advocate and Journal (New York)
Christian Recorder (Philadelphia)
Church Advocate (Lancaster, Pennsylvania)
Cincinnati Daily Commercial
Cincinnati Enquirer
Cincinnati Gazette
Daily Cleveland Herald
Darke County (Ohio) Democrat
Decatur (Indiana) Eagle
Delaware County (Indiana) Free Press
Franklin (Indiana) Democrat
Hancock (Ohio) Courier
Hancock (Ohio) Jeffersonian
Independent (New York)
Indianapolis Daily Journal
Indianapolis Daily State Sentinel
Indianapolis Witness
Lawrenceburg (Indiana) Democratic Register
Lima (Ohio) Weekly Gazette
Milwaukee Daily Sentinel
National Intelligencer (Washington, D.C.)
Newark (Ohio) Advocate
New Castle (Indiana) Courier
New York Evangelist
New York Times
North-West (Napoleon, Ohio)
Norwalk (Ohio) Experiment
Presbyter (Cincinnati)
Putnam (Indiana) Republican Banner
Ripley (Ohio) Bee
Rushville (Indiana) Jacksonian
Scioto (Ohio) Gazette

Star in the West (Cincinnati)
Toledo Blade
Toledo Commercial
Western Christian Advocate (Cincinnati)
Wisconsin State Register
Zion's Herald and Wesleyan Journal (Boston)

SERMONS

Bailey, Silas. *The Moral Significance of War. A Discourse Delivered in the Baptist Meeting House in Franklin, Indiana, on the Occasion of the National Fast, September 26, 1861*. Indianapolis: Dodd & Co., 1861.

Baldridge, Samuel C. *The Martyr Prince. A Sermon on the Occasion of the Assassination of President Lincoln, Delivered in the Presbyterian Church, Friendsville, Sabbath Morning, April 23d, 1865*. Cincinnati: Jos. B. Boyd, 1865.

Barr, E. *Fast-Day Sermon. Preached by Rev. E. Barr, Pastor of the Presbyterian Church Frankfort, Indiana, April 30, 1863*. Indianapolis: Indianapolis Journal Company Printers, 1863.

Bittinger, J. B. *A Sermon. Preached before the Presbyterian Churches of Cleveland, on the National Fast Day, September 26, 1861*. Cleveland: F. Cowles & Co., 1861.

Carey, Isaac. *Discourse of Rev. Mr. Carey, on the Death of Abraham Lincoln. Preached on the Day of his Funeral, April 19th, 1865, in the First Presbyterian Church in Freeport, Illinois*. Freeport: n.p., 1865.

———. *God Doing Wonderful Things in Behalf of the Nation. A Discourse. Preached on the National Thanksgiving Day, November 26th, 1863, in the First Presbyterian Church of Freeport, Illinois*. Freeport: Judson & McCluer, 1863.

Chubb, Rolla. *A Discourse, Upon the Death of President Lincoln. Delivered at Greenwich M. E. Church, Huron County, Ohio, June 1st, 1865*. Mansfield, Ohio: Herald Book and Job Printing, 1865.

Collins, H. B. *God and our Country, or The Higher Law Doctrine Illustrated and Insisted Upon. A Fast Day Sermon, Preached in the Presbyterian Church, Franklin, Ind., April 30th, 1863*. Indianapolis: Indianapolis Daily Journal Co., 1863.

Corning, James L. *Religion and Politics. A Discourse Delivered on Thanksgiving Day, November 29th, 1860*. Milwaukee: Strickland & Co., 1860.

Curran, R. *A Sermon Preached by Request of the Pastor and Official Board of Wall Street Methodist Episcopal Church, Jeffersonville, Ind., Thursday (Fast Day) August 4, 1864*. Louisville: L.A. Civill, 1864.

Duffield, George. *Humiliation and Hope: Or, The Christian Patriot's Duty in the Present Crisis of Our National Affairs. A Discourse, Delivered November 14, 1862, The Day of Fasting, Humiliation and Prayer*. Detroit: O. S. Gulley, 1862.

———. *The Nation's Wail. A Discourse Delivered in the First Presbyterian Church of Detroit, On Sabbath, The 16th of April, 1865, The Day After Receiving the Intelligence of the Brutal Murder of President Abraham Lincoln, By a Brutal Assassin*. Detroit: Advertiser and Tribune Print, 1865.

———. *Our National Sins to be Repented Of, and the Grounds of Hope for the Preservation of our Federal Constitution and Union. A Discourse Delivered Friday, January 4, 1861, on the Day of Fasting, Humiliation and Prayer Appointed by the President of the United States.* In *Secession: Its Cause and Cure.* Detroit: Free Press Mammoth Book and Job Printing House, 1861.

———. *A Thanksgiving Discourse. The Rule of Divine Providence Applicable to the Present Circumstances of Our Country, Delivered in the First Presbyterian Church of Detroit, Thursday November 28, 1860.* In *Secession: Its Cause and Cure.* Detroit: Free Press Mammoth Book and Job Printing House, 1861.

Eddy, Thomas. *Abraham Lincoln. A Memorial Discourse, by Rev. T. M. Eddy, D.D., Delivered at a Union Meeting, Held in the Presbyterian Church, Waukegan, Illinois, Wednesday, April 19, 1865, the Day upon Which the Funeral Services of the President were Conducted in Washington, and Observed Throughout the Loyal States as One of Mourning.* Chicago: Methodist Book Depository, 1865.

Fairfield, Edmund B. *Christian Patriotism: A Sermon Delivered in the Representatives' Hall, Lansing, Michigan, February 22, 1863.* Lansing: John A. Kerr, 1863.

Funk, John F. *Warfare: Its Evils—Our Duty. Addressed to the Mennonite Churches Throughout the United States and Canada, and All Others Who Sincerely Seek and Love the Truth.* Markham, Ontario: Economist Office, 1863.

Gaddis, Maxwell. *Sermon upon the Assassination of Abraham Lincoln. By Rev. M. P. Gaddis, Pastor Sixth Street M. P. Church, Delivered in Pike's Opera House, April 16, 1865.* Cincinnati: Times Steam Book and Job Office, 1865.

Giles, Chauncey. *The Problem of American Nationality, and the Evils Which Hinder Its Solution. A Discourse Delivered on the Day of the National Fast, April 30, 1863.* Cincinnati: Wighton & Co., 1863.

Glover, L. M. *The Character of Abraham Lincoln. A Discourse Delivered April 23d, 1865, at Strawn's Hall, Jacksonville, Ill.* Jacksonville: Journal Book and Job Office, 1865.

———. *National Sin and Retribution. A Discourse Delivered on the Occasion of the National Fast, January 4, 1861.* Jacksonville, Ill.: Catlin & Co., 1861.

Goodrich, William H. *A Sermon, on the Christian Necessity of War.* Cleveland: Fairbanks, Benedict & Co., 1861.

Goodspeed, E. J. *Funeral Discourse on the Death of Abraham Lincoln. Preached Sunday, April 23rd, 1865, in the Second Baptist Church, Chicago.* Chicago: Church, Goodman & Connelley, 1865.

Grant, C. Norris. *"Praise Ye the Lord"—David. A Thanksgiving Sermon, Preached in the Congregational Church, in Tallmadge, November 24, 1864.* Akron: Beebe & Elkins, 1864.

Gurley, L. B. *Sermon on the Victory at Fort Donelson, and Moral Aspects of the Rebellion. Delivered in Galion, Ohio, February 23, 1862.* Cincinnati: Methodist Book Concern, 1862.

Gurley, Phineas D. *Man's Projects and God's Results. A Sermon: Preached by the Rev. P. D. Gurley, D.D., on Thursday, August 6, 1863, being the Day of National Thanksgiving, Praise and Prayer.* Washington, D.C.: Wm. Ballantyne, 1863.

Hawley, S[ilas]. *The Fall of Sumter: Its Intent, And Portent. An Address Given at Plymouth Church, St. Paul, Sunday Evening, April 12th, 1863, the Anniversary of the Attack on Fort Sumter.* Saint Paul: Office of the Press Printing Co., 1863.

Hayden, William B. *A Brief Abstract of Remarks by Rev. Wm. B. Hayden. At the New Jerusalem Church, on the Funeral of the President, April 19, 1865.* Cincinnati: Mallory, Power & Co., 1865.

Hibbard, A. G. *In Memory of Abraham Lincoln. A Discourse Delivered in the First Congregational Unitarian Church in Detroit, Mich., Sunday, April 17th, [sic] 1865.* Detroit: O. S. Gulley, 1865.

Hitchcock, Henry L. *God Acknowledged, in the Nation's Bereavement. A Sermon Delivered in Hudson, Ohio, on the Day of the Obsequies of Abraham Lincoln, April 19th, 1865.* Cleveland: Fairbanks, Benedict & Co., 1865.

Hovey, Horace Carter. *The National Fast. A Sermon, Preached at Coldwater, Mich., January 4, 1861.* Coldwater: Republican Print, 1861.

———. *Freedom's Banner. A Sermon Preached to the Coldwater Light Artillery, and the Coldwater Zouave Cadets, April 28th, 1861.* Coldwater: Republican Print, 1861.

Hughes, D. L. *President Lincoln's Death. A Sermon Delivered at the First Presbyterian Church in Des Moines, Iowa, on Sunday Evening, April 23, 1865.* In *Lincolniana: In Memoriam.* Boston: William V. Spencer, 1865.

Hull, Moses. *Death of President Lincoln. A Discourse Delivered Before the 'Friends of Progress,' in Stuart's Hall, Battle Creek, Mich., April 19, 1865.* In *Lincolniana: In Memoriam.* Boston: William V. Spencer, 1865.

Lamb, E. E. *Sermon on the Death of President Lincoln. Preached in the Congregational Church of Rootstown, By Rev. E. E. Lamb, Sabbath Morning, April 23, 1865.* n.p., 1865.

Little, George O. *The Mission of Our Government. A Fast-Day Sermon, Delivered at the 2d Presbyterian Church, Fort Wayne, Aug. 4th, 1864.* Fort Wayne: D. W. Jones, 1864.

Lowrie, John M. *Christian Loyalty. A Discourse, Preached Before the Synod of Northern Indiana at the Opening of its Sessions.* Indianapolis: Indianapolis Journal Co., 1861.

———. *The Lessons of Our National Sorrow. A Discourse Delivered in the First Presbyterian Church, of Fort Wayne, Indiana, On the Sabbath Morning, April 16th, 1865, Succeeding the Death of Abraham Lincoln.* Fort Wayne: Jenkinson & Hartman, 1865.

MacEl'rey, J. H. *The Substance of Two Discourses, Occasioned by the National Bereavement. The Assassination of the President, The Position, the Lesson, and the Duty of the Nation, Delivered in the St. James Episcopal Church, Wooster, Ohio, Easter Day, 1865.* Wooster: Republican Steam Power Press, 1865.

Mather, D. D. *National Greatness. A Discourse Delivered in Zanesville, Ohio, April 19th, 1865, on the Occasion of the Death of Abraham Lincoln.* Zanesville: John T. Shryock, 1865.

Mayo, A. D. *The Nation's Sacrifice. Delivered on Sunday Morning, April 16, and Wednesday Morning, April 19, 1865, in the Church of the Redeemer, Cincinnati, Ohio.* In *Two Discourses.* Cincinnati: Robert Clarke & Co., 1865.

McCoskry, Samuel A. *Trust in God the Strength of a Nation. A Sermon Preached in St. Paul's Church, Detroit, on the Day of the National Fast, January 4, 1861*. Detroit: Free Press Book and Job Printing House, 1861.

McIlvaine, Charles Pettit. *The Necessity of Religion to the Prosperity of a Nation. A Sermon Preached on the Day of Public Thanksgiving and Prayer, November 29th, 1860, in St. John's Church, Cincinnati*. Cincinnati: Bradley & Webb, 1860.

Morehouse, H. L. *Evil Its Own Destroyer. A Discourse Delivered Before the United Societies of the Congregational and Baptist Churches at the Congregational Church, in the City of East Saginaw, April 19th, 1865, on the Occasion of the Death of President Abraham Lincoln*. East Saginaw, Mich.: Enterprise Print, 1865.

Northrop, Henry H. *A Sermon in Commemoration of the Assassination of Lincoln. At Washington, April the 14, A.D. 1865*. Carthage, Ill.: Carthage Republican, 1865.

Ottman, Sefferenas. *God Our Leader. A Discourse Delivered on Occasion of our National Thanksgiving August 6th 1863 to the United Congregations of Edwardsburgh, Michigan*. Niles, Mich.: Book and Job Rooms of the Berrien County Freeman, 1863.

Paddock, Benjamin H. *Our Cause, Our Confidence, and Our Consequent Duty. A Sermon Preached in Christ Church, Detroit, Sunday After Ascension, May 12th, 1861, before Company A, First Regiment Mich. Volunteers*. Detroit: Daily Advertiser, 1861.

Platt, James M. *Light in the Darkness. A Sermon Preached to the United Congregations of the First and Second Presbyterian Churches of Zanesville, Ohio, on Thanksgiving Day, November 24th, 1864*. Zanesville: Daily Courier Office, 1864.

Powell, E. P. *Sermon, Appropriate to the Obsequies of Abraham Lincoln*. In *Sermons on Recent National Victories, and the National Sorrow*. Adrian, Mich.: Smith & Foster, 1865.

Prime, G. Wendell. *A Sermon. Delivered in Westminster Church, Detroit. On Sabbath Morning, April 16, 1865, After the Death of President Lincoln*. Detroit: Advertiser and Tribune Print, 1865.

Rice, Daniel. *The President's Death—Its Import. A Sermon Preached in the Second Presbyterian Church, Lafayette, Indiana, April 19, 1865, On the Day of President Lincoln's Funeral*. n.p., 1865.

Robinson, E. T. *Christianity and War*. Cincinnati: American Reform Tract and Book Society, n.d.

Senour, F[aunt Le Roy]. *The Hand of God, As Seen in the Present Great Rebellion, The Hope of our Country and a Reason for Thanksgiving*. Rockford, Ill.: Register Steam Printing Press, 1862.

Simmons, James B. *The Cause and Cure of the Rebellion: Or, How Far the People of the Loyal States Are Responsible for the War*. Indianapolis: Werden and Co., 1861.

Smart, James S. *National Fast. A Fast Day Sermon, Delivered in the city of Flint, January 4th, 1861*. Flint, Mich.: William Stevenson, 1861.

Swing, David. *The Death of the President. Sermon by Rev. David Swing. Preached in the Presbyterian Church at Hamilton, O., April 16, 1865*. Hamilton: Hamilton Telegraph Print, 1865.

Thompson, M. L. P. *Discourses. Preached in the Second Presbyterian Church, Cincinnati, Ohio.* Cincinnati: Gazette Co., 1861.
Wilson, William. *A Nation Nonplussed, But Enlightened, Extricated, & Victorious, By Turning its Waiting Eyes upon God. A Sermon, Preached in the City of Xenia, On the National Day of Fasting, January 4, 1861.* Cincinnati: B. Frankland, 1861.
Windsor, William. *Justice and Mercy. A Sermon Preached at a United Service Held in the Methodist Episcopal Church, of Davenport, Iowa, on the National Fast Day, June 1st, 1865.* Davenport: Gazette Steam Book and Job Rooms, 1865.
Yourtee, Samuel L. *A Sermon. Delivered in the Central M. E. Church, Springfield, Ohio, April 19th, 1865, on the Occasion of the Funeral of Abraham Lincoln, President of the United States.* Springfield, Ohio: News and Republic Job Printing Rooms, 1865.

OTHER PUBLISHED PRIMARY SOURCES

Anderson, James, ed. *Life and Letters of Judge Thomas J. Anderson and Wife.* [Columbus, Ohio]: F. J. Heer, 1904.
Becker, Carl M., and Thomas, Ritchie, ed. *Hearth and Knapsack: The Ladley Letters, 1857–1880.* Athens: Ohio University Press, 1988.
Bergeron, Paul H., et al., eds. *The Papers of Andrew Johnson.* 15 vols. Knoxville: University of Tennessee Press, 1967–99.
Burlingame, Michael, ed. *An Oral History of Abraham Lincoln: John G. Nicolay's Interviews and Essays.* Carbondale, Ill.: Southern Illinois Press, 1996.
Clopper, E. N., ed. "Country Life during the Civil War: Selections from the Diary of Sarah Elizabeth Rogers of Butler County, Ohio." *Bulletin of the Historical and Philosophical Society of Ohio* 9 (July 1951): 171–96.
Cox, Florence Marie Ankeny, ed. *Kiss Josey for Me!* Santa Ana, Calif.: Friis–Pioneer Press, 1974.
Cox, Samuel S. *Emancipation and Its Results—Is Ohio To Be Africanized? Speech of Hon. S. S. Cox, of Ohio. Delivered in the House of Representatives, June 6, 1862.* Washington, D.C.: L. Towers & Co., 1862.
Davis, Barbara Butler, ed. *Affectionately Yours: The Civil War Home-Front Letters of the Ovid Butler Family.* Indianapolis: Indiana Historical Society Press, 2004.
Dee, Christine, ed. *Ohio's War: The Civil War in Documents.* Athens: Ohio University Press, 2006.
Dennett, Tyler, comp. *Lincoln and the Civil War in the Diaries and Letters of John Hay.* New York: Dodd, Mead & Co., 1939.
Elder, Donald C. III, ed. *Love amid the Turmoil: The Civil War Letters of William and Mary Vermilion.* Iowa City: University of Iowa Press, 2003.
Ellis, Richard N., ed. "The Civil War Letters of an Iowa Family." *Annals of Iowa* 39 (1969): 561–86.
Fletcher, Calvin. *Diary of Calvin Fletcher.* Ed. Gayle Thornbrough et al. 9 vols. Indianapolis: Indiana Historical Society, 1972–83.

Foroughi, Andrea R., ed. *"Go If You Think It Your Duty": A Minnesota Couple's Civil War Letters*. St. Paul: Minnesota Historical Society Press, 2008.

Holcomb, Julie, ed. *Southern Sons, Northern Soldiers: The Civil War Letters of the Remley Brothers, 22nd Iowa Infantry*. DeKalb: Northern Illinois Press, 2004.

Kiper, Richard L., ed. *Dear Catherine, Dear Taylor: The Civil War Letters of a Union Soldier and His Wife*. Lawrence: University Press of Kansas, 2002.

Larimer, Charles F., ed. *Love and Valor: The Intimate Civil War Letters between Captain Jacob and Emeline Ritner*. Western Springs, Ill.: Sigourney, 2000.

Lincoln, Abraham. *The Collected Works of Abraham Lincoln*. Ed. Roy P. Basler et al. 9 vols. New Brunswick, N.J.: Rutgers University Press, 1953–55.

Locke, David Ross. *The Nasby Papers: Letters and Sermons Containing the Views on the Topics of the Day, of Petroleum V. Nasby*. Indianapolis: C. O. Perrine, 1864.

Mills, George, ed. "The Sharp Family Civil War Letters." *Annals of Iowa* 34 (1959): 481–532.

Minutes of the Fourteenth Annual Session of the North-Western Indiana Conference, of the Methodist Church. Cincinnati: Methodist Book Concern, 1865.

Minutes of the Indiana Conference of the Methodist Episcopal Church. Cincinnati: Methodist Book Concern, 1862.

Minutes of the Nineteenth Session of the North Indiana Conference of the Methodist Episcopal Church. Cincinnati: Methodist Book Concern, 1862.

Minutes of the Tenth Session of the North-Western Indiana Conference of the Methodist Episcopal Church. Lafayette, Ind.: Courier Steam Book and Job Printing, 1861.

Minutes of the Twelfth Annual Session of the North-Western Indiana Conference, of the Methodist Episcopal Church. Lafayette, Ind.: Daily Courier Steam Printing House and Book Bindery, 1863.

Minutes of the Twenty-Seventh Anniversary of the Washtenaw Baptist Association. Detroit: O.S. Gulley, 1862.

Moody, Granville. *A Life's Retrospect: Autobiography of Rev. Granville Moody, D. D*. Ed. Sylvester Weeks. Cincinnati: Curts & Jennings, 1890.

Perkins, Howard Cecil, ed. *Northern Editorials on Secession*. 2 vols. New York: American Historical Association, 1942.

Skidmore, Richard S., ed. *The Alford Brothers: "We All Must Dye Sooner or Later."* Hanover, Ind.: Nugget Publishers, 1995.

Welles, Gideon. *Diary of Gideon Welles: Secretary of the Navy under Lincoln and Johnson*. Ed. John Torrey Morse. 3 vols. Boston: Houghton Mifflin, 1911.

SECONDARY SOURCES

Ahlstrom, Sydney E. *A Religious History of the American People*. New Haven: Yale University Press, 1972.

Andreasen, Bryon C. "'As Good a Right to Pray': Copperhead Christians on the Northern Civil War Home Front." Ph.D. diss., University of Illinois, 1998.

Armstrong, Warren B. *For Courageous Fighting and Confident Dying: Union Chaplains in the Civil War.* Lawrence: University Press of Kansas, 1998.

Atlas of Rush County, Indiana, To Which Are Added Various General Maps, History, Statistics. Chicago: J. H. Beers & Co., 1879. Reprint, Knightstown, Ind.: Bookmark, 1974.

Attie, Jeanie. *Patriotic Toil: Northern Women and the American Civil War.* Ithaca: Cornell University Press, 1998.

Austin, James C. *Petroleum V. Nasby.* Twayne's United States Authors Series, ed. Sylvia E. Bowman. New York: Twayne, 1965.

Barrows, Frederic Irving, ed. *History of Fayette County, Indiana: Her People, Industries, and Institutions.* Indianapolis: B. F. Bowen & Co., 1917.

Barton, William E. *The Soul of Abraham Lincoln.* New York: George H. Doran Co., 1920. Reprint, Urbana: University of Illinois Press, 2005.

Berens, John F. *Providence & Patriotism in Early America 1640–1815.* Charlottesville: University Press of Virginia, 1978.

Bernstein, Iver. *The New York City Draft Riots: Their Significance for American Society and Politics in the Age of the Civil War.* New York: Oxford University Press, 1990.

Berwanger, Eugene H. *The Frontier against Slavery: Western Anti-Negro Prejudice and the Slavery Extension Controversy.* Urbana: University of Illinois Press, 1967.

Blum, Edward J. *Reforging the White Republic: Race, Religion, and American Nationalism, 1865–1898.* Baton Rouge: Louisiana State University Press, 2005.

Borden, Morton. "The Christian Amendment." *Civil War History* 25 (1979): 156–67.

Boritt, Gabor. *The Gettysburg Gospel: The Lincoln Speech That Nobody Knows.* New York: Simon & Schuster, 2006.

Brodrecht, Grant R. "'Our Country': Northern Evangelicals and the Union during the Civil War and Reconstruction." Ph.D. diss., University of Notre Dame, 2008.

Budd, Richard M. *Serving Two Masters: The Development of American Military Chaplaincy, 1860–1920.* Lincoln: University of Nebraska Press, 2002.

Butler, Diana Hochstedt. *Standing against the Whirlwind: Evangelical Episcopalians in Nineteenth-Century America.* New York: Oxford University Press, 1995.

Butler, Jonathan M. *Softly and Tenderly Jesus Is Calling: Heaven and Hell in American Revivalism, 1870–1920.* Chicago Studies in the History of American Religion, ed. Jerald C. Brauer and Martin E. Marty. Brooklyn: Carlson Publishing, 1991.

Capps, Donald. "The Death of Father Abraham: The Assassination of Lincoln and Its Effect on Frontier Mythology." In *Religious Encounters with Death: Insights from the History and Anthropology of Religions,* ed. Frank E. Reynolds and Earle H. Waugh, 233–44. University Park: Pennsylvania State University Press, 1977.

Card, Nan. "Experience of Death in the Civil War: Sandusky County, Ohio." M.A. thesis, Bowling Green State University, 2001.

Carwardine, Richard J. *Evangelicals and Politics in Antebellum America.* New Haven: Yale University Press, 1993. Reprint, Knoxville: University of Tennessee Press, 1997.

———. *Lincoln.* Harlow, U.K.: Pearson, 2003.

Cashin, Joan E., ed. *The War Was You and Me: Civilians in the American Civil War.* Princeton, N.J.: Princeton University Press, 2002.

Cayton, Andrew R. L., and Peter S. Onuf. *The Midwest and the Nation: Rethinking the History of an American Region.* Bloomington: Indiana University Press, 1990.

Chesebrough, David B. *"God Ordained This War": Sermons on the Sectional Crisis, 1830–1865.* Columbia: University of South Carolina Press, 1991.

———. *"No Sorrow like Our Sorrow": Northern Protestant Ministers and the Assassination of Lincoln.* Kent, Ohio: Kent State University Press, 1994.

Churchill, Robert. "Liberty, Conscription, and a Party Divided: The Sons of Liberty Conspiracy, 1863–1864." *Prologue* 30 (1998): 295–303.

Cimbala, Paul A., and Randall M. Miller, ed. *An Uncommon Time: The Civil War and the Northern Home Front.* New York: Fordham University Press, 2002.

Clebsch, William A. "Christian Interpretations of the Civil War." *Church History* 30 (1961): 212–22.

Coggeshall, William T. *Lincoln Memorial: The Journeys of Abraham Lincoln.* Columbus: Ohio State Journal, 1865.

Corrigan, John. *Business of the Heart: Religion and Emotion in the Nineteenth Century.* Berkeley: University of California Press, 2002.

Curran, Thomas F. *Soldiers of Peace: Civil War Pacifism and the Postwar Radical Peace Movement.* New York: Fordham University Press, 2003.

Cutter, Barbara. *Domestic Devils, Battlefield Angels: The Radicalism of American Womanhood, 1830–1865.* DeKalb: Northern Illinois University Press, 2003.

Donald, David Herbert. *Lincoln.* New York: Simon & Schuster, 1995.

Douglas, Ann. "Heaven Our Home: Consolation Literature in the Northern United States, 1830–1880." *American Quarterly* 26 (1974): 496–515.

Dunham, Chester Forrester. *The Attitude of the Northern Clergy toward the South, 1860–1865.* Toledo: Gray Co., 1942.

Endres, David J. "Rectifying the Fatal Contrast: Archbishop John Purcell and the Slavery Controversy." *Ohio Valley History* 2, no. 2 (2002): 23–33.

Engs, Robert F., and Corey M. Brooks. *Their Patriotic Duty: The Civil War Letters of the Evans Family of Brown County, Ohio.* New York: Fordham University Press, 2007.

Escott, Paul D. *"What Shall We Do with the Negro?" Lincoln, White Racism, and Civil War America.* Charlottesville: University of Virginia Press, 2009.

Etcheson, Nicole. *The Emerging Midwest: Upland Southerners and the Political Culture of the Old Northwest, 1787–1861.* Bloomington: Indiana University Press, 1996.

Fahs, Alice. "The Sentimental Soldier in Popular Civil War Literature, 1861–65." *Civil War History* 46 (2000): 107–31.

Farber, Daniel. *Lincoln's Constitution.* Chicago: University of Chicago Press, 2003.

Farrell, James J. *Inventing the American Way of Death, 1830–1920.* Philadelphia: Temple University Press, 1980.

Faust, Drew Gilpin. "The Civil War Soldier and the Art of Dying." *Journal of Southern History* 67 (2001): 3–38.

———. *This Republic of Suffering: Death and the American Civil War.* New York: Knopf, 2008.

Foner, Eric. *Reconstruction: America's Unfinished Revolution 1863–1877.* New York: Harper & Row, 1988.

Foote, Shelby. *The Civil War: A Narrative.* 3 vols. New York: Random House, 1958, 1963, 1974.

Fornieri, Joseph R. *Abraham Lincoln's Political Faith.* DeKalb: Northern Illinois University Press, 2003.

Fox-Genovese, Elizabeth, and Eugene D. Genovese. *The Mind of the Master Class: History and Faith in the Southern Slaveholders' Worldview.* New York: Cambridge University Press, 2005.

Frank, Stephen M. *Life with Father: Parenthood and Masculinity in the Nineteenth-Century American North.* Baltimore: Johns Hopkins University Press, 1998.

Fredrickson, George M. *The Inner Civil War: Northern Intellectuals and the Crisis of the Union.* New York: Harper & Row, 1965.

———. *The Black Image in the White Mind: The Debate on Afro-American Character and Destiny, 1817–1914.* New York: Harper & Row, 1971.

———. "The Coming of the Lord: The Northern Protestant Clergy and the Civil War Crisis." In *Religion and the American Civil War*, ed. Randall M. Miller, Harry S. Stout, and Charles Reagan Wilson, 110–30. New York: Oxford University Press, 1998.

Gallman, J. Matthew. *The North Fights the Civil War: The Home Front.* Chicago: Ivan R. Dee, 1994.

Geary, James W. *We Need Men: The Union Draft in the Civil War.* DeKalb: Northern Illinois University Press, 1991.

Gedge, Karin E. *Without Benefit of Clergy: Women and the Pastoral Relationship in Nineteenth-Century American Culture.* New York: Oxford University Press, 2003.

Glatthaar, Joseph T. *The March to the Sea and Beyond: Sherman's Troops in the Savannah and Carolinas Campaigns.* New York: Yew York University Press, 1985.

———. "Duty, Country, Race, and Party: The Evans Family of Ohio." In *The War Was You and Me: Civilians in the American Civil War*, ed. Joan E. Cashin, 332–57. Princeton, N.J.: Princeton University Press, 2002.

Goen, C. C. *Broken Churches, Broken Nation: Denominational Schisms and the Coming of the American Civil War.* Macon, Ga.: Mercer University Press, 1985.

Goodrich, Thomas. *The Darkest Dawn: Lincoln, Booth, and the Great American Tragedy.* Bloomington: Indiana University Press, 2005.

Goodwin, Doris Kearns. *Team of Rivals: The Political Genius of Abraham Lincoln.* New York: Simon & Schuster, 2005.

Graham, Preston D. *A Kingdom Not of This World: Stuart Robinson's Struggle to Distinguish the Sacred from the Secular during the Civil War.* Macon, Ga.: Mercer University Press, 2002.

Grant, Susan-Mary. "Patriot Graves: American National Identity and the Civil War Dead." *American Nineteenth Century History* 5 (2004): 74–100.

Greenberg, Amy S. *Manifest Manhood and the Antebellum American Empire.* New York: Cambridge University Press, 2005.

Griffen, Clyde. "Reconstructing Masculinity from the Evangelical Revival to the Waning of Progressivism: A Speculative Synthesis." In *Meanings for Manhood: Constructions of Masculinity in Victorian America,* ed. Mark C. Carnes and Clyde Griffen, 183–204. Chicago: University of Chicago Press, 1990.

Grimsley, Mark. *The Hard Hand of War: Union Military Policy toward Southern Civilians, 1861–1865.* New York: Cambridge University Press, 1995.

Grossjean, Paul Eugene. "The Concept of American Nationhood: Theological Interpretation as Reflected by the Northern Mainline Protestant Preachers in the Late Civil War Period." Ph.D. diss., Drew University, 1977.

Guelzo, Allen C. *Abraham Lincoln: Redeemer President.* Grand Rapids, Mich.: Eerdmans, 1999.

———. *Lincoln's Emancipation Proclamation: The End of Slavery in America.* New York: Simon & Schuster, 2004.

Gunderson, Robert Gray. *The Old Gentlemen's Convention: The Washington Peace Conference of 1861.* Madison: University of Wisconsin Press, 1961.

Guyatt, Nicholas. *Providence and the Invention of the United States, 1607–1876.* New York: Cambridge University Press, 2007.

Hall, Susan G. *Appalachian Ohio and the Civil War, 1862–1863.* Jefferson, N.C.: McFarland, 2000.

Harrell, Carolyn L. *When the Bells Tolled for Lincoln: Southern Reaction to the Assassination.* Macon, Ga.: Mercer University Press, 1997.

Harris, William C. *With Charity for All: Lincoln and the Restoration of the Union.* Lexington: University Press of Kentucky, 1997.

———. *Lincoln's Rise to the Presidency.* Lawrence: University Press of Kansas, 2007.

Hart, D. G. "The Spirituality of the Church, the Westminster Standards, and Nineteenth-Century American Presbyterianism." *Premise* 4, no. 3 (1997): 15 pages; accessed January 13, 2004, at http://capo.org/premise/current/p971005.htm.

Hatch, Nathan O. *The Sacred Cause of Liberty: Republican Thought and the Millennium in Revolutionary New England.* New Haven: Yale University Press, 1977.

———. *The Democratization of American Christianity.* New Haven: Yale University Press, 1989.

Hay, Robert P. "Providence and the American Past." *Indiana Magazine of History* 65 (1969): 79–101.

Haynes, Stephen R. *Noah's Curse: The Biblical Justification of American Slavery.* New York: Oxford University Press, 2002.

Hein, David. "A Sermon Lincoln Heard: P. D. Gurley's 'Man's Projects and God's Results.'" *Lincoln Herald* 89 (1987): 161–66.

Herrick, H. N., and William Warren Sweet. *A History of the North Indiana Conference of the Methodist Episcopal Church, from Its Organization in 1844 to the Present.* Indianapolis: W. K. Stewart Co., 1917.

Hess, Earl J. *Liberty, Virtue, and Progress: Northerners and Their War for the Union.* New York: New York University Press, 1988.

Hickey, Donald R. *The War of 1812: A Forgotten Conflict.* Urbana: University of Illinois Press, 1989.

History of Rush County, Indiana, From the Earliest Times to the Present, with Biographical Sketches, Notes, Etc., Together with a Short History of the Northwest, the Indiana Territory, and the State of Indiana. Chicago: Brant & Fuller, 1888. Reprint, Knightstown: Eastern Indiana Publishing Co., 1966.

Hoffert, Sylvia D. "'A Very Peculiar Sorrow': Attitudes toward Infant Death in the Urban Northeast, 1800–1860." *American Quarterly* 39 (1987): 601–16.

———. *Private Matters: American Attitudes toward Childbearing and Infant Nurture in the Urban North, 1800–1860.* Urbana: University of Illinois Press, 1989.

Hoffman, Harold Richard, and Max I. Briggs. *A Light in the Forest: A History of the First Baptist Church of Indianapolis, Indiana 1822–2003.* 2d ed. Carmel, Ind.: UN Communications, 2005.

Holifield, E. Brooks. *Theology in America: Christian Thought from the Age of the Puritans to the Civil War.* New Haven: Yale University Press, 2003.

Hopkins, Charles Howard. *The Rise of the Social Gospel in American Protestantism 1865–1915.* Yale Studies in Religious Education. New Haven: Yale University Press, 1940.

Howard, Victor B. *Religion and the Radical Republican Movement 1860–1870.* Lexington: University Press of Kentucky, 1990.

Hurt, R. Douglas. *The Ohio Frontier: Crucible of the Old Northwest, 1720–1830.* Bloomington: Indiana University Press, 1996.

Jacoby, Stewart Olin. "Of Nationalism and Nativism: The God Amendment Movement Begins, Xenia, Ohio, February 1863." *Old Northwest* 13 (1987): 143–61.

Jones, Howard. *Union in Peril: The Crisis over British Intervention in the Civil War.* Chapel Hill: University of North Carolina Press, 1992.

Kete, Mary Louise. *Sentimental Collaborations: Mourning and Middle-Class Identity in Nineteenth-Century America.* Durham: Duke University Press, 2000.

Klement, Frank L. *The Copperheads in the Middle West.* Chicago: University of Chicago Press, 1960.

———. *The Limits of Dissent: Clement L. Vallandigham & the Civil War.* Lexington: University Press of Kentucky, 1970.

———. *Dark Lanterns: Secret Political Societies, Conspiracies, and Treason Trials in the Civil War.* Baton Rouge: Louisiana State University Press, 1984.

Klingaman, William K. *Abraham Lincoln and the Road to Emancipation, 1861–1865.* New York: Viking, 2001.

Laderman, Gary. *The Sacred Remains: American Attitudes toward Death, 1799–1883.* New Haven: Yale University Press, 1996.

Lawson, Melinda. *Patriot Fires: Forging a New American Nationalism in the Civil War North.* Lawrence: University Press of Kansas, 2002.

Leckie, William H., and Shirley A. Leckie. *Unlikely Warriors: General Benjamin H. Grierson and His Family.* Norman: University of Oklahoma Press, 1984.

Lehman, James O., and Steven M. Nolt. *Mennonites, Amish, and the American Civil War*. Baltimore: John Hopkins University Press, 2007.

Long, E. B., with Barbara Long. *The Civil War Day by Day: An Almanac 1861–1865*. Garden City, N.Y.: Doubleday, 1971.

Manning, Chandra. *What This Cruel War Was Over: Soldiers, Slavery, and the Civil War*. New York: Knopf, 2007.

McDannell, Colleen, and Bernhard Lang. *Heaven: A History*. New Haven: Yale University Press, 1988.

McKivigan, John R. *The War against Proslavery Religion: Abolitionism and the Northern Churches, 1830–1865*. Ithaca: Cornell University Press, 1984.

McPherson, Edward. *The Political History of the United States of America, During the Great Rebellion*. 2d ed. Washington, D.C.: Philp & Solomons, 1865.

McPherson, James M. *Battle Cry of Freedom: The Civil War Era*. New York: Oxford University Press, 1988.

———. *For Cause & Comrades: Why Men Fought in the Civil War*. New York: Oxford University Press, 1997.

———. "Afterword." In *Religion and the American Civil War*, ed. Randall M. Miller, Harry S. Stout, and Charles Reagan Wilson, 408–12. New York: Oxford University Press, 1998.

Mead, Sidney E. "The 'Nation with the Soul of a Church.'" *Church History* 36 (1967): 262–83.

Means, Howard. *The Avenger Takes His Place: Andrew Johnson and the 45 Days That Changed the Nation*. Orlando, Fla.: Harcourt, 2006.

Miller, Charles C., ed. *History of Allen County, Ohio and Representative Citizens*. Chicago: Richmond & Arnold, 1906.

Miller, Randall M., Harry S. Stout, and Charles Reagan Wilson, ed. *Religion and the American Civil War*. New York: Oxford University Press, 1998.

Miller, Robert J. *Both Prayed to the Same God: Religion and Faith in the American Civil War*. Lanham, Md.: Lexington Books, 2007.

Mitchell, Reid. *The Vacant Chair: The Northern Soldier Leaves Home*. New York: Oxford University Press, 1993.

Morel, Lucas E. *Lincoln's Sacred Effort: Defining Religion's Role in American Self-Government*. Lanham, Md.: Lexington, 2000.

Moorhead, James H. "Henry J. Van Dyke, Sr.: Conservative Apostle of a Broad Church." *Journal of Presbyterian History* 50 (1972): 19–38.

———. *American Apocalypse: Yankee Protestants and the Civil War 1860–1869*. New Haven: Yale University Press, 1978.

———. "'As Though Nothing at All Had Happened': Death and Afterlife in Protestant Thought, 1840–1925." *Soundings* 67 (1984): 453–71.

———. *World without End: Mainstream American Protestant Visions of the Last Things, 1880–1925*. Bloomington: Indiana University Press, 1999.

Mullin, Robert Bruce. *Episcopal Vision/American Reality: High Church Social Thought in Evangelical America*. New Haven: Yale University Press, 1986.

Nagel, Paul C. *One Nation Indivisible: The Union in American Thought 1776–1861.* New York: Oxford University Press, 1964.

———. *This Sacred Trust: American Nationality 1798–1898.* New York: Oxford University Press, 1971.

Nation, Richard F. *At Home in the Hoosier Hills: Agriculture, Politics, and Religion in Southern Indiana, 1810–1870.* Bloomington: Indiana University Press, 2005.

Neace, Estel Leroy. "A Study of Methodism in Indiana during the Civil War." M.A. thesis, Butler University, 1961.

Neely, Mark E., Jr. *The Fate of Liberty: Abraham Lincoln and Civil Liberties.* New York: Oxford University Press, 1991.

———. *The Last Best Hope of Earth: Abraham Lincoln and the Promise of America.* Cambridge: Harvard University Press, 1993.

Nelson, Jacquelyn S. *Indiana Quakers Confront the Civil War.* Indianapolis: Indiana Historical Society, 1991.

Noll, Mark A. "'Both...Pray to the Same God': The Singularity of Lincoln's Faith in the Era of the Civil War." *Journal of the Abraham Lincoln Association* 18, no. 1 (1997): 1–26.

———. *America's God: From Jonathan Edwards to Abraham Lincoln.* New York: Oxford University Press, 2002.

———. *The Civil War as a Theological Crisis.* Chapel Hill: University of North Carolina Press, 2006.

O'Malley, Michael. *Keeping Watch: A History of American Time.* New York: Viking, 1990.

Paludan, Phillip Shaw. *"A People's Contest": The Union and Civil War 1861–1865.* New York: Harper & Row, 1988.

Parish, Peter J. "The Instruments of Providence: Slavery, Civil War, and the American Churches." *Studies in Church History* 20 (1983): 291–320.

———. "From Necessary Evil to National Blessing: The Northern Protestant Clergy Interpret the Civil War." In *The Civil War and the Northern Home Front*, ed. Paul A. Cimbala and Randall M. Miller, 61–89. New York: Fordham University Press, 2002.

Parrillo, Nicholas. "Lincoln's Calvinist Transformation: Emancipation and War." *Civil War History* 46 (2000): 227–53.

Peterson, Merrill D. *Lincoln in American Memory.* New York: Oxford University Press, 1994.

Potter, David M. *The Impending Crisis 1848–1861.* New York: Harper & Row, 1976.

Rabinowitz, Richard. *The Spiritual Self in Everyday Life: The Transformation of Personal Religious Experience in Nineteenth-Century New England.* Boston: Northeastern University Press, 1989.

Reck, W. Emerson. "Mr. Lincoln's Growth in Faith." *Lincoln Herald* 92 (Spring 1990): 6–11.

Richard, Patricia L. *Busy Hands: Images of the Family in the Northern Civil War.* New York: Fordham University Press, 2003.

Robertson, James I., Jr. *Soldiers Blue and Gray.* Columbia: University of South Carolina Press, 1988.

Rotundo, E. Anthony. *American Manhood: Transformations in Masculinity from the Revolution to the Modern Era.* New York: Basic Books, 1993.

Rowell, Geoffrey. *Hell and the Victorians: A Study of Nineteenth-Century Theological Controversies Concerning Eternal Punishment and the Future Life.* Oxford: Cambridge University Press, 1974.

Ryan, Mary P. *Cradle of the Middle Class: The Family in Oneida County, New York, 1790–1865.* New York: Cambridge University Press, 1981.

Saum, Lewis O. "Providence in the Popular Mind of Pre-Civil War America." *Indiana Magazine of History* 72 (1976): 315–46.

———. *The Popular Mood of Pre-Civil War America.* Westport, Conn.: Greenwood Press, 1980.

———. *The Popular Mood of America, 1860–1890.* Lincoln: University of Nebraska Press, 1990.

Schecter, Barnet. *The Devil's Own Work: The Civil War Draft Riots and the Fight to Reconstruct America.* New York: Walker Publishing, 2005.

Schlabach, Theron F. *Peace, Faith, Nation: Mennonites and Amish in Nineteenth-Century America.* The Mennonite Experience in America, vol. 2. Scottdale, Pa.: Herald Press, 1988.

Schultz, Jane E. "Healing the Nation: Condolence and Correspondence in Civil War Hospitals." *Proteus* 17, no. 2 (2000): 32–41.

Sherley-Price, Leo, ed. and trans. *The Imitation of Christ.* London: Penguin, 1952.

Silber, Nina. *Daughters of the Union: Northern Women Fight the Civil War.* Cambridge: Harvard University Press, 2005.

Simeone, James. *Democracy and Slavery in Frontier Illinois: The Bottomland Republic.* DeKalb: Northern Illinois University Press, 2000.

Smith, Craig R. *Daniel Webster and the Oratory of Civil Religion.* Columbia: University of Missouri Press, 2005.

Smith, Gary Scott. *Faith and the Presidency: From George Washington to George W. Bush.* New York: Oxford University Press, 2007.

Smith, Mark M. *Mastered by the Clock: Time, Slavery, and Freedom in the American South.* Chapel Hill: University of North Carolina Press, 1997.

Stampp, Kenneth M. *And the War Came: The North and the Secession Crisis 1860–1861.* Baton Rouge: Louisiana State University Press, 1950.

———. *Indiana Politics during the Civil War.* Indianapolis: Indiana Historical Bureau, 1949. Reprint, Bloomington: Indiana University Press, 1978.

Stannard, David E. *The Puritan Way of Death: A Study in Religion, Culture, and Social Change.* New York: Oxford University Press, 1977.

Stewart, Charles J. "Lincoln's Assassination and the Protestant Clergy of the North." *Journal of the Illinois State Historical Society* 54 (1961): 268–93.

———. "The Pulpit and the Assassination of Lincoln." *Quarterly Journal of Speech* 50 (1964): 299–307.

———. "Civil War Preaching." In *Preaching in American History: Selected Issues in the American Pulpit, 1630–1967*, ed. DeWitte Holland, 184–205. Nashville: Abingdon, 1969.

Stoltzfus, Grant M. *Mennonites of the Ohio and Eastern Conference: From the Colonial Period in Pennsylvania to 1968*. Studies in Anabaptist and Mennonite History, no.13. Scottdale, Pa.: Herald Press, 1969.

Stout, Harry S. *Upon the Altar of the Nation: A Moral History of the Civil War*. New York: Viking, 2006.

Stowell, Daniel W. *Rebuilding Zion: The Religious Reconstruction of the South, 1863–1877*. New York: Oxford University Press, 1998.

Striner, Richard. *Father Abraham: Lincoln's Relentless Struggle to End Slavery*. New York: Oxford University Press, 2006.

Swanson, James L. *Manhunt: The Twelve-Day Chase for Lincoln's Killer*. New York: William Morrow, 2006.

Sweet, William Warren. *The Methodist Episcopal Church and the Civil War*. Cincinnati: Methodist Book Concern, 1912.

Syrett, John. "The Confiscation Acts: The North Strikes Back." In *An Uncommon Time: The Civil War and the Northern Home Front*, ed. Paul A. Cimbala and Randall M. Miller, 280–325. New York: Fordham University Press, 2002.

Temple, Wayne C. *Abraham Lincoln: From Skeptic to Prophet*. Mahomet, Ill.: Mayhaven, 1995.

Thornbrough, Emma Lou. *Indiana in the Civil War Era 1850–1880*. Indianapolis: Indiana Historical Society, 1965.

Trefousse, Hans L. *Andrew Johnson: A Biography*. New York: W. W. Norton, 1989.

Turner, Thomas Reed. *Beware the People Weeping: Public Opinion and the Assassination of Lincoln*. Baton Rouge: Louisiana State University Press, 1982.

Velde, Lewis G. Vander. *The Presbyterian Churches and the Federal Union 1861–1869*. Cambridge: Harvard University Press, 1932.

Voegeli, V. Jacque. *Free but Not Equal: The Midwest and the Negro During the Civil War*. Chicago: University of Chicago Press, 1967.

Volpe, Vernon L. "The Frémonts and Emancipation in Missouri." *Historian* 56 (1994): 339–54.

Waugh, John C. *Reelecting Lincoln: The Battle for the 1864 Presidency*. Cambridge: Da Capo Press, 2001.

Weber, Jennifer L. *Copperheads: The Rise and Fall of Lincoln's Opponents in the North*. New York: Oxford University Press, 2006.

Wells, Cheryl A. *Civil War Time: Temporality and Identity in America, 1861–1865*. Athens: University of Georgia Press, 2005.

Wells, Robert V. *Facing the 'King of Terrors': Death and Society in an American Community, 1750–1990*. New York: Cambridge University Press, 2000.

Welter, Barbara. "The Cult of True Womanhood: 1820–1860." *American Quarterly* 18 (1966): 151–74.

Wert, Jeffry D. *The Sword of Lincoln: The Army of the Potomac*. New York: Simon & Schuster, 2005.

White, Ronald C., Jr. *Lincoln's Greatest Speech: The Second Inaugural.* New York: Simon & Schuster, 2002.
———. *The Eloquent President: A Portrait of Lincoln through His Words.* New York: Random House, 2005.
Wills, Gregory A. *Democratic Religion: Freedom, Authority, and Church Discipline in the Baptist South, 1785–1900.* New York: Oxford University Press, 1997.
Winger, Stewart. *Lincoln, Religion, and Romantic Cultural Politics.* DeKalb: Northern Illinois University Press, 2003.
Woodworth, Steven E. *While God Is Marching On: The Religious World of Civil War Soldiers.* Lawrence: University Press of Kansas, 2001.

Index

Adams, Kelsey, 208
African-Americans, 216, 243, 254, 311n16
 arguments for equality of, 25, 31–32, 41, 177, 222, 235–36, 264, 268
 arguments for inequality of, 53, 97, 117, 170, 183, 235
 colonization of, 50, 53, 58, 171, 283n35
 white opposition to, 52–53, 68–69, 114, 143, 220, 234
 as soldiers, 171, 221
African Methodist Episcopal church, 58, 113, 180, 200, 216, 232, 234, 237, 254
Agenbroad, John, 46
Alford, Franklin, 37, 42–43, 147, 150, 152–53, 155, 158–60, 191–92, 197, 209
Alford, Lafayette, 152–53, 191–92
Alford, Virginia, 195
Alford, Warren, 147, 150, 155, 158–60, 191–92
Alford, Wayne, 147, 191–92
Ames, Edward, 33, 180–81, 280n7
Anderson, Robert, 23, 26, 244
Anderson, Thomas J., 146
Andersonville prison, 239–40

Ankeny, Henry and Joseph, 146, 159
Antietam, battle of, 67, 69, 192
Antioch College, 114, 291n27
Aplin, Elvira, 82, 86, 88, 91–94, 118–19, 199, 210–11, 234, 246, 259
Aplin, George, 82, 86, 93, 199, 211
Appomattox Court House, 244, 252
Atlanta, Ga., 226
Avery, George Smith, 30, 52–53, 89
Avery, Lizzie (Little), 26, 29–30, 52–53, 59, 64, 89, 104, 212, 240

Bailey, Silas, 45
Baldridge, Samuel, 259
Baptists, 21, 43, 51, 56, 98, 111–12, 186–87
Barland, Thomas, 28–29, 151
Barnes, H. N., 224
Barr, Edward, 120
Bass, Mary, 200
Bates, Mercy, 88
Beauregard, P. G. T., 23
Beebe, Joseph, 47–48, 156–57
Beecher, Edward, 265
Beecher, Henry Ward, 259
Bender, Margaret, 75

Bereman, Eleanor, 198, 218–19
Bible, 25, 32, 103, 126, 179, 188, 190, 222, 238, 240
  appropriation of for political purposes, 17–18, 59, 110, 117–18, 164–65, 177, 189, 223, 229, 233, 250, 252, 269–71
  civilian citation of, 69, 76, 124, 150, 154, 163–64, 175, 195, 211, 239
  and slavery, 168–70
Bingham, Abel, 23, 48–49, 65–66, 109
Bingham, Angie, 131–32
Bingham, Hannah, 48, 65, 77–78, 87–88, 94
Bingham, Joseph J., 262–63, 313n31
Bittinger, J. B., 40–41
Bitzel, Peter, 111
Blanchard, Jonathan, 54
Blinn, Dorothy, 89, 203
Bolton, R. H., 169–70, 182–83
Booth, John Wilkes, 246–47, 252, 256, 259–60, 264
Borton, Ira, 57
Borton, Samuel, 111
Bowler, Lizzie (Caleff), 54, 83, 86, 207, 220–21, 247
Bowler, Madison, 54, 83, 86, 220–21
Boyd, J. L., 144–45
Bradford, Lucy, 91
Brenneman, Daniel, 136
Brenneman, John M., 125–27, 187–88, 235–36
Brookville College, 31
Brough, John, 158, 172
Brown, Ethan, 108, 200
Brown, Eunice, 195
Brown, F. T., 48
Brown, Jerome, 99, 157
Brown, Richard, 119
Browning, Orville, 62, 68
Bryan, Thomas, 29, 261
Buchanan, Claude, 48, 74, 82
Buchanan, James, 13–14
Buchanan, Sophia, 64–67, 74–75, 82, 85, 104, 109, 131, 252–54, 257, 259

Burke, William, 224
Burnside, Ambrose, 104, 107, 221
Burt, N. C., 57
Buswell, Milton, 54, 98, 231–32
Butler, Ovid, 135, 230–31, 238

Cameron, Simon, 23, 45
Carey, Isaac, 177, 255, 260
Carlisle, Maria, 258
Carrington, Henry B., 117
Catholics, 129–30, 170, 174, 258
Catholic Telegraph, 129, 170, 174
Cavins, Ann, 55
Chancellorsville, 121–22
Chandler, Zachariah, 253
Chapin, Alice, 75–77, 85, 88, 94, 124, 136, 203, 207, 209, 213
Chapin, Ally, 77, 85
Chapin, George, 202–03, 206
Chapin, John, 203, 224
Chapin, Lucius, 76, 85, 88, 94
Chapin, Sarah, 77, 202, 206, 209
Chaplains, 86, 145–46, 238–39, 295n13
Chase, Cornelia, 73, 112
Chase, Salmon, 35
Chastening, 16, 37–38, 41, 66–67, 122, 188, 215, 265
Cheney, Mary, 82, 122
Chesterton, G. K., 271
Chittenden, Amanda, 80, 93
Chittenden, George, 80
Chittenden, Mary, 37–38, 209
Christian republicanism, 20–21, 276n3
Christian Union, 179
Chubb, Rolla, 263–64
Churches. *See also* names of specific denominations
  spiritual decline in, 32, 43, 112, 161–62, 183, 185
  and discipline of members, 55–56
  and division over politics, 110–11, 172, 177–79, 185–87, 224, 237
  and revival, 54–55, 112–13, 179–80, 237
  and Unionism, 4, 25, 56, 162, 182

Church of God, 169, 172, 179, 182–83
Cincinnati Daily Commercial, 100–01, 104, 179, 262–63
Cincinnati Enquirer, 100–01, 103–04, 122, 145, 169, 173–77, 182, 184, 188–89, 222–23, 227, 242
Clannard, Henry, 269, 314n7
Clark, Alexander, 245
Clendenning, John, 186
Cline, William, 37
Cobb, Ann, 99
Cobb, Antoinette, 78–79, 99
Cobb, Henry, 99–100, 212
Cobb, Newton, 99
Cold Harbor, 217
Collett, Mary, 87
Collins, H. B., 120, 295n13
Confederacy, 23, 44, 51, 67, 117, 230, 232, 239, 250–52, 255–56, 264, 267–68
Confiscation Acts, 38, 50–51, 60–61, 64, 67–68
Congregationalists, 14, 21, 117, 121, 184, 216
Conkling, Ann, 28, 57, 81, 119
Conner, Charlotte, 105
Constitution, U.S., 15, 18, 40, 64, 99, 103, 120, 133, 157, 270–71, 309n44
  13th Amendment, 235–36
  14th Amendment, 268, 270
  15th Amendment, 268
Copperheads, 211, 226–27, 231, 234–35, 250, 258, 268
  opposition to, 111, 114–16, 124, 129–30, 136, 162–63, 171–73, 183, 189, 215, 217, 223–24, 229, 251
  and violence, 128–29, 220
Corbett, Boston, 260
Corning, James, 15
Cotton, Ann, 83–84, 91–92, 114, 217, 221, 227, 286–87n17
Cotton, Dexter, 83–84, 134
Covington, S. F. and Mary, 198, 214
Cox, Samuel S., 59
Crane, O. J., 202

Creighton, William, 202
Cress, Randie, 238, 261
Crooks, Adam, 202
Cumings, Charles, 239

Dart, Almira, 86, 94, 199–200
Davidson, A. H., 30–31
Davis, Jefferson, 23, 30, 45, 108, 171, 218, 230, 233, 254, 266, 268
Day, Henry, 232–33
Dean, Drusilla, 194
Death, 77, 123, 175, 192–93
  and anonymity of on the battlefield, 201–02
  God's control over, 195–99
  "Good Death," 199–200
  and condolence letters, 200–01
  preparation for, 194–97, 199
  of Christian soldiers, 203
  and last words, 201
Declaration of Independence, 25, 97, 222–23
Demaree, David, 164
Demaree, George Whitefield, 164
Demaree, Henry, 26
Demaree, Peter, 43–44
Democrats, 57, 100, 110, 130, 218, 225–26, 228–32
  criticism of Republicans, 25, 31–32, 116, 173–74, 183–84, 227, 241–42, 258, 269
  as disloyal, 30, 133, 172, 251
  and providence, 31
  War Democrats, 115, 164, 226
Dempster, John, 121
Denny, Margaret, 210, 212, 246, 260
Devil. *See* Satan
Disciples of Christ, 22, 71, 120, 230
Dispensationalism, 238
Dooley, Atellus, 201–02
Dooley, Rufus, 82, 92–93, 147, 150, 201
Dooley, Sarah, 82, 91–93, 114–15, 133, 199, 201–02, 228–29
Dooley, Silas, 147–48, 150
Doolittle, James, 23, 99

342   INDEX

Draft, 99–100, 143, 220, 228
Duffield, George, 11–12, 15, 106, 250, 290n15
Duncan, Elizabeth, 81, 136
Dunham, Cyrus, 117
Dunham, John, 43
Dunn, Louisa, 224

Eddy, Thomas, 260
Eggleston, Rhoda, 74, 91, 210
Elections
  of 1862, 100
  of 1863, 158, 171–74
  of 1864, 228–229, 231–32
Eliot, Emily, 206–07
Elstine, Therese, 28, 30, 75, 253
Ely, Emma, 50
Ely, Frances, 44, 211
Emancipation
  in the District of Columbia, 58–59
  and Frémont, 38–39, 280n6
  opposition to, 59, 68–69, 99, 108, 157
Emancipation Proclamation, 106, 108, 157, 236, 255
  Preliminary Emancipation Proclamation, 64, 69–70, 98–99
Enrollment Act, 125
Episcopalians, 14, 101, 103, 111–12
Este, David, 218, 257
Evans, Amos, 142–43
Evans, Andrew, 142–43, 155
Evans, Sam, 142–43
Everett, Edward, 175

Fanning, Eliza, 206
Fast and thanksgiving days, 14–15, 40–42, 119–21, 135–38, 166–67, 219, 221–22, 263
Fletcher, Calvin, 18, 23, 45–46, 60, 113–14, 120, 242
  and politics, 100, 231
  and prayer, 17, 42, 108, 184, 228
  and providence, 16, 26–27, 33, 37, 44, 48, 50, 61, 123, 132, 134, 194, 204
  and slavery, 17, 20, 39, 51–52
  and war, 38, 67, 131, 243

Fletcher, Elijah, 23, 28–29, 37, 50, 278n28, 282n22
Fletcher, Emily Beeler, 194
Fletcher, Keys, 113
Fletcher, Miles, 204–05
Foot, C. C., 202
Foote, Andrew H., 50
Fort Donelson, 50, 282n22
Fort Henry, 50
Fort Pillow, 216
Fort Sumter, 23, 26–27, 174, 244–45
Foster, Josephine, 196
Fredericksburg, battle of, 107
Frémont, John C., 38–39, 218–19
French, John, 144
Frey, Augustus, 229, 246–47, 251, 254
Funk, John F., 21, 24, 32–33, 54, 127–28, 243, 280n10

Gaddis, Maxwell, 248, 251
Gary, Kate, 252
Gettysburg, 131, 175, 257
Gettysburg Address, 175–76
Giles, Chauncey, 119
Gleichmann, Emilie, 73–74, 89, 220
Gleichmann, John, 89
Glessner, Lewis, 145, 166
Glessner, Will, 166–69, 242
Glover, L. M., 15, 256
Godfrey, Hattie, 79
Godman, William, 131
Goodrich, William, 24
Goodspeed, E. J., 256
Goodwin, Edward P., 129
Goodwin, W. R., 185
Gordon, Permelia, 107
Graham, William, 112
Grant, C. Norris, 232–33
Grant, Ulysses S., 50, 122–23, 184–85, 217–18, 221, 225, 244, 252, 256
Greeley, Horace, 67, 306–07n9
Grierson, Alice, 39, 42, 56, 71–72, 85, 92–95
Grierson, Benjamin, 71–72, 85, 92–95
Griffin, John, 75, 123
Griffith, Lizzie, 207

Gurley, L. B., 50
Gurley, Phineas D., 137, 294n62, 312n22

Hall, Perry, 22, 57, 277n17
Hall, S. A., 177–78
Hall, Sarah, 105
Halleck, Henry, 131, 204
Hamilton, Charles, 208
Hammond, Abram A., 21
Hancock Courier, 145, 166–67, 242
Hancock Jeffersonian, 165, 167
Harrell, Eliza, 113
Hatch, C. M, 51
Hawley, Henry, 261
Hawley, Ransom, 147, 159–60
Hawley, Ransom E., 140–41, 147, 159–60
Hawley, Silas, 117
Hayden, William, 257–58
Heaven, 191, 211
  conditions of, 208–209, 212
  entrance into, 209
  God as emphasis of, 206–07
  family as emphasis of, 207
  infants in, 207–08
  Abraham Lincoln in, 256–57, 311–12n22
  soldiers in, 210
Helmer, C. D., 135
Hendricks, Thomas A., 117, 251
Hibbard, A. G., 250
Hibbard, Samuel, 120, 194
Hill, James, 75, 85–86
Hitchcock, Henry, 257
Hitchcock, Reuben, 35–36, 46, 66
Hobbs, Mary Ann, 73
Hogan, John, 181
Honnell, J. G., 186, 300n36
Hooker, Joseph, 121–22
Hovey, Horace, 14–15, 24
Hudelson, Amanda, 207
Hudson, Alonzo, 51
Hughes, D. L., 255–56
Hull, Moses, 260
Huntington, Elisha M., 11, 16–17, 20, 28, 33, 37, 39, 68
Hyde, N. A., 251

Indiana Asbury University, 23, 42, 204, 228
Indianapolis Daily Journal, 14, 239, 248
Indianapolis Daily State Sentinel, 119, 262
Ingram, Andrew, 16–17, 20, 27, 29, 204

Jackson, Thomas J. "Stonewall," 60, 121–22
Jackson, William, 230
Jessup, William, 133
John, Martha, 202
John, Samuel, 202, 303n19
Johnson, Andrew, 229, 252–56, 263–64, 267–68, 270, 313n4
Johnson, W. G., 20, 112
Johnston, Ella, 69, 114
Jones, J. R., 207
Jones, Smith, 30–31
Judgment, 216
  on earth, 238, 251
  in eternity, 30, 126, 210–11, 255

Kalb, John S., 167–68
Kellar, Harrison and John, 147–48, 150, 153, 156, 210
Kemper, Helen, 203, 206, 208
Kennon, William, 56
Ketcham, John L., 17, 108, 155–56, 197, 226, 239, 267
Ketcham, Willie, 155–56, 158, 239
Kidwell, Abiram, 247
King, William, 243
Knights of the Golden Circle, 115–16, 129
Kohlsaat, Christian, 110, 141–42
Kohlsaat, Reimer, 141–42
Kohlsaat, Sarah, 112, 141

Ladley, Alice, 120
Ladley, Mary, 114
Laird, Francis, 268–69
Lamb, E. E., 254–55
Lamon, Ward Hill, 19
Lankford, W. S., 175
Larimer, George, 56

344 INDEX

Lee, Robert E., 60, 65, 69, 104, 107, 121–22, 130–31, 243–44, 250
Leggett, Marilla Wells, 134
Lewis, Cyrus, 125, 134
Lincoln, Abraham, 37, 51, 101, 121, 151, 171, 173, 181, 188–89, 230, 232
 civilian opinions of, 44, 46, 98, 108, 126, 183, 215, 218, 225, 227, 229, 236, 245–46, 253–55, 258–59, 262
 and colonization, 58, 283n35
 death of, 160, 245–52, 256, 260–63
 and emancipation, 58, 61, 63–64, 67–70, 220, 243
 and proclamations of fast and thanksgiving days, 40, 118–19, 135–36, 184, 226
 and providence, 17, 19, 40, 62–63, 70, 118, 131, 216
 and religion, 5, 105, 137, 185, 218, 257, 264, 294n62, 312n22
 and slavery, 18, 50, 225
 speeches of, 6, 19, 108–09, 175–76, 231, 234, 240–42, 246, 271
 and war, 23, 39, 104, 122, 217, 219
Little, George, 222
Livermore, Lark, 151, 296n21
Locke, David Ross, 165, 167, 231
Logan, Mary, 44, 197, 211
Longnaker, Letty, 55
Lough, Albert, 201
Lough, David, 155, 188, 201, 206, 209
Lough, James, 155, 201
Lough, Levi, 185
Lowrie, John, 43, 249
Lozier, J. H., 248
Lynch, A. D., 202
Lynd, S. W., 24
Lytle, William Haynes, 196

McCarty, John, 257
McClellan, George B., 39, 60, 225–27, 230–31
 civilian opinions of, 45, 104, 226
McCormick, Cyrus, 27, 218
McCormick, Nettie Fowler, 28
McCoskry, Samuel, 14
McCullough, John, 45–46
McCune, C. W., 250
McDonald, Joseph E., 251
McIlvaine, Charles P., 14, 101–04, 120, 136, 181–82, 185, 261
McKee, J. S., 180
McLean, Sarah, 91
McMullen, J. W. T., 204, 223–24, 229
McPheeters, Alexander, 153, 155, 196–97
McPheeters, Anna, 257–58
McPheeters, Henry, 138
McPheeters, John, 153, 225
McPheeters, Mollie, 91, 123, 133, 195, 225, 231, 234, 253, 266
McPheeters, Samuel, 181
McPherson, James B., 195
MacEl'rey, J. H., 250
Mahoney, Dennis, 258
Maine, John, 28
Manassas, First, 32–33
Manassas, Second, 62, 65
Marsh, Milton, 33
Mason, James, 44
Mathews, J. T., 226–227
Matlack, L. C., 145
Mauck, Jane, 203
Mayo, A. D., 256–57
Meade, George, 131
Mears, Eliza, 75
Medill, Joseph, 221
Meeks, J. A., 166–69
Meharry, James, 54
Mendenhall, Elizabeth, 88
Mennonites, 125–28, 136
Merick, Jane, 16
Methodists, 14, 39–40, 42, 51, 57, 97–98, 112–13, 120–21, 144–45, 171–72, 180–81, 184–85, 222, 227, 230, 237, 251, 255, 257, 266
Meyer, Edward, 183, 202
Millennialism, 25, 28, 47, 54, 105, 138, 156, 230, 233, 243, 249–50, 263–64

INDEX 345

Mills, Benjamin, 148, 152–56
Mills, Caleb, 146, 148–56, 216, 234–35, 247, 252–53
Mitchell, Nancy, 110
Monfort, J. G., 3, 40, 145
Moody, George, 267–68
Moody, Granville, 31–32, 37, 267–68, 270, 313n4
Morehouse, H. L., 260
Morgan, John Hunt, 132–34
Morris, Huston, 187, 300n37
Morton, Oliver P., 115, 133, 141, 204, 229, 251
Mount, Charles, 48, 84, 287n18
Mount, Phebe, 48, 84
Mumford, Mary, 212

Nasby, Petroleum V., 165–66, 231
 see Locke, David Ross
Newspapers, 24, 113, 162, 173, 175–76, 181, 196, 200, 229, 239–42, 248, 254, 258, 262–63
 criticism of politicized religion, 120–21, 130, 166–68, 269
 religious themes in secular press, 11, 25–26, 48–49, 99, 116, 173–74, 177, 189, 221–23
New York City draft riots, 132
Nicholson, Valentine, 217
Nisbet, Alfred, 259
Nold, Jacob, 125
Northrop, Henry, 249–50
Noyes, Joseph, 146

Ogburn, Calvin, 56
Olds, Edson, 100–101, 164–65, 178
Osborn, J. W., 196, 218
Ottman, Sefferenas, 137

Pacifism, 21, 125–27, 157, 187–88, 242
Paddock, Benjamin, 24
Patrick, William, 27, 32, 46, 173
Patton, William W., 41, 54, 63, 121, 127, 280n10

Peirce, Catharine, 195, 208, 229
Petersburg, Va., 217, 221, 243
Pinkerton, Allan, 19
Platt, James, 232
Plattenburg, Ellen, 230, 244
Political preaching, 5, 15, 24, 42, 56, 119–20, 259
 opposition to, 14, 21–22, 31, 57, 110, 112, 120–21, 130, 166–67, 181–82, 221–22, 258, 268
Pomeroy, Marcus "Brick," 269
Pope, John, 65
Porter, Eliza, 74, 208
Potts, Jemima, 246
Poucher, John, 23, 26–28, 228
Prayer, 74–76, 183–85, 234
Presbyter, 3, 32, 40, 145
Presbyterians, 11, 15, 22, 24–25, 40, 43, 55, 57, 98, 106, 111, 113, 137, 145, 161–62, 172, 176, 182, 186, 224, 231, 255
Prime, G. Wendell, 249
Proclamation of Amnesty and Reconstruction, 217
Providence, 4, 12–13
 and assassination of Lincoln, 245–47, 253, 256, 261–63, 313n31
 and human responsibility, 17, 29, 156
 and protection of soldiers, 74, 155, 191
 and secession crisis, 11, 15–16
 and slavery, 25, 58, 61, 98, 106, 117, 227
 and war, 26–28, 31, 33, 36, 46–47, 64–65, 104–05, 109, 122, 131, 137, 156, 177, 188, 205, 216, 219, 223, 231–32, 235, 238–39, 241–42, 244–45, 265
Pugh, George E., 171
Purcell, Edward, 129–30, 170
Purcell, John, 174, 293n48
Putnam, Mary, 232

Quakers, 32, 62, 85, 125, 133–34, 292n43

Reconstruction, 216, 256, 266–68
Remley, George, 147, 150–51, 201
Remley, James, 147, 150–51, 153, 156, 198, 208
Remley, Jane, 203
Remley, Lycurgus, 147, 151, 153, 156, 198, 201, 203, 208
Republicans, 14, 25, 30–31, 35, 39, 215, 218, 242–43
    Radicals, 59, 218–19, 253, 266–68, 270
Revels, Willis R., 58, 61, 113, 204–05, 232, 283n35
Rice, Edwin, 54
Rice, Eliza, 114
Rice, Lizzie, 111
Rice, Robert, 104–05
Richmond, Va., 243
Ritner, Emeline, 210
Robinson, E. T., 47
Robinson, Mary, 162–63
Rosencrans, Sylvester, 174
Rosencrans, William S., 181
Ross, Margaret, 46, 196

Sabbath observance, 39
Satan, 109, 124, 132, 149–50, 163–64, 223, 237, 240
Scoland, J. S., 39, 45
Scott, Winfield, 45
Seawright, Anna, 86, 210–11
Secession, 13–14, 16–17
Semple, Louisa, 74, 188
Senour, Faunt Le Roy, 106–07, 290n16
Sermons, 22, 24, 43, 47–48, 50, 54, 56, 106, 117, 135, 223–24, 226–27, 245, 303–04n20
    assassination, 247–51, 254–57, 260–64
    fast and thanksgiving day, 41–42, 45, 119–20, 137, 222
    Thanksgiving Day, 11–12, 14–15, 47, 106–07, 177, 232–33
Seven Days' battles, 60
Seward, William, 35, 44, 63–64, 176, 252, 258, 281n15
Shackelford, James, 134

Shanks, Martha, 199–200
Sharp, Helen, 209
Shaw, Virgil, 178
Shelton, Walter, 255
Sherman, John, 59, 61
Sherman, William T., 226, 233–34, 238–39, 251
Shively, Sarah, 114
Simmons, James, 21, 41–42, 277n16
Simpson, Matthew, 227, 261
Sioux uprising, 68, 74
Slavery
    civilian attitudes toward, 19–20, 25, 28, 51–54, 59–60, 68–69, 98, 156, 163, 238, 243, 284n42
    clerical attitudes toward, 15, 32, 41, 51, 106, 119–20, 137, 170, 174, 222, 235, 265, 280n10
Slidell, John, 44
Sloane, William, 18
Smart, James, 14–15
Smith, Henry Parker, 246–47
Smith, Margaret, 73
Social Gospel, 265–66
Society of Friends. *See* Quakers
Soldiers
    and Bible, 81, 94, 150–51
    clergy as, 144–45
    evangelism of, 85–88, 153–55
    funerals of, 202–03
    and Christian manhood, 139–40, 146–47, 160
    and relations with chaplains, 151–53
    and temptations of camp, 89–94, 147–50
Sons of Liberty, 223
Southerners, 17, 29–30, 32, 50, 110, 180, 215, 217, 219, 223, 226–27, 233–34, 238–41, 244, 254–56, 263, 266–68
Southworth, Eli, 85
Southworth, Rhoda, 60, 65, 69, 82, 85, 88–89
Southworth, Sophia, 98
Spiritualism, 212–213
Spirituality of the church, doctrine of, 21, 162, 277n16

Stanton, Edwin, 45, 180–81, 231, 252
Starr, Anna, 85, 89–90, 207
Stevens, Elizabeth, 90–91, 200
Stevens, Emma, 75, 138
Stevens, Simeon, 200–01
Stoneburner, J. H., 124
Stork, Mary, 85–86, 92–94
Sutherland, Asa, 124
Sutton, Mary, 129
Swedenborgians, 119, 212, 257
Swing, David, 249

Talbert, Martha White, 16, 29, 132
Thanksgiving Day, 176–77, 232
Thompson, M. L. P., 41, 115, 245, 249, 261–62, 313n31
Thorna, Jacob, 55, 228
Thorpe, Franklin, 61, 208–09, 230
Tod, David, 133, 173, 175
Trent Affair, 44
Trumbull, Lyman, 51
Tuthill, George, 14, 22, 108, 244, 261
Tyler, John, 35

Union
 compared to Israel, 24, 48, 56, 106–07, 226, 232
 as sacred, 4, 16, 22, 24–25, 37, 46–47, 188, 215, 266, 271
United Brethren in Christ, 172, 178–79
Upfold, George, 111–12

Vallandigham, Clement, 110, 116, 158, 165–66, 171–74, 182–83, 220, 226, 268
Van Anda, C. A., 164–65
van den Tak, Jane, 199
Van Dyke, Henry, 57
Vannest, John, 157
Vannest, Joseph, 157–58
Vannest, Mary, 158
Van Scyoc, Jane, 237
Van Sellar, Henry and Sallie (Pattison), 90
Vermilion, Mary, 135, 173, 195, 211

Vicksburg, 122–23, 131

Washington, George, 19, 104–05
Washington Peace Conference, 35
Wabash College, 140, 146, 159
Wade-Davis bill, 219
Ward, B. C., 145
Webb, Benjamin, 32
Webb, Clement and Clarissa, 200
Weed, Thurlow, 242
Weiler, James, 116, 220
Weishample, J. F., 144
Welles, Gideon, 63–64
Western Christian Advocate, 61, 97, 144, 169–70, 176, 178, 230, 232, 235–36
Wheeler, Henrietta, 115
Wilderness, Battle of the, 184
Williams, Ammi, 50
Wilson, Amanda, 44
Wilson, Henry K., 30–31
Wilson, S. R., 15
Windsor, William, 264
Women
 and benevolence, 81–82
 and childrearing, 84–85
 and encouragement of soldiers, 89–95
 and evangelism, 85–89
 and faith, 72–74, 76–77
 and patriotism, 82–84, 123–24
 and politics, 158, 225
 and prayer, 74–76
 and views of salvation, 77–81
Woodruff, George, 16, 198
Woodworth, Ellen, 82, 86, 91, 188
Woodworth, Samuel, 86
Wright, Harvey, 187, 300–01n37
Wright, Nathaniel, 144, 190, 247, 252–54, 266
Wright, Serena, 38, 65, 68, 80–81, 107–08, 131
Wright, William, 144

Yourtee, Samuel, 256, 311n19